CHILDREN AND YOUTH
Social Problems and Social Policy

CHILDREN AND YOUTH
Social Problems and Social Policy

Advisory Editor

ROBERT H. BREMNER

Editorial Board
Sanford N. Katz
Rachel B. Marks
William M. Schmidt

THE CHILD LABOR BULLETIN, 1912, 1913

ARNO PRESS
A New York Times Company
New York — 1974

Reprint Edition 1974 by Arno Press Inc.

Reprinted from copies in
  The University of Illinois Library

CHILDREN AND YOUTH
Social Problems and Social Policy
ISBN for complete set: 0-405-05940-X
See last pages of this volume for titles.

Manufactured in the United States of America

CONTENTS

CHILD LABOR AND EDUCATION (Reprinted from *The Child Labor Bulletin,* Vol. I, No. 1, June, 1912), New York, 1912

CHILD LABOR AND POVERTY (Reprinted from *The Child Labor Bulletin,* Vol. II, No. 1, May, 1913), New York, 1913

The Child Labor Bulletin

VOLUME ONE
NUMBER ONE

CHILD LABOR
AND
EDUCATION

J. J. LITTLE & IVES COMPANY
NEW YORK

The Child Labor Bulletin

Volume I JUNE, 1912 Number 1

TABLE OF CONTENTS

	PAGE
NATIONAL AID TO EDUCATION . . . . *Felix Adler*	1
A SUBSTITUTE FOR CHILD LABOR . . . . *Hon. P. P. Claxton*	6
CHILD LABOR AND VOCATIONAL WORK IN THE PUBLIC SCHOOLS . *E. O. Holland*	16
CHILD LABOR AND VOCATIONAL GUIDANCE . . . . . *Dr. Helen T. Woolley*	24
CHILD LABOR AND THE FUTURE DEVELOPMENT OF THE SCHOOL . *Carroll G. Pearse*	38
THE DANGERS AND POSSIBILITIES OF VOCATIONAL GUIDANCE . *Alice P. Barrows*	46
RELATION OF INDUSTRIAL TRAINING TO CHILD LABOR . . *William H. Elson*	55
ECONOMIC VALUE OF EDUCATION . . . . *M. Edith Campbell*	66
NEED OF COMPULSORY EDUCATION IN THE SOUTH . . . . . *W. H. Hand*	73
A FEDERAL CHILDREN'S BUREAU . . . . . *Congressman Andrew J. Peters*	85
FEDERAL AID TO EDUCATION A NECESSARY STEP IN THE SOLUTION OF THE CHILD LABOR PROBLEM . . . . *Dr. Samuel McCune Lindsay*	97
PART TIME SCHOOLS . . . . *Mrs. Florence Kelley*	106
SOCIAL COST OF CHILD LABOR . . . . *John P. Frey*	113
CHILD LABOR AND DEMOCRACY . . . . *Dr. A. J. McKelway*	121
EXTENDING MEDICAL INSPECTION FROM SCHOOLS TO MILLS . *G. F. Ross, M.D.*	128
CHILD LABOR IN THE CANNERIES OF NEW YORK STATE . . . *Z. L. Potter*	135
HOW TO INTEREST YOUNG PEOPLE . . . . *Mrs. Frederick Crane*	140
THE EDUCATIONAL TEST FOR WORKING CHILDREN . . . *Richard K. Conant*	145
A LEGISLATIVE PROGRAM FOR SOUTH CAROLINA . . . . *John Porter Hollis*	149
REJUVENATION OF THE RURAL SCHOOL . . . . . . *Prof. Ernest Burnham*	183
RURAL CHILD LABOR . . . . *John M. Gillette*	154
SYMPOSIUM: UNREASONABLE INDUSTRIAL BURDENS ON WOMEN AND CHILDREN.	161
I. Mrs. Florence Kelley	
II. Mrs. Millie R. Trumbull	
III. Rev. John A. Ryan, D.D.	
IV. Jean M. Gordon	
REPORT OF THE GENERAL SECRETARY FOR SEVENTH FISCAL YEAR	187
PROCEEDINGS OF THE EIGHTH ANNUAL CONFERENCE	203

ANNOUNCEMENT

WITH the publication of the following papers and proceedings of the Eighth Annual Conference on Child Labor, the National Child Labor Committee introduces the first number of "The Child Labor Bulletin." During the past eight years the principal publications of the Committee have been issued in annual volumes by courtesy of the American Academy of Political and Social Science in its Annals; and through this channel the principles for which the Committee stands, as well as the progress of its work, have become well known.

The demand for more frequent publications, however, has led the Committee at this time to undertake the publication of its own documents, rather than further rely on the generous courtesy of others. "The Child Labor Bulletin" will appear as a quarterly publication, edited at the office of the National Child Labor Committee, and sent regularly to all members and subscribers. In addition to the publication of papers dealing with the various aspects of child labor reform and the progress of the movement throughout the country, the Bulletin cordially solicits news items and specific reports from its readers everywhere. We shall undertake to publish such communications as in our judgment are of general interest to our readers, and designed to promote the cause of which "The Child Labor Bulletin" becomes the official organ.

NATIONAL CHILD LABOR COMMITTEE.

New York, June 10, 1912.

NATIONAL AID TO EDUCATION

By Dr. Felix Adler,
Chairman National Child Labor Committee and Founder Society for Ethical Culture, New York City.

No one can approach the subject I have chosen for my address in a light-hearted or dogmatic spirit. "National Aid to Education in the States" is the subject. National sentiment in this country has been steadily growing ever since the Civil War. Never have we so keenly realized the fact that we are one body politic and that we have, as we believe, one great destiny.

This does not imply that the loyalty each of us bears toward his own State is in any sense lessened. The contrary is true: our loyalties somehow enhance each other. That which we feel toward our State is caught up, as it were, into a higher potency, and blended with the loyalties of all our fellow-citizens of other commonwealths.

But the question before us is whether the power of the nation shall advance into what has hitherto been regarded as the almost exclusive domain of the separate States. It is true that certain colleges have been aided by the national government and we were told the other evening that three per cent. of the educational fund has gone to the support of schools in the various States. But a large subsidy of education in the commonwealths to be applied to the public schools has hitherto not been contemplated.

I wish to present to you certain reasons why it seems that we must now face the necessity of advancing in this direction.

First, education, as I hold, is a national concern. The whole nation is interested in the intelligence and the usefulness—usefulness in the highest sense—of each and every citizen. The training and the education of the children of Kentucky is undertaken not merely in the interest of Kentucky, but is undertaken by Kentucky as the steward or deputy of the United States. And the same is true of New York, of Massachusetts and of all the rest.

Education, I hold, is a national concern, and the meaning of this statement will become more explicit if we reflect upon the object for which a nation exists. A nation is a people organized for a certain object. The means it employs are political, legislative, judicial, administrative. But what, we must ask, is the object of the nation's existence? The current answer is, To secure the welfare of the people. And this definition we may accept provided we are on guard in two directions.

In the first place, when we use the phrase "the welfare of the people," we are not to understand only the people now living. The nation exists to secure the welfare not only of the men, women and children at present constituting the people of these United States, but to secure the welfare of all those others who will live on this broad continent after you and I and every one of us that breathes here shall have passed away. The nation possesses a certain immortality of existence. That welfare which is to be secured is not the welfare of our contemporaries merely, but of our successors as well. The nation stretches out its arms to take in the unborn as well as the living.

In this respect we have been greatly at fault. We have been wastrels and spendthrifts of the resources of the country. We have wasted the soil. We have cut down the forests. We have polluted the waters. We have lived as if "the welfare of the people" meant of the people that are now alive.

And secondly, the welfare of the nation does not mean the wealth of the nation merely. Unquestionably, material wealth is the basis of any civilization whatsoever. Wealth is an indispensable thing and we require far more of it than we have. But it is a means and not an end. A means to what?

Here is the answer, roughly outlined, of the end for which the wealth is a means, of the object for which a nation exists.

Every people has certain gifts, certain special aptitudes, a certain genius. The purpose of national existence in the highest sense is to develop those gifts and aptitudes which the nation collectively possesses. No one can fail to observe that the type of civilization produced by the German people has a singular, distinctive complexion of its own. So has the civilization of France, so has that of England, and of Italy. England, Germany, France,

Italy have existed in order to bring to the birth the peculiar thing which we call their civilization. Germany has existed in order that it might produce Kant and Bach and Beethoven; and Italy that it might produce its Dante, and its Cavour, and its Mazzini; and so on. Or rather, every one of these nations has existed in order to produce the type of human nature, that is, of civilization of which these names are crowning illustrations.

And so we dream of and believe in a peculiar American civilization that is to come. There will be a new art, of the American type, a distinctive American literature, an American science. (Compare the predictions of Darwin in this respect.) And best of all, we believe that there is to come a distinctive social and political life in America in harmony with that vast ideal which we call Democracy. Democracy is sometimes defined as a government in which each citizen has a share in making the laws which he obeys. But a still better definition of Democracy, it seems to me, is that it is not merely a government, but a point of view, a point of view that takes effect in social and political institutions, a point of view from which every human being is regarded as a spiritual investment of the human race and of his nation, in which every individual, however humble, is treated as if he had something to contribute toward the upbuilding of the new civilization.

Decentralization in Education

Now, if what has been said be true, if the object for which the nation exists is to develop a specifically American civilization, then my contention is valid that education is a national concern. For the whole nation is at work on this problem of producing a distinctive culture, and the whole nation is interested in seeing that every citizen shall be so educated as to be able to assist in the task.

But having asserted my first thesis, I wish to dwell with equal emphasis on the second, namely, that on the whole, decentralization in education is wiser than centralization. The several commonwealths should be allowed absolute independence in the construction and regulation of their educational systems. The separate States should be viewed as organs of the nation, charged severally with the function of promoting this public, this national concern, but it is best that they should be unhampered by national supervision in discharging their responsibility, for the following reasons: First, because any centralized system would soon fall into the ways of routine, because we need experiment, originality and constant improvement; second, because the system of education should be adapted to local needs and conditions; and, third, because the responsibility placed upon the commonwealths, of providing for the education of their citizens, is itself educative in the highest possible degree.

Lastly, my proposition is that if any one of the organs of the body politic be found temporarily too feeble to discharge its function in the most adequate manner, it is for the interest of the whole that it should be assisted in so doing. I repeat, the State is the proper organ through which national aid is to be imparted. But it is an *organ* of the nation. And if, as is actually the case in many of our commonwealths, the State is too heavily burdened with imperative obligations in other directions, adequately to fulfill its educational mission, the nation should step in to aid it. We have heard much of late as to the menacing evil of illiteracy. I have just seen the latest illiteracy statistics of the Census of 1910. It seems that there are more than six millions of illiterates in the United States at least ten years old. What a perfectly appalling situation is thus revealed! How shall we deal with this load that weighs us down? Can we expect those of our States, in the South, for instance, that are struggling along and staggering under their own burdens, that carry so many responsibilities which they find it difficult to meet—can we, I say, expect within the near future that these States will really be able to do justice to the educational responsibilities that are imposed upon them? The burden is too great, the load of illiteracy is too heavy, and the demand for ever larger and larger expenditure on the public schools is too urgent. The schools must be not only built and equipped, suitable teachers trained and salaried, but provision must be made for agricultural and industrial education as well, the curriculum must be enlarged, a higher grade of teaching ability must be employed. We must go to vastly greater expense for our schools than we have ever done in the past.

And there is no time to lose. A school generation occupies

from five to ten years. Every five or ten years during which we postpone the needed improvements, one more generation of school children will be defrauded of its rights. Every five or ten years, a new generation passes by the doors and finds them closed or enters and finds inadequate provision made. Germany spends hundreds of millions on her army and navy. Shall we not love our schools as Germany loves her army and navy? Will not the nation step in and hold up the hands of the States so that they may discharge the task which they are incompetent wholly to perform at the present day?

A SUBSTITUTE FOR CHILD LABOR

By Hon. P. P. Claxton,
United States Commissioner of Education.

We are all agreed that all institutions should be for the welfare of children. The only thing that makes every other enterprise valuable is the development of child life. Water power, forests, mines, fields, factories have no value except as they minister to the development of manhood and womanhood. There is only one fundamental primary good in the world, the human good. Everything else finds its value in proportion as it ministers to this.

Therefore, any people who shall at any time to any extent forget the welfare of children in trying to obtain the means of living are lifting the means above the end and are striving not for the ultimate things and things of primary value, but for those which have only secondary values.

The home, the church, the state, all exist for the children; and the future of all these institutions depends on what we do for the children of this generation.

The ancient philosopher was right when he told us that the noblest science known among men is the science of politics and that the highest art of the politician is in making the material from which states are made. But states are not made from rocks and trees. A republic is not built of prairies and rocky mountains. It can be built only of the spirit. Again, the individual good is, after all, the high thing for which the coöperative good, the state, exists.

In a dream and vision of the night, an ancient monarch saw on the plain a magnificent statue with head of resplendent gold, breasts and arms of silver, belly and thighs of shining brass, the legs and feet of iron, strong to endure. There it stood, a magnificent statue, the glory of the plain and a joy to those who looked upon it. But with the iron in the feet and the toes of the feet, clay was mingled. This alloy was not in the head of gold, nor in the breasts and arms of silver, nor in the belly or thighs of brass, nor even in the legs of iron; only in the feet and in the toes of the feet, down in the dust and unseen. Then a little stone, hewn from the mountain, rolled down across the plain and struck the statue, not on its head of gold, not on its breasts and arms of silver, not on its belly and thighs of brass, not on its legs of iron, but on its feet, and because clay was mingled with the iron in the feet and the toes of the feet, the feet were broken and unsupported, the statue fell headlong upon the plain and was broken into powder and dust, which the winds of the desert drove away as it drives away the dust of the threshing floor. It is the vision and prophecy of the future of our own proud republic, as it has been of so many great nations of the past, if we are foolish and forgetful enough to mingle clay with the iron even in the toes of the feet.

The Danger

The danger does not come in this republic from those who are in high places; it does not come from that which is most the subject of observation. There is little or no danger for years to come from invasion from without. The danger is in our forgetting the children of the poor and the obscure, in the slums of our cities where the fires of hell burn hot and furious, in the mountain cove, where 30 per cent. of them cannot read or write, where they live and grow up in ignorance, and down in our factories where we weave their blood into cloth, so that to one with an eye to see there is a crimson tinge in its web.

I believe in the mills; I believe in material wealth; I hope to see the day come when in this country of ours there shall be wealth enough for every man, woman and child to have a sufficient share of the material things necessary for human welfare. I welcome the factory, I welcome every means of turning raw materials of nature into wealth, that which wealeth, that which doeth good. But we must hold above all this the physical, the intellectual, the moral and the spiritual good of the children. It is for the children we must all work, and for them would I speak.

I believe in democracy which means, if it means anything, equality of opportunity. Every child born into our democracy must have an equal opportunity with every other child for the development of its physical, mental, moral and spiritual nature, an equal opportunity with every other child to prepare itself for good living and for producing honestly the means necessary thereto. In a democracy like ours, there can be no safety except in universal salvation. Those who founded our Government and thrust upon us this new untried experiment, well understood this. Therefore did Jefferson plead with his compatriots that they would preach a crusade against ignorance and illiteracy, and strongly maintained that democracy could exist only on the basis of universal intelligence of a high order.

Dr. Charles W. Eliot is right when he says that a fundamental element in virtue is physical health. Many educated men of his acquaintance, he says, have gone far astray, but if their physical health endures, have finally come back to something like virtue and respectability.

I am in hearty sympathy with the laws the Child Labor Committee and its agents have advocated in regard to the labor of children in the mills and mines. I am in hearty sympathy with the release of children everywhere from grinding labor. But I think of the problem from the educator's standpoint. We must have in mind not merely freeing children from labor, not merely keeping them out of mills and mines, but we must provide all that tends toward the building of strong manhood and womanhood, toward producing the units of which a great republic may be built.

Educating for a Democracy

We cannot educate children for a republic like ours, for democratic government in an age like ours, if we have them in the schools only through the years of childhood and previous to adolescence. In these years of childhood we might fit them to become citizens of an autocratic government in which a Little Father rules from above and in which the people are required only to follow their leaders and do as they are bid, having to decide for themselves no complex problems of politics such as come to us. Even a generation ago in our own country this might have been possible to a degree. The population was sparse and rural; people lived in the open country and there were no great cities; no great organizations of labor on the one side and of capital on the other; there was little foreign commerce; no great accumulations of wealth; every man was to a large extent his own employer and his own employee; each little community produced what it consumed and consumed what it produced. Children lived with their parents and parents with their children. There were no great international problems. Each State was a backwoods state in a backwoods nation, protected by its double oceans, and had not drifted away from its moorings and its sheltered eddy out into the great stream of world-wide politics.

Today difficult and complex problems are crowding upon us. Men with the ballot at the polls, men and women who help to make public sentiment which finally gets itself written into law, which judges of the law, once it is written, and which demands or refuses its enforcement—all who have to do in any way with civic problems must have power to think, to collect evidence, to sift and analyze it patiently, to interpret it, to arrive at tentative conclusions on which they act if they must, but which they hold in suspense and ready to be revised whenever there may be more evidence, or they have been able to analyze more closely and think more completely. In our democracy men and women must be so educated as to have self-guidance and not be reduced to the necessity of following leaders and being guided by authority. Authority from above is not sufficient when they face new problems till now unsolved. This kind of education must be universal and not the heritage or possession of the fortunate few. Therefore, in some way must the children be kept under right educational influences, not only through the years of childhood but also through the years of early and middle adolescence at least, when the powers of reason are beginning to develop—the time which I like to call the infancy of manhood or womanhood, just as the first six years of life may be called the infancy of childhood. In this second infancy the ideals are being formed and principles wrought out by which the man or woman is to be guided in mature life.

Purposeful Activity

In order that they may attain to the fullest manhood or womanhood, children must live a life of joyous activity. Jean Paul was right when he said that the most important thing in the life of any individual is to have a happy, joyous childhood. Joy is the sunshine in which everything grows except vice. Those who know children best know that this joy does not come from idleness, nor from what is usually called pleasure. Not even from play, but from working with the hands and accomplishing some worthy task. The highest feeling of joy is the result of a difficult task accomplished. It is not well that children should merely be restrained from work. No child should live in idleness. All children should have a reasonable amount of work to do of a proper kind. Out of this purposeful activity will come the experience so necessary for intellectual and moral development. Education is not a thing to be brought down out of the heavens nor imported from the ends of the earth. It is not a thing to be fitted on to children or rammed down their throats. It is rather an uplifting, an outsifting, a refining, an organizing, an interpreting and enriching of their experience. The fuller and richer the individual experience, the more abundant and valuable the material to be used by the educator. The most real of all experiences are those which come from labor performed willingly for the accomplishment of some worthy and interesting task, which the child recognizes as having a relation to its present life. Such experiences do not come alone or chiefly from tasks of the school.

We should also not forget that it is just as possible to injure the child by compelling it to labor unceasingly in the great school factory as it is by compelling it to labor in the cotton mills. I believe no one will accuse me of not believing in schools. Thirty years of my life have I spent pleading with the people of the Southern States to establish better schools with longer terms, and to put more of the children in the schools. But it is possible to injure the child by excessive work under insanitary conditions in school. It is not natural for children to sit for long periods restraining their physical activities, working with their undeveloped brains. They thrive best physically, mentally and morally, in the open air. Valuable results may come from intelligent, well-directed labor on the farm, in the field, in the forest.

The fundamental sin of our modern world is the desire to have something for nothing; the desire to eat one's bread in the sweat of another man's brow. Men and women in all ranks of society need to have the lesson driven home, that every individual must produce in some way as much as he consumes, must at least give in exchange for the production of the labors of the hands of other men and women something of equal value. This lesson should be learned in childhood both by the children of the rich and the children of the poor.

A Plan Worth Trial

Many years ago, before the National Child Labor Committee was organized, I dreamed of a plan I believe worth practical trying out. Possibly a brief statement of this plan may be helpful in enabling this Committee to attain the worthy aims for which it is working so nobly. In the Carolinas I have seen children under ten years of age working their lives away in the mills. Their pale faces haunt me still. I saw little boys eight years old drinking black coffee at midnight to keep awake until the end of their shift at four or five o'clock in the morning. Then they went out of the hot, steaming, noisy mill into the cold air of the morning to their homes probably for a little fitful sleep and a drowsy, joyless day, only to come back at night and grind again through the long dark hours.

In the cotton mill section of the South the climate is mild and vegetables will grow in the open nine or ten months in the year. The land is cheap in and about the cotton mill towns. Frequently there are thousands of acres of unused land in the immediate vicinity of the village. The tenant houses placed in long rows on either side of the barren streets have from a quarter to a half acre in front and rear yards; frequently more than this. This vacant land is devoted to trash piles and grows up in weeds.

The families in these mill towns have, as a rule, recently come from their homes and little farms in the hills of the Piedmont section or in the mountains. There they lived most of the time outdoors, cultivated the soil, and produced at least sufficient food to keep them from want. They had vegetables from their gardens, corn from their fields, meat from their hogpens, eggs from their poultry yards, and milk and butter from the cows that ran on the range, in the pastures, and on the mountain sides. Their clothing was poor and coarse, but sufficient to keep them warm. The children lived in the sunshine a good part of the year, filled their lungs with air, ran and played about the fields and forests, and gained physical strength and health. One day an agent of the mills came to the country home and said to the father that he would give him $1.50 or $2.00 a day if he would go to town and work in the mills; he also promised that he would give employment to three or four of the half dozen children in the family. To the father, who had never possessed more than a few dollars at a time, this offer brought visions of wealth. So with his wife and children he moved to the factory town and began to work. He then found that he must pay money for the rent of his house, a thing which he had never done before. He must pay money for the clothing of the children, twice as costly now as that which seemed sufficient when they lived at their country home. He must pay money for all food, a thing of which he had never thought. He has no garden, no cow, no poultry yard, no orchard, no hogpen—everything must be bought. Soon his monthly salary of $40.00, together with the small addition made by the wages of his children, is exhausted, and he finds himself in debt at the end of the month. Instead of a variety of meats, fruit, and vegetables, his table is supplied chiefly with Western bacon, cornbread, black molasses and coffee. There is only one remedy—either the younger children or the mother must go into the mill. The laws will not permit the children to go, therefore the mother must go, though her going may mean serious injury to her unborn child. Under these circumstances you can well understand that few more children will be born into this family, nor will children be born into the families of younger married men and women who have observed the conditions and circumstances of those with larger families of children.

School and Profitable Outdoor Training Combined

What is the solution of this? It seems to me quite simple. Let us put into the schools of the mill towns, and of the suburbs of manufacturing cities, teachers who know city or town agriculture, who know how to cultivate soil in the way to get the largest return from it in such things as will be most useful on the table and in the pantry. During the fall and winter months this teacher will teach the principles of horticulture and extensive and intensive agriculture to the children in the schools. In February, and earlier in some sections, he will encourage and assist the children in preparing the soil in their back yards, on vacant lots, and in such of the waste land about the village or town as can be had for this purpose. He will help to select seeds and will show them how to plant. As the days become longer and warmer, the hours in school will be lessened and more time left for work outdoors. The teacher will then go from home to home, from garden to garden, and from field to field encouraging the children, directing and assisting them in planting and cultivating their small crops. This teacher should be employed for the entire year. There should be some form of school work for the children—an hour or two every day, or three or four hours on two or three days of the week—throughout the summer. The lessons during this time should have special reference to agriculture and the problems of outdoor and indoor home life, and the teacher and children should spend the remainder of the hours and days of the week applying them in the cultivation of their crops and the care of the home. This teacher will also encourage and help the children with their chickens, showing how to make them most profitable. In many instances a cow might be kept, and about every home there should be flowers, fruit trees and grape vines. These will not only prove profitable in supplying food, but will add much to the beauty of the town and to the attractiveness of the home. Children working in this way, in coöperation with nature, may contribute more to the support of the family than they could by working in the mills. Parents and children will have good, wholesome food. The wages received by parents and older children can be used for rent, clothing, books, and for establishing and maintaining an ever-increasing bank account. The children working in the open sunshine, their feet in the soil and their lungs filled with fresh air, will not grow pale and sallow but strong and ruddy. Working at real tasks, with a good purpose and in obedience to the laws of nature, they will gain not only intellectual development but an understanding of the most fundamental moral principles.

The Experiment Tried

Something like this has already been done in many cities, towns and mill villages. Last year a woman in Memphis, whose heart goes out to the unfortunate, attempted to work out some such plan for one of the schools in the suburbs. With the assistance of a woman's club and a commercial organization, she raised an amount of money sufficient to employ for this school a teacher of the kind I have just described. He began work on the first of February. On the first of April, 62 gardens had been started by children at or near their homes, and some had proven very profitable. A girl of twelve had at this time sold, from her small garden plot, vegetables at the rate of $3,000 per acre, which is pretty good farming. I do not know, but I think it probable most of these had been sold to her own father. She had enjoyed the work; her lungs had not been filled with dust, her nerves had not been racked by the roar of the mill, and her mind had not been stunted by the monotonous work of watching spindles turn and mending threads. The program is very simple; but I am sure it would prove effective. Had I, as Commissioner of Education, $15,000 a year with which to employ a small group of men and women to work out the details of the plan, and to bring it properly before the people in the manufacturing cities and towns, I could, in a few years, revolutionize the character of their school work and do much to solve this vexed problem of child labor and the economic conditions of the mill workers. No doubt it would soon come about that the working day of the older children would be shortened to such an extent that they might have some time left in which to do similar work under the direction and instruction of teachers. This would be for them the best possible recreation, both for body and mind. In this way also these children might have some schooling throughout the years of early and middle adolescence, which, as I have already pointed out, are so important in the education of the child. Permit me to add that I believe the principle involved in this may also be applied very effectively to the solution of the negro problem in Southern cities and towns.

Similar work with vegetables, fruits, flowers, poultry, and with the indoor work of the home should be provided for the girls, and there should, of course, be in the school as teacher a woman who knows how to do this work.

CHILD LABOR AND VOCATIONAL WORK IN THE PUBLIC SCHOOLS

By E. O. Holland
Superintendent of Public Schools, Louisville, Ky.

In 1790 there were in the United States but six cities with a population of over 8,000 inhabitants, representing but 3.4 per cent. of the total population. In 1900 there were 545 cities with 8,000 or more inhabitants, representing 33.1 per cent. of the entire population of the country. With the enormous increase in urban population has come a demand for a different preparation for the work of the city, the factories, the shops, and the whole commercial life of the country.

Meantime, a most profound change has affected both the home and the church. No longer do the main educational agencies center in the home, and many contend that the church is no longer the great inspirational force it used to be in the realms of religion and ethics. Those of us who work in cities realize that there is a profound need for a change in our educational aims and methods.

In most States the compulsory education law holds the child until the age of fourteen, sometimes to the age of sixteen, but we know that this school-leaving age is too young. As a great German educator has put it, "the premature release from school discipline means for most pupils a complete cessation of all systematic education, and this cessation occurs at an age when the demoralizing influences of an uncontrolled life may have the most baleful effect on the budding moral character." If this assertion is half true, how can the American people permit thousands of children from eight to twelve years of age to labor from ten to fourteen hours a day in factories and cotton mills?

Doctor David Snedden, Commissioner of Education in Massachusetts, says: "It has been pointed out in the report of the Douglas Commission (of Massachusetts) as well as elsewhere that the period from 14 to 16 is a critical one in the vocational development of large numbers of children. This is the period when economic necessity or ambition tempts children into callings which are temporarily quite remunerative (for children), but which are essentially non-educative. The outcome is the unskilled worker."

Solving the Industrial Problem

In the United States in 1900, according to the census, 1,750,178 children under sixteen years of age were employed in gainful occupations. Such a vast army of little ones whose future is in jeopardy cannot be ignored. In many respects this is the most important educational and social problem that is presenting itself for solution to-day. Where have we been compelled to turn for guidance in meeting this difficult question?

As in many other things, we find that the German people have come more nearly than any other civilized nation to solving their industrial problem. Let us consider the progressive German empire for a moment. A giant hand could take up the German empire and one-half the State of Kentucky and find room for this territory in the single State of Texas. In our entire country we have at present but eighty-five million people, while the German empire has to-day a population of sixty-five million, with an annual increase of 750,000 a year. The natural resources of the German empire do not compare with those of this country, yet we find less pauperism, and crime, and lawlessness in this monarchy than can be found in almost any other civilized country.

A few years ago S. S. McClure, the author and publisher, discovered that in the city of Chicago there were four times as many murders committed each year as in Berlin, a city of the same size. He further discovered four times as many convictions for murder in Berlin as in Chicago. A recent article in *Collier's Weekly* shows but ten murders annually to every million inhabitants in Germany; in the United States there are eighty-five murders to every million inhabitants. Obedience to law and deep respect for human life are direct corollaries to an efficient public school system such as Germany has had for nearly a century.

The story is told that a number of years ago the Earl of Shaftesbury took the famous Arnold of Rugby to the East Side of

London, where thousands of people live in want and squalor and misery, and where both lawlessness and disease are rampant. These two spent nearly the entire night going from hovel to hovel, and as they proceeded the famous schoolmaster could hardly believe they were walking through the streets of the largest and wealthiest city in his own country, for until then he could not believe that civilization was able to produce and tolerate such misery. As he and Shaftesbury were leaving the district as the early dawn was breaking, he turned to Shaftesbury and said: "Many years ago the Vandals or Goths of northern Europe swept down and destroyed the civilization of Italy. If we Englishmen do not take thought of these thousands of workers, another horde here in our own midst will rise up and destroy all that our civilization holds sacred. We can no longer ignore these poor helpless beings as they have been ignored in the past."

Yet the conditions that Arnold and Shaftesbury saw in the London East Side were in many respects no worse than we can find in many larger cities of this country, and no worse than many conditions that are bound to arise in many of our Southern cities where factories are springing up by the score. Spargo states that from 1880 to 1900 the value of Southern manufactures increased from less than $452,000,000 to $1,463,000,000,—an increase of 320 per cent. According to one expert this growth was due "chiefly to her supply of tractable and cheap labor."

A few years ago I had an opportunity to inspect the Elmira reformatory and examine the classes of young men confined in that institution. I discovered that 58 per cent. of the 1,600 young men in that reformatory came from the single borough of Manhattan, and that 73 per cent. were from the city of New York. At once you might imagine that this large percentage from New York city was mainly composed of foreigners who were not able to adjust themselves to the conditions in a great city. But this is the very thing I did not discover. In fact, practically all these young men were American born, though it is true that most of them were of foreign-born parentage.

You will agree, however, that many of these young delinquents were the product of city life rather than of social and economic conditions in the home itself. This mal-adjustment of

social and economic conditions which develops hundreds of criminals each year in the single city of New York was more largely due to inadequate city administration, and unsuitable educational opportunities than to indifference on the part of parents who had come to this country from foreign lands.

We must learn that it does not pay to permit either parent or city prematurely to exploit childhood. In the end the family and the city will suffer, and the state eventually will be disrupted. If we believe that self-preservation on the part of the State is of first consideration, we then may proceed to a consideration of how to meet this problem.

Experiments in Germany looking toward a different curriculum for children who must work in factory, store, and on the farm, have been eminently successful. The director of the public schools in Munich, Doctor Kerschensteiner, has developed a type of school considered in many respects the model for both Europe and the United States. Doctor Kerschensteiner states that the first aim of education for those leaving the primary school is the "development of *trade efficiency* and *love of work,* and with this the development of those elementary virtues which effectiveness of effort and love of work immediately call forth—conscientiousness, diligence, perseverance, responsibility, self-restraint, and dedication to a strenuous life."

"In close connection with this," he states, "the second aim must be pursued: to gain an insight into the relations of individuals to one another and to the state; to understand the laws of health, and to employ the knowledge acquired in the exercise of self-control, justice, and devotion to duty, and in leading a sensible life tempered with a strong feeling of personal responsibility."

American Continuation Schools

Have the educators in the United States developed a primary school system that fulfills these aims in the education of the factory child? The answer is an emphatic negative.

First of all, the older type of night school, still to be found in many larger cities, has failed to add materially to the equipment of the factory folk who are growing so rapidly in numbers. In the main, their work has been negative rather than positive, and, as a consequence, only a very small percentage of the boys and girls attending this type of night school in American cities has been able to complete the work.

In a few places here the work of the continuation schools in Germany has been imitated. Some splendid experiments have been tried recently under the direction of the University of Wisconsin in the work shops and factories of Milwaukee and Beaver Dam. Very recently vocational and continuation schools have been established in various parts of Massachusetts where there is great need for such schools since thirty thousand boys and girls leave the common schools each year at the age of fourteen to take up some trade.

Recently the University of Cincinnati and the public schools of that city have worked together to solve this very important juvenile and industrial problem. After some experimentation under private initiative, conferences were called between the leading manufacturers and the Board of Education, and the whole question of vocational education was discussed in detail. Finally, it was agreed that the city was to provide the necessary teachers and the proper equipment for a school of industrial education. At the same time, the manufacturers pledged themselves to send a sufficient number of apprentices to justify the city in establishing and maintaining such a school. This school was opened in September, 1909, and has paid for itself in many ways.

According to statements made by city officials, the attendance in this school averages at this time about 200 a week. The boys come in groups of about twenty each, and remain for half a day or for four hours each week. The employers of these boys pay them their usual wages for attendance. When the boys return to the shops for regular work they are questioned by workmen and foremen in order that the lessons in school can be understood and applied to the definite work of the shop. Many older workmen have become interested in this vocational work and, as a consequence, many attend night school where definite instruction is given and various shop problems discussed.

This experiment is similar to what has been tried with eminent success in many industrial centers of Germany, and it will not be long before other cities will awaken to the needs of the factory boy and girl. In imitating the continuation schools of Germany still further, a part of each day is given to general culture and to talks on hygiene and civics.

Such continuation schools should be in every city. They should have the direction of all working children between the ages of fourteen and sixteen. For some time, because of the economic conditions in many families, it will be impossible for the city or the State to monopolize the time of the child from fourteen to sixteen. It is likely that a compromise will have to be effected, and during these two years only from four to eight hours of each week required of the child. If this much time can be given to continuation work, expert industrial training can be furnished boys and girls upon whom the economic demands are already pressing heavily.

Commercial Supremacy Demands Better Equipped Workers

In the past, the natural wealth of this country has been so bountiful that we have easily met the competition of the industrial classes in other countries. But much of this natural wealth has been consumed, and much more has been wasted. As a consequence, if we are to maintain our position of commercial supremacy, we must see that the working class is reinforced by young people splendidly equipped, and more intelligent and better protected than were their fathers from any dangers of exploitation on the part of the manufacturer.

The commercial and industrial supremacy of this country demands this; moreover, our democracy depends upon it. We must have a working class that is intelligent, that has industrial skill, and is not lacking in steadiness and sobriety. A democracy standing upon any other industrial organization will fail, as will the sanctity of the home, when these qualities are lacking among the industrial classes. Certainly it can be said that the primary school, established at the beginning of the 19th century, no longer adequately meets the requirements of society at the beginning of the 20th, when economic, social and political conditions have completely changed.

As Jane Addams has stated in her wonderful book entitled "The Spirit of Youth and the City Streets": "We may either smother the divine fire of youth or we may feed it. We may either stand stupidly staring as it sinks into a murky fire of crime and flares into the intermittent blaze of folly, or we may tend it into a lambent flame with power to make clean and bright our dingy city streets."

If to-day one of us should see a man on the streets of a city beating a child or mistreating even a donkey or a horse, we would interfere. Yet, we are willing to permit the exploitation of boys and girls in our factories and mills and shops. We are willing to permit these children to be enslaved even before the adolescent period and this means that they will never become strong, vigorous men or women, or be able to enjoy to the full the civilization of which we are so proud. The beating of a child on the streets of Louisville, from which the child may recover within a few hours or a few days, cannot be compared with the irreparable injury done to the same child by permitting ignorant parents to sell the very body and soul of that child for a few paltry dollars.

Germany has found that from the financial standpoint the exploitation of childhood is indefensible. Philanthropists and educators have raised their protests from the standpoint of social and moral progress, and our democracy will not much longer endure such a terrible violation of the rights of our children. Certainly our economic progress cannot continue unless we are able to develop as skillful and intelligent workmen as does Germany and other European countries.

Let us go back to our homes and lend our aid against the folly and the injustice of exploiting childhood in our factories. Let us interest the leading men of our community—the ministers, the editors, the doctors, the lawyers, and the laboring men—in this great question. Have them comprehend what frightful toll inevitably comes from compelling a child to take up the burden of the adult. Let the religious forces of your community understand that the saving of souls is not possible if the body is broken in the terrible grind of factory toil. Let us wage a campaign for the children of the South. Let us demand that those children be given the same opportunities in the way of thorough economic preparation and higher conceptions of civic duty that are given the child of the German laborer. The social, economic and political future of this country demands that the exploitation of youth be discontinued.

Many years ago a famous artist looked out upon a field and saw there a dull-minded, broken-spirited man toiling with his hoe; and in his imagination he saw back of this toiler the injustice that had come upon the individual and the thousands of his brothers who had been held in the ranks of serfdom.

His picture has aroused the sympathy of the world. It has done its part with Rousseau and the other social leaders in the awakening of public conscience to a realization of such injustice. Those of us who are engaged in educational work should understand that we also can do our part in arousing the public to adopt effective measures for the protection of the children of our country.

CHILD LABOR AND VOCATIONAL GUIDANCE

By Dr. Helen T. Woolley
Director, Survey of Children at Work, Cincinnati, Ohio.

When I first began to consider what I should say in response to the question as to what the school can do to solve the child labor problem, I thought to myself: "Well, there are a few recommendations on which I can rely as universally acceptable to all those interested in child labor." But a little further reflection made me more skeptical. I am afraid that even within the body politic of those interested in child welfare, there are divisions of opinion as radical as those which my small daughter found within her own little body. She was about to have her morning bath, which happened to be a tepid bath. Her feet were quite warm and her hands were cold. She stepped into the bath with her little feet warm, and, of course, it felt cold, and then she stooped down and put her hands into the water. She looked at me with a surprised smile and said: "My feet think my bath is cold, but my hands think it is warm." Now, I fear there are differences of opinion quite as radical as that among those who are interested in the problems of child labor.

Most of us would agree that it is very desirable to raise the age and schooling requirements in all states to the maximum now attained, i. e., fourteen years of age and the completion of the fifth grade of public school, but I know a few prominent educators who believe that fourteen years is too old, that labor under that age does not injure the child, provided the labor is properly regulated, and that our efforts ought to go toward regulation rather than toward increasing age and schooling requirements. Perhaps the only plan of campaign which would meet with universal approval, is the general one of obtaining more information. I think we would all agree that there are certain facts we ought to know in order to come to an intelligent decision on many problems of child labor, which we do not as yet know. There is still another reason for insisting on the importance of collecting more information, and that is that even with regard to points of which we feel certain in our own minds, it is impossible to convince the public by quoting a personal opinion. One must have facts in statistical form, behind even what seem to us obvious statements, before we can get for them a general recognition which will influence action. In the absence, then, of any accepted creed on the subject, let me express my own faith.

The School's Opportunity to Solve the Child Labor Problem

The two recommendations I should like to make as to what the school can do to solve the child labor problem, are, in the first place, that the school authorities should take an active part in working for an increase of the statutes in those states in which they are below the maximum, until we get more uniform conditions. I think it is possible for the schools to have great weight in influencing legislation on that subject. In obtaining our present excellent child labor law in Ohio, the school authorities seconded the efforts of the child labor workers very effectually.

My second recommendation is that the school ought to feel responsible for gathering facts with regard to working children. I believe the child labor law ought to throw the supervision and control of working children into the hands of the school by the following measures: The law should give school authorities responsibility of issuing the work certificates to children. That responsibility should fall not on the teachers or principals, but on a school officer under the direction of the Board of Education. In the second place, the regulation we have in Ohio which requires children to return to the work certificate office to have their positions registered every time they change positions, should be a part of every child labor law. That gives us an opportunity for collecting the actual facts with regard to the conditions of occupation during the years in which children are required to have certificates.

In the third place, I believe we should work for the establishment of continuation schools, which insure not merely the slight degree of oversight which is given by requiring children to return for certificates, but a certain measure of control and greater opportunity to know the conditions of employment.

Ohio's Test

I am discarding modesty completely in these recommendations, for that is just the state of affairs we have at present in Ohio, and it does seem to me about the best program the schools can establish for helping solve child labor problems. We are trying to take advantage of this child labor law in Cincinnati by gathering information which we hope is going to be valuable not only for child labor legislation but for the problems of vocational guidance and industrial training as well.

The law gives the power to issue work certificates, to the superintendent of schools or to a person to whom the superintendent shall delegate his authority. In Cincinnati Dr. Dyer has delegated his authority to Mr. Conant, and at this point I think I would better give you a brief history of this whole movement to make you understand the relationship which at present exists.

When this new child labor law was passed in 1910, Mr. Clopper, Secretary of the National Child Labor Committee for the Mississippi Valley, and Miss Campbell, Director of the Schmidlapp Fund of Cincinnati, saw the possibilities it offered for carrying out a piece of sociological research on working children, and getting a valuable mass of statistics. They took the responsibility—and I am sure I can say nothing more for their genius than the fact that they succeeded—of collecting enough funds from private sources to finance such an undertaking. The contributors were J. G. Schmidlapp, James N. Gamble, L. A. Ault, Edward Senior, Harry M. Levy, Omer T. Glenn, Sidney E. Pritz, Messrs. Alms & Doepke and Mrs. Thomas J. Emery. Dr. Dyer is thoroughly in sympathy with the work, and he has delegated the authority to issue work certificates to Mr. Roger L. Conant, who is paid by the private bureau of research. The study is under the direction of the writer. Mrs. Martin Fischer, Miss Ruth Levi, Miss M. Louise Boswell, Miss Annis E. Alden and Mr. William A. Spencer also assist in this work. The bureau consists of Mr. Clopper, Miss Campbell, Dr. Freiberg and a few others. The research was planned by Miss Campbell and Mr. Clopper. The control of the work certificate office makes it possible to get the material. Within our office, accordingly, there are two quite distinct things going on, one is the regular work of the work certificate office, which is a part of the public school system; the other is a piece of private research carried out with part of these working children. It is impossible to get an office force large enough to carry out this program of research with all, but we are taking as many as we can.

We are trying really to enforce the child labor law, and we are doing it in the following ways: We are requiring genuine credentials of age and schooling. We require a birth certificate either from the church in which a child was baptized or from the board of health of the town where he was born, and accept an affidavit of parents only when convinced that neither of these records is in existence. In the vast majority of cases we have an actual, legal record of age for these children.

The second provision of the law which we try to enforce is that which requires the children to register every time they change positions. That is not an easy thing to enforce. The measures we take are the following; every employer is instructed when he employs a child, that when the child leaves his employ he must send the certificate by mail to our office, not give it to the child. Every child is instructed carefully when he receives a certificate that when he leaves his position he must request the employer to send the certificate back to us, and that he must let us know as soon as he leaves. Here is the folder of instructions about work certificates:

INSTRUCTIONS

For getting a Certificate allowing a Child to Work.

SAVE YOURSELF TROUBLE BY READING ALL OF THIS!

Who Cannot Get Certificates. 1. Those not 14 years old. 2. Those not promoted to the sixth grade.

Who Do Not Need Certificates. Those 16 years old and over. They should, however, give the employer legal proof of age: 1. A church certificate of birth; or, 2. A Health Department certificate of birth; or, 3. An affidavit of parent or guardian giving child's birth-date and birthplace.

Who Can Get Certificates. Those who are 14 years old AND have been promoted to the sixth grade, and are in good health.

How to Get a Certificate. Get from the principal of the last school you went to: 1. A card to be filled out and signed by the firm that is going to hire you. 2. A card, on the back of which the pastor of the church at which you were christened or confirmed, or the clerk of the Bureau of Vital Statistics, will fill out and sign your birth certificate. When you have obtained these two records, take them to the principal of your school, who will fill out and sign your school record on the front of the birth record card. If you cannot get a proof of age as called for above, go to the office where the work certificates are issued with one of your parents or your guardian, taking with you the school record and the card signed by the employer.

Where to Get a Certificate. On the second floor of the old Hughes High School, West Fifth St., foot of Mound.

When to Get a Certificate. Any week day, except Saturdays and legal holidays, from 8.30 A. M. to noon, and from 1 P. M. to 3 P. M.; Saturdays, from 9 A. M. to noon.

Continuation School. Every child under 16 years of age who has not successfully completed the 8th grade must attend a continuation school four hours a week, between 8 A. M. and 5 P. M.; hence, attendance at a night school cannot be accepted instead. The child must report to the school to which it is assigned within 24 hours of receiving the certificate. Employers are responsible for compliance with these instructions.

When You Quit Your Job you must report the reason immediately to the office where you got your certificate. This report may be made by postal. If you do not get a new job within two weeks, or have been guilty of misconduct or inconstancy, you may be required to go back to school for the rest of the year.

Help and Employment may be obtained through the office that issues the certificates. The law requires that the office keep a file containing the name, address, age, etc., of every child in whose favor a certificate has been issued. EMPLOYERS in need of help and CHILDREN out of work are urged to apply to this office for assistance in meeting their needs. Every effort will be made to serve the interests of both.

Before Allowing the Child to Begin Work the employer is required by law to have the child's work certificate in his possession.

Return of the Certificate to the child by the employer is forbidden by law. Within 48 hours of the time employment ceases the employer must mail it to the issuing office, giving the reason for the child's withdrawal or dismissal. This report may be made on a slip of paper attached to the certificate, and should state: 1. Left without notice. 2. Voluntarily—if exact reason is not known. 3. Discharged, for this or that reason.

Hours of Work for boys under 16 and girls under 18 must not be more than 48 a week, nor more than 8 hours in any one day, nor before 7 A. M. or after 6 P. M.

Rate of Pay and hours of work must be stated to the child in writing by the employer before it is allowed to begin work; and retention of any part of child's pay, because of presumed negligence, violation of rules, breakage of machinery or incompetence, is forbidden by law.

These folders are distributed to all schools, to all children who are to have certificates, and to all employers. We have then two chances of getting the certificate when a child leaves a position. One is that the employer will send it back spontaneously, and the other is that the child will report to the office that he has left his position, and we can then ask the employer for the certificate. By verifying the employment records of a series of 630 children who had been studied, we find that in only about five per cent. of the 630 we failed to get the certificate when it should have been sent in.

With regard to the question as to how many children are going to work without certificates, or are taking second positions without them, we have as yet no full data. That is not so easy to find out, because even after the certificate is surrendered to our office we do not know what has become of the child in case he fails to call for the certificate; whether he has taken another job without his certificate, or has gone back to school, or is still at home. It takes some time through the efforts of the truant officers and factory inspectors to get records of that sort.

In enforcing the regulation about not working without certificates, we are entirely dependent on the coöperation of truant officers and factory inspectors, and the factory inspectors have certainly been very faithful in sending in all children whom they find who have no certificate. Whenever she goes into an establishment where children are employed, Miss Hagerty, who does most of that work, demands to see the certificates. If the employer cannot show them, the children are sent at once to our office.

We have also been enforcing the law which requires that children shall not work more than eight hours a day, or before seven in the morning or after six at night. Every child who brings us an employer's agreement card, which he must have before he goes to work, has to tell us for what hours he is to be employed, and if the hours stated are not legal he is sent back and either has the hours changed or else is told that he is not allowed to take the position. When they come back to change positions, we ask them if they were worked overtime. Very few report that they were. I believe the eight-hour law is being very well enforced. Another aspect of enforcing the law is that of preventing children from going into illegal occupations. Of course we never accept an employer's agreement contract for an illegal occupation.

Other Valuable Data

The second part of the work of the office consists in collecting statistics with the hope that they will serve as a basis of judgment about the general problems of child labor. We have in the office a great many more statistics than we have yet had time to formulate, but I have here those that are worked out.

The total number of children who received certificates during the school year August 31, 1910, to August 31, 1911, was 2,800. Of those slightly more than half—50.7 per cent.—were girls, and 49.3 per cent. boys. Those certificates may have been obtained by children anywhere between the ages of fourteen and sixteen. Almost 80 per cent. got their certificates before the fifteenth birthday and only 20 per cent. after they were fifteen. Twenty per cent. of the whole number went to work within a month after they were fourteen. Of the 2,800 children who received certificates, 78.5 per cent. came from schools in the city of Cincinnati, 21.5 per cent. from schools outside the city. Of the children who came from the city schools, 57 per cent. were from public schools, 43 per cent. from parochial schools. The enrollment of the public schools is about two and one-half times that of the parochial schools.

The statistics with regard to the school grade from which children came are as follows: 28 per cent. have just finished the fifth grade, 30 per cent. the sixth grade, 25 per cent. the seventh grade, 13 per cent. the eighth grade, and only a little over 2 per cent. had finished a grade above the eighth. A normal fourteen-year-old child ought to have finished the eighth grade. I believe that in estimating retardation, Dr. Dyer allows a year's leeway—that is, if a child has finished the seventh grade by fourteen he does not call him retarded. On that basis, about 40 per cent. of these children are up to grade and 60 per cent. are retarded one or more years. These figures are a bit too small, because both fourteen and fifteen-year-old children are included in the table, and, of course, the fifteen-year-old children are one more year retarded than the fourteen-year-old, so that it would probably be fair to say that between 65 and 70 per cent. are retarded and the remaining ones are up to grade, allowing a year leeway.

With regard to the occupations into which these children go: We found that of the 2,800 children, the shoe factories of Cincinnati took 509, or 18 per cent.; retail stores, 499, also about 18 per cent.; the clothing trades, 281, or 10 per cent., and the messenger service, 136, or 5 per cent. The other 50 per cent. are scattered through so very wide a range of occupations that the percentages do not mean very much.

On wages paid to children, we have a great many more records in the office than appear in the table I have here. This record is based on 2,000 certificates, issued between March 20 and November 9, 1911, and the statistics record only what the children were told they would be paid when they took their first positions. Of these 2,000 children, almost half did not know what they were to be paid. They had not even asked. One thousand and sixty of these children had been told what they were to be paid, and the groups are as follows: First, 1 per cent. of the boys and 28.5 per cent. of the girls were to be paid less than $2.50 a week; 46 per cent. of the boys and 41 per cent. of the girls, which is the largest group, $2.50 and less than $3.50; 38 per cent. of the boys and 27 per cent. of the girls, $3.50 and less than $4.50. And at $4.50, and above, there are 14 per cent. of the boys and 3 per cent. of the girls. If you make the dividing line $3.50 a week, there are 47 per cent. of the boys and 70 per cent. of the girls getting less than $3.50 a week.

These figures are a bit too high because they represent only what the children had been told they would be paid and not what they actually were paid. A child is sometimes docked for continuation school, or is engaged at so much a week, but is soon changed to piece work, and finds he cannot earn on that system as much as he was promised on a time basis. In the office we make a record of what the children actually were paid, because whenever they come back we ask about it.

I have here the number of changes of position recorded in our employer's agreement file for each of 1,268 children for one year. The great majority have but one position recorded. Only 30 have more than four positions recorded. The figures are misleading because many of those for whom only one position is recorded, have not held that position for a year, but have either gone back to school, stayed at home, or moved away. I think the figures indicate that the changes of position are not so frequent as many people suppose. We hope soon to have more adequate statistics on this subject also.

Complete Facts About a Selected Group

Those are all the statistics we have at present with regard to the regular work of issuing certificates. We have taken children of fourteen years so that we would have at least two years to follow them before they got through with their work certificates. We have taken those who have just left school and those who are going into paid occupations. We are trying to fill out for each child six schedules which seem to us to cover the main facts that one ought to know about working children. The first schedule gives a record of the information we need for issuing the certificates, supplemented by questions about the schools they have attended, what studies they liked best, why they left school, and whether they worked out of school hours before they were fourteen. The answers to these questions will throw some light on the street trades which have been discussed at this Conference, and we can find how many pursued street trades before they went into regular occupations, and then find how that modified their school records and their subsequent industrial histories. Here is schedule I in full:

STUDY OF CINCINNATI WORKING CHILD.

SCHEDULE I.

NAME ....
ADDRESS ....
AGE........................Date of Birth..........................
    Birth-place ....
CREED ....
    Name of Pastor or Priest..

OCCUPATION: (a) FATHER ....
             (b) MOTHER ....
SCHOOL ATTENDED ....
    Last Day .... Grade........................
STANDING:
    Reading ....Spelling ....Writing.............
    Eng. Grammar........Geography ....Arithmetic ....
SCHOOL ATTENDANCE RECORD...
SPECIAL TRAINING:
    Manual ....Domestic Science....................
CONDUCT ....
                (If troublesome, state reason.)
APPLICATION ....Punctuality ....
REMARKS ....
....
....
....
Source—Age and schooling certificate records......................
WHAT SCHOOLS HAVE YOU ATTENDED?...................................
....
WHAT STUDIES DO YOU LIKE BEST?....................................
WHAT STUDIES DO YOU LIKE LEAST?...................................
WERE YOU ABSENT MUCH?..............If so, why?...................
WHY HAVE YOU LEFT SCHOOL?...
WORK BEFORE AGE OF FOURTEEN?..............Age...............
    Before school.......After school.......Errand......Peddling.......
    Selling papers.........Bootblacking ....Other earnings.........
WHY ARE YOU GOING TO WORK?..
....
....
....
    1a. Father's birthplace and race..............................
     b. Same for mother ....
    2a. Languages spoken by father ....
     b. Same for mother ....
    3. Language of home ....
    4a. Mother a wage-earner at home? ....
     b. Outside of the home?......................................
    5. Number of rooms occupied by family ....
    6. Lodgers? ....

In answer to the question as to why they left school, we get some very interesting material. Of course, most of them say their families need their help. That we shall verify later by home visiting. Then we ask: "Would you rather have stayed in school or did you really want to leave school, anyway?" And the majority say they wanted to leave, anyway. Just what that means I have not time to discuss, but it is worth thinking over from various points of view.

The second schedule is a physical examination which we give the child in the laboratory when he comes for his certificate. It is not as thorough as I wish it could be, because it is not made by a physician. It is only the best the regular workers of the office can do. We make some measurements such as height, weight, vital capacity, chest measurement, temperature and pulse rate, and we observe their tonsils and adenoids and the condition of their teeth—which is deplorable in at least ninety per cent. of these children—and of their glands and mucous membranes. We get what we can of the family history with regard to disease, and of the child's personal history. Here is schedule II:

PHYSICAL EXAMINATION.

SCHEDULE II.

Name ....
Number ....Sex ....Height ....Weight ....
Family History:
    Number of other children................No. of child................
    Mother's condition ....
    Father's condition.........Rheumatism ....Cancer ....
    Tuberculosis ....Syphilis ....Heart disease............
Personal History:
Mumps .... Measles .... Whooping cough.. Scarlet fever.....
Diphtheria .... Typhoid .... Pneumonia ....Health during past year ....
Present Condition:
Earache .... Headache .... Eyes ....Cough ....
Expectoration .... Night Sweats ... Sort Throat......Appetite ....
Fatigue .... Color ....
Examination:
Tonsils .... Adenoids .... Cervical glands....Gums ....
Thyroid Gland ... Teeth .... Mucous membrane Expiration ......
Chest .... Lungs .... Inspiration ....Pulse Rate.......
Excursion .... Vital Capacity..... Heart ....Posture ....
Rhythm .... Temperature ..... Spine ....
Feet .... Skin .... Rash ....

    The third schedule is psychological. We have a psychological laboratory in connection with the work-certificate office, and each child who is being specially studied is put through a psychological examination. Here is the schedule. There are a few tests which do not appear on it.

PSYCHOLOGICAL.

SCHEDULE III.

NO. SCHOOL GRADE NAME

VIS. AC. { V. R. E. AUD. AC. { RIGHT GRIP { RIGHT
V. L. E. LEFT LEFT

TAPPING—RIGHT. TAPPING—LEFT.

Seconds.	Taps.	Seconds.	Taps.	Seconds.	Taps.	Seconds.	Taps.
1-15		1-30		1-15		1-30	
15-30		30-60		15-30		30-60	
30-45		1-60		30-45		1-60	
45-60		Index of fatigue.		45-60		Index of fatigue.	

MEMORY

SUBSTITUTION Series. 7 place. 8 place. 9 place.

SECTION 1 2 3 4 1
TIME 2
ACC. AV.
INDEX SPAN

STEADINESS Form Board Test

HAND RIGHT LEFT A TEST { Time Opposites. { Time
HOLE Acc. Acc.
CONTRACTS Index Index

CARD SORTING.

TIME ERRORS
ACC.
INDEX

SENTENCES { 1—No. Done. 2—No. Correct (a) Incorrect (b)
3—No. Simple (a) Complex (b) 4—Av. No. Wds. 5—Time
6—Pauses (a) 2 (b) 3-5 (c) 6-10 (d) 11-20 (e) 21-60
7—No. Ideas 8—Index

DATE ....OBSERVER...................

We hope to reëxamine these children both physically and mentally from year to year for five years, and then compare the series with a corresponding series of children who stay in school. We will take school children of as near the same economic status as possible.

The fourth schedule is an industrial history, much more detailed than the one we get for the rest of the children. We have a complete record of the dates of taking and leaving positions, of the child's use of unemployed time between positions, of his kind of work, hours of work, whether he worked overtime, his earnings, what he did with them, his reasons for leaving the job, and the employer's reasons for letting him go. Here is the schedule in full:

INDUSTRIAL HISTORY.

SCHEDULE IV.

No. Jobs.	Date of Taking.	Leaving.	Use of Unemployed time.	Industry.	Kind of Work.
1.					
2.					
3.					
4.					

		Earnings.			Child's Reason for leaving.	Employer's Reason for his leaving.
Hours.	Overtime.	Time. Piece. Weekly.	How found.			
1.						
2.						
3.						
4.						

JOBS.   1   2   3   4
   1. Ease of finding..
   2. Fatigue: { At first? ....
              { After becoming accustomed? ....
   3. Earnings: { How much to family? ....
               { How much spending money? ....
   4. Apprentice: { Learning a trade? ....
                 { What trade would you like to learn? ....
   5. Continuation of Education: Classes attended?.............
   6. Relation of Studies to Work ....
   7. Enjoyment of Work ....
   8. Free Time, Use of ....
   9. Work and School { In which do you think children learn most?......
                     { ....
                     { Which do you like best?..........................
  10. Combination of Work { Would you prefer a combination to all or either?
      and School   { ....

The schedule for the home visit is not yet in form to be printed. The information is recorded under the following heads: character of neighborhood, and of the tenement itself, the way in which the home is cared for, number of people in the family, its income, expenditures, and history; the child's place in the home, the responsibility thrown on him, and the parent's attitude toward the child.

The sixth schedule records the study of the children's occupations. That also is not yet ready for publication. We try to record the physical conditions under which children work in the various trades, the wages paid them, the possibilities for increase of earnings, and for learning the trade; in fact, the whole industrial outlook for children in the trade, the class of workers employed, their number, and the provisions made for the comfort of employees.

We hope the information we are collecting will have a wide and useful application to many problems of child labor, of industrial education, and of vocational guidance. Perhaps the outcome in which this conference is most interested is the information bearing upon the mental and physical effect of labor on children who begin work at fourteen. We hope to be able to compare a large group of working children with a corresponding group of school children. It would also be desirable to compare children working in one trade with those in another, but there are only a few trades in which enough children are employed to make this at all possible within the limits of the present study. After norms are established, it may be possible to make special investigations of the separate trades.

CHILD LABOR AND THE FUTURE DEVELOPMENT OF THE SCHOOL

Carroll G. Pearse,
Superintendent Public Schools, Milwaukee, Wis., and President National Education Association.

Children leave school earlier than they ought, chiefly for two classes of reasons. The first has to do with parental attitudes and necessities; the second, with the attitude and the real or fancied necessities of the children themselves.

In many instances, family conditions are such that the small sum the boy or girl of thirteen, fourteen or fifteen can earn is very important; in some cases, under present-day industrial conditions, it is necessary. With the father out of employment, or so poorly paid that family necessities cannot be met; with the father dead, or a deserter of his wife and family, so that either the mother must be breadwinner while an elder child cares for the little ones, or the immature boy or girl must earn that the mother may stay in the home; with illness of the breadwinner so that income stops; with illness of other members of the family so that expenses for doctor or surgeon and medicine make terrible inroads on the slender income: for such withdrawals from school, society, not the school, is to blame; and society must readjust industrial conditions and assume responsibility to remedy them. The State or the city can, if it will, do much to help the man who is out of work find employment; and society can shape conditions so that starvation wages will be less common. Impoverished widows and deserted wives may be made the care of the State—to such an extent, at least, that the home shall not be broken up and may be kept worthy of the name until the brood has been fitted decently to take up the struggle of life; and better organization for the relief of families temporarily in distress, can greatly lessen the necessity for taking immature children out of school for work.

In other cases, parents do not realize the importance of schooling and are neglectful; or they consider a child a family asset—a heaven-given means of increment to the family income. If there are five or six of these, the father may not have to work at all, but can live on the earnings of the children. Generations of European peasants have practiced the theory that, after a child is "confirmed," he is to go to work and produce income for the family, either in the home, or in the father's shop, or by turning over the small wages he gets by working for some one else. Many such families take a child from school to use his wages in paying installments on a house and lot bought to rent out as a means of income. These cases, also, are for society to deal with, either by its agent, the attendance officer, who shall educate the careless or immigrant parent to American standards concerning the duty of parents to children; or by its fiat of law, which compels the greedy or short-sighted parent to permit America to be the land of opportunity for his boy.

The School's Responsibility to the Individual Child

But other children leave school, because they do not care to stay. The boy's crony, the girl's chum, is at work, and has a part or all of the week's wages for spending money; the cheap theatre, the picture show, the dance, the bit of finery, appeal; the hold of the school is not strong; no teacher has the personal touch, or is in such relation as to give the word of counsel needed; the exaggerated sense of independence which adolescence often brings enters into the situation, and the youngster makes the great mistake —he is swept out into what is likely to prove for him the wilderness of labor. Or the pupil is a misfit in the school; he does not like what the school gives him; he does not like the conditions or the discipline, or the studies and exercises, or the teachers; he is old enough to get out, if he tries; he is uncomfortable where he is, and he leaves to go to work, or to loaf.

For these latter classes of children the school, and not society at large, is responsible; for the first class, because some one in the school is not closely enough in touch with the pupil, and if necessary, with the home, to show the more excellent way, and influence to a right decision; for the second class, because it is the province of the school to so study its problems as to understand not only general conditions but individuals—not only the usual, normal individual pupil, but also that one who is non-normal, a little twisted in disposition, a little "under-powered" in mentality, a little queer in tastes, or in previous experiences, a little better able to do things with his hands than to read books or solve problems—and having so studied and understood, to so re-shape and adapt its course of instruction and school exercises that the school may supply the educational need of children to-day; not merely the need of ordinary children, but of all children.

First, without any special changes in curriculum or methods except in the attitude of the teacher toward his work and "material" (the pupils), and in intelligent understanding of that material, the school can do much for a great number of the children who have been failing; for the pupil who fails to keep with his class in grammar school grades, or who fails and does not get on into those grades when most children of his age and apparent strength pass on, is a pupil who begins to think of leaving school, and frequently does leave. After a pupil has failed once or twice and begins to find himself surrounded by children considerably younger, it usually requires a firm application of the compulsory attendance law to keep him in school; and when he does stay he too often becomes a trouble maker; he makes the school pay for his humiliations by becoming a nuisance to the other pupils and a disturber of the teacher's peace of mind.

If teachers were careful to watch the beginnings of lagging, to note the first signs of lack of interest or lack of understanding, to see that no child was allowed to fall behind when by rekindling his interest or his courage, or by making clear something over which he had become confused, or by helping him overcome an easily besetting tendency to inattention or idleness, a surprisingly large proportion of the pupils who now fail to keep up with their classes might be kept from falling behind. It is from among these "repeaters" that the mills and factories, the "cash girl" and "messenger boy" jobs take their heaviest toll.

The schools must realize their responsibility for "keeping in touch" with each pupil, and keeping him "in condition" as trainers do their athletes. It is worth while, for victories in the proper work of the school are as important as victories on the track or diamond. If necessary, and it will usually be necessary as our schools are now organized, the teacher must be allowed some time to be set apart each day for such study of individual pupils, and the giving of such individual help as will keep those members of the class who need individual help, working up to their best.

Present Educational Needs

Once the school had simple responsibility—to teach reading, writing, ciphering—little more. The banker or the merchant taught his young employee the details of accounting or salesmanship; the youth was educated in the business by his employer. The girl learned the household arts in her mother's house and garden; the boy on the farm or in the shop got such training of his hands and such mastery of common tools as served to develop his motor activities and the nerve tracts and brain areas that preside over them; that which came in the line of daily duty built up in him the strength and balance to be obtained only in that way, and made him "a man of his hands," whatever his later calling might be. But the school to-day is confronted by the necessity for giving education which a generation or two ago was received from many different instrumentalities.

It is clear that the State's interest is to see that the general intelligence which all citizens require to be useful and able to act advisedly in public matters, is given in the schools. Those elements of the knowledge common among civilized men, and of the history and machinery of government, must be taught without fail. But we, to-day, must do more. The importance of our commerce increases day by day; more and more young men and women are called to be its ministers—to sell goods and make account of the sales, to record items, extend amounts and make footings.

Elementary schools are not now called upon to train for vocations. I do not think they ever will be. But all boys and girls will be trained more effectively than now to make the common computations and records required in business, and to write down more clearly and tersely what they wish to say—not to be accountants, but to have better grounded in habit and practice the ability for accuracy and attentiveness and prompt effectiveness.

The boys will have a good course of training in the use of common hand tools. They will not be carpenters, blacksmiths or machinists; the elementary schools have no call to turn out such. But they will have the benefits of hand-work training, they will be able to use the hammer, saw, plane, auger, ax, chisel and file with understanding and effectiveness in the common affairs of life. They will not be helpless in the presence of situations requiring a little judgment and resourcefulness. They will be able readily to go on and learn to be good craftsmen, if their tastes lead in that direction.

Each girl will be given time and teaching to acquire the elementary household arts, sewing and cooking, sweeping and scrubbing, washing the clothes, caring for kitchen, laundry, bedroom, sitting room, bathroom and cellar. She will learn to buy as well as to cook and sew; to care for the sick; to look after, wash, dress and feed babies and little children.

Some ground will be found wherein boys and girls can plant things, and when the things they have planted come up, protect and cultivate and harvest them. They will get the blessed smell of the soil in their nostrils and wholesome dirt between their fingers and toes; and they will get some first hand elementary knowledge of the mysteries of that ancient and honorable craft whereby, since the dawn of time, men have enriched themselves from the bounty of the soil. And on this ground, through the exercises and the sports and games in which they may engage, nature, through the ministry of fresh air and by means of the exercise at work and play, will be the better enabled to build up for them strong muscles and steady nerves, vigorous hearts and lungs and stomachs.

And when we are able to convince parents and children that school exercises are of real value; when not merely the average "good" child can find satisfaction and pleasure in the work of the school, but also that lad whose taste is toward business, and that one whose thoughts find expression more readily and effectively in the work of his hands than in the words of his mouth,—then we shall have gone far to solve the problem of keeping in the schools, until they can receive its benefits, those children who are now very often found tugging so fiercely at the bonds designed to hold them within its "influence."

Training for Vocation

The school will not have done its duty until it provides a way for the pupil who has finished the elementary school to fit himself for a vocation. Many high schools send out efficient bookkeepers and clerks and stenographers; soon the high schools of all cities will recognize the propriety and necessity, and will establish courses to turn out efficient office employees, instead of merely turning out, like the elementary schools, young people with good habits of attention and accuracy, able to begin to learn to be efficient office help. To meet all the need, the schools must also establish industrial, as well as commercial vocational schools; schools of trades for boys, where the product shall be capable machinists, electrical workers, bricklayers or blacksmiths, ready to go out and earn the wages of a beginning journeyman; schools of trades for girls, where they may become competent milliners, dressmakers, power machine operators or household cooks; schools of agriculture, where both boys and girls may learn the arts of farm life, and how to render the life of the farmer more comfortable as well as more prosperous.

Continuation Schools

But many young people must and will leave school before it has done for them as much as it ought, either to make them commercially and industrially useful, or to render them as likely to be intelligent citizens and members of families. The school system must provide a way to continue their education. In continuation schools or classes, they must learn such application of mathematics and science and drafting to the trades they are learning, or get such knowledge of the geography of commerce as will make them better and more successful at the employment they have chosen. These schools must also give such instruction as will make the young people more generally intelligent as citizens, better able to judge of public questions, with knowledge of and a taste for enjoyments of a superior character—better house-fathers and house-mothers.

Readjusting the Curriculum

So far this paper may have given the impression that its author considers it an evil for children to labor. But do not so conclude. The school has that to offer which is of great value to youth; and they should not fail to possess themselves of its benefits. Yet children have labored since Adam delved and Eve span; and the labor has generally been good for their bodies and for their souls. We pass laws to keep children from working. We do this not because work is an evil; it is only an evil when performed under bad conditions and at the expense of the benefits the school should bestow. It is an evil when the physical or moral conditions are unwholesome; when tender bodies are taxed through weary hours, which sap vitality; when the work is done without the oversight and companionship of elders interested in the child and thoughtful for his well-being; when by it he is deprived of education for the mind and of the joy of life. If every child could work in the home, under the eye of a wise and interested father or mother, at tasks suited to his age and strength, and for a reasonable time each day, no greater boon could be conferred. And that boy or girl who, upon the farm or in the household or in the family shop or place of business, bears daily responsibility for the performance of reasonable tasks, is fortunate beyond youth's realization.

But such opportunities for the boys and girls of our towns are pitifully few; and so we pass child labor laws to keep children in school and save them from coal breaker and loom, glass blower's furnace and factory, from sweat shop, department store and mill.

No question more appalling confronts the thoughtful school administrator to-day than the question of a proper readjustment of the school curriculum, school hours, and school equipment, so as to make our public educational system fit the need of the child to-day. The value of labor as a deterrent and prophylactic is so well known that in schools for delinquent or semi-delinquent children, as much time is given to useful labor as to usual school studies. Students of education understand that the benefits of suitable labor to normal children, in developing a balanced and robust physique and a mind and character of similar quality, are quite as great as those conferred by labor upon children who need correction or reform. Whether this opportunity is to come through some extra-school agency, where children can work under suitable conditions for a suitable time each day, devoting the necessary time to lessons at school; or whether as a development of the school and its facilities whereby children may do real work and bear real responsibility, no one can now say. But to train up a citizenship worth while we must not only keep boys and girls from coal breakers and out of sweat-shops and mills, but, either in connection with some agency to be developed and coöperating with the school, or through some further development of the school itself, our young people must have restored to them the opportunity for suitable and wholesome, but real and regular work, as part of a sound and rounded education.

THE DANGERS AND POSSIBILITIES OF VOCATIONAL GUIDANCE

By Alice Prentice Barrows,
Director, Vocational Guidance Survey, New York City.

Vocational Guidance is the second great chapter in the history of Child Labor—the "thou shalt" rather than the "thou shalt not" of that great movement; and it is also the *motif* or running accompaniment of the industrial education revolution. How that chapter is to be written depends upon whether those interested in vocational guidance realize that it is only a chapter and not a volume in itself; what the spirit of that *motif* is to be depends upon whether those interested in the newer movement realize that one of its great opportunities is to aid in developing industrial education along the most democratic lines. It is therefore well that those interested in child labor, industrial education, and vocational guidance should make common cause, for the dangers of vocational guidance are the dangers of child labor and industrial education, and in the possibilities of vocational guidance lie the greatest aids to the abolishment of child labor and the founding of fundamental systems of industrial training.

The Danger of Vocational Guidance

Probably the greatest danger of vocational guidance at the present time is that its supporters may endeavor to guide children into vocations. The object of half this paper will be to try to explain that paradox.

"Vocations" and "Guidance" are dangerous words, both because they are vague and because they sound impressive. I have never been able to find a satisfactory definition of vocation, and it certainly does not seem to be a word descriptive of actual conditions. There are "jobs" and there are positions, but one of the problems of vocational guidance is to find out what a vocation is at the present time. "Guidance," on the other hand, has an ecclesiastical tang that is particularly dangerous to the cause of democratic education. It is most questionable whether, under any circumstances, any one has the right to guide children systematically into vocations. Giving guidance is one thing, and giving information so that there will be greater freedom of choice is quite a different thing. At present we cannot give even this information about vocations because we do not know enough about actual conditions to give it. Yet it sometimes seems as though the whole tendency of vocational guidance at the present time were to give some information, any information, because the lack of it is felt so keenly—just as a layman in the presence of an ill person might snatch something, anything, from the doctor's black bag and give it to the patient, thereby possibly injuring him for life. The fact that he did it because he could not bear not to do something would hardly exonerate him in the eyes of the world. The fallacy of the point of view back of this attempt to meet the situation by immediate action may be found in tracing the history of the movement, and there also we may find the justification of the movement.

When an irresistible force meets an immovable object, tradition has it that one or the other goes out of business. The irresistible force, industry, is swinging along at a destructive pace toward the immovable object—education. Each has begun to send off danger signals. Vocational guidance is only one of those danger rockets. Whether it is to be merely a rocket or, to let the metaphor fall to pieces, whether it is to become a real searchlight, remains to be seen. The fact is that industry has advanced by geometric progression and education by arithmetic progression. No one sees that better than the educators of the present time. Given the difference in the rapidity of changes in industry and education, and given a sudden awakening on the part of industry to the fact that it needs better workers, and on the part of education that it has not kept pace with social and industrial changes, and add to this a praiseworthy desire on the part of the schools to make up for lost time, and on the part of industry a realization that their demand for the training of workers is part of a new popular movement in which their judgment as "practical men" will carry weight, and we have the scene set for a more subtle and indefinable exploitation of children than the world has ever seen—subtle and indefinable because all would be done in the name of the "good of society and of the child"; exploitation because the employment of children of fourteen is as much exploitation as the employment of children of ten. The chief difference seems to be that, in the case of fourteen-year-old children there is a likelihood of exploitation of their minds at the most important period of development, that is when they are first beginning to use them consciously, and when they consciously long for training; while with children of ten, exploitation means the premature death of any ambition for training. That is the significant fact in this newer movement for child labor reform and industrial education. That is the second great chapter of the child labor movement.

I am open to correction, but I should say that to arouse the ambition and interest of a child of fourteen by promising him "trade training" the value of which is dubious, and then a job where he "can work up" when we have no facts to prove that he can work up, and a distinctly uncomfortable feeling that he probably cannot, is after all even worse than stunting a child by premature labor so that you cannot arouse his ambition at all. Any one who has ever taught knows how worse than disastrous it is to stimulate a vivid interest in children and then fail to satisfy it. It is their first taste of disillusion, and a teacher of any sensitiveness who has once seen that does not readily forget it. It behooves us not to start Vocation Bureaus too soon and thereby arouse hopes in the children who are now leaving school by promises of training or of jobs which we cannot fulfill. It behooves us to make sure that our trade courses are worthy of the time and money of the children, and that the jobs are fit occupations, before we urge them to enter either.

All the present talk about "blind alley" occupations expresses the sense of maladjustment between the school and society, and the realization that mere finding of jobs is not the solution of the problem. "We must not let our children go into blind alley occupations but direct them into the skilled industries," is a phrase often heard. But what are the skilled industries, and what is the skilled work in them? What are the blind alley occupations? By that term is usually meant an unskilled occupation which has a limited number of processes easy to learn and leading nowhere, but a highly skilled industry may be a blind alley for the majority of workers in it. "The instrument trade is a highly skilled trade," said one boy, "but you may do the same kind of work from the time you enter until you leave. You can't even get a chance at anything else. Of course they can get out more goods, I suppose, if the fellow who has got the habit of doing one thing keeps on doing it." A girl in a dressmaking establishment who is making sleeves may be in as much of a blind alley as the girl in a paper box factory.

What is the real significance of this concern about blind alley employments? Does it not represent an awakening to the fact that social and industrial conditions have changed to such an extent that even legalized employment may be dangerous unless the occupation is known? But is there not also danger that we may then rest back comfortably on the fancied discovery that occupations may be divided into blind alley employment and "skilled trades," with the resulting determination to prepare children for "skilled trades"? Do we know any more about "skilled trades" than about blind alley employments? Is it not important to know before we prepare children for them? Can we afford not to investigate the facts—not to send out scouting parties, in other words, to explore conditions? If there is really such a chasm between the schools and industry, it should be remembered that chasms are not usually crossed by leaping into the air supported by a great desire to reach the other side. Even if you succeeded in crossing, you might land in the enemy's camp. Moreover, before bridging this chasm, it is desirable to study the topography of the country on both sides. After that is done, we may know what should be the approaches to the bridge, how it should be supported, and whether its terminal is correctly located.

Such failure to realize the need of a preliminary survey of the ground before making a constructive plan is the fundamental danger of vocational guidance. It is the source of all the immediate dangers.

Some Immediate Dangers of Vocational Guidance

It should be remembered that throughout this article, I am referring to vocational guidance among children leaving the elementary school, or the fourteen to sixteen-year-old group. Probably the greatest imminent danger for this group is the formation of employment bureaus as a solution of the problem. This is the quick and easy method, one might almost say the lazy method. It is always so much easier to systematize than to construct. This is one of the chief forms that the movement took in England, almost inevitably growing out of special conditions in that country. It is interesting to read in Reginald D. Bray's book on Boy Labor and Apprenticeship the following paragraphs (the italics are mine) :

"Until the year 1910 the provision of openings in suitable occupations was not considered among the duties of the State. It is true that here and there, usually in coöperation with voluntary associations, education committees made some attempt to place out in trades the boys about to leave school. But any expenditure in this direction was illegal, and under no circumstances was it possible to do anything for those who had already left school. But in the year 1910 the State, *without premeditation, has found itself committed* to the duty of finding openings for children and juveniles. *The revolution was upon us before we had seen the signs of its approach.*

"This assumption of a new duty was the unforeseen result of the establishment of Labour Exchanges. The Act of 1909 thought nothing, said nothing about juveniles. It was passed as a measure intended to deal with the problem of adult unemployment. Now, there is no problem of unemployment in connection with boys and youths; the demand of employers for this kind of labour appears insatiable. Nevertheless, no sooner were labour exchanges opened, than the question of juveniles came to the front. Employers asked for juveniles, and the manager of the local labour exchange, eager to meet the wishes of the employer, searched for and found juveniles. Enthusiastic about this work, and prompted by the laudable desire to show large returns of vacancies filled, it did not occur to him that the problem of the juvenile and the problem of the adult had little in common. He was not permitted to remain long in this condition of primitive ignorance. Questions were asked in the House, letters were written to the papers, deputations waited on the President of the Board of Trade, all complaining that the *Labour Exchange was becoming an engine for the exploitation of boy labour.* In the case of adults, no bargain as to conditions was struck with the employer; the man had to make his own terms. But the boy could not make his own terms, and public opinion had for some time been uneasy about the increasing employment of boys in occupations restricted to boys, and leading to no permanent situation when the years of manhood were reached. Returns showed that it was largely into situations of this character that lads were being thrust by the Labour Exchange. The Board of Trade rapidly realized the evil, and set itself to work to repair the unforeseen mistake."

Is there any reason why we should not profit by the mistakes of England? Cannot we prevent the State here from finding itself committed to the questionable duty of finding work for children who are not prepared for it?

The second immediate danger is the establishment of bureaus for giving advice about occupations. This is merely a more subtle form of the labor exchange evil. Bureaus of information about occupations would be most desirable, but it seems unfortunate to attempt to give advice when we do not possess the information. The third danger is closely allied to this, that is, the publication of bulletins about occupations, founded upon inadequate investigation. Bulletins about occupations would be most helpful, of course, but their helpfulness is in proportion to the thoroughness of the investigation. An investigation covering all details of a single occupation by its very conditions takes time. In our eagerness to give information we are in great danger of publishing bulletins founded only upon general information. But general information for a boy whose whole problem is specific is sorry comfort when he is engaged on one small part of a large trade—at three dollars a week.

The fourth danger lies in the encouragement of short cuts in industrial education, such as training for specific trades at the age of twelve, or short time trade courses because the child "has to go to work." The fifth is the failure to recognize that it cannot be taken for granted that a child "has to work." The sixth is the tendency not to realize that even if we had information about the trades, vocational guidance is an educational problem and reaches down into the regular school as well as forward into special training.

Some Possibilities of Vocational Guidance

After such a marshalling of the dangers of vocational guidance, and after stating that our chief danger is that we exist at all, it seems as if the second part of this paper were superfluous. And yet, if the dangers of vocational guidance are great, the possibilities of service seem to me infinitely greater. Granting that vocational guidance is simply the outward and visible sign of the maladjustment between the school and society, and granting that the real question is whether the State shall give over the care of children leaving school to the forces controlling industry or the forces controlling education, we have in vocational guidance one of the best means of correcting that maladjustment.

Some years ago business descended upon the schools and captured commercial education. Since that time, we have been trying to undo the effects of that assault. The market has been flooded with inefficient workers to the exasperation of employers, the despair of teachers, and the misery of the children. The reason for the assault was natural. The schools were said not to be "practical." They did not prepare for life, which was spelled "business." But the attempt to give the children a narrow commercial education and then find them "jobs" was probably the most impractical thing ever done by business. Vocational guidance is the popular warning of the same danger in regard to industrial training, and the history of its rise and the cause of it must be considered if the same disaster is not to follow. The previous experience would seem to suggest that finding jobs for children who are not trained is a stupendous and futilely repetitious task. It also suggests that too narrow an interpretation of the word "practical" is most impractical, and that a short cut to knowledge is a long way round to efficiency.

Vocational guidance, on the other hand, is the means of sparing the community that expensive lesson. That is the great possibility of vocational guidance. It is the warning to take thought in a complex and disturbing situation. And it has some practical suggestions of how to attack the problem, that is if the term is interpreted broadly enough. If it arises out of a real need of readjustment between the school and society, it is evident that we must know the factors in that readjustment—the children, the schools, and the trades. To meet the dangers of vocational guidance, I should suggest the following safeguards.

Instead of starting employment bureaus, it would be good business to analyze the problem more exactly, to make a thorough study of the children and schools in a given locality in order to know the elements in the situation. Such work would take time, but concrete study of the actual conditions, although limited in scope, would be suggestive for larger application. It would mean a large staff, organized work in the schools, regular interviewing of children, and systematic home visiting. To be successful such a study must be both scientific and thoroughly social. You cannot get information unless you can win confidence, and it is impossible to win confidence unless you have both honesty and real interest in each individual situation. Before issuing bulletins and starting bureaus of information, committees should be organized to make a continuous study of trade conditions and demands. Such investigations would be of more value to vocational schools and children applying for working papers than anything at present in existence. Such a study of a given locality combined with such a study of the trades would settle certain points necessary to determine before establishing vocation bureaus. We should find out whether children leave school on account of economic pressure; we should discover the good and bad points in the employment certificate law and the importance of tests to determine a child's fitness to leave school, and we should gain a knowledge of the occupations that would enable us to forestall the exploiting of young workers, and show in what trades they might work.

If, through such information, vocational guidance can succeed in bringing the school into closer relation with the life of its children, it will, by so doing, impel the school to bridge the chasm between industrial and school life. But when that work is accomplished, vocational guidance may cease to exist as a distinct movement, just as the campaign against child labor will be unheard of when the system causing it has departed. In other words, the function of vocational guidance is probably to make itself superfluous by correcting fundamentally a social maladjustment so that the machinery of the newer education may run automatically. In the meantime, it must not be overlooked that there is a practical need for vocational guidance, and if it is to be successful it must have the coöperation of those interested in child labor and industrial education. The Child Labor Committee is legislating for the same group that is the chief concern of those interested in vocational guidance, that is the fourteen to sixteen-year-old children leaving school to go to work. Could not representatives from the two organizations be mutually helpful in making these laws more adequate? On the other hand, it is useless for vocational guidance directors to attempt to guide children into vocations unless they can aid them in getting training for those vocations. Guidance for training is probably the only really legitimate guidance. But if such assistance is to be given, the training must be obtainable. Is it not important that representatives of the industrial education committee and of vocational guidance should pool the results of their work with the same group of fourteen to sixteen-year-old children? I can think of nothing that would help vocational guidance more than such a standing committee consisting of representatives of child labor and industrial education and vocational guidance committees. If this were done it might be possible another year to report, not only upon the possibilities and dangers of vocational guidance, but upon its accomplishments.

RELATION OF INDUSTRIAL TRAINING TO CHILD LABOR

By William H. Elson,
Formerly Superintendent of Schools, Cleveland, Ohio.

Needs of Youthful Wage Earners

Whatever gives the best preparation for life, in view of opportunity and outlook, and tends to prolong the period devoted to school, minimizes the problem of child labor. I believe industrial training does this. It goes without saying that children destined early to enter the ranks of the laborer are in need of a school that will not only train the mind but will also train hand and eye. Obviously such a school offers a better composite called education, as a preparation for the life these children are to live, than one that devotes itself merely to books. For in such a school children learn how to go about work, how to lay out work; they acquire some knowledge of and skill in design, and they learn the properties of materials. Moreover, they learn patience and carefulness, for they have constantly before them the results of the exercise of these qualities. In dealing with material things a mistake is always in evidence; it is often costly, and is ever present; while errors of speech in mere lip service are evanescent and soon forgotten. Indeed, children do not regard these as important because of their evanescence. On the contrary errors in hand work persist. This is one of the large values in teaching children to express ideas in things as well as by words.

New Meaning of Education

Tradition associates books with education and pays little or no attention to experience. In consequence we are not inclined to think of the training of the shop as education. It is, however, impossible to distinguish between education through books and education through experience; both are factors in the product which we call an educated person. A school should offer instruction that makes for intelligence and insight, but it should also furnish opportunity for pupils to gain such control of materials and of tools as will enhance their earning power and fit them to render helpful service in the world of work. A school that combines theory and practice, correlating the two; that is both academic and industrial; that finds uses in the shop for applying book knowledge, and that stimulates its pupils to know more in order to do more, is not one nor the other, but is a composite of the two ingredients that make for a new definition of education. For pupils within the compulsory age limit, the problem of school administrators is to determine the composition of the ingredient best suited to the needs of the group of children in hand, in view of their aptitude, outlook and probable destination. This means segregation of those having similar needs. Whatever tends best to fit children for intelligent and helpful service when they may withdraw from school we must regard as education.

The Claims of Industrial Training

An industrial school demands recognition on the ground that it meets changed and changing conditions in the economic life with its growing demand for efficiency in industrial pursuits, and further because of the well-established fact that many, if not most, failures of children in the work of the schools are due, not to lack of ability on the part of the children, but to failure to consider the needs of hand-minded or practical-minded children by the school which gives distinctly one-sided attention to the language-minded and imaginative, relying upon the imagery of words and abstractions, neglecting to give attention to the actualities of everyday concrete life, both in learning and doing. Industrial schools have shown again and again that hand-minded children who have gained in their classes the reputation of being dullards and have lost faith in their ability may be restored to confidence and courage in themselves, and led to make satisfactory progress even in previously distasteful subjects, by giving them opportunity to exercise their powers in matters that appeal to them as worth while. If such children are to be given an opportunity to make the most of themselves, they must be approached from the side of the practical; must learn to do by doing and in order to do. Such children can be led to the "cultural," to an appreciation of the value of knowledge, only through the medium of the practical. The industrial school rests its claim to recognition upon these well-established facts.

Need of Data

To what extent industrial training tends to attract and hold the pupils in school is not known. Obviously it materially lengthens school life for many children. But, unfortunately, school administration in this country is based largely upon mere personal opinion, rather than upon known facts. This is true of the influence of industrial training in extending the school life of children beyond the age limit of the compulsory school law. Two cases furnish *actual data* bearing upon this point. One relates to the elementary grades, the other to high schools.

Elementary Industrial School

In 1909 an elementary industrial school for seventh and eighth grades was established in Cleveland, to which pupils stranded in the sixth, and not less than two years behind grade, were admitted. The principals were requested to send a given number of girls and boys who in their judgment were likely soon to withdraw from school, and who would, in their judgment, profit by such school. The consent of parents was obtained chiefly on the ground that the children were to be given a better chance for progress and promotion.

In this way a school for ninety-three boys and forty-three girls was organized in eight classes; five for the boys and three for the girls. The school was not to be a mere vocational or trade school. Industrial considerations were, indeed, to lead and the practical tendencies of the pupils were to be appealed to and emphasized both in hand-work and in academic work. They were to revel, as it were, in practical efficiency. Yet no effort was to be spared to touch and stir the deeper springs of personality, of manly and womanly qualities in the pupils, to lead them to an appreciation of the social and æsthetic value of work, to spiritualize their growing efficiency with elements of good-will and joy.

The Course of Study and Time Schedule

The course was planned for two years, covering seventh and eighth grades. The school-day extends from 8.30 A. M. to 3.15 P. M. It is divided into nine periods, one of which is assigned to luncheon. This leaves forty periods per week for instruction and practice. One-half of these are devoted to academic work in English, mathematics, geography, history and hygiene of a thoroughly practical character. The other half is devoted to industrial work, domestic economy and gymnasium practice. There are shower baths, a swimming pool and an auditorium for assembly exercises—rhetorical, musical, stereoscopic and general. The classes are segregated and no attempt is made to give classes of boys and girls the same treatment in any subject.

The Course for Girls

On the industrial and economic side, the course for girls includes cooking, laundering, and other household arts, sewing and garment-making, millinery, drawing and design, and applied art. The care of the sick-room and other features of home nursing receive attention; also plumbing, the care of traps, of the sink, refrigerator, bathroom, etc. Household accounts are treated—cost of food, fuel, service, rent, typical family budgets. Class visits are made to markets and house-furnishing establishments, to factories and shops.

A room was set aside which serves consecutively as living-room, dining-room, bedroom, sick-room. In the furnishing of this the boys and girls coöperate. Its subsequent management is in the hands of the girls.

The Course for Boys

The industrial course for boys includes mechanical and freehand drawing, woodwork, pattern-making, design and craft. Throughout, the work is closely related to corresponding industrial pursuits. In woodwork problems are given, presenting the systematic use of tools and general principles of construction. Simple projects are made with reference to use and beauty, and correlated with this is the work in metal, mechanical and free-hand drawing. Commercial problems are offered in appliances for school garden, window boxes, bulletin boards, frames for schoolrooms, etc. House-furnishing receives consideration in conjunction with the work of the girls in their model room, as well as in connection with individual needs. Fundamental problems in building construction are solved in miniature to be later applied in actual work. Metal fittings for woodwork, stains, paints and finishes are studied and applied. Class visits are made for definite purposes to shops and drafting rooms, to buildings in process of construction, paint manufacturers, etc. Stress is placed upon business methods, time-card, expense and checking system, measuring, estimating cost, bills, letters, materials and contracts.

The Effect Upon Pupils

After a thorough investigation of the work of this school, Dr. William N. Hailmann, former Superintendent of Indian Education in the United States, summarizes the work of the school in the following words:

The effect of the new work upon the pupils is full of encouragement. Under the stimulus of kindly and consistent discipline, and of faith in their ability on the part of their teachers, and under the influence of work in both departments of the school that dealt with directly intelligible problems and appealed to tangible interests, the children soon found themselves, discovered that they possessed abilities heretofore doubted, detected in their academic studies values bearing upon their immediate interests and turned to these studies with feelings of good-will heretofore foreign to them. As they gained in confidence they gained in poise. With increasing self-respect, there came to them increasing respect for the school and its work. With growing recognition of their social value and efficiency, they gained in individual self-assertion, coupled with a deepening sense of responsibility.

Pupils Gain in Academic Studies

Significant is the gain of the pupils in their academic work. Indifference yielded to intelligent interest; discouragement and apathy in the presence of difficulty to determined persistence and the fervor of achievement. Parents who came to visit the school expressed themselves as much pleased, praised the growing interest and ability of their children in academic as well as economic subjects, seemed to enjoy the new sensation of pride in the work and progress of their children.

A concomitant result of this growing appreciation of the value of the school is found in the steady increase in regularity of attendance. The significance of this gain is enhanced when it is remembered that many pupils come from great distances involving trolley trips of from six to seven miles, and, on the part of some, daily walks of three or four miles to and from school.

It must be noted, too, that these children came from the homes of day laborers, that the average age was 14.3 years, and that not more than 30 were *required* to attend school by reason of the compulsory school law. Notwithstanding these facts, in June, 1911, a class of 55 graduated from this school, 20 of whom registered for high schools, an awakening that was truly marvelous.

A lingering prejudice, due to misapprehension that membership in the school implied dullness, has been overcome so completely that the opening of the second year brought a number of voluntary applications from "bright" children. Moreover, a number of pupils, some of whom had lost interest in school education, are now eager to prepare for entrance in the Technical High School.

OPINIONS OF PUPILS

Reports from Girls

A second-year class of twenty-seven girls was requested to state freely in a letter, without revision by the teacher, what benefit, if any, they had derived from transfer to the school, and what were their favorite subjects of work and study.

The following extracts from letters received will indicate the spirit of their answers with reference to the first point:

"Arithmetic and geography I never could understand in grade school, but since I have come here I am interested." "I like the school because the teachers teach the studies we most need, especially the boys and girls who want to earn their own living." "I find that I have improved in the subject which seemed to halt my progress in school. This subject was arithmetic, and I am grateful to the teacher and the school for their help." "I like the school because it has helped me to get good marks in school and be good to home folks." "The school has taught me to be more useful in the home and to be neater in my work than I used to be." "I hope this school will help me more every day, so that I may be more useful when I grow older." "Here we learn how to sew and cook, and we learn arithmetic and geography that we will use out in life." "Our arithmetic and other studies are given us in a way that will help us when we are grown up." "This school has helped me to wish to be helpful to others, and it has taught me work that, when I am home, I can help my mother." "The teachers here speak to us like grown-up sisters. They tell what we should do in a way that makes us feel at home." "I enjoy coming here, because the lessons are more businesslike." "Since I came here I have learned more than in the seven years at grade school, especially in arithmetic." "I like this school because I never could have learned anything, and I am more use in the world. I learned how to be a lady." "Out in the grade school I felt as if I just wanted to stop, but here the work is so interesting that I don't like to leave it." "The school has helped me in what I needed most, obedience and behavior."

Cooking and sewing were mentioned as favorite subjects by twenty-one; gymnasium practice and swimming by eight; geography by six; arithmetic by ten; English by nine; drawing by five. Six of the girls are looking forward with eager interest to the millinery of the second-year course.

Reports from the Boys

Letters similarly obtained from a class of thirty-seven boys yield the following extracts:

"The lessons were so interesting that I felt as if I was taking a new hold in life." "I am more business-like than I was before, and can do my work much better." "Mechanical drawing I like best, because you have to be neat and accurate." "It has taught me what an education means in life." "We do not sit in one room all the time, and have the privilege of changing classes." "The school has made me be more of a man; it has made me have more self-respect and responsibility." "I like the shop-work because it gives me something to do with my hands." "The six hours in this school pass quicker than the five hours in the other school." "It makes me more respectful, and the work is more of the kind I like." "If the industrial school continues to be used to make men of boys, it will soon be of great value." "In making things at home I have more confidence in myself." "It has learned me to have better manners and to do better arithmetic and lots of other things." "The work I like best is arithmetic, because I did not know any at all before I came here." "I learned to be more obedient and my parents say: 'You seem to be learning more now than you used to learn.'" "The school has made a man of me." "The school has helped me to think and to get my work more easily." "Shop-work and drawing I like best, because they teach me to be accurate." "I like it because it is the line of work I will follow." (Several boys express this thought; others see in the work good preparation for the Technical High School, and one of these for subsequent attendance upon a course in scientific farming at the O. S. U.) "It has not only helped me in learning a trade, but to get along better in my other studies." "It has taught me to like school. I like all the work we have."

Among favorite subjects mechanical drawing is mentioned by twenty-six, woodwork by eighteen. Seven boys praise the fact that they do not have to sit in one room all day. One boy criticises "the poor location" of the school, but is otherwise much pleased.

Summary of Gains

Clearly, there was distinct awakening in the life of those children under the stimulus of the new work. There were evidences of gain in sustained interest and purposeful effort extending even to so-called academic work. Stress is laid by the children on their gain in general interest, on the practical value of the school, on their gain in obedience and "behavior," in self-respect and confidence, in efficiency, in a conviction that they amount to something. A few attribute this to the industrial and economic features of the work; others to the helpful attitude of the teachers; still others to the departmental organization which does away with the feeling of constraint in being confined in one room "the whole day," and gives opportunity for the mental relief that comes from change of environment. Evidently the feeling of dawning manhood and womanhood with its "sweet responsibilities" had come to these children. They had tested the proud privilege of self-education. Their school was to them no longer a fancied *preparation* for life, but had every ear-mark of *actual* life.

Moreover, this school has demonstrated that industrial training as a child-saving measure has marvelous power to extend the school life of children, even under the press of economic need. It is not too much to say that none of these original 136 pupils, stranded in the sixth grade, would ever have seen the eighth grade, much less the high school, had it not been for the impelling interest and influence of this industrial school.

High School Data

The second instance furnishing actual data as to the influence of industrial training in attracting and holding pupils, thereby extending their school life, relates to the high school field.

Previous to 1909, Cleveland had six high schools of the usual or literary type, preparing pupils for college. In 1909 vocational high schools were started by the opening of a technical high school with courses preparing for work and not for college. This school enrolled 729 pupils at once, of whom 484 had just completed the grammar grades, 122 were transferred from other high schools in the city, and 123 were recruited from shops and factories, pupils who had quit school and gone to work, but who were attracted by a practical school of this kind. The year following a High School of Commerce was established along similar lines of practical efficiency. The following table tells the story in a graphic way:

ATTENDANCE IN CLEVELAND HIGH SCHOOLS.

Year	1906	1907	1908	1909	1910	1911
Academic	4983	5059	4989	4787	4436	5293
Vocational				729	1560	2005
Total	4983	5059	4989	5507	5996	7298

Notice that in the three years before 1909, high schools did not grow, yet the city was growing at the rate of 2,000 school children each year as shown by the school census. In 1909 vocational high schools were started, the Technical High School in 1909, the High School of Commerce in 1910, and the West Technical in 1911. The result is a growth from 4989 in 1908 to 7298 in 1911, almost 50 per cent. gain. Moreover, it is to be noted that the vocational high schools have started growth in the academic

Number of Pupils in Cleveland High Schools

Vocational School Reports began in 1909
Almost 50% growth since 1908.

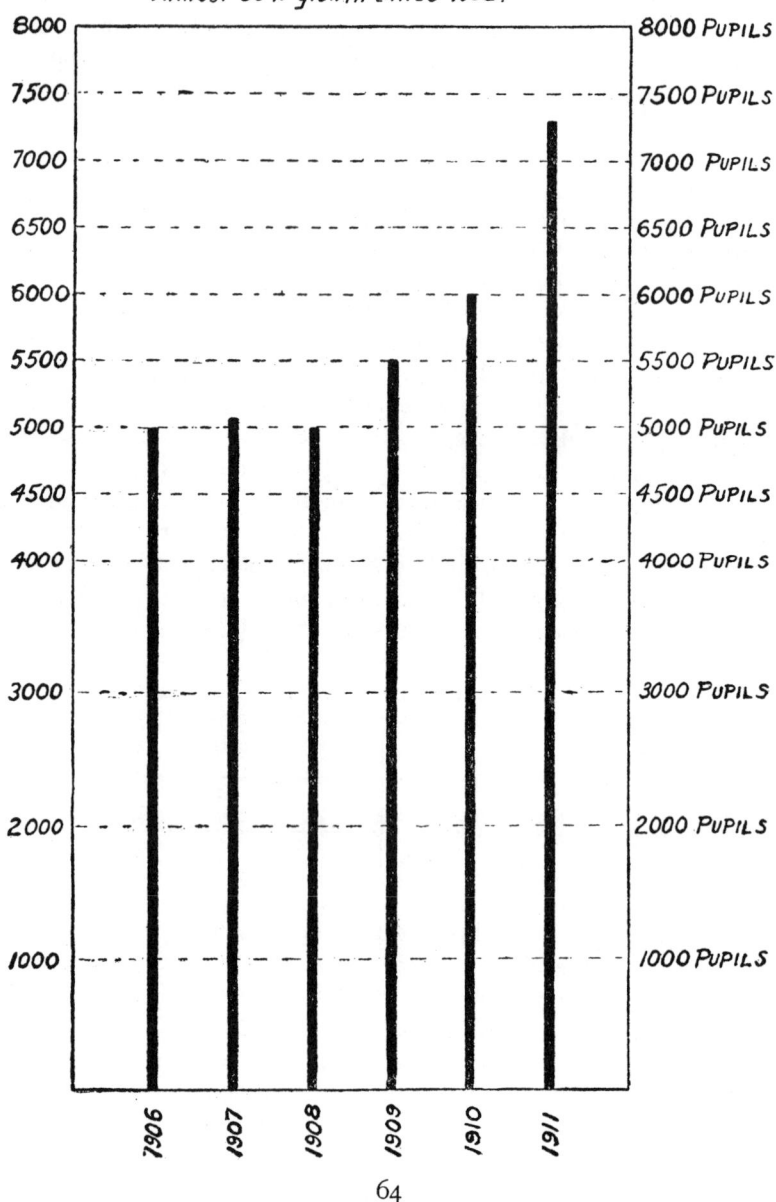

high schools. While for three years previous to the opening of vocational high schools the academic schools did not grow, yet they reached their highest enrollment in 1911, notwithstanding the fact that more than 2000 pupils were in attendance at the vocational high schools.

We need more data showing the actual influence of industrial training on school attendance and in extending the school life of needy children. Of its value to the youthful wage-earner there can be no doubt. These cases of actual data available bear strong testimony to the holding power of industrial training. What we now need is not more theory along this line, but more facts giving actual measure of the commanding influence of industrial training and its consequent relation to the problem of child labor.

ECONOMIC VALUE OF EDUCATION

By M. Edith Campbell,
Director, The Schmidlapp Bureau for Women and Girls, Cincinnati, Ohio.

The life of a little girl who recently came under our notice is haunting my memory with unusual insistence. She lives alone with her father in two small basement rooms, from where she walks two miles to school every morning. She has made few, if any, friends in school, either among teachers or pupils, because of her extreme timidity, which amounts to a positive fear of people. Her father, a night watchman, earns $12 or $15 a week, out of which he gives the child $1.00 a week for all her expenses, including clothing. He is opposed to her attendance at school, because it interferes with her preparing lunch for him, and other home ministrations to his comfort. This opposition explained her silence and fear of talking with people as well as the shadow of a catastrophe which always seems to be hanging over her. So far as we could secure her confidence, this dreaded catastrophe was the loss of her beloved school hours, for which she was making such heavy sacrifices, and to the retention of which her every effort was bent with a silent, stoical fortitude unsurpassed in its pathos and heroism. Thinking of the child's lonely, inexplicable struggle for education, I ventured to wonder if, after the completion of high school, she presented herself at our employment desk we could reward her perseverance. Could the great public school system of Cincinnati demonstrate to her how her efforts would pay in the great *industrial* system of the city? Could we place her for $2.00 or even $1.00 more a week than we could if she had come to us from the seventh or eighth grade? When one has sat at the desk of an employment bureau and has seen from 20 to 30 children and young women a day who are coming in for advice and information, you wish most profoundly, as we did in this case, that we could turn to that infallible file of a 5-by-8 card, and that we could have one drawer, which said, "Children who have completed High School," and another drawer, "Children who have not," and that one drawer would be so good as to show us a fair wage scale, and the other drawer would be so good as to show us a low wage scale. But these drawers are not in our office; perhaps they are in yours. Consequently when we think of the economic advantage as purely a material advantage to the child, we are perplexed and dumbfounded at the results.

But I keenly realize the danger in even discussing some of these apparent results—the danger of being understood as depreciating training and education; and also my lack of authority in the matter. In fact, when I saw the very convincing chart [1] of educational and non-educational "hills," I felt quite like Artemus Ward, whom I heard Mr. Dyer laughingly quote not long ago, when he was asked to speak on a specialty not in his line. He said that Ward in passing a snake hole remarked, "This 'ere hole belongs to this 'ere snake," and walked *around* the hole. The discussion of this subject certainly belongs to those of you who have taught and worked with children longer and more intelligently than I have. Consequently, I have only to offer you the benefit of the very limited experience of the Schmidlapp Bureau for Girls, which will certainly be "walking around" the unfathomable "hole" of education and its economic value. The Bureau has three departments:

1st. The Charlotte R. Schmidlapp Fund, a loan fund, available to young women for educational purposes.

2d. The Employment Department, through which young women secure positions.

3d. The Vocation Department, issuance of age-and-schooling certificates for city, and testing of children for future vocations. In this department we are coöperating with Mr. Edward N. Clopper.

We have not found, as far as women and girls are concerned, that we can use the educational department for a standard for the other two departments. We cannot point to the educational department and say "here is a group of 250 girls whom we are helping, whom we are putting through college, whom we are encourag-

[1] See page 142*a*.

ing to finish high school, whom we are advising to enter some professional form of training; here is a group of girls we can absolutely rely upon as far as increase in efficiency, in general intelligence, in good taste, in simplicity of dress, in culture"—we cannot take this group as a whole and feel that there we have the correct standards for the girl of the employment class or the high school or eighth grade, or even the girl of the fourth or fifth grade class.

Just why this is we cannot tell. There may be three reasons why the educational department, or why the educational standards are not always to be used as the norm that we are trying so hard to reach.

No Economic Advantage

In the first place there is, of course, the failure of education, and whenever we have nothing else to do we jump on the system of education and say that it is a total failure. Dean Schneider was telling me the other day that in connection with his work on the New York School Commission, he was lunching with three or four employers, two or three college men and one or two men of other professions. In the course of the discussion, one of these men said, "Well, why don't we come out flat-footed and say that the whole system of public school education is wrong from the foundation up?" To which every single man at that luncheon agreed; there was not a dissent. This failure seems further illustrated in a recent investigation made by the Woman's Educational and Industrial Union of Boston, under the direction of Miss Kingsbury. This disclosed the fact that many college women were working for salaries far below women who had never entered even high school, and that the wage of the college woman is often below $1,000. Using the term economic advantage in the sense of financial advantage, we find a similar failure in the early education of the child. There is, of course, a vast difference between the child of the fifth grade, and the child of the high school. That is, there is no question but that we are finding some advantage, even material advantage in the child who completes the fifth and sixth grade over the child who is allowed to go into work without any educational requirements at all. And for that reason we believe that in the few States where we have the educational requirement, we can show in a few years some material advantage coming to the child for having completed at least the sixth or seventh grade. But there seems to be an inexplicable lack of superiority in the high school graduate over the child of the seventh and eighth grade. The occupation of stenographic or clerical work may be used as an illustration, an occupation where we would expect to find a distinct economic value in three or four years' additional schooling. We find, for instance, in going over our files of the girls who are securing $9 or $14 or $15 a week, that they have secured that wage because they have been with the firm a great number of years; because of reliability; because of their usefulness or because of some natural aptitude for the work, and we have found almost invariably that the girl who is making this wage is just as apt to be an eighth grade girl as she is to be the graduate of a high school. This fact is clearly shown in the recent most excellent and thorough report on Vocational Training made by a committee [1] for the Chicago City Club. In a questionaire presented to business men concerning office or clerical employees, 60 per cent. replied that high school pupils were not efficient. Among other criticisms the employers claim in these employees "a lack of knowing how to apply what mathematics they have learned," "deficient general education," "miserable penmanship and not thorough in anything." In the reasons given by the pupils for leaving school at fourteen these deficiencies in the present system are recognized. In his summary (p. 9) Mr. Mead says: "Finally we have taken into account the economic loss to children and their parents if they remain in school after the age of fourteen and are thus deprived of the opportunity of earning."

Analysis of Industrial Situation Lacking

While he shows that the return which boys who leave school at fourteen bring into the home is negligible, he also demonstrated

[1] George H. Mead, chairman; E. A. Weidt, W. J. Bogan. Published since the Child Labor Conference, but before the revision of this paper; p. 258, pp. 9-11.

that the parent does not find a financial reward in compelling the child to remain in school until he is sixteen or eighteen. A large share of this failure or the second failure of the educational standard can certainly be attributed to a lack of analysis of the industrial situation. For years we have been turning out children day after day from these schools of ours, plunging them into a life of which the makers of the curriculum knew absolutely nothing, for they had never stopped to make an analysis, not even through the great implement which was right at their hands, the issuance of work certificates. This opportunity for analysis has been entrusted again and again to boards of education, without their seizing the chance to understand the child's first wage-saving experience or to gain an intimate, accurate knowledge of industrial conditions surrounding the child worker. A patient, careful analysis of the trades and professions open to the boy or girl, cannot fail to clarify our insight and to make us face conditions as they are. We will at least reckon with "enervating" and "energizing" trades, as Dean Schneider calls them. In the continuation schools in Cincinnati we find we cannot train the children using their trade as a guide, because there is often nothing in the trade for which to educate them. Many of the trades are so distinctly automatic, part of the process so evidently enervating, that the child's mind can only be stimulated by presenting some line of thought as far removed as possible from the occupation. On the other hand, when a trade has been found to be energizing, this mental stimulation can be secured by presenting to the child information about the difficulties of this trade over which the child is puzzling, and in which there is no chance for advancement without an intelligent efficiency. These trades are often disclosed by the question which the children in the continuation schools ask—questions showing an awakened mind which had hitherto lain dormant. Such an analysis may not only show distinct classification in trades, but it may show that the majority of our children are entering upon work so automatic and so mechanical that the State will be compelled to raise the working age; to allow the child of fourteen to work only part time; or to pay the heavy, unthinkable price of our working children being physically, morally and mentally degenerated.

The third reason which may be given for the seeming failure

of the educational standard is, of course, the ever-present human equation, which, in spite of our faith in class reforms, and in educational systems, thwarts plans and baffles the most reasonable of theories.

General Economic Value

May we now turn and attempt to enlarge our definition of economic value, which we have so far used as purely material and financial value. For as faulty as our educational system may be, we have certainly enormously increased the child's economic asset by making a better individual than he would have been without his school years. We may call this value a spiritual one, an ethical one, or one which makes character, or the "unknown quantity" in education, but in any case in so far as this value increases the physical, moral, mental or spiritual power of the individual, it cannot but increase the economic and industrial power of the community. Because of this belief we are tenaciously clinging to the theory that a "general education" is as necessary as a special or vocational course of study to the development of the individual. How else can we give the child reserve power, resourcefulness, a "cultivated imagination," and the ability not only to *meet* the exigencies of life, but to *rise above* their sordidness? Mr. James has said in a recent essay that education "should help you to know a good man when you see him." This can only be accomplished by bringing the child into contact with "superiority" in history, literature, and every field of human endeavor. He can thus be taught to differentiate between "sound work, clean work, finished work; feeble work, slack work, sham work," and to "acquire standards of the excellent and durable."[1] The opportunity to bring the child into contact with superiority is ever present also in the personality of the teacher. And I often marvel, as I pass through the great buildings of our school system, at the unhesitating and enormous expenditures in stone and wood when the amount invested in people is so comparatively small. Too little is done toward building up strong, splendid personalities in our teachers, thus making sure of

---

[1] William James, Memories and Studies, New York, 1911. Essay on the College Bred.

the most powerful influence of which we know, the influence of personality. This great body of workers is too often underpaid, overworked, and not given the chance to gain a wider vision and deeper insight into the needs of the child. We must not let equipment or material demands make us forget that the eternal, *known* force in education whether it be general or vocational is *personality*.

While our schools have accomplished wonders in thus developing the child's character and resourcefulness, there is yet much to be done. Yesterday there came to my desk a young woman who applied for work to do at home in the evening. Finding her intelligent, well dressed and refined, and knowing of the comfortable circumstances of her family, as well as of her own excellent wage as a stenographer, I expressed my surprise that she needed to do such work. She insisted that she must have it, but when I told her that because of my disapproval, I could not place such work at her disposal, she exclaimed: "Well, then, what shall I do with my evenings?" This girl, a high-school student, had missed the lesson of resourcefulness! And have we not with us the problem of teaching the child some use of "evenings" as much as teaching her the use of the day for making a living? By a constant, patient, keen analysis of the demands of industry, saving the child from wasted years in "blind-alley trades," by a quick adaptation of our educational system to the present needs of the child, we can at least begin to untangle vocational riddles. By a fearless acknowledgment and training of the "sixth sense"—mysticism, imagination, resourcefulness or, however you may define it, that sense which enables the child to find the secret of life in his own interpretation of its brilliant lights and dark shadows, we can give to education its only economic value.

NEED OF COMPULSORY EDUCATION IN THE SOUTH

By W. H. Hand,
State High School Inspector, Columbia, S. C.

The need of compulsory school attendance in the South is so nearly axiomatic as to render its demonstration almost superfluous. One is forced to wonder that discerning men and women ever question the need of anything so manifest. The long train of evils consequent upon illiteracy is patent to the most casual observer or superficial thinker. One of the most remarkable facts connected with the history of education in the United States is that our Southern States have persistently refused to enact such compulsory attendance laws as have been found necessary and have been enacted by every other State in the Union, and by nearly all the leading culture lands of the world. Of all the Southern States, Kentucky and Arkansas are the only ones with compulsory attendance laws which may be considered general and effective, and none of the five Southern States with any kind of compulsory law has had the law long enough to have made any marked decrease in its illiteracy. We are still debating in a purely academic way the need, the wisdom, and the feasibility of something which has been tested and accepted by the majority of English, German and French-speaking peoples. Nevertheless, the mere fact that other sections of the Union and other countries have enacted such laws is of itself not conclusive evidence that we should enact them. Any logical argument for or against compulsory attendance must be based on conditions as they exist.

To some persons statistics are not only dry but meaningless. Generally the same persons are more or less impervious to facts whenever the facts happen to be distasteful. However distasteful the facts concerning our illiteracy (and to no one are they more distasteful than to the writer), I am compelled to introduce them. It is highly regrettable that we must use in the main figures from the census report for 1900. The figures dealing with illiteracy in 1910 will not be available for several weeks. It is to be devoutly hoped that the census report for 1910 will reveal the greatest advance against illiteracy made in a century. However, some of the deductions from the published data are not altogether reassuring. In at least four Southern States, widely separated geographically, the decennial increase in school attendance, as shown by reports of State Superintendents of Education, is very little in advance of the decennial increase in white population for the corresponding period. These figures do not indicate any very marked decrease in the illiteracy of these States.

Confining ourselves to the native white population, I beg to direct your attention to the actual conditions in the Southern States, and to the relative illiteracy between the South and other parts of the United States and four foreign countries.

Exhibit A—Native White Illiterates Ten Years of Age and Over

	Per Cent.
North Atlantic States (all under compulsory laws)	1.7
North Central States (all under compulsory laws)	2.8
Western States (all under compulsory laws)	3.4
South Atlantic States (mostly without compulsory laws)	12.0
South Central States (mostly without compulsory laws)	11.6
Southern States alone	12.4

Exhibit B—Native White Illiterate Males of Voting Age

	Per Cent.
North Atlantic States	2.1
North Central States	3.5
Western States	2.8
South Atlantic States	12.2
South Central States	11.5
Southern States alone, 307,236 persons	12.2
France, male adults	4.7
England, male and female adults	3.0
Scotland, male and female adults	2.4
German Empire, male adults	0.5

Exhibit C—Showing Rank of Each Southern State in Percentage of Illiteracy of Native Whites Ten Years of Age and Over

Texas (highest in rank)	35th	Kentucky	43rd
Mississippi	37th	South Carolina	44th
Florida	38th	Tennessee	46th
Virginia	40th	Alabama	47th
Arkansas	41st	Louisiana	48th
Georgia	42nd	North Carolina	49th

Compulsory Education in the South

In the next exhibit the eleven so-called Southern States are taken as a group with no compulsory attendance laws until very recently. Virginia, North Carolina, South Carolina, Georgia and Mississippi are taken as representative States of the South, with practically no compulsory attendance. Massachusetts, Rhode Island and Connecticut are taken as representative of New England, each with a compulsory attendance law enacted years ago and requiring long terms of attendance enforced by rather heavy penalties. Michigan is taken as a type of the newer West, with a compulsory attendance rather rigidly enforced. West Virginia and Kentucky are taken as specimens of recent compulsory attendance laws at first mild in form and not very rigidly enforced.

Exhibit D—Native White Illiterates Ten Years of Age and Over

	Persons.	Per Cent.
Southern States	959,799	12.4
Virginia	95,583	11.4
North Carolina	175,325	19.6
South Carolina	54,177	13.9
Georgia	99,948	12.2
Mississippi	35,432	8.1
Massachusetts	3,912	0.5
Rhode Island	1,196	1.0
Connecticut	1,958	0.6
Michigan	12,154	1.5
West Virginia	63,008	10.4
Kentucky	166,822	13.9

Exhibit E—Native White Male Illiterates of Voting Age

	Persons.	Per Cent.
Southern States	307,236	12.2
Virginia	35,057	12.5
North Carolina	54,208	19.0
South Carolina	15,643	12.6
Georgia	31,914	12.1
Mississippi	11,613	8.3
Massachusetts	1,927	0.6
Rhode Island	550	1.2
Connecticut	1,040	0.9
Michigan	6,406	2.2
West Virginia	23,024	11.2
Kentucky	62,182	15.5

These figures, rightly interpreted, can have but one meaning—that compulsory education reduces illiteracy, and that the South sorely needs to have hers reduced. In a monarchy, the primary object in educating its citizens has been to make good, intelligent, loyal subjects. In a democracy, such as ours, the primary object in educating the people is to make good, intelligent, loyal and prosperous citizen-sovereigns. Admittedly we are making "the most stupendous experiment in government" that the world has ever seen. We are making of practically every man a citizen, clothing him with the power to make and to administer the laws of a great nation, and to direct and to control all the forces and resources of our institutional life. To meet successfully such tremendous responsibilities requires intelligence and training of the highest constructive order.

If our government is to achieve and maintain that eminence among the powers of the earth to which we pledge our faith, it must secure for itself an intelligent, efficient, and orderly citizenship. Intelligence and efficiency lie at the very foundation of any people's greatness; intelligent and efficient citizens are a State's fundamental asset, and the State which has the largest percentage of illiteracy has relatively the smallest percentage of effective citizens. Ambassador Bryce has repeatedly emphasized the fact that America has put unlimited power into the hands of the people, and if the people are to enjoy that power without abusing it, they must be educated. By the people is meant all the people. The South could once boast of an aristocracy capable, broad minded and highly trained—in the language of Henry W. Grady, "almost feudal in its grandeur." The conditions conducive to such a society have been swept away, and the South to-day is preëminently the land where training and fitness of the masses are indispensable.

No sound-thinking man would for a moment contend that education in the common acceptation of that word is a panacea for political and social ills, nor would he claim that an illiterate man is necessarily not a good citizen. But in a democracy where manhood suffrage practically prevails, institutional life is exposed to tremendous dangers when twelve per cent. of the voting population are unable to read the names printed on the ballots they are supposed to cast intelligently for the government of the State.

Compulsory Education in the South

Ignorance stands for narrowness, bigotry, selfishness and stagnation; intelligence stands for liberty, liberality, tolerance, sympathy and growth. We must choose between the two.

The advocates of compulsory education among us are being constantly admonished to wait for the thirteenth census report (1910) for proof that we do not need compulsion. Reference has already been made to the probable disappointment which that report holds for us. Many of us had our hopes blasted by the revelations made by the twelfth census. It may not be amiss to take a glance at the decrease in illiteracy of our Southern States between 1890 and 1900:

Exhibit F—Showing the Actual Decrease of Native White Illiterates Ten Years of Age and Over, Between 1890 and 1900

	1890.	1900.	Decrease.
Virginia	102,669	95,583	7,086
North Carolina	173,128	175,325	*2,196
South Carolina	58,782	54,177	4,605
Georgia	113,384	99,948	13,436
Mississippi	44,284	35,432	8,852
West Virginia	64,017	63,008	1,009
Kentucky	175,308	166,822	8,486

The opponents of compulsory attendance insist that our people will send their children to school without being compelled to do so, if only they are shown their duty and their obligation to their children. These opponents declare that the younger generation of our white children are already in school. Neither contention is true. The credulity of a man already wedded to a delusion is something marvelous. For twenty years our ablest and safest leaders, men and women whose names stand high in the nation, have been tireless in their efforts to get the children of the South into the schools; yet more than twenty-five per cent. of the native white children between the ages of ten and fourteen are not in school at all. In 1900 the South Atlantic States had 2,472,895 white children between the ages of five and twenty years; the

*This increase of white illiterates in North Carolina comes in the decade following one of the most strenuous educational campaigns ever waged in the State.

white attendance for the same year was 1,176,976, or fewer than one-half the total number. Let us make one other comparison:

Table G—Native White Illiterates Between Ten and Nineteen Years of Age

	Persons.
Southern States	262,590
Virginia	23,108
North Carolina	45,632
South Carolina	17,839
Georgia	25,941
Mississippi	10,212
Massachusetts	416
Rhode Island	100
Connecticut	160
West Virginia	11,628
Kentucky	33,400

People of the South, shall we be content to send out into the world at the unseasoned age of twenty years more than a quarter of a million illiterate native white boys and girls? Can we afford to thrust these illiterate white boys and girls out into a world enriched by the progress in the arts and sciences reaching back over a century rich in discoveries and inventions? How can we expect them with vagrant minds and untrained hands to win in competition with brain-guided hands and muscle-aided brains? Our young Samsons have their hands bound with the withes of ignorance while the pitiless Delilah, dogged conservatism, cuts off their last lock. Poverty and stress of war can no longer be urged as a palliative for the illiteracy of the South's children who ought to be in school. The material prosperity of the present South is one of the marvels of modern times. The faith and courage with which our people rebuilt their ruined homes, reclaimed their neglected fields, bridged the rivers, tunneled the mountains, built factories and constructed railroads challenge the admiration of the civilized world. In that struggle to rise from the ashes the greatest hindrance has been our load of illiteracy, and to-day it is our heaviest burden.

Who are these illiterate white children of the South, and why are they not in school? Some are the sons and daughters of parents themselves ignorant and unable to appreciate or to understand what education means to their children and to the State; some are the children of sordid fathers and mothers who are more than willing to make wage-earners and breadwinners of their untaught offspring. Many of these children are at work on the farms, in stores and shops at a few cents a day, or in the cotton mills making good wages for children; while hundreds of others are roaming the streets and country lanes, the training grounds for idlers, vagrants and enemies to law, order and decency. Many of these children are the descendants of Walter Page's *forgotten men.* They became the *neglected mass,* and the neglected mass has become the *indifferent mass.* When any considerable number of people in a state become indifferent to the intellectual, moral and social conditions of themselves and their offspring, the situation becomes alarming, for illiteracy, like every other evil, tends to perpetuate itself. And one of the most unpromising features of this already gloomy prospect is that in most of the Southern States the illiterate females outnumber the illiterate males. An illiterate mother does not augur well for the child of to-morrow.

Has the State the right to compel a parent to send his child to school? On this point we have many valiant knights ready to do battle for the so-called inalienable rights of a free people, among them the right to keep their children in the bondage of ignorance. These knightly statesmen grow hysterical over the word "compulsory." They are exceedingly anxious lest we should introduce into our government machinery something practiced by some ancient aristocracy or suggested by some modern monarchy. These statesmen fail to see that compulsory education is in its spirit and purpose modern and democratic. Years ago we accepted without much serious question the doctrine that popular education is necessary to the growth and permanence of our republican institutions. Since all classes of our heterogeneous society are active factors therein, the State maintains schools for all the children of all the people. The schools exist primarily for the benefit of the State rather than for the benefit of the individual. The State seeks to make every citizen intelligent and serviceable. The State compels the rich man to pay taxes to help support the schools, not because he owes the poor man's child an education, but because the State needs the intelligent services of that child. The schools are democratized by compelling the rich and the poor alike to pay taxes according to their ability for something necessary to all.

When the State has provided schools for all the children, it has performed only a part of its duty. If a universal school tax is justifiable on the ground that popular education is a necessity, compulsory attendance by the State is also justifiable. The State has no right to levy and collect taxes for a specific purpose, then permit that purpose to be defeated at the hands of indifferent or selfish parents. In this connection we hear much about the sacred rights and personal privileges of the parent who neglects or refuses to send his child to school. Has the helpless child no sacred rights? Has the State not some privileges? No one regrets more than I the tendency to shift from the home those functions which properly belong there. One of those functions is to train the children for their duties and responsibilities in the social organism. Society itself is imperiled whenever its members are unfit. One of the essentials of fitness is what we call education. Therefore, whenever the home refuses or neglects to prepare the child for society, it is not only the privilege but the duty of the State to see that the child is fitted for its part in society. Argument against the right of the State to send a child to school is specious and superficial. Those who make such argument would not for one moment deny the right of the State to compel the parent to vaccinate his child, to compel the parent to feed and clothe his child, or to compel him to fight for his country, and to shoot him if he deserted. The State has the right to carry the law-breaking child to the reformatory or to jail to protect society. Has not the State as much right to carry the child to the schoolhouse to save him from the reformatory or the jail and to train him to benefit society? Those who deny the right of the State to compel the parent to send his child to school are too frequently the offending parents themselves, sentimental theorists or vacillating politicians.

When the State compels the parent to send his child to school, it is simply compelling the parent to put the child in possession of his own rightful inheritance. In a narrow sense that inheritance is his right to the benefit of what the State has collected and set apart for him: in a wider and truer sense it means his opportunity to make of himself all that his God-given abilities will permit him to become; in the broadest sense it is his becoming fitted to take his place in the State to perform the sacred duties of an intelligent citizen in the broadest meaning of that term.

Objection is often made that compulsory attendance would work hardship in the homes of the poor. Is it not a fact that the poor child is the very one who most needs the aid of the State to bring him into possession of his own? He it is who must soon face the complexities of modern life and the insistent demands of citizenship with none of the advantages common to birth or wealth. He is the very one whom the State ought to help, because he himself is helpless. The child of the poor must work; but it is neither right nor humane that he should be forever denied his share in his inheritance in order to be a breadwinner for a selfish, unfeeling father, as is so frequently the case.

Over and over we are told that a compulsory law could not be successfully enforced. That is begging the question. Why not the same skepticism about the enforcement of any other law? The opponents insist that a compulsory law could not be enforced, because the people are not ready for such a law. Would there be any use for this law or any other law, if all the people were ready and waiting to obey it? Laws are enacted to compel men to do that which they ought to do, but will not do voluntarily. Tens of thousands of people in America are not obeying the Ten Commandments. Are we to justify this disobedience on the ground that the people are not quite ready for the Decalogue? Or is the Decalogue a piece of unwise and premature legislation, because some of us do not obey it? Will any law enforce itself? Will any law be enforced until an honest effort has been made to do so? And what is meant by successful enforcement? Can the enforcement of a law be called unsuccessful so long as it is violated by the few? In every civilized land there is a law against homicide. There are many violations of that law. Shall we for that reason call that law a failure and repeal it? To argue that a compulsory law could not be enforced is to argue that we ourselves are not law-abiding.

It is further argued that a child forced to attend school would derive but little benefit from the school. Those who argue thus forget that the compulsion is not in bringing to the school the unwilling child, but in forcing an indifferent, mercenary, recreant parent to let his child go to school.

Another contention is that compulsory laws could not be enforced without truant officers, and that such officers must be paid out of the school funds. I at once admit the necessity for the truant officer and that he must be paid. The city of Louisville would no doubt save thousands of dollars every year in the way of salaries if it would dismiss its policemen, its constables, and its detectives. But these officers are necessary to perform for the people services more valuable than the sum of their salaries. So it would be with the truant officers. We are perfectly willing to pay an officer of the law to arrest little negro boys in a ten-cent crap game; but it is too much to pay an officer of the law to see that a lazy, selfish father sends his child to school. We are paying today in actual money every year five times as much in tribute to the industrial supremacy of other sections as it would cost to keep every white child in the South in school for six months in the year. What economists we are! What philosophers we try to be!

Frequently the opponents insist that we have not enough schoolhouses and teachers to take care of the thousands of children whom a compulsory law would add to the attendance. Then the situation should be alarming to even the opponents. These opponents, if they be farmers, would likely oppose any increase in the yield of their cornfields because, forsooth! their corncribs would not hold the crop. Such argument is absolutely worthless unless we are prepared to admit that the white people of the South are actually unable to take care of their own children—an admission I am not ready to make. Shall the schoolhouses ever be built or the teachers employed until there is need for them? Whenever the children knock at the door of the schoolhouse it will be found open and a sympathetic teacher ready to receive them.

Temporizing patriots, with one ear listening to the call of duty and the other listening to the hostile rabble, declare for compulsory education when pressed to take a stand, but they usually add that the people are not quite ready for it. Who are the people not quite ready? Why are they not quite ready? When shall they be quite ready? Are they not the same people who were not quite ready for education at public expense, and were not quite ready for the foreign mission movement, and were not quite ready to vote for waterworks, electric light plants, and other public utilities? In fact, these people are not quite ready to do anything which their forefathers did not do, and some of them would not be quite ready to vote for compulsory education twenty years hence, though every child they should have be signing his name with a cross mark. These temporizing patriots must know that by compulsion alone we shall get all the children into the schools, yet they are hindering the day which they admit ought to come. They justify their course by saying that they are leading the people instead of attempting to drive them. These men ought to know that leaders must be men of determined purpose and strength—mere temporizers never. They mistake timidity for discretion. Parents in the bonds of ignorance, indifference, greed and stifling cupidity are not easily lured into educating their children. The experience of other sections and other countries has been that compulsion had to be applied. In the end the South will have to apply compulsion. Neither bonuses nor local option laws will put the children into the schools. We might as well face the facts.

The argument against compulsory education on account of the negro has been worn threadbare; surely the time has come to let it drop. Some phases of it are pathetic. Is it wise or expedient to permit thousands of white boys and girls to grow up in ignorance, lest in forcing them to school we should awaken the aspirations of the negro child? Shall we remain ignorant in order to encourage the negro to remain ignorant? Is it better for white and black to remain ignorant than to have both intelligent? The only logical conclusion to such argument is that the ignorant white man can compete successfully with the ignorant negro, but that the educated white man cannot compete with the educated negro. Then what becomes of the boasted superiority of the white man? Has the white man so nearly reached the zenith of his possibilities that he cannot keep well in advance of the ambitious negro?

I know that there are among us many who contend that the educational conditions in the South are matters for congratulation. I yield to no one in the matter of pride over what the South has done in the past forty years. To me it is a source of constant delight to see and to hear so many evidences of educational progress in the Southern States. Increased taxation for schools, new school buildings, larger and better equipment, longer school terms, and better paid teachers occupy enviable places in all these pictures. But what about a substantial decrease in our illiteracy? Increased enrollment and the increased attendance do not always keep pace with the natural increase in population. The truth is that in a few of the Southern States the total white illiteracy has remained practically unchanged for thirty years. Of what value are all of your taxes and your elegant buildings and your improved schools to your thousands of boys and girls who never enter the door of a schoolhouse?

Men of the South, it is high time to end our academic discussions and specious arguments, to quit our quibbling, and to throw aside our political sophistries. We know the facts, we know the conditions, we ought to know our duty, and we ought to have the courage to do it.

A FEDERAL CHILDREN'S BUREAU *

By Congressman Andrew J. Peters, of Massachusetts

The child of to-day is the Nation's ruler of to-morrow. The children of the present are the citizens of the future. Our civilization advances in exact proportion to our success in putting children upon a plane a little higher than that on which their parents stood. It is the glory of our civilization that more and more we consider the welfare of the child. No taxes are levied, no public money is spent with greater popular approval than the vast sums contributed for education by the States, while private benevolence directed to the same end is always warmly applauded. But there are many problems of child life outside of the educational problem, questions that call for authoritative answers, for a proper understanding of which every possible facility should be afforded. It is therefore proposed to establish in the Department of Commerce and Labor a children's bureau.

Each year Congress produces masses of legislation upon subjects too extended to enumerate. Of all subjects to be considered, can one be found in a representative government so important as the individual—the citizen on whose intelligence and mental and moral health the whole nation rests? The problem of our children is one that can no longer be treated by guesswork, or by casual movements inspired by local feeling and directed perhaps by warm hearts, but too often by untrained vision. The study of children is becoming a science, and its students need information and data for analysis. To-day the most vital questions affecting our children are decided on a lack of information that in no other subject would for a moment be tolerated.

*Bill passed Senate January 31; passed House April 2; signed by President Taft April 9. On April 17 Julia C. Lathrop, of Hull House, Chicago, was appointed chief of the Bureau.—Ed.

Objects of the Bill

The objects of the bill to establish a children's bureau are stated clearly in the bill itself. I quote from Section 2:

> The said bureau shall investigate and report upon all matters pertaining to the welfare of children and child life, and shall especially investigate the questions of infant mortality, the birth rate, physical degeneracy, orphanage, juvenile courts, desertion, dangerous occupations, accidents and diseases of children, employment, legislation affecting children in the several States and Territories, and such other facts as have a bearing upon the welfare of children. The chief of said bureau shall from time to time publish the results of these investigations.

The bureau, upon the principle of first aid to the injured, shall, in brief, collect such facts as have a bearing upon the health, efficiency and character of the children of the Nation, our future citizens and rulers.

History of Legislation

The bill providing for a Federal children's bureau is to-day before both branches of the Federal Congress. Senator Borah has introduced in the Senate a measure, Senate 252, providing for a children's bureau, and in the House I have introduced a similar measure, H. R. 4964.

This is far from being the first Congress in which such measures have been considered. At the request of the National Child Labor Committee the first children's bureau bill was introduced in the Fifty-ninth Congress. President Roosevelt himself specifically indorsed the measure, and it was approved as well by Secretary Hitchcock of the Department of the Interior, in whose department it was intended at that time to establish the bureau. President Roosevelt, in his message to Congress on December 5, 1905, called attention to the need of a particular study of the conditions of the children of the nation.

The measure was brought before the Sixtieth Congress and referred to the House Committee on Expenditures in the Interior Department and to the Senate Committee on Education and Labor. Each of these committees, after hearing the subject, reported the bills favorably without any amendment.

A Federal Children's Bureau

In the Sixty-first Congress the children's bureau bill was again introduced and very much the same routine was gone through with. The interest in the bill had so much increased that at that time the possibility was considered of establishing not a bureau but a department, but it has been thought more advisable to urge the establishment of a bureau rather than a department on account of the difference in cost.

In this, the Sixty-second Congress, the bill is introduced in both bodies and has already been reported favorably by each of the committees to which it has been referred. Introduced in the last four Congresses, the bill has been heard and reported favorably by the committees of the House and Senate in the Sixtieth, Sixty-first and Sixty-second Congresses, or by six committees. In the present Congress the bill was reached in the Senate on December 11, 1911. Senator Borah asked unanimous consent to take up the bill at that time, but its consideration was postponed until January 8, when it again came before the Senate. At this time Senator Borah made a brief but pointed speech in support of the bill, in which he was repeatedly interrupted by Senator Heyburn, whose objections to the passage of the bill could hardly be considered as complimentary to his colleague, the junior Senator from Idaho, and to others who are in favor of the measure. I quote from Senator Borah's speech, which answers effectively the typical objections which have had to be met. Senator Borah said:

> I would be somewhat discouraged if such an attack (referring to the remarks of Senator Heyburn) were made on this bill, and this bill alone, by my colleague. I believe it was Job or some one to Job who said, "Hast thou restrained all wisdom unto thyself?"
>
> Now if there is any specific objection to this bill, I should think it would be fair to those who are supporting it to offer some specific objection. It is not fair to those men who take such measures as this and go through them in the committee to come here upon the floor of the Senate and assert that they are being urged for an ulterior motive and that righteous sentiments are being used under which to cover up appropriations and to provide offices and so forth. It is a general declaration which anyone can make, but which everyone would not wish to make.

The bill again went over. It came up for debate on January 24, and after some dispute on its merits it was unanimously agreed that it should be considered and finally disposed of on Tuesday,

January 30. It is to be strongly hoped that its passage will be assured in the Senate as it passed that body in the last Congress, and only through misfortune failed to get consideration by the House. The bill which I have introduced, H. R. 4694, was reported favorably to the House by the Committee on Labor on January 17, 1912. The report of the Committee concludes with this statement:

> The (whole) committee believes that the need for such a Bureau has been established, that it will be of great benefit to the children of this country and we therefore recommend the passage of this bill.

This bill is now on the Union Calendar, and is next in order upon the call of the Labor Committee, and is likely to be reached in a short time.

Operation of the Children's Bureau

In its operation this bureau would concern itself chiefly with infant mortality, diseases of children, child labor, and infant delinquency. Take the question of infant mortality, for example, a problem that relates to the very existence of children after they are brought into the world.

The bulletin of the Census Bureau on Mortality Statistics for 1910, issued less than a week ago, presents interesting data on infant mortality.

For the total number of children in the so-called registration area (which has been used by the Census Bureau to refer solely to the area in which registration of deaths was satisfactory, and which now includes data for a little over one-half of the total population of the United States) under five years of age, the average number of deaths per 100 deaths at all ages is 27.

Of the different States included in the "registration" area, California, with 16, has the lowest number of deaths, per 100 deaths, for children under five years. Next comes Vermont with 18, next Colorado, Maine and Washington with 22, then there are variations all the way up to 32, which obtains in North Carolina and Rhode Island, and then Pennsylvania, the highest, with 34.

Registration cities present, of course, an even more varied

record for deaths among infants as compared with deaths among all others.

In New York State, Albany shows but 19, while Amsterdam records 41 and Lackawanna 79. In New York City, the Bronx Borough, 23, the Manhattan, 34. In New Hampshire, Concord, 11; Berlin, 60, and so forth. The table giving these statistics is followed by a statement explaining two of the most extreme cases. I quote in part:

> The low ratio for California may be ascribed in part to the large number of deaths from tuberculosis, most of which are of adults, and in general to the unusually small proportion of children in the population. . . . Some exceptionally high ratios may be explained by the existence of infant homes or institutions. For example, the high proportions shown for Lackawanna, N. Y., are due to the deaths of infants from the city of Buffalo.

This is followed by a more general statement of some fifteen lines to the effect that no conclusions can be drawn from the statistics except those of a most superficial nature.

The explanation is a satisfactory one so far as it goes, but there is necessarily little in it that could not have been concluded by a most casual examiner of the data furnished. The explanation, however, goes as far as it is expedient for the Census Bureau to go in a matter of this kind. The Census Bureau has collected information which presents possibilities of further study. What is needed now is an organ in our government—and the Children's Bureau will be that organ—which will go back of these figures and find out in detail just what accounts for this wide divergence in the death rate of young children who ought normally at that early stage in life to be, from community to community, in very much the same condition in respect to their possibilities of successfully battling with the ills that beset childhood.

Is the death rate of 15 per cent. of the total deaths, in contrast with a death rate of, say, 35 per cent., due to a difference in the regulations of the different health departments, or is it due to the inability of working people to employ competent doctors at childbirth in place of the poorly trained midwife? Or is it the result of conditions peculiar to a certain stage in the development or decline of different localities? Or was there an epidemic of children's diseases, or is it, perhaps, true that the seeming difference is but the result of the comparative care taken in the registration of births and deaths?

It is this sort of information which we wish to obtain, and this is the sort of information which we may expect to have available for our mutual education and betterment when the Children's Bureau has been instituted.

Think of the truth and pathos, as applied to many of our children, of Mrs. Browning's words:

> "It is good when it happens,"
> Say the children,
> "That we die before our time."

A government bulletin, prepared by some medical expert of long experience, could be sent into every quarter of the Nation, just as our agricultural bulletins are sent out. Our blind asylums are now full of children, supported at great expense to the States and to private philanthropy, who could have been saved their fate in early infancy, except for the general ignorance on this subject. How they must wish that there had been knowledge instead of ignorance! But hundreds of children are being born every year who will not be saved from blindness without a proper knowledge of causes and the remedies. Let not future generations curse us for our neglect or indifference as to their fate! Let us not postpone the organization of a government bureau to give this needed information to our people. Take the subject of the occupational diseases and accidents to children. Surely it is important for us to know, as we do not know now, whether certain occupations in which grown people may work with impunity are in themselves harmful for children. I see it is asserted in one of the hearings before the House Committee that in one occupation the accidents to children were 400 per cent. more in number than the accidents to adult workers.

The census will stand as the only national authority for ten years more, perhaps to our discredit as a Nation, unless we have some agency charged especially with inquiring into the reason for such differences as may exist as respects this evil, whether the laws are defective or not well enforced in one State or another, and to record the advances that are being made. In short, we shall be able to get the information necessary for every State to correct its own abuses, not from the writers in the magazines intent upon making a sensation, but from an authorized bureau of this Government belonging to all the people, so that the people directly concerned, without a feeling of resentment at an exaggeration of the conditions, may go about the work of correcting abuses known to prevail and the righting of the wrongs of childhood.

Consider another problem that has been widely studied within the last few years, the problem of juvenile delinquency and reform. Some of the principles of dealing with the child criminals, if we may call them such, have been established by such men as Judge Ben B. Lindsey, of Denver; Judge Julian W. Mack, of Chicago, and others. Both these gentlemen are earnest advocates of this bureau. Judge Lindsey declared that it took the time of two stenographers in his office to answer the questions that came to him regarding his children's court. But why should people be compelled to write to Denver, rather than to Washington, to find out from one locality where conditions may be peculiar concerning the proper method of dealing with delinquent children all over the country?

While a member of the judiciary committee of the Massachusetts State Senate, I helped investigate the question of establishing in that State the juvenile court which is now in operation there. The lack of a body to turn to for proper information as to what other States were doing was to our work a great hindrance, and a bureau of this kind could have rendered assistance of the greatest value.

No Infringement of State Jurisdiction

Each of our States has sought in its own way, without the benefit of the common experience, to protect its children by legislation in their behalf. The states are recognizing more and more the responsibility which they have for the care and uplift of their children, and each is endeavoring to give to these problems a more intelligent understanding. The need most acutely felt by those engaged in the study and solution of these various problems of childhood is to have adequate and full information as to the conditions to be met, and as to what has been done by other States in meeting these conditions. It is not only the duty, but the high privilege of the National Government to furnish this desired information, to the saving of waste and misapplied energy, to the curbing, sometimes perhaps, of undisciplined zeal, and to the stimulation of every community to the recognition of the abuses of childhood that these abuses may be ended.

It would be as difficult for the States, even if all could be persuaded to act together, to secure this needed information, as it would be for them to take a census under 46 different varieties of standards of the population of the United States.

That publicity through a national children's bureau would tend to bring views and methods into harmony concerning these humane questions cannot be doubted. The present laws respecting neglected children, delinquent children, the children who toil, the unfortunate children of every kind who make the appeal of their helplessness to the State or the community, are conflicting and confusing. It should be the function of this bureau, in studying the legislation of the different states, to present expert opinion as to the best standard of legislation to be adapted by each state to its local conditions. The experience of all will be the guide of each.

No one could be more jealous than I to preserve to the States their sovereign rights over their people. The constitutional objections to a national child-labor law I fully recognize, and to such a measure I am unalterably opposed, but a bureau of this nature is the strongest force in preserving to the States their rights over their own citizens. Its power to enable the States to obtain information on this subject will strengthen and uphold their hands in progressive legislation, and by increasing their efficiency in dealing with their citizens will be the strongest force against the encroachment on the States by the Federal power. It is claimed the States are not meeting the full responsibilities to their citizens. No greater aid than this could be given them to do so. Absolutely opposed to national regulation, I support no less firmly the collection of national information.

European Nations in Advance of Us

Far beyond the United States other nations have already advanced in this important matter. Perhaps the nations of Europe feel the pressing need of the care of the children more keenly than we, from the fact that these children are to be the future defenders of the nation in the war that always threatens those nations who must be kept in a state of continual defense.

The experience of England during the Boer war, on account of the degeneracy of a large part of her population, especially the factory population, was a bitter one. One of the results of the investigations of this subject, which fill a whole series of "blue books," was the enactment by Parliament of a "children's charter," as it is popularly called. It has the double function, under the British system of government, of investigation and administration. The children's bureau, outlined in this bill, is confined to the first duty alone, except that it may report such facts as Congress may legislate upon within proper Federal jurisdiction in the District of Columbia and the Territories. To the States must be left the duty of administration. Germany also, with an eye to its future citizens and soldiery, has a very complete and thorough system of research and publicity concerning all the facts relating to child life. Our own students of these problems have been compelled to gather their information about many of these questions from foreign sources, with more or less applicability to American conditions.

While Europe is an armed camp, this Republic is at peace. It is an even nobler duty to prepare for the victories of peace than to provide for the exigencies of war.

Self-preservation is spoken of as the first law of nature, and when the welfare of a nation rests, as ours, on universal suffrage, the care and bringing up of the children to healthy men and women can assume to no other duty a second place.

It is objected that we already have too many bureaus. There are in the nine great departments represented in the Cabinet thirty-two bureaus. But the argument is the other way. If we have not neglected the creation of any bureau dealing with material things, what further excuse have we for neglecting the most precious asset of national life, the children?

Comparative Statement of Appropriation Required

If it is a question of expense let us look at the outlay which this last year has been authorized by the Government in some of the bureaus tabled below, and contrast that as a whole, or item by item, with the amount asked for under the present bill.

For this last year we have appropriated for the investigation of plant diseases and pathological collections $22,930; for the control of diseases of cotton, truck and forage crops, $24,860; for investigation and improvements of tobacco and methods of production, $26,630; for control of diseases of orchards and other fruits, $42,075; for experiments and investigations in animal husbandry, $47,480; for eradication of Southern cattle ticks, $250,000. The total expenditures for the Bureau of Animal Industry are $1,654,750, and the total expenditure for the Bureau of Plant Industry is $2,061,686, and in contrast with that we ask for the establishment of this bureau an appropriation of only $29,440.

Considering the confessed lack of knowledge on the vital questions concerning American children which I have briefly indicated, and the importance of reliable information about them for the use of all public and private agencies that are attempting to deal with these problems, the expense involved is insignificant. I will give you an exact list of the expenses of the children's bureau, as asked for in my bill (H. R. 4694), which is as follows:

Chief	$5,000
Assistant chief	2,400
Private secretary	1,500
Statistical expert	2,000
Two clerks of class 4, $1,800 to $2,000 each	4,000
Two clerks of class 3, $1,600 to $1,800 each	3,600
One clerk of class 2, $1,400 to $1,600	1,600
One clerk of class 1, $1,200 to $1,400	1,400
One clerk	1,000
One copyist	900
One special agent	1,400
One special agent	1,200
One messenger	1,440
	$27,440
Annual rent not to exceed	2,000
Total	$29,440

The study of bugs no doubt has its importance, but we can at least afford to spend one-eighth of the amount we expend on bugs for the study of the problems of our children.

It is admitted that with increased appropriations and the specification of new duties some of the already established bureaus might deal with some of these questions, but none of them is fitted to deal with them all. One of the most powerful reasons for concentrating such work in one bureau, with its significant name, "The Children's Bureau," is that the general public would know at once where to apply for the needed information. For example, one official of the Marine Hospital Service is believed to have discovered the cause of a very common and debilitating disease among the children of certain sections of the South, and a very simple and cheap remedy for the affliction. But the unsophisticated would hardly think of applying to the Marine Hospital Service for information about a disease of the children of inland Carolina. We increase the opportunities for valuable publicity many fold by centering the information about children in one bureau, whose very name is an index to the character of its work.

Public sentiment is arousing itself on this subject, and each day more and more interest is evinced in the objects of this bill. The press of the entire country, with scarcely an exception, is advocating the support of this measure, and letters and petitions from every part of the land have been rushing to the hands of Members of Congress. There are no selfish or mercenary interests behind this measure, and the expression of opinion which is reaching us is the outgrowth, spontaneous and sincere, of the feeling for the children of our country.

The exploitation of childhood and the withering of little lives must stop, and to stop it the first and most necessary step is to proceed with intelligence and understanding.

Political equality and civic rights, obtained through years of struggle, have brought with them great responsibilities as well, and the future of our country depends upon the way our citizens will assume the responsibilities so placed upon them. Democratic government cannot exist by itself, and the proper exercise of the suffrage and the development of the ideas of the framers of our Constitution necessitate the active interest of all the people of the country. Upon the quality of that citizenship the strength of our Government will depend, and the standard can never rise above the aims and ideals on which it rests. A good government can never be legislated by us or upon us. The only sure basis on which to rest our Government and from which we can look to the future with calm confidence is the basis of high and enlightened citizenship. To insure the preservation of our national ideals we must have citizens healthy and active, both in mind and body, and to develop from our children the highest types of men and women must be the first duty of our State, and it is a duty which this bill, to establish a children's bureau, will help each State to perform. Let us take now the final step in offering to the children, our future citizens, the assistance of this measure.

FEDERAL AID TO EDUCATION A NECESSARY STEP IN THE SOLUTION OF THE CHILD-LABOR PROBLEM

By Samuel McCune Lindsay, LL.D.,
Vice-Chairman, National Child Labor Committee,
Professor of Social Legislation, Columbia University.

Every advance in the protection of childhood, and every success in securing better child labor legislation means greater demands upon the public school. Every State and locality will need more schools, more kinds of schools, and better schools, and especially a much more costly system of elementary education, just as soon as it succeeds in taking its children out of factories, mills, work shops and street trades where they do not belong and putting them where they do belong, namely, in schools that are adequately equipped to give them education both for citizenship and industrial efficiency.

Dr. Felix Adler, in his address as chairman of this meeting, has well said: "The appeal of the child labor cause is fundamentally a moral appeal." That is one reason for feeling very certain about its ultimate outcome. There is no question that can be stated clearly to the American people as an appeal to the conscience, that will not be settled eventually and settled right. But it is one of the peculiarities of any movement that rests in part upon an emotional appeal, that in order to be effective it must constantly formulate many definite things, to which energies may be directed so as to give expression to the moral enthusiasm that it arouses by the appeal. The atrocities committed upon little working children in all parts of the United States may well arouse strong feeling which, if properly directed, will achieve great social results. One way to answer the inevitable question of what we can do about it, is to look back for a moment upon the history of the various stages that have marked the progress thus far of the child labor movement.

In the early days of the nineteenth century when England

worked with this problem as a great public question and when Robert Owen, Lord Ashley, Oastler, Sadler and others in public life were fighting for the recognition of the right of the State to intervene on behalf of the child and won their great victory on that point, they found, difficult as it was to get that right recognized, questions presenting still greater difficulties confronted them. In proportion as child labor was eliminated from certain industries, it came to the front in other forms of industry. Restricted or prohibited in the larger mills and factories, it appeared in greater magnitude in the small factories and workshops. When successfully attacked and reduced in organized industries child labor became more and more prevalent in home industries and in the street trades where it often assumed forms that were even more menacing than the old forms. It was well on to the end of the nineteenth century before, in England, where they have been engaged longer in the struggle against child labor and have gone farther in governmental regulation than we, they discovered that the educational questions raised at every stage of progress became increasingly important. We are beginning to experience precisely the same thing in this country. Legislation seeks to prevent premature employment and to eliminate the child from harmful and dangerous trades and occupations. If such legislation accomplishes its purpose, or in proportion as it does, the question necessarily arises what are we doing for the children thus removed from industry? How are we going to give them more effective training and prepare them for efficient industrial activity later? The addresses at this very meeting by the Louisville Superintendent of Schools, Dr. Holland, and by the President of the National Education Association, Dr. Pearse, amply sustain and illustrate my point that every gain in progress in the child labor movement creates a new and larger demand upon the public school and requires new experiments in education. This means that new resources for the financial support of public education must be found. We know from bitter experience what it means to press the claims of child labor reform in industries where we touch the pocketbook of the manufacturer who finds child labor profitable. Will the tax-payer be less sensitive or more generous when we appeal to his pocketbook for the infinitely greater sums necessary to make our schools what they ought to be in order to take care of the child laborers of the country when industry gives them up. We know that whatever success we have means that we must inevitably in the long run touch the pocketbook of every citizen and of every taxpayer. We must have larger funds for both the old and the newer types of education to make the common schools more efficient, and to do the things that our superintendents of schools tell us must be done in order to meet demands already pressing as a result in part of the reform work that we are doing in restricting child labor in mills and factories.

The School Revenue

Where have the resources of education come from in this country thus far? Very largely from local taxation. We spent during the school year 1908-09 in the United States, as far as we can judge from the very meagre and inadequate data furnished by the Bureau of Education at Washington (Report, 1910, Vol. II), $403,647,289. Of that amount, 71.5 per cent. was derived from local taxation; 15.7 per cent. from State taxation; 3.3 per cent. from what are called the permanent school funds, mostly derived from gifts from the federal or national government, largely in the shape of lands; and 9.5 per cent. from miscellaneous sources.

PERCENTAGE ANALYSIS OF THE SCHOOL REVENUE (1908-09)

	Permanent funds and rents.	State tax.	Local tax.	Other sources.
United States	3.3	15.7	71.5	9.5
N. Atlantic Division	.7	12.3	76.2	10.8
S. Atlantic Division	1.1	36.0	54.4	8.5
S. Central Division	9.9	36.1	48.0	6.0
N. Central Division	4.6	9.9	75.9	9.6
Western Division	4.3	20.7	68.3	6.7
New Hampshire	2.6	2.7	85.1	9.6
Massachusetts	1.2	1.1	96.3	1.4
New York	.6	9.2	85.8	2.4
South Carolina	...	4.0	89.6	6.4
Iowa	8.0	...	87.8	4.2
Kansas	8.8	...	86.6	4.6
Colorado	2.7	...	87.2	10.1

The Federal government inaugurated the policy of national aid to education as early as 1785 and 1787, and has followed it consistently since, but unfortunately thus far the funds available from national sources have been limited to receipts from the sale of public lands given to the States, to the general distribution from the surplus in the National Treasury in 1836-37, and to the distribution of the proceeds of later sales of the public lands of the United States through the Hatch and Morrill Acts chiefly for the encouragement of agricultural education and the mechanic arts as represented in colleges or secondary schools.

The lands or funds thus received from the National Government have been used by the States generally to establish permanent school funds or to increase such funds already established, the income of which only is used for the support of the schools. Receipts from the Hatch and Morrill Acts are of course an exception, and are used for equipment or current expenses of the institutions to which they are given.

Some of the older States began a similar policy even before the Federal Government established its land grants in aid of schools and sporadically throughout their history nearly all the States have attempted to develop permanent school funds in addition to annual grants from taxation.

Dr. E. G. Dexter, in his "History of Education in the United States," pp. 203-204, says:

"In the early days the financial support of the schools was wholly local, either through fees, town taxes, or private bequest. In some instances, as in North Carolina with the excise fees, and in Boston and Burlington, New Jersey, where lands were set apart as a source of revenue, and in Plymouth, where fishing rights were disposed of for the same purpose, the school had some particular franchise to depend upon, but such cases are comparatively rare. Public lotteries were also sometimes made use of as sources of school support, though usually for purposes of higher education. But it was the general rule for the parents of the pupils to pay for the schools outright. As time went on, the custom became general for States to set apart public lands for school purposes. As early as 1733 Connecticut set apart a considerable area to the 'perpetual use of the schools.' In 1795 the same State turned

Federal Aid to Education

over to the school fund $1,000,000, the proceeds of the sale of lands in the 'Western Reserve.' In 1786 New York set apart two lots in each township of unoccupied lands for the uses of the schools, and in 1801 established a permanent school fund by the sale of 500,000 acres of vacant land. Twenty years later Maine disposed of twenty townships for school purposes, while New Hampshire at about the same time, instituted a tax upon all banks in the State to the same end.

"In most of the older States school funds were established from one source or another; in Virginia (1810), South Carolina (1811), and North Carolina (1825), by direct State appropriation; in Alabama, Florida, Kentucky, Louisiana and Tennessee by apportionment of lands. By various acts of Congress, all States admitted to the Union previous to 1848 received the sixteenth section in each township for school purposes, and in those admitted subsequent to that time, the thirty-sixth as well (Utah receiving four sections), making in all 67,893,919 acres, which, at the traditional price of $1.25 per acre, makes a perpetual endowment of nearly $85,000,000. The States have all made material additions to the fund, so that in the year 1901-02 the total income from the general funds amounted to $10,522,343.

"In 1836 the twenty-seven States then organized received from Congress the sum of $42,000,000. Sixteen of them devoted their quotas, in part or in whole, to the public schools, eight turning over the whole sum (Alabama, Delaware, Kentucky, Missouri, New York, Ohio, Rhode Island and Vermont).

"Apart from the national bequests, the entire support of the public schools has come from within the States, either from State taxes, local taxes, or tuition, etc."

Limited State Revenues

The older States have already found that they can no longer meet the educational demands even for elementary education from the resources of local taxation and are voting large sums each year from their State revenues, but these again have about reached their limit. The hardest task of the governor in such States as New York and Pennsylvania, which may typify the most favored and wealthy States industrially, after each legislature adjourns, is to scale down appropriations to keep them within expected revenues. Such a system is unsatisfactory and must, in the long run, work to the disadvantage of school appropriations as schools are removed more and more from political control. National resources are, relatively speaking, untouched, compared with the strain the people feel to pay their State and local taxes. President Taft said recently, in speaking of the work of his Economy and Efficiency Commission, that he often wished that he might discuss our national budget and national revenues with the finance ministers of the leading European countries and see how their mouths would water when they understand how easy it is for us to raise revenues for our legitimate national expenses. That means that where modern nations are taxing every conceivable resource to meet their national expenses, partly due to their heavier charges for armaments, that we do not need, and partly also because they do more for education and have a correspondingly less illiteracy rate and the prospect of a greater future industrial efficiency, we have hardly touched our possibilities of revenue from national resources. In the United States, industry has become nationalized on a scale scarcely dreamed of in Europe, and the Federal Government has many sources of revenue that the States cannot reach. They will go untaxed and not contribute their share unless the National Government adopts a fiscal policy to include them. Is there any purpose for which our nationalized industries might be asked to pay taxes more appropriate than the support of education for industrial efficiency? We should not increase national revenues to pile up a surplus, nor to encourage wasteful expenditures. If the Economy and Efficiency Commission is sustained in its important work, many millions that are now wasted will be available and many more can easily be added to them and made productive in the highest sense, if those of us who are interested in child protection and education develop the right sort of a national educational program.*

* Since this address was delivered the Page Bill pending in the United States Senate has been amended as the result of serious deliberations initiated by the National Society for the Promotion of Industrial Education, and now proposes to authorize the annual expenditure of sums varying from a little over two million dollars in 1913, increasing in each subsequent year to over

National Aid Urgent

The important and urgent thing for the National Government to do now, and for which conditions everywhere are ripe, is to really grip the educational situation with the purpose of standardizing the benefits of the free public school and equalizing the burdens of its cost, as well as its advantages for the people of the entire nation. One of the greatest evils growing out of our reliance upon local taxation almost exclusively for the support of elementary schools has been that those communities are the richest in resources usually where the need and the demands for public education are least, and vice versa, where the greatest need is found there we usually have the greatest poverty of educational funds. The governments of Germany and England have pursued a very different policy with respect to the local support of public education and very important results have been achieved, not merely in the equalization of the burdens of taxation that have been brought about through national subsidies or national support for education, but even to a greater degree by the raising of standards through the influence of the national purse. Mr. Sidney Webb has recently shown in a remarkably interesting little book, entitled "Grants in Aid," how great has been the improvement in standards both in education and in many other forms of social work in England through the conditions that have been attached to these grants in aid from the national purse which now amount to something like one hundred million dollars a year. It is probably not possible and certainly, in the opinion of many, would not be desirable that our

thirteen and a half million in 1921 and annually thereafter for the maintenance of instruction in agriculture, the trades and industry, and home economics in schools of secondary grade; for the support of extension divisions of existing state colleges of agriculture and the mechanic arts; the training of teachers for such work and the cost of national administration, distribution to the states and supervision of the funds to be distributed. This may be a necessary and commendable forward step in the rational development of the policy already begun by the Federal Government in aid of Agriculture and Mechanic Arts, and would doubtless make it possible to bring its great benefits within the reach of pupils in the secondary schools. It does not touch, however, the greater problems of primary and elementary education. Its plan of distribution avoids some of the pitfalls that wrecked the proposals of the Blair bill so vigorously discussed years ago.

Federal Government should be given power of legislation over the elementary schools of the several States and localities, but a national board of education thoroughly representative of the best educational life of each State in the nation might well be organized under the presidency of the United States Commissioner of Education. If it did its work through a small executive commission constituted from its own membership, and if Congress placed in its hands an annual appropriation which might aggregate many millions of dollars for distribution to the States to aid the educational machinery of the several States in support of elementary schools, such a board could practically revise our educational system and strengthen it at every point without diminishing one iota of the local effort or support. In England and Wales, the annual expenditures for elementary education for the five years, 1905-1909, averaged 20.5 million pounds sterling, of which 9.8 million pounds, or 48 per cent., came from local rates, while 52 per cent. came chiefly from the national exchequer in parliamentary grants. Germany and France make about the same showing with respect to their relative reliance upon national and local taxation for public schools.

It is not the purpose of this paper to present a detailed plan for national aid to education. It would have to be worked out by a thoroughly representative commission to harmonize with our political system, but I do feel that the National Child Labor Committee has not emphasized sufficiently the cost to the nation of the great reform which it is seeking to accomplish. Child labor we are willing to condemn and our efforts in this direction win new converts every day. Child labor is an anachronism in our present industrial system. It must be abolished and it will be abolished; but the cost of its abolition will not be merely what we are willing to pay for educational propaganda to arouse resentment and to crystallize our feeling against child labor into prohibitive legislation. It must also include the cost of wise provision for the enforcement of such legislation, which, to be efficient, is destined to become very much more costly than anything we have yet contemplated, and it must include a willingness to meet the proper burdens of taxation which will provide an adequate and suitable scheme of public education in which the greater freedom of the child will find expression through wiser provision for the conservation of his health, his energy and his mental development for the highest possible usefulness to society. That is a vision of child labor reform that many of us who have been working for this cause have seen from the beginning. It is, I believe, our duty to present it more widely and forcibly to the general public. Why should not the National Child Labor Committee itself either work out a plan to present to Congress, or ask Congress to establish a commission to study the whole question and elaborate a plan and prepare the necessary legislation to inaugurate national aid for the public schools.

PART-TIME SCHOOLS

By Mrs. Florence Kelley, New York,
General Secretary, National Consumers' League.

Fifteen years ago in Chicago I was teaching in a night school near Hull House, because in those days the people of the second city in this Union, citizens of the third great manufacturing State in our industrial republic, were content to have the immigrant children go to school three nights in the week, two hours in the evening, and accept that as attendance under the compulsory education law. There was required proof of the age of children when they left, they were nominally fourteen years old. There was no required acquisition, they were simply compelled to come and sit on the school benches in a dirty, ill-ventilated, unattractive, old building condemned by the building department of Chicago as unsafe. These were working boys and girls, recent immigrants, and that was the educational opportunity forced upon very reluctant recipients.

Sometimes the children did not come, a given boy would not come for a week at a time. I said to such a boy: "Where have you been?" "Oh," he said, "I've been 'waifing it.'" I did not know what he meant. At last I found that he had been taking a vacation, living at the Waifs' Mission, because he was tired of taking care of a bed-ridden father, and was sick of my attempt to teach him English. So he had been a waif two or three weeks, and when he was rested had come back because he was afraid that, if the truant officer should find him he might be sent to the country, to a compulsory education continuing throughout the year, which these children knew and dreaded because they hated to leave the excitement of the city streets.

I think all our great cities have discarded that kind of part-time education in these fifteen years. I do not know one great city which to-day accepts evening school attendance in lieu of day-school attendance. I think that evil old chapter in our educational history is closed.

We have one survival of it in New York now, in the provision that boys fourteen years old having worked eight hours in the factory or workshop, or nine hours in the store, must go to school three evenings in the week at least until they finish the work of the eighth grade of the schools.

This is not in lieu of all primary school education, it is additional to the work of the first five years which they must have completed before they can work. It is a cruel provision, because in industry as it is carried on to-day, a boy works so strenuously eight hours in the factory or workshop, or nine hours in the store, that it is a weary body and a weary mind that come to the night school. It was not the New York Child Labor Committee who put that provision into the law requiring boys to come to school three nights a week after their work, and we are trying to get it out, because it is cruel that, after children have worked eight hours in the day they should then be required to go to school in the evening. They need the evenings for recreation if they really earn their wages.

In England it has been discovered that children very largely forget after they leave school the elementary work that they have done in the scant time allotted to school attendance alone. And a great influential committee, with Mrs. Sidney Webb at their head, have been working for years to establish on a national scale in England the requirement that, to the nineteenth birthday, boys and girls shall regularly be carried on the school rolls, and their working day shortened in proportion as their educational opportunity is increased. The idea is to have 48 hours in the week of required work all told, a part of it devoted to wage-earning after the children are sixteen years old, and the rest devoted to education along three lines, to building up the degenerating physique of the working children, to teaching hygiene, and to promoting carefully systematized education in the duties of citizenship—this threefold education being provided by the local authorities at the national expense, and the requirement made of the employer that he should give the time, treating these children as school children until they reach the nineteenth birthday.

This provision is not actually in force in any English city. The English cities are still making the mistake that we are making in New York, letting the children work eight hours a day and then taking their weary minds and bodies to the great polytechnics at night. We do not, either in England or America, as some of the German cities do, require that the employer shall allot time out of the regular working week during which the children shall go to school.

There are reasons why in England and Germany they can do that very much better than we. They want skilled labor. We have little market for it in our manufacturing States, and our tendency is to want less of it instead of more.

I am a member of two little committees which administer scholarships for boys and girls. One has scholarships for children who would suffer hardship without them, because the law requires a certain amount of school work, even though that keeps the children in school until they are sixteen years of age. The other committee is interested in discovering children who have special talent or aptitude, to give them an opportunity for higher technical education. The necessary schools are there. We have certain public schools giving commercial and mechanical advanced courses. We have art schools and music schools; we are not desperately poor in the opportunity for education. But the baffling thing is that after the children have been given school opportunity, there is no place open to them. It is the hardest thing in the world to find an employer wanting a girl or boy who has had this additional training, and willing to pay for it. What our American industry calls for increasingly is common labor, unskilled labor. We should make a blunder if we set about to provide, certainly in any compulsory way, for employers to surrender a part of the time of working children with any idea that the employers would be rewarded by being required afterward to pay higher wages for a skill which they had not called for, as the German and English industries do call for it.

We boast of our perfected machinery. We turn out wonderful products up to a certain level of perfection which the machine can achieve. But the by-product of our industry is an ever-increasing mass of unskilled, common laborers.

Some years ago I took our philosopher, Henry Demarest Lloyd, to see the greatest can factory in this country, just out of Chicago. I wanted to show him a group of little boys who had been sitting fourteen hours a day on a shelf in midair, every boy crooking his back and compressing his lungs because of the attitude in which he was compelled to sit on this shelf for the purpose of watching interminable rows of can lids—of tincan lids for condensed milk and tomatoes, and all such precious commodities. The little fellows had only the lids to look after. Every boy looked, in the course of a year, after some millions of lids of tomato cans and milk cans, coming down in a procession. It was the function of the bright eyes of the boys to see any defect in the lid of a can. They were constantly cutting themselves, crippling their hands, and cutting off the tops of their fingers in this work, because they had to seize these sharp-edged things and take them out of the procession of cans if there was any defect in the lids.

But that was the least of their troubles. At the end of fourteen hours of crouching on this wretched shelf, the boys were so tired that they often could not drag themselves home, but slept in the fields nearby and went back to their work the next day without ever having gone home, because they were too weary at the end of the work. That was the level on which these young boys were working.

These were young boys who lived in a suburb where they were not even required to go to the evening school, as my neighbor boys were required to do. But I never got Mr. Lloyd as far as that shelf of boys, because on the way he came upon a man of about his own age who had sat for twelve years on the same stool watching an interminable procession of millions of cans to which the lids belonged. This man had given twelve years of his life to looking for dents in tomato cans. Heaven only knows how many cans had passed under his eyes and how many dents he had discovered. But that philosopher of American democracy, as Dr. Adler has been interpreting it to us to-night, was so horribly fascinated at the spectacle of a man of his own years who had spent twelve years in doing that work, that the spectacular shelf full of little boys who were beginning at ten, and eleven, and twelve, and thirteen years old, to spend their lives at equally valuable work, failed to draw him away.

Do not understand me as saying that the making of cans is an uncommonly monotonous and horrible occupation. It is not. Our industry tends all the time to that standard of work, to such complete perfection of machinery that the work of the human observer of the machine is simply to sit passive and use the eye to discern occasional defects and pick out occasional defective products. The human being in that way becomes a truly monstrous by-product of industry.

We must face the fact that we cannot conduct a republic made up of citizens who spend nine, ten, twelve, fourteen or sixteen hours in twenty-four in that way. But the tendency of industry is to that end. Our education will have to be deliberately shaped in recognition of the fact that, if we let little girls turn their backs upon school when they are fourteen years old and go, nominally self-directing citizens of this republic, into industry under the pressure of competition as we have it, we shall not last long as a civilized nation, if that procession of little girls continues to increase as it has continued to increase during the fifteen years that I have been watching it.

In the year 1911 about 20,000 little girls went out of the schools of New York legally, between the ages of fourteen and sixteen years, to enter into industry, of which it can be safely said that the watching of the tops of tomato cans coming in interminable procession down through a slot, is a fair type. There is little more educational influence coming to those 20,000 little New York girls than came to those wretched little boys on their shelf in the tomato can factory fifteen years ago. Since we are a self-governing nation with an industry developing in that direction, our education must be truly recreational. We must enable the children to renew the active quality of their minds and bodies during the hours when they are not employed, and we must give them so short a working day that the recreating, educational hours will really make up to them in some measure for the stupefying influence of their work.

We do not do that now. In the best cities, in the States that have the best legislation, in New York, in Ohio, in Nebraska, in

Illinois, and some Western States we give the children eight hours only of this stupefaction. But in the other States it may be nine hours, or ten; in some States there is no effective limit. In Georgia, I think, there is no limit whatever on the working day. In South Carolina, when the eleven hours' day was agreed to by the Legislature, and factory inspectors were created to make sure that the working day of the young children did not exceed that, Governor Blease vetoed the appropriation for factory inspectors, and the working day is unlimited, as long as it suits the convenience of the mill owners to have the work go on.

We cannot give to young girls and boys eight hours of stupefying work and then save them for an intelligent citizenship by adding evening school work to that. It cannot conceivably be sufficiently recreational.

We must establish the eight hours' day in those industries in which we have not yet got it. Then we must provide in the rest of the time for undoing the injury to the growing mind and growing body that those hours of utterly stupefying work inevitably inflict.

It is one of the horrors of our education to-day that our school authorities live in the world, but not of it; that they do not know the mills from the inside; they do not know tenement-house work from the inside, they do not recognize the tomato can as a destroyer of childhood. They do not know what willow plumes and artificial flowers and the tips of shoestrings, and all the kinds of things that we wear and eat and use, mean for the children who make them. I have within six months heard leading educators—to their shame—urging that we should let the children go out into industry at the age of twelve years, on condition that, in addition to their work, they attend continuation classes.

First, we must realize from the inside what industry does to wreck the young body and the young mind by stupefying monotony, then I am quite sure our educators will talk an entirely different language, that they will go in, as the State of New York is at last doing, for establishing recreation as a daily part of the routine of the children, that they will gradually increase that share of the day and diminish the share in which we surrender the children to work. In the meantime, the most modest demand that any Child Labor Committee, or any Consumers' League, or any thinking citizen of this republic ought to make, is for a prompt reduction of the working day of the children to eight hours.

SOCIAL COST OF CHILD LABOR

By John P. Frey,
Editor, Moulders' Journal, Cincinnati, O.

It affords me great pleasure as a workman and as a member of organized labor to stand here and indorse as heartily as it is possible for an individual to indorse the National Child Labor Committee.

I presume that no group of citizens in the United States have taken a deeper interest in what the National Child Labor Committee is doing, and what it aims to do than the organized workmen of our country, and I presume there is no group who understand better what the child-labor problem means than those who earn their weekly wages by the sweat of their brow.

I have been asked to say something about the Social Cost of Child Labor, and it would give me a great deal of pleasure if I could discuss that question and use American statistics as a basis for my argument. But unfortunately, in our country we have no statistics which are national in character. The question of child labor has not been one that has interested our lawmakers very much until of recent years, and I believe if it had not been for the activity, for the public consciousness which this National Child Labor Committee has been able to awaken, we would not have even the meager statistics we have to-day.

Some time ago the Department of Labor was instructed to make an exhaustive investigation into child and female labor in this country. That investigation has been made, and the report is contained in some nineteen volumes, but instead of this being made a report of the Department of Labor and Commerce, it has been made, I believe, a Senate document, and Senator Smoot, of Utah, who is chairman of the Committee on Finance of the Senate, has taken a position which prevents the printing and sending of these reports to all those who so desire them, and in order to get statistics on which to base a few moments' discussion on the social cost of child labor, it will be necessary for me to go to another country, which, perhaps, after all, is the best one that we can go to, in order to understand just what a terrible thing, just what an appalling thing child labor under the factory system is.

Now, there is something so utterly inhuman about child labor under the modern industrial system, that we become so interested in our sympathy for the unfortunate victims of that system, our sympathies become so aroused over their own unfortunate condition, that we lose sight of the bigger and the broader question involved in child labor.

We are all familiar, I believe, with the question of the conservation of national resources. Some of our most prominent citizens have been calling our attention to what it means to carelessly destroy our forests and allow our water power to fall into private hands, preventing the rapid development, for the people, of the wealth that lies in this water power.

We have had a civic awakening and a national awakening on the question of conserving our national resources.

But it seems to me we have not been giving the attention and thought we should to our greatest national resource—the children; because it is the child of to-day who will take our place 25 years from now.

The civilization, the culture we are creating to-day rests upon a foundation formed by those children, and that civilization must be carried on their shoulders 25 odd years from now. And if they are not as competent as we, then whatever we may build up will rest on a very insecure foundation.

So one of the greatest countries the world has ever known has realized that through child labor it has weakened its foundation, and it realizes that the greatest problem perhaps that it has is that of the progressive physical deterioration of a large group of its people owing to child labor.

I do not want to lay a mass of figures before you. I know how difficult it is to remember figures if they come in too large a number; but there are one or two that I desire to give you this afternoon in the hope that you will carry them away as one of the strongest, most powerful evidences of the terrible national results of unrestricted child labor in the industries.

The factory system and child labor, as we discuss it to-day, that is, the child in the factory, had its origin in England. And as the factory system developed, the child went into the factory, went in at eight or nine or ten or twelve years of age. Orphan asylums and other eleemosynary institutions found it profitable to take their little charges and put them into factories where they would become a source of profit, and the child's welfare was lost sight of in the pecuniary gain, and those little children, working under unsanitary conditions, working long hours, working under the monotonous whirr of machinery, had the results of these conditions stamped upon their bodies and in their minds. Then when the next generation of child workers had grown to be adults, they married and their offspring followed them. So we have in Great Britain to-day the fourth and the fifth generations of factory workers who have been affected by unregulated child labor.

In order that what follows may not be misunderstood, let me say that it is almost impossible to separate the question of child labor and female labor. It is difficult to separate the one from the other because they are inter-related, and their results are very largely the same.

What happened in Great Britain? Any one who has ever been in the large manufacturing cities, who has walked through the streets of Birmingham, Manchester, Liverpool, and other factory districts, knows that there is a different type there than is found elsewhere, a different type from what you will find on the hills and out in the open country. And it is the type that strikes your mind, strikes your eye, because instead of its being the full-chested, rosy-cheeked, powerful British beef-eater, such as we are accustomed to picture the Englishman, we find that they are small and under-sized and flat-chested, with lack-luster eyes, and that they go slinking down the street—there is no life, there is little vitality left. And that is the result of one or two or three or four generations of child labor, each generation having a little more vitality taken away from it, until the present factory worker bears no resemblance at all to the strong, sturdy ancestry he sprang from.

Physical Effects

It would be impossible to-day for any Duke of Marlborough to go through the English factory towns and recruit the regiments of soldiers that the famous Duke was able to lead at Blenheim. Now, England has realized the price that she has been paying. England has been gathering statistics, and in the city of Bradford, where a large number of females work in the mills, it has been found that among these female workers the death rate for children under one year of age is 160 per thousand. In the same city, in the homes where women are not factory workers, the death rate of children under one year of age is 40 per thousand. We find there a difference of 400 per cent. in the proportion of deaths of children among mothers who are workers in factories and mothers who are kept at home.

Back of that there seems to be a great deal more, because if 400 per cent. more children die, born of mothers who were factory workers, what about the vitality and strength of the remainder who do not die? Certainly it cannot be as high as that of the children born in more fortunate families.

A few years ago the British government made a very exhaustive study to discover the difference between the child who worked in the factories and the child brought up without being a factory worker, and for every age beginning from eight years they secured the average height and weight of these children for each year up to sixteen years. The difference between the vigor and vitality of the boys who were not factory workers and those who were, was this:

The factory worker at sixteen years of age was 3.37 inches shorter than his more fortunate brother, and he weighed 19.67 pounds less. Think of the difference at sixteen years of age. Think more of what the moral condition or the moral fiber of those unfortunate factory workers must have been. Think of the physical difference between the two, and picture to yourself what it means for a nation to suddenly wake up to the fact that a large proportion of its citizenship has been degraded physically, mentally and morally.

An English author, in a book written a short time ago on the question of child labor and the rapid physical deterioration of the

British workman, said that in 1845, the minimum height of the recruits in the British army was 5 feet 6 inches. Now, that is not supported by the reports of the War Department as to the recruits and their minimum height for enlistment at that time, and we would not expect the War Department of any country to officially and publicly announce the physical deterioration of a nation. But we do know that in 1885 the minimum height for recruits was 5 feet 2 inches, and that in 1901 "Specials" were enlisted at 5 feet. There is the evidence of what child labor has accomplished when the child has been exploited for private profit instead of being conserved and protected and guarded as the nation's most valuable asset.

Other European countries have not done the same. The German child has not had to go through the experience of the English child. Neither have the children of the other manufacturing nations of central and northern Europe.

We, too, have a child labor problem. We do not know what the effect is going to be. We have not yet reached the third and fourth and fifth generation of child workers. But as a working man and as one interested in studying this question upon the ground, I have seen the little unfortunates, with bare feet, pinched features, colorless faces, no hope in life, and but very little prospect of developing into robust manhood and womanhood, or developing into proper fathers and mothers for the type of citizens America should be proud of. And if it were not for the influence of such an organization as the National Child Labor Committee, if it were not for the moral influence and the persistent efforts of the organized workmen of this country to protect the children, I do not know but that we might have a condition in this country a great deal worse than England has experienced.

A Bid for Child Labor

Only a few years ago some of the States believed nothing would bring capital into their borders more quickly than a large supply of child labor, and to say, "Child labor is cheaper here; it can be secured on easier terms here than in any other State in the union." And just as a State will advertise its rich grazing lands, as it will advertise its mineral and its other natural resources to bring capital within its borders, so have some States of our nation advertised the fact that children within that State were helpless and could be used by private capital for private profit without restriction.

I have an interesting little document in my hand. I do not care to mention the name of the State, because this was issued in 1898, and I know this particular State has been trying to redeem itself, or rather I know that some of its leading citizens are trying to redeem it, but I want to give you an idea of how one State in this Christian nation of ours within the last 12 years has advertised its natural resources. This circular, which was placed in almost all correspondence being sent out to the North and the East, read in part as follows:

"No strikes, no laws regulating the hours of employment and the age of employees. Cheap labor and the home of the cotton plant."

When the statesmen of a community, or the business men of a community feel that it is profitable to advertise the fact that there is absolutely no regulation or restriction of child labor, I think the State is not only in most unfortunate hands, but is in the hands of those who are willing to scatter its most valuable assets to the winds in order to gain temporary financial advantage and to bring capital temporarily within its borders.

In one of the States where the public conscience was being awakened to the vital importance of this child labor question, where the Legislature was on the point of enacting a measure which would regulate child labor, which would say that no child under a certain age—and this age was twelve years—would be permitted in the industries, the cotton interests of that State held a banquet in the capitol city and they invited the Legislature there to discuss the question. And I know that some of the arguments used were these:

"When we brought our capital from the North to operate mills in this State, we were guaranteed that no legislation would be enacted which would in any way limit our right and our opportunity of employing children, no matter what the age might be."

We must look this question fully in the face. If we want a

nation where the child will be used in the industries before it is developed, then we must expect to draw our future well-developed workmen from other countries. If we do our duty, as we should, we will realize that the child of to-day is the nation's most valuable asset, and we are going to do what we can, not only to give that child a strong body, and a strong mind, but we are going to do what we can to develop both, so that the citizens of twenty years from now will average up better physically, better mentally, and better morally than the citizens of to-day.

We want to go ahead. We don't want to go backward. These children can do nothing for themselves. The legislation which is going to give them the opportunity must be enacted by the citizens of to-day.

Trade Unions vs. Child Labor

Just one word more, so that the attitude of the trade union movement may be thoroughly understood. I know of no movement in this country which has been so many years actively working in the cause of the child as the trade union movement. You are not familiar perhaps with the fact that the public school system we think so much of to-day came into existence in this country, not through the interests of educators primarily, although they lent all of the influence they could, but through the agitation of organized workmen in 1820, though men like Horace Mann, and others helped the movement along. It was the organized workmen of Boston, of New York, of Philadelphia, and of other cities, who, through the mass meetings they held, through the agitation they carried on by insisting that the welfare of America demanded that the poor man's son should receive the opportunities for education equal to those of the more fortunate child—it was due to trade union activity that we got our free public schools in the beginning. The trade unions got behind that movement, and would not be denied; so to-day we enjoy our public schools. But unfortunately, in many places in the South, I have seen little colored children going to school, and little white children of the same community going to the cotton mill.

We cannot discuss these questions quietly. It is not a question which should be spoken of in the most polite terms and in a sort of indifferent manner. We cannot afford to use altogether the most polite terms, and the most diplomatic language in discussing such a question as the labor of children in factories. It is too important a question. It means not only something for the child itself, it means not only that a little child should have the opportunity of growing up as the Almighty Father fully intended that it should, not only that there should be some sunshine and some pleasure and a chance for the child to kick up its heels and play the way the little animals do, but it means a great deal more than that. It means the welfare of this Nation of ours, it means the determination of the type of citizen who is going to follow us. Unless that type, unless the mass of labor in this country has a high standard of living, then it seems to me the work of our universities, and of our statesmen, will amount to but very little.

We have the experience of the past. We have had civilizations as great as our own, civilizations that have handed down to us some of the most priceless principles of democratic forms of government. We have had Greece, Rome, with their genius and with their statesmen, but those empires fell, not for lack of genius, but for lack of a solid foundation composed of the working man of those countries who would sustain the structure that the statesman was endeavoring to establish.

So when we plead for the children we are not pleading alone for the little child, we are pleading for the nation, we are pleading that we may have a better and higher standard of living for the mass of our workers than we have to-day. We are pleading that for every little child the law will say, "You shall have an education and neither an ignorant parent nor a greedy manufacturer shall take away from you the opportunity offered by the public schools."

The animals never exploit their offspring. When they have reached a certain stage, the parents may turn them loose to forage for themselves; but they never force their offspring to work for the parents' welfare.

The savages do not allow their young offspring to go out and hunt for them or to work for them. It has remained for civilized man, for the Christian nations of the earth to give us the most terrible examples of exploitation of the little child for private profits.

CHILD LABOR AND DEMOCRACY *

By A. J. McKelway,
Secretary for the Southern States, National Child Labor Committee.

Describing, in his "French Revolution," the death of Louis the Fifteenth, Carlyle says: "Borne over the Atlantic, to the closing ear of Louis, King by the Grace of God, what sounds are these; muffled, ominous, new in our centuries? Boston Harbor is black with unexpected tea; behold a Pennsylvania Congress gather; and ere long on Bunker Hill, Democracy, announcing in rifle volleys, death-winged, under her star banner, to the tune of Yankee-doodle-doo, that she is born, and whirlwind-like, will envelop the whole world!"

We suppose that it was not within the vision even of that seer that the opening years of the Twentieth Century should behold democracy striving to assert itself in Russia, in Turkey and in Persia, or the Chinese Empire changing into a Republic. How much lies between the birth of democracy in America and the formal abdication of the Chinese Emperor is too familiar historic ground to be more than touched on this occasion; but that Democracy "will envelop the whole world," is a prophecy far nearer realization than could have been known in Carlyle's day. In America itself we need not blind ourselves to the fact that the term "democracy" is beginning to take on new meanings. "Westward the course of empire takes its way," according to the poet. In the United States "Eastward the course of democracy takes its way." Whether we will or not, the people are more and more determined to take into their own hands whatever of the processes of Government they believe to be necessary for the carrying out of the popular will. It was my good fortune a little more than a year ago to attend the Constitutional Conventions of the new States which have just added two stars to the American flag, New Mexico and Arizona. I call to your attention the fact that

* Read by title.

even in New Mexico, with sixty per cent. of the population men of Spanish blood, the citizens recently voted by an overwhelming majority to make their constitution easily amendable on the demand of the people; while in Arizona there is a breath of freedom in the very air, inspiring almost to a degree of intoxication. The old order changeth. The issue is not, I take it, whether a pure democracy shall take the place of representative government, but rather that government shall be representative of the will of the majority in a sense in which it has never yet been in American history.

It is doubtless true that a people at any particular epoch has the government which it deserves to have. Where a people is unfit for self-government to any degree, to that degree will it be ruled for good or for ill by those who can assume the reins of government, and the King is the one who can. The trouble with the most of us, said William Allen White, not long ago, is that we did not get beyond the fifth grade at school; but every year more and more are getting beyond the fifth grade. Two proverbs of Thomas Jefferson come to mind in this connection, companion proverbs, and the first is, "The remedy for the evils of democracy is more democracy," and the second, "Preach a crusade against ignorance." A democracy in which there is a large enough element of ignorance to turn the balance one way or another between those who struggle for the common good and those who demand special privilege, is constantly in a position of unstable equilibrium; while a democracy in which there is a large uneducated electorate is itself a prey to the self-seeker and the demagogue and a menace to civilization itself. Not only are we beholding in these times the beginnings of a more direct rule of the people in governmental affairs, but there is a movement for the democratization of industry itself, and here also there is a demand that more of us should go beyond the fifth grade in school. Not that I believe education to be the panacea of all ills. It is only another name for opportunity. But with this growing sense of the responsibility of the electorate to do more than to choose between two sets of public officials, duly selected for them, and to assert their will even in the initiation and veto of legislation itself, there arises the very instinct of self-preservation against unknown ills, and that instinct manifests itself most potently in the demand that the electorate shall be intelligent. In a democracy, rightly so-called, no one liveth to himself or dieth to himself. Moreover, we have in America a double citizenship. We owe proper allegiance both to our State and to our Nation. While the majority must rule, a minority may hinder social progress. Therefore, ignorance is the curse of a democracy, and not alone the ignorance that accompanies illiteracy, but that which is satisfied with a little learning and feeds on half-baked theories of government. The ignorance of these who have already attained citizenship cannot be cured. What every State in the Union, what the Nation itself has suffered, by an unenlightened suffrage, is beyond calculation. We who patriotically glory in the America that is, may well hang our heads for shame at the thought of the America that might have been. That we have had some narrow escapes from almost irremediable disaster is certain. That we have had a Civil War that was a bloody blunder is history. But when we speak of childhood, we project our thoughts toward the future. What of the citizens of the future? What great question, vital to the well-being of the Republic itself, may be decided by a vote of those who are now the children of the sweat shops of New York City; of the coal mines of Pennsylvania; of the cotton mills of the Carolinas? This is an aspect of the child labor problem which, it seems to me, has been almost lost sight of. It is a comparatively easy task to harass the minds of an audience like this with what are called "human interest" stories concerning the abuses of childhood, that appeal to our sense of pity first, but to which we become hardened, unless at the same time we have some practical outlet for our emotions. I am striving here and now to appeal to the patriotic instinct, which, in its last analysis, is an instinct of self-preservation. In the noble words of Ben Hill of Georgia, "Who saves his country saves all things, saves himself, and all things saved do bless him; who lets his country die, lets all things die, dies himself, ignobly, and all things dying curse him."

Fruits of Child Labor

The perpetuation of the system of child labor means the perpetuation of ignorance and poverty and their multiplication through succeeding years. Wherever there is a demand for the labor of children, unchecked by a stern law, and its vigorous enforcement, that demand empties the schools of the children. Nor are the physical effects of premature toil to be overlooked in this connection. If, ordinarily, the sound mind is found only in the sound body, then the child labor system is doing more than to rob the children of their rightful opportunity by denying to them an education. It is poisoning their bodies, while it is starving their minds, for we have come to know in these later years that fatigue itself is a poison. The medical authorities speak now of the toxin of fatigue, and when children are forced to work for hours which would be long even for the adult man, the society that permits such an abuse can be indicted at the bar of civilization for the wholesale poisoning of children. The latest figures we have concerning the employment of children in America are from the Census of 1900. Perhaps, unless Congress shall reverse a position it has recently taken, and will allow sufficient appropriations for the publication of the occupation schedules, these may also be the last figures we shall have. But the figures for 1900 compared with those of previous decades prove that there was a large increase in the employment of children in the United States. It is perhaps a conservative estimate to say that there are a million children to-day under the age of 16 years who are employed in the various industries of this country, with more or less regulation of such employment, in addition to another million in agriculture, only a part of whom were assisting their parents on the farm. It is safe to say that for all children under the age of 16 their employment has interfered more or less with their education in the schools. Do we realize that this great army of children comprises about one-fourth of all the children of the country from 10 to 15 years of age? Certainly we all agree that all the children from 10 to 14 years of age should be pupils at school. Yet one out of seven of these is at work.

Child Labor Means Low Wages

The cotton manufacturing industry, and, in fact, the whole textile industry, including the woolen and silk mills, has always been cursed with child labor, with its attendant evils of long hours and low wages. Here comes in another economic law which has had abundant illustration and which needs only to be stated to be accepted by common sense, and that is, that the industries which depend to a considerable extent upon the labor of children are low wage industries, the obvious reason being that where a child can do adequately the work of the adult, the adult must take the wages which are deemed sufficient for the child. So that child labor means family labor, means either the turning of the home into a workshop, significantly called a sweat shop, or means that the mother with the father and all the children who are allowed to work by the law or by the employer must work in order to earn the necessary income for the family. Therefore, in the child employing industries we have a feudalism instead of a democracy. |The children who begin work at an early age are likely to remain children in all but years.| The whole process of evolution is disrupted by the child labor system. The progress of the race itself has been often shown to depend upon the prolongation of the period of childhood. |The child labor system shortens the period of childhood.'| Hence we have in many industrial centers a population growing up with only the smallest opportunity for an education, and this in an age when the movement of civilization itself is becoming accelerated at an enormous pace. They retain the helplessness of childhood. It is not merely that the rest of us must go on and leave these unfortunates behind, though they form no inconsiderable portion of our population, but they hold us back, they are a drag upon the wheels of progress.

Child Labor and Crime

There is another aspect of the problem which is near akin to that which we have been considering. It is the relation between child labor and criminality. I have had frequently quoted to me by the opponents of child labor legislation, in legislative halls, the proverb, "Satan finds some mischief still for idle hands to do," as if it were a message from Holy Writ, like those other two texts of Scripture which are frequently quoted: "He tempers the wind to the shorn lamb," and "Cleanliness is next to Godliness." But the inexorable figures show that to put a child to work too soon is to embitter him for life. When you rob the child of his childhood, you have taken something that cannot be replaced and you have sowed the seeds of rebellion against all law and order. There has only been a partial investigation of this subject, and this is found in Volume 8 of the report of the Bureau of Labor on the Condition of Woman and Child Wage-Earners in the United States, entitled "Juvenile Delinquency and Its Relation to Employment." The cases of several thousand children were studied, who had passed through the Juvenile Courts of a few of our cities. In Boston, for example, of the children at work, 10 to 15 years of age, nearly 16 per cent. were found to be delinquent children, while of the children at school, 10 to 14 years of age, only 1½ per cent. were found to be delinquent. This is a larger proportion of delinquent children than was found in other cities, but in every city the percentage of the working children who were delinquent was several times larger than that of school children who were delinquent. Of the whole number of delinquents, whose records were kept as to their employment, it was found that nearly 22 per cent. were newsboys and over 20 per cent. errand boys and messenger boys, and these figures are even more significant when we consider how small a class the newsboys and errand boys in any city are. Now society is at war with criminality. The criminal is both a menace and a burden. So far as child idleness is concerned—if idleness means freedom from breadwinning toil, then I make bold to affirm the right of the child to be idle and his right to play. Certainly in our modern school systems we cannot consider the child in school an idle child, and so far as the right to play is concerned, I have heard Jane Addams testify that the introduction of children's playgrounds in certain quarters of Chicago, at the expense of the taxpayers, so diminished the expenses of the Juvenile Court that there was a cash balance on the right side of the ledger so far as the public was concerned.

I took it upon myself to make some study of the children who were employed by the Blue Bird Company when the play was last given in Washington. Instead of having all the comforts of a first-class hotel, of carriages waiting at the door to carry them to their place of abode, of a tutor to see that their lessons were not neglected, of Pullman cars when they travel (and these have all been widely advertised by the theatrical association interested), upon following a troupe of these children home from the theatre, I found that they walked several blocks at midnight, attended by two young ladies, who were employed on the stage themselves, to a third-class hotel, where they were lodged certainly not under the best environment, and then I saw them board an ordinary day coach for their transportation back to New York; not that that was any particular hardship, but it was a failure of the specifications. Nor is the claim at all founded on fact that the majority of great actors went upon the stage as children. We have abundant testimony to the contrary, and again it stands to reason that the best preparation for the stage, as for any other occupation in life, is the school. The vast majority of children who entered upon a stage career as children have become so much human waste and the real question is whether we shall tolerate even for our amusement or our improvement, the sacrifice of childhood.

To sum up the case of child labor versus democracy, I present the following indictment against the child labor system, namely, that child labor means racial degeneracy, the perpetuation of poverty, the enlargement of illiteracy, the disintegration of the family, the increase of crime, the lowering of the wage scale, and the swelling of the army of the unemployed.

It is incumbent upon society for its own preservation to give every child a chance in life, a chance

> "To seek! Not to be bound and doomed in the dust!
> And the seekers, the millions far-lifting,
> In the dim new ages we know they shall fail—
> Some crushed, some self-lost, some drifting
> Back down the slopes—but the chance shall be theirs
> And ten thousand, touching the sun,
> Shall pull the race upwards to the City of Brothers
> Till on earth God's will be done.
> Till our streets shall be sunned with the joy of children
> Aud our shops be busy with men
> Toiling together great ends of the Earth,
> And our homes be hallowed again
> With the Mother, the Child! Till our schools shape souls
> For an earth-life ending in skies,
> Till we know that a Soul is a Soul, and as such
> Is holy before our eyes."

EXTENDING MEDICAL INSPECTION FROM SCHOOLS TO MILLS

By George F. Ross, M. D.,

Superintendent of Health, Guilford Co., N. C.

The subject of this paper is an entirely new one to most people in the South, although it has been tried in many Northern industrial plants, especially in those of Massachusetts, and has met with considerable success.

In North Carolina, we have comparatively little systematic medical examination of children, and that little is confined to school children of larger towns and to those of the rural schools of Guilford County. But, as North Carolina is one of the largest industrial centres and employs thousands of children in her cotton mills, cigar factories, etc., all who have to do with public life and public health are realizing more and more the need of such work.

For years, this idea of examining school children has been growing in favor throughout the country, because people realized that such supervision was not only to help the child himself, but to prevent the rapid spread of infection among those who were meeting together in intimate contact *five* days in the week. These infections, in the past, often gained an epidemic form before the proper notice was taken. Now, those same people are realizing that the mill children are meeting together *six* days of the week in large numbers under less favorable conditions than those of the school children.

I call your attention to the fact that there is a close relationship between the mill sections and the rural districts because many of these mill children were either themselves born in the country or their parents were. Many families whose heads failed to thrive in the country because of poor work or poor management, removed to the mill towns in order to put at work their poor, pale, pasty-faced children, that a living might be had through these young hands.

The old-fashioned idea that country children are stronger and healthier than those of the large towns and cities is a mistaken one, and the sooner educators, teachers, physicians and parents realize this fact the better it will be for these children. There are several reasons why this is true:

(1) Many do not have the proper food, or they have the food improperly prepared, or they do not have sufficient clothing, or the proper home surroundings.

(2) These children are often handicapped because of ignorance or indifference of parents toward diseases, and disease is often allowed to get a strong hold on the children before a physician is consulted.

Ignorance and Indifference

The following are instances of this ignorance or indifference: About one year ago a father brought his 12-year-old son to me and said that for eighteen months the boy had been "puny," and that six months before coming to me he had taken him to a doctor, who said, without giving the boy an examination, that he had consumption, because of his cough, loss of weight, etc. Under treatment for consumption he grew no better, but worse. I gave him a thorough examination and found no consumption, but a typical case of hookworm disease, which was cured by two doses of thymol. In this case, the father had waited one year to consult the first physician, didn't believe my diagnosis, but agreed to give one dose of thymol, when he then saw the worms for himself. There are many similar cases.

Another instance was one of consumption. A girl in a family of six had a "cough" for months, with loss of weight, night sweats, etc., and it was not until she was bedridden that the parents consulted a physician, then the physician's diagnosis was not credited and no precautions taken, with the result that now three other members of the family have that disease.

In my work of examining school children, I find many handicapped because of noses and throats filled with adenoids and tonsils. Although these children are being robbed with every breath of something more important than money, there are many parents who will "wait a while," hoping the children will "outgrow" the defects. These may appear extreme cases, but I meet the same almost every day, only in a lesser degree. I do not mean to give the impression that parents in the country or mill section do not coöperate, for they do, but their resistance to medical legislation is greater than among people of the larger towns and this is the *third* reason why country school children are not the healthiest. It is to help overcome this "resistance" and the ignorance already mentioned that those who drafted the Health Bill which passed our last legislature specifically stated that a part of the duties of the Superintendent of Health was that of education by lectures, addresses, papers, etc. And it is for this reason that, during the five months just passed, I made over thirty talks to fathers and mothers of school children throughout Guilford County and reached nearly twenty-five hundred people. These talks were illustrated with stereopticon pictures—many being of local interest.

Medical Examination in Guilford County

Last August, Guilford County started a movement to give its country-school children what the larger towns and cities are giving theirs; that is, medical examination, and thus became the only county in the United States, so far as I can learn, to take such a step. I began by having the teachers of the eighty-five schools send in a list of names (10 per cent. of their total enrollment) of those children so defective as to be apparent to the laymen. So far, over 900 names have come in, and this means that *one* out of every *nine* is seriously handicapped. I have been able to examine only about three hundred of these children, but have learned some interesting facts. Nearly every one of the three hundred is pale, under weight and under size, 98 per cent. of them have tonsils and adenoids so enlarged as to deprive them of a good deal of the air they should be getting. Eight per cent. are deaf, probably from the nose and throat condition, and many have various eye troubles, doubtless for the same reason. Several cases of tuberculosis and malaria were found, and of those examined for hookworm, 12 per cent. showed the disease. Nearly one-third of these children are in the mill schools. Since education is not compulsory in North Carolina, a large percentage of the children of the mill section do not come under school inspection.

My work among these children, while covering so far only a period of a few months, has been amply sufficient to convince me that the work is of vital importance, in order to have a coming generation of strong men and women.

I. A very little work with factory school children will be necessary to convince any one that they and those in the factories need medical attention even more than those living in the rural sections. Their whole mode of life is different from that of those in the country. The boys in the country may spend the same number of hours at work as the factory boy, but usually a country boy's work is outside, while the mill boy works in a steam-heated building, where air is hot and moist or dust laden, a condition conducive to enlarged tonsils and adenoids, which predisposes to lung trouble, and lowers his powers of resistance for other infections.

II. Then, in the mill sections all over the State, many children alternate a period of school work with a longer period of work in the mill. This is unsatisfactory from the point of view of both teacher and physician; for the child coming from work to school is below par mentally and physically. A child working in a mill soon becomes so familiar with the work and so skilful as to be almost machine-like. Such work, as somebody puts it, is "enervating," while if he went to school regularly, with the gradual increase in the severity of his studies and with gradual sharpening of his mental faculties, he would be doing work which would be "energizing." Physically, his powers of resistance are lowered from long hours in the mill, from the usual throat and nose condition, etc.

III. Another reason for medical examination of mill children is because of night work. In some mills where there are night shifts, young boys and girls are allowed to work, and with the long hours at a time when children, of all people, should be asleep, with their lunch at midnight, improperly prepared and hurriedly eaten, and with their broken rest the day following, these boys and girls cannot get their normal development.

IV. Many children begin life handicapped because their mothers, either through necessity or desire, are allowed to work in mills, either day or night, expending physical strength at work and in standing—strength which should go toward developing and growing the unborn children; these children come into the world below par as the mother's physical strength is far below what it should be.

V. There are three diseases which are more or less prevalent both among factory children and those in the country: three diseases whose onsets are so insidious that they often get a strong hold upon children before anything is done: these are tuberculosis, malaria and hookworm disease. Many children both at work and in school are suffering from one of the three infections, but in such a low degree of infection that they are not acutely sick, have no pain to attract attention, but are sick enough for their strength and resisting power to be sapped. If these diseases could be looked after and controlled, a great deal of suffering and poor work would be averted. In my opinion, these three diseases do more harm than do the ten long hours of work each day, hard as this day's work is.

There are children at work in many factories spending ten hours a day at actual labor indoors plus the energy it takes to stand, when they should be outside, studying some, but playing and growing more. This condition is brought about because the State does not require enough for her children and because of the ignorance and indifference of parents.

Still another reason why children both in the mill sections and in schools should be examined and kept under constant supervision is the exposure to consumption while at work and in the schoolroom and because of predisposition to this disease. Statistics show that 207 male and 144 female operatives in every 100,000 and 144 male and 106 female teachers in every 100,000 die annually from tuberculosis.

Protective Laws

Examination and treatment even will not bring about the desired results unless certain other things are done.

(1) We should have laws fixing for all States the age limit for all kinds of work for the women and minors, with no night work for any save male adults, and with these laws rigidly enforced by men whose sole interest is the child.

(2) We should have compulsory registration of births in all

States and it should be necessary to present the birth-certificate when a child wishes to work in a factory. This would stop the perjury of many parents and many of the evils of child labor under legal age.

(3) We should endeavor to improve the home surroundings of children by educating parents. I am glad to say that there are several factors already at work toward this end, namely, systematic, practical health lectures, monthly medical bulletins sent to each home, free of charge—bulletins which treat in a simple, comprehensive way of such subjects as consumption and typhoid fever, their cause and prevention, the why and wherefore of enlarged tonsils and adenoids, hookworm disease, etc. The other factors are The Betterment Associations, Mothers' Meetings, trained nurses and domestic science teachers.

The Betterment Associations which have been and are being organized at different schools, are doing much for the education of people in showing them how to improve their homes, not only from a sanitary, but also from an artistic point of view. Many of these Associations through North Carolina are paying particular attention to the sanitary surroundings of their school buildings. Several have furnished these buildings, provided water coolers and individual drinking cups, put the grounds in good order, secured a good water supply for the pupils and have put in sanitary closets approved by the State Board of Health. All these things taken together will be a good example for the homes of these sections.

The Mothers' Meetings in some mill sections are doing good work. Here these women meet and pass a pleasant hour or two in conversation, in sewing, in learning how to cook nutritious food or in discussing questions in regard to their homes or the welfare of their children: all this under the guidance of one or two capable women who are usually the wives of mill owners. Some mills have trained nurses whose sole duty it is to go from house to house, giving practical aid and instruction in caring for the sick and in preparing suitable food for them.

The Domestic Science Departments which have been established by some of the mill owners are under the guidance of well-trained teachers and have classes for the married women as well as for the girls.

It would be a good thing if the cotton mills, cigar factories, and overall factories, where many girls are employed, had rest rooms in charge of matrons, and also would allow their female employees to walk out each month, with no questions asked, and be absent, on pay, for one to three days. Many girls are seriously handicapped because of enforced work during this time. Some of the mills of the North have adopted this plan and do not experience any loss from it.

(4) Added to the forces mentioned above for bettering the condition of these people, we should have *compulsory education* of the proper kind not only for the children in these industrial centres, but also for the children of the rural sections. In 1900, there were over 51,000 illiterate children in North Carolina, and in certain mill sections of the State there are boys and girls who began work earlier in life than the law allows and who are unable to read and write. With compulsory education, these children by the time the working age was reached would have stronger bodies and a mental training which would save many from being the machine-like beings they are now, and would relieve the country children of the serious handicap with which so many start out in life.

These conditions will not only be of untold value to the child, but will be of material advantage to the mill owners. For instance, in a meeting of owners of eight of the largest mills in North Carolina, a physician asked them to put in figures the amount lost each year from preventable diseases among their operatives, and it was found that the eight mills lost from $55,000 to $60,000 during twelve months.

With these plans for bettering child life in general carried out, with the improvement of homes and of school life, and with medical supervision of all children both in school and at work, not only will the scope of usefulness of the present generation be materially widened, but the generation to come will be able to begin life without the handicap we see each day among these young breadwinners.

CHILD LABOR IN THE CANNERIES OF NEW YORK STATE

By Zenas L. Potter,
Field Secretary, New York Child Labor Committee.

We have been accustomed to look on the child labor laws of New York State as among the best in the country. As far as child labor in canneries is concerned we rank with the "tail-enders." We put up a good appearance. Our law reads: "No child under the age of fourteen shall be employed, permitted, or suffered to work in or in connection with any factory." It makes no exception and grants no favors. An exemption in favor of the canners has, however, been read into the law by a former Attorney General. Among the thirteen States leading in the canning industry we rank, in reality, with Delaware, the only State which in law not only grants the canners special rights to exploit children of any age, but permits them to be worked unlimited hours.

In 1908, when the State Labor Commissioner first attempted to enforce the law in its application to canneries, Mr. J. P. Olney, President of the State Canned Goods and Packers' Association, secured, through the Labor Commissioner, a ruling of Mr. Julius Mayer, then Attorney-General, which, in effect, held that work in the shed of a canning factory—the place where the vegetables and fruits are prepared, the beans snipped, corn husked, etc.—was not factory work, nor was it work "in connection with a factory," for then it would have come under the prohibitions of the law: but that work in the shed of a canning factory was agricultural in character, and, therefore, altogether free from restrictions upon the age of workers or the hours of their labor. In spite of the fact that the Labor Department, in an official investigation, since determined that of 63 cannery sheds reported, 41 were connected structurally, or by power, with the rest of the factory, that 49 contained from one to seven different machines each, and that all but 14 were provided with artificial light for night work, local courts have steadfastly held the opinion of the Attorney-General as indisputable.

The result is that children five, six, and seven years of age may be found working in cannery sheds upward to 14 hours a day. I speak from experience, for the New York Committee has had persons working as laborers in the canneries for the last two summers, and I have been one of them.

Let me quote a few facts from the daily reports of investigators:

Oneida, August 7th.—"In the shed were about 100 snippers of whom 60 or 70 were children, and of those fully 45 were children under 12. There were a number—say, 30—who couldn't have been over 10. They began at from 6.30 to 7 A. M., and the weigher said they would work till 9 or 10 o'clock at night."

Canastota, August 12th.—"Shed ran from 11 A. M. to 10.30 P. M., 20 odd children working."

August 16th.—"Shed ran from 7 A. M. to 10.45 P. M. There were over 50 children in the shed in the afternoon, including many small tots hardly able to walk."

August 17th.—"Shed ran from 7 A. M. to 10.30 P. M. At 9.45 P. M. I counted 22 children at work. Most of these were Italians, several being very small."

August 18th.—"Forty children in shed to-day. It ran from 7 A. M. to 7 P. M."

August 19th.—"Shed ran from 7 A. M. to 10.30 P. M., children working."

August 20th.—"Shed ran from 7 A. M. to 10 P. M., children working."

Brockport, August 16th.—"On a porch or shed there were 16 children under 10, and 5 over 10 at work. Inside the building were four boys of 10 or 11 working at the sorting tables."

Forestville, August 22d.—"Shed ran from 6.30 A. M. to 10 P. M. At 7.30 P. M. there were 23 children under 14, about 20 being under 10, at work."

August 23d.—"There were 22 children working in the shed to-day. It ran 13½ hours from 6.30 A. M. to 10 P. M. At night 29 children worked."

August 24th.—"Eighteen adults and 23 children snipped beans and husked corn to-day. Shed ran from 6.30 A. M. to 10 P. M. Mothers beat children for working too slow and not working at all. The names of these children are Tony Pollino, age 7, his sisters, aged 11 and 13, Joe Sacci, age 13."

These Conditions Not Typical

The New York Child Labor Committee has information concerning 15 different canneries employing children under 14 years of age. One point, however, should be made absolutely clear: these conditions are not typical of the canning industry of New York State, nor do they exist in the majority of factories. We have information concerning the conditions in 26 factories which employ children seldom, if ever. In contrast to the above facts, let me quote the views of some canning factory owners and superintendents who not only refuse to take advantage of the former Attorney-General's ruling, but are opposed to child labor in the industry:

From a cannery southwest of Buffalo, superintendent said: "We live right up to the letter of the child labor law, and employ no children anywhere under 14. When the law was passed we thought it would be death to the industry. We thought children were our best workers, but it has proved a blessing, and we are better off without them."

From a cannery southeast of Rochester, superintendent said he was opposed to all child labor. He said he had worked in canneries from the time he was a mere lad, and knew what long hours and hard work meant.

From an officer of the Canners' Association, Mr. ———, told me he had often opposed, in meetings of the Canners' Association, having it given out to the public that the industry depended on the labor of children.

From a cannery between Buffalo and Rochester, superintendent told me he used no children either in factory or shed, but provided a place for them, and hired a boy to watch them. He said he had been at the factory six years, and that during that time it had never paid less than 5 per cent., and that in 1910 it paid 22 per cent.

From the owner of a large cannery east of Rochester, Mr. B. told me he was absolutely opposed to child labor in the canneries, and knew that it was unnecessary.

Such facts give us an optimistic outlook and faith in human nature.

The Canners' Arguments

In answer to the contentions of the Child Labor Committee, however, the canners who employ children advance four arguments:

First: They claim that the life of the industry in the State depends on the labor of children. Our answer that at least 26 canneries, among them some of the largest in the State, operate without children, seems a sufficient and conclusive reply.

Second: They maintain that the labor of the mothers, which cannot be secured unless the children are permitted to accompany them to work, is necessary to the life of the industry. Again the fact that 26 canneries use no children seems a sufficient reply. Several of the owners of these factories furnish a room for the children, and hire a woman to take care of them. Others have not found even this necessary. Any difficulty on this point can be easily overcome, and it cannot be urged as a justification for existing conditions.

Third: The canners attempt to disclaim responsibility for these conditions: "Pay is by the piece," they say, "and children are free to come and go as they please." Whether the child exploitation which exists is due to the greed of canners or parents, or to mistaken ambitions on the part of the child, the latter must be protected; and whatever the method of employment or payment, the fact remains that the work is done on the property of the canner, for him, and that only by holding him responsible, as the law holds other manufacturers responsible, can present conditions be remedied.

Finally: Some canners say the work does not hurt the children physically, and since it is summer work, does not interfere with their schooling. Courts of law the country over, the great conservative agencies of government, have upheld as public health measures, laws which restrict the hours of labor for children under 16 years to 8 per day. They have even decided that a law limiting the hours of women in factories to ten per day is justified on the same grounds. I do not believe the sound judgment of the business, professional and laboring people of New York State will agree with the canner who claims the vitality of a child of five, or even of ten or twelve years, is not impaired by work for ten, twelve or fourteen hours a day.

The Educational Loss

The claim that the schooling of cannery children is not interfered with, is based on misinformation: Many canneries operate into October. A considerable number run into the Christmas holidays. The result is that children who go out from the cities for the summer's work often lose from two weeks to three months' schooling. Last year the New York Committee made a special study of 100 of these children in the Buffalo schools. Twenty-four lost from one to twenty-five days' schooling; 55 from twenty-five to forty-nine days', and 21 from forty-nine to seventy-one days'. As a result 36 per cent. lost a class outright, and 54 per cent. either lost a class or were conditioned. Probably only half of these children completed a term's work during the school year. These are some of the children who, with only a primary grade education, are leaving our schools every year to become citizens.

With the facts in hand, the New York Committee is in better position than ever to meet the canners' argument, and we hope the time will not be long till New York joins the ranks of those States which grant to no industry a special right to exploit children.

HOW TO INTEREST YOUNG PEOPLE

By Mrs. Frederick Crane, New York

It is not enough to set the child in the midst to be examined with telescope and microscope, to be discussed, classified, tabulated and chronicled; but in addition an earnest effort must be made to interest the child itself in the child labor situation, and its relation to child welfare.

This is necessary partly because children are active agents in creating the situation where they are eager to leave school and earn money; partly because those others who are in no danger of industrial exploitation should have their active sympathies enlisted for the less fortunate; and even more because in the hands of the children of to-day lies the fate of the nation's children of to-morrow.

This effort to interest young people should aim definitely to arouse an impulse strong enough to result eventually in action. The young are peculiarly susceptible to such impulses, even as early as the kindergarten age. An old lady dates her life-long enthusiasm for foreign missions from the day when, barely six years old, she was shown some curios from mission fields. Nevertheless, whoever undertakes to awaken and guide youthful enthusiasm must possess certain natural gifts as well as certain acquired qualifications.

The natural gifts are fortunately more or less common, and are capable of considerable development. The most important are:

A sense of humor.

Imagination.

Sensitiveness to the moods of the audience or group, and enough versatility to capture and make use of these moods.

These four characteristics tend to induce a crisp, incisive, sympathetic manner; an avoidance of over-elaboration and monotony; and freedom from sentimentality in describing the pathetic phases of the subjects.

In addition to these natural gifts, there are at least three qualifications which it is essential to acquire:

1. A dominating belief in the subject itself. Young people are too shrewd to be caught by the chaff of simulated enthusiasm. When your own revolt against the enormity of child labor is absolute and complete, then you are well on the way to convince young people of its enormity.

2. A mastery, both of your subject and of the language in which to present it. One is as important as the other. This means much study and research, followed by skillful adaptation of your material. You may have learned, and may think the young should know also, that "many of the foremost physicians, jurists, publicists, etc., concur in the deduction that an early assumption of industrial responsibility is deleterious," but to express it in Chinese would be almost as clear to them and much more interesting.

3. A fundamental belief in young people and their potentialities. The importance of this cannot be over-estimated, for none is more sensitive and responsive to such a belief than the young person.

To illustrate: A worried father complained to a bank president that notwithstanding all opposition his son was determined to leave school and enter the bank. "Let me talk with him," said the banker. When the boy appeared, he asked: "So you want a position in this bank? What are you planning to make of yourself?" "A bank president," was the immediate and emphatic answer. "That is right," exclaimed the banker, sincerely gratified. "Aim for the highest every time. But you are going about it the wrong way," and he explained to the boy how much preliminary school education was necessary for such an office, and ended by assuring him a position in the bank when he had fulfilled school requirements. To this evidence of confidence in his ability, and especially in his honesty of purpose, the boy's response was complete, for the father testified that he immediately became as eager to attend school as he had been to leave it.

Visualization

Now, as to methods. First and indispensable is what, for want of a better title, we will call Visualization.

The child already mentioned as an enthusiast on missions, was impressed through her eyes. To this day her recollections centre on the curio-cabinet and its contents. The appearance and words of the gentleman in charge are forgotten. It was therefore neither his personality, nor his persuasiveness that influenced her, but his showing objects adapted to interest her. The appeal to the eyes, therefore, must be as carefully adapted to the degree of intelligence behind them as is the appeal to the ears in the choice of language. This visualization may be accomplished:

1. By means of exhibits of charts, pictures or other objects with or without speech.

2. By illustrative strokes on a blackboard while speaking.

The National Child Labor Committee has prepared an exhibit for an itinerary of the boys' departments of the Young Men's Christian Associations. One of the younger lads was so absorbed in the pictures and explanatory placards that he refused to be drawn away by the offer of a chance at the billiard table. Here are two of the charts included in that exhibit. (See pp. 142a and 142b.)

They are what every teaching chart should be, simple and obvious, yet attractive. Why could not copies be hung in the elementary grades of every school and used as the bases of arithmetical problems? If children were set at computing how many more hours, especially Saturday hours, would be spent in factories than in school during given periods, they would, while acquiring the science of numbers, be automatically acquiring a wholesome sense of the comparative freedom from irksome confinement in school life. And could they have a series of problems based on the other, they would gain an impression which no amount of telling would give of the unwisdom of beginning work with insufficient education. Charts on other phases of the subject could be devised and used in connection with the regular school training, which would at the same time teach many wholesome lessons, both to restrain the child who is eager to go early to work, and to awaken the sympathy of the more fortunate toward those forced into the industrial grind.

The blackboard has so long been an indispensable adjunct to pedagogy that it is surprising that speakers to children, or even to

MILESTONES IN THE LIFE and EARNINGS OF WORKMEN

What you can earn if you go to school to learn a — AND — What boys earn if they go directly into a trade after you leave grammar school.

STATISTICS: Massachusetts Commission on Industrial Education—U. S. Census, 1900.

Note.—Between ages of 14 and 25 the study is based on 799 cases.

Do the Hours You Spend at School Seem Long to You?

See how much longer they are for children who work in the Factory.

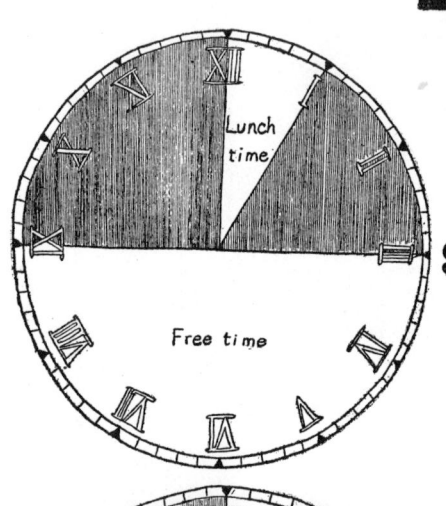

In school
9 months of the year
for 5 hours a day.

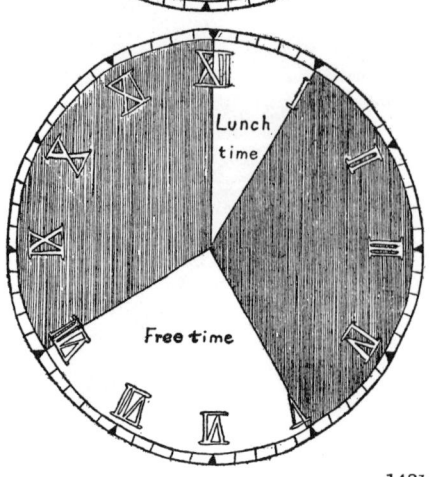

In the Factory
12 months of the year
for 8 hours a day.

adults, do not oftener avail themselves of this simple and effective means of appealing at once to the understanding and memory, by illustrative strokes while speaking.

But even where material aids are lacking, the attention may be held by using explanatory gestures in combination with vivid word pictures. A stereopticon lecture on child toilers was advertised in a Vermona village. Too late for repairs, it was discovered that a dangerous defect in the apparatus would prohibit the use of the lantern. So, to hold the eyes of the young people, the speaker used gestures illustrating the various trades described. Afterward the son of a farm hand, a boy under twelve, commented, "Yes, I liked the lecture. She told a lot of things I never knew before. If that's what they mean by a lecture I'd like to hear another!"

Dramatization

Visualization may be combined with Dramatization. Such simple stage properties as a piece of muslin, another of silk, a chunk of coal, a glass bottle or lamp chimney have held the eyes spellbound while Miss Cotton told her tale; followed by Mr. Anthracite; then Miss Silk had her little say, and Mr. Glass closed the symposium. After listening to one of these talks a boy of nine years, son of a prominent professor, said to his mother, "Mamma, why do they make children work? When I get to be a man, they shan't."

Another method, particularly effective, is to have the children themselves do the dramatization. It was the use of this expedient which saved one meeting from disaster. The group of children to be addressed were badly officered and did not have the initial conception of orderliness. Finally, the most restless were picked out, and set to imitating motions of the child laborers of whom they had just been told. This kept them all interested until the improvised breaker boy cried, "Huh! I'm tired." The others promptly followed suit, which gave the speaker the opportunity to point out that it tired them even to play at the work others no older than themselves actually had to do.

In this same manner, why could not younger children in a school personate the different States, mention their products, and tell what share children have in producing them? This would be a combination lesson in physical and industrial geography, with a touch of States' rights thrown in.

There are thousands of ways by which children and young people, who are so ardent in their sympathies, so generous in their impulses, so shrewd in their insight, may be not only interested to avoid and suppress child labor, but may be made so intelligent concerning the child labor situation that by the time the boys are voters and the girls are suffragists, there will be no doubt as to the correctness of their position, and their stand-patness on this issue.

THE EDUCATIONAL TEST FOR WORKING CHILDREN

By Richard K. Conant,
Secretary, Massachusetts Child Labor Committee.

What educational test ought the child to pass in order to obtain a permit to work? Here seems to me the commonest practical relation of Child Labor and Education. In the office of the superintendent of schools, or whatever authority issues working papers, Child Labor meets Education.

The meeting is often not a cordial one. Education has a few perfunctory questions to ask Child Labor. Child Labor is somewhat embarrassed, and Education too diffident, but the meeting has to be gotten through with and Education generally smooths matters over with smiling corrections, and then dismisses Child Labor with a wave of the hand.

Yet, in truth, this meeting place is the accessible ground where many of the important questions discussed at this conference may be controlled. In any ideal system of education and restriction of child employment, the law can at this meeting place perform its effective regulation through the educational test for working children. Whether your ideal be industrial education or general education, part-time schooling or vocational guidance, the law should set educational standards for the child before he can become a workman. Physical and age standards are necessary, but the educational standard is also indispensable. If the schools should develop to the point where the children would in the grades grow in natural directions leading to different occupations, and if the wisest vocational guidance should be given the children as they approach the proper working age, we should still need to develop to perfection the educational test. For each occupation there would then be a separate test, but adequate educational preparation would be insisted upon before the child could begin his work. So, too, if there should be inserted in the educational scheme a transitional period of part-time at school and part-time at work, the school ought to demand **appropriate** examinations before releasing the child entirely.

In any ideal system then we should have adequate educational preparation for work. How near that ideal have we approached? In an average state the educational preparation required before the working child may enter upon his vocation is that he be able to read and write simple English sentences. That is all. That is the requirement in ten States. Twenty-nine States have even less than that, they have no requirement. Only nine States have a higher requirement and in many of those States the requirements are not enforced.

More Than Mere Reading and Writing Needed

The Uniform Law prescribes five yearly grades in reading, spelling, writing, English language, geography and arithmetic to and including fractions. This is certainly a sane, practical, minimum requirement. That much schooling is due to the possible geniuses among the next generation—that slight glimpse of the possibilities of life is due to all these little people who march into the mill for years of drudgery. Without elementary education they have no outlook, cannot move even from department to department of their own industry, and they become parts of the machinery. Many are soon worn out and cast upon the scrap-heap of drifting idlers.

Stimulate their intelligence enough to give them the possibility of a happy and useful life. They need more than the simplest reading and writing—they need geography to teach them of other lives than their own, other industries, other people, other places, to give them ideas of the world which they can use to improve their condition of servitude. They need arithmetic to brighten their dull listlessness. They need books to interest them, things to think of. It is just the elementary need of having thoughts pass through the brain to wake it up. They need a conception of civics and of hygiene, if we ever learn to teach those subjects,—they need to know how to live economically and properly, and to be efficient members of a republic.

In my own State, and I presume in some others, the immigrant presents the big child labor problem. Just before coming here I visited Lawrence, where there is now a tremendous textile strike. I had known Lawrence for a quiet New England city with many great mills which hummed peacefully. The stores and sidewalks presented ordinarily the appearance of a good American city. But now that the brick walls of the mills can no longer cover up their multitudes of almost foreign slaves, the city surges with fifteen thousand strikers, crowding the streets and sidewalks, jabbering different languages—Poles, Lithuanians, Syrians. I am told that fifty-five different languages or dialects are spoken in one of the mills. The city is alarmed at this new population now disclosed, always before shut up in the neat brick walls, or sleeping or eating or herding together in their isolated slums. Massachusetts is alarmed, and it may well be. Lowell, New Bedford, Fall River, Ludlow, Maynard, North Adams, Chicopee, Palmer, Northbridge and many more of its cities and towns—nearly all of the places where there are large mill populations,—would, if they could see their laborers on strike, be similarly aghast. The children grow up in isolated foreign communities, soon forgetting the little English required of them, having small conception of American ideals.

If we must receive so many foreigners, and I would be hospitable, as our mill owners are, we must insist on more education before the minors become day laborers. It is not enough that they read "John chases the butterfly." They should at least meet the educational requirement of the Uniform Law, five grades of school work, and they need also more training in civics and hygiene. This elementary education is necessary to make them Americans.

The need for the educational test is not, however, confined to immigrants. To our shame, we must admit that many children of the older races in different sections of our country are growing up in just as dense ignorance as these children of recent immigrants. These more American, but more pitiable children, need the same educational test before they are allowed to become day laborers. They need adequate educational preparation for life, and they are in many cases not even taught to read and write their native tongue. They need brain-quickening arithmetic, reading and broadening elementary geography.

In the ideal future then we may hope for a comprehensive educational test based upon the careful preparation of the child for the work he is to do. At present we can at least demand an educational test of five grades in order to assimilate the children of recent immigrants and to build up the intelligence of many of the children of the older races. In this way we can help preserve and increase our American standards of civilization.

A LEGISLATIVE PROGRAM FOR SOUTH CAROLINA

By John Porter Hollis,
Special Agent, National Child Labor Committee,
Rock Hill, S. C.

It seems generally agreed that the evils of child labor are greater in no industry than in cotton textile manufacturing. A backward glance into the history of child labor legislation will reveal the fact that the wrongs inflicted upon laboring children became first glaringly apparent in the cotton factories of both Old and New England. And in South Carolina it is the children in the cotton factories who call for the immediate attention of the friends of child labor reform; for there are no coal mines, tobacco factories or canneries in the State, and but one glass factory of any consequence; there are comparatively few children in street trades, since the State has but two cities worthy the name. But in the manufacture of cotton, the State ranks second only to Massachusetts, and it is a safe statement that one-fifth of our white population live in cotton mill villages. In some counties the proportion is even as high as one-third.

This indicates to what extent the cotton industry affects the mass of the people—that is, the white people,—and when it is attempted to suggest any working legislative program, certain complicating factors compel attention. These factors are not altogether peculiar to South Carolina and the South, but they are not so extensive in the older cotton manufacturing States of New England.

First, there is the powerful influence of the cotton mill presidents and stockholders, which has always, heretofore, been directed strenuously against all efforts to improve the condition of factory children. It is but natural to find that these mill owners occupy positions of commanding influence in the community. They are the local "colonels" of industry and have played the leading rôle in bringing about the passing of the community from a purely agricultural to a **manufacturing** status. Moreover, they have played on the ambitions of the towns for increased population and succeeded remarkably in assembling the local savings as subscriptions to cotton mill stock. These promoters are largely concerned with earning dividends, to the neglect of the welfare of the operatives, and many local holders of factory stock feel precisely the same way. If, to this very considerable element, we add those who are gratified to see enterprises established in their respective communities, and who look upon the promoters as benefactors who did so much in such an opportune time to rehabilitate the State after the ravages of war, we have a strong combination in opposition.

Workers Not Organized

Then there is the attitude of the mill operatives themselves. It is difficult to say just what the desire of the factory workers in South Carolina is, regarding the exploitation of their children by mill corporations. But it will hardly be contradicted that up to the present those who have resisted every effort to restrict child labor have often successfully used the supposed opposition of the workers as a powerful club. The mill people of South Carolina are not organized into labor unions, and we are deprived of this effective channel of information as to their real desires regarding child labor. My own belief is that, barring a comparatively inconsiderable element of dinner-toters, the mill people of the State do not favor the "feeding of their children to the machines." Yet they are not in position to declare their wishes and assert their rights. Without organization there is little opportunity for concerted action. Moreover, whether there has been intimidation from sources higher up or not, it will hardly be disputed that a condition of potential intimidation constantly exists. For a cotton factory organization in the South is but a species of modern feudalism, with the mill president and mill worker standing in the relation respectively of lord and vassal. The mill corporation owns the house in which the operative lives and generally controls all the activities about the premises. The vassal is dependent upon the lord for both bread and shelter, and generally dares not oppose his wishes, especially if well-defined and positively made known. I do not mean to say that intimidation prevails to a marked degree in practice. I do mean, however, that a condition of potential intimidation constantly exists.

In the face of these conditions, what practical way presents itself to the workers for child labor reform? The present child labor law of South Carolina prohibits employment of all children under 12 in daylight and of all children under 16 at night. There is also a factory inspection law. The pressing needs are a 14-year age limit for daylight employment; a law prohibiting employment of boys in the night messenger service and of children on the stage; an effective compulsory school attendance act and birth registration. Birth registration has a bearing on the child labor question in that it will aid in determining the true age of working children. At present a parent's affidavit to the child's age is final. A false affidavit is easy to make and is apparently made without scruple in South Carolina, judging from the number of tots to be seen in some of our factories. I do not think we can hope to see under-age children entirely removed from the mills and the child labor law effectively enforced, until a system of birth registration is installed. The legal importance of the registration of births and deaths, as well as its importance for reasons of public health, is recognized by a large number of our people. A vital statistics bill is pending before the legislature now in session, but its chances of becoming law are slim. There is also pending a bill to prohibit the employment of minors by messenger companies,[1] and of children under 16 on the stage.

Need for Compulsory Education

With birth registration and the messenger service properly cared for, there are still left the knotty problems of compulsory education and higher age limit. The State stands next to the foot in the column of literacy, with about 19 per cent. of the population not able to read and write. This is an alarming situation and demands heroic measures. Consequently there is a very considerable

[1] Passed; prohibits employment of boys under 18 at night, under 14 during day, in delivery of goods and messages: cities of 5,000 and over.

sentiment in favor of an immediate compulsory education law. Some think a well-enforced compulsory education law will remove any further demand for more child labor legislation. It cannot be denied that the two matters are closely related, and that the one has a decided bearing upon the other. But no compulsory education law can be made to answer the needs of child labor reform in South Carolina. At best the school term would last but a brief period, after which the mills would absorb the children as at present. Nevertheless, friends of child labor reform would probably do well to turn this pronounced compulsory education sentiment to their own account as far as possible. They might at least for the present join in with this sentiment and do what they can to aid in securing a compulsory attendance law, and in the event such a law cannot be enacted, then that class of mill presidents and stockholders who proclaim their keen desire for compulsory education will have been disarmed for future opposition to better child labor laws. In this compulsory education struggle there might at least be obtained an educational qualification for the employment of children up to the standard age of 14 years. Such child labor legislation as has been so far enacted in South Carolina has been after compromise and by very short steps with long intervals between.

As conditions now exist, I suggest that the friends of child labor reform join forces with the friends of compulsory education in a strenuous effort to pass an effective school attendance bill. If after a vigorous campaign the bill fails, then let the same united forces work for an amendment to the present child labor law, which will provide that children under 14 years shall not be permitted to work in factories unless they can read and write. In case both these bills fail, all flank movements will have been exhausted and the only course left open will be a front attack.

There are in South Carolina two principal, powerful classes which may be depended on to resist to the very last any attempt to raise the age limit, viz., the factory owners and the operatives themselves. The opposition of the operatives is the more to be dreaded. It is difficult to help a class of people who do not see, or at least pretend not to see, their need of help, and who resent any sort of interference with or regulation of their domestic affairs. To all our appeals for raising the age limit, the mill owners have heretofore returned the specious answer that they did not wish to work little children, but that it was better to place the children in the mills where they could be controlled, than to turn them out on the streets where they would grow up in idleness and ignorance and learn mischief. We should not force the children out of the mills unless we force them into the schools. This is a safe position for them to take, since compulsory education has so far been a dream. In short, the mill capitalists say "Give us first compulsory education," the mill laborers say, "Let us alone," and this combined opposition we have so far been unable to overcome.

The task before us is to awaken the mill people to their danger and to win them to our way of thinking. I believe this can be done more speedily by appealing, not to their sense of responsibility to their children, but to self-interest. Let them be brought to see that the cheap labor of children in competition with their own labor tends inevitably to drag down their own wages. This, you will say, is a sordid appeal, but I believe it is the only practical one that will yield early results.

RURAL CHILD LABOR

By John M. Gillette,
Department of Sociology, University of North Dakota.

It has been the customary assumption that the child labor evil is confined to our cities and manufacturing villages. Undoubtedly the more vigorous and unwarrantable conditions relative to youthful workers do entrench themselves in those places. Another familiar assumption is that the child labor performed on the farm is entirely wholesome and is therefore to be encouraged. But it is largely the product of those who are ignorant of farm life, or of those who have seen agriculture at a distance or in certain favored regions. There are many persons having large experience and intimate acquaintance with country conditions who recognize the darker phases in the situation.

There is no contradicting the fact of rural child labor. The special census bulletin of 1907 reported 1,750,178 child workers in continental United States of whom 60.2 per cent. were on the farm. Four-fifths of these youthful agricultural laborers were reported as assisting their parents. The special investigation which the National Child Labor Committee conducted into the number of such workers fully substantiated the census estimate. The only question at stake, consequently, is whether that labor in itself or in its consequences is sufficiently injurious to be seriously considered.

It can hardly be questioned that much of the work which farm children do is a distinct advantage to them. Work which is suited to the growing boy and girl is conducive to a better development of body and mind. The chores about the house and barn and the lighter forms of labor which may be engaged in outside of school hours are distinctly favorable to the establishment of a disciplined ability to carry on useful activities, which is sadly lacking in urban children. It is one of the recognized defects of city life that there is nothing at which to set the boys outside of school hours and in vacation periods. Idleness and idle habits, bad associations, and irregular wayward tendencies are the familiar fruits of that situation. Shiftlessness and criminality in manhood, together with other undesirable and anti-social qualities are often directly traceable to this void in city boy life. It is not the adjusted, timely work of children in the country which is in question.

There is far more labor of an excessive nature placed on children, particularly boys, who live on farms than we would suspect. I have observed a number of cases where boys of eleven, twelve or thirteen years of age were performing the full work of men. This could be but an infinitesimal fraction of one per cent. of all the cases which occur in this broad country. In some instances they were large, strong, and active, eager to be at something. The father found it convenient to indulge them. In most cases the work was required, notwithstanding the physical inability which was apparent in some cases or of the effect on the larger interests of the child. It is well known that there are parents in cities who look upon their children as economic assets and one phase of the struggle against child labor there is to counteract that view. It should not seem strange, then, if many parents living on farms view the work of the child as an investment.

It might be sufficient to remark that no boy under the age of 17 or 18 can do the heavier work of a man on the farm without suffering bad physical consequences. The State rural school inspector of North Dakota insists that many country boys are overstrained, and that they manifest various asymmetrical physical effects. From our present knowledge of the influence of early labor of a severe sort in mining and industrial populations, we should expect exactly these results. Here is a line of investigation and study for which provision should be made by some of our scientific foundations or by the Children's Bureau.

Arrested Educational Development

Undoubtedly the greatest evil attendant on rural child labor appears in the form of arrested educational development. There is a large recognition of widespread elimination from the country schools, especially in the case of boys. We do not know exactly how extensive this elimination is. Several studies of city schools have been made with a view to determining the extent to which urban elimination proceeds. A difference in the conclusions exists in the case of the various interpreters. Thus Thorndike found that 90 per cent. of the school children in cities of 25,000 people or more completed the fourth elementary grade, 80 per cent. the fifth, 70 per cent. the sixth, and 55 per cent. the seventh, and slightly over 40 per cent. the eighth. Strayer's conclusions follow along slightly above these. Ayres' findings are considerably higher. He finds practically no elimination up to the beginning of the fifth grade. According to his study 90 per cent. of the city school children conclude the fifth grade work, nearly 75 per cent. the sixth, and somewhat less than 55 per cent. complete the eighth grade. Strayer finds that the elimination of boys, especially in the later grades, far exceeds that of girls.

Unfortunately there has been no general, authoritative investigation into the extent of elimination in rural schools. Observations by experienced students of the matter make it far larger than takes place in cities. It is evidently extensive enough to demand profound consideration. Moreover it is not confined to one section. I quote a reply which I received from Mr. Charles W. Holman of Dallas, Texas, editor of *Farm and Ranch,* in response to a letter of inquiry: "Notwithstanding the fact that we have a Texas law, no effort has ever been made to prevent the labor of young children in the fields during the cotton picking and the cotton hoeing seasons. The result is that the whole of our common school system in country districts is based upon the fact that the child will be at work until late in the fall and must leave school early in the spring. * * * To understand the child labor problem you must understand the larger problem of land tenure. Since a majority of the farmers are renters and since the cotton crop imposes such an enormous tax upon labor, it is impossible for us to eradicate this evil until we pass compulsory education laws which will provide for adequate inspection of truants, and until we completely revolutionize our field cropping system, an evil which has grown out of land tenure."

The more facts we are able to obtain about rural school attendance the more evident it becomes that boys in the late years leave far in excess of girls. As an indication of this I will quote from an address of the North Dakota Rural School Inspector, Mr. N. C. McDonald, made by him at the last meeting of the State Educational Association. "In twenty-five one-room schools that I visited during the months of September and October there were enrolled in the upper grades (fifth, sixth, seventh and eighth) 111 pupils. Of these 103 were girls. Eight were boys! In October

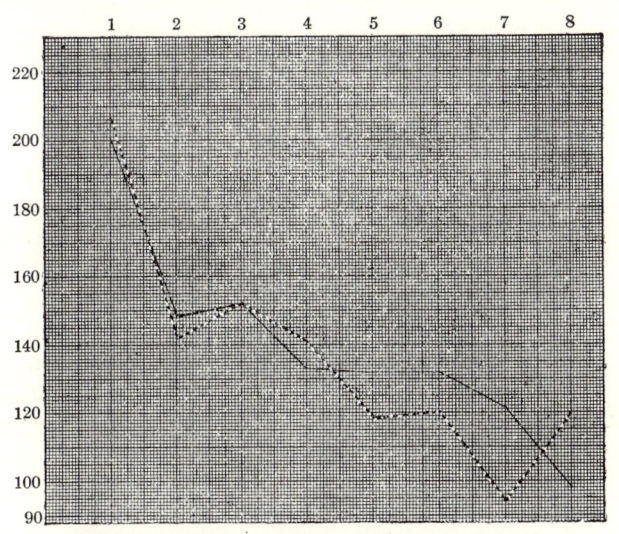

Rural school enrollment by sex in Grand Forks County, North Dakota, 1910-1911.

Dotted line represents girls. Straight line represents boys.
Numerals at top indicate grades. Numerals at side indicate enrollment.

and November thirty-five one-room schools inspected showed 148 pupils enrolled in these same upper grades. There were 136 girls and 12 boys! In one graded rural school, in the sixth, seventh, eighth and ninth grades 23 girls were enrolled and no boys. In a one-room rural school the fifth, sixth, seventh and eighth grades showed six girls and not a boy. In another, in the same grades, there were eight girls and not a boy. In other schools visited during these months about the same ratio obtained." Yet in that State the number of boys exceeded that of girls in the population.

In order to obtain more exact data on rural school elimination I have had one of my graduate students, Miss Hattie Listenfelt, make an investigation of rural school attendance and enrollment of Grand Forks County, North Dakota. In that county there are 121 rural schools with an enrollment of 1097 boys and 1095 girls, a total of 2192. Of these 32 boys and 31 girls attended school less than ten days in the year, and are omitted in the estimates. The accompanying graphic representations portray the enrollment of the two sexes grade by grade and also the per cent. of average attendance of boys and girls in successive grades.

The great drop in the lines of enrollment is probably to be explained as the result of making the first grade a clearing house or waiting place for unclassified pupils and also from the fact that many children do not make the second grade and thus remain in the first. This phenomenon occurs in all the schools of the State as is to be observed in the reports of the State Superintendent of Public Instruction. The enrollment of the second and third grades is practically identical, with about 150 pupils of each sex. As compared with that, the eighth grade has lost 30 girls and 50 boys. There is no means of discovering an explanation for the erratic drop in the line representing the enrollment of the girls in the seventh grade.

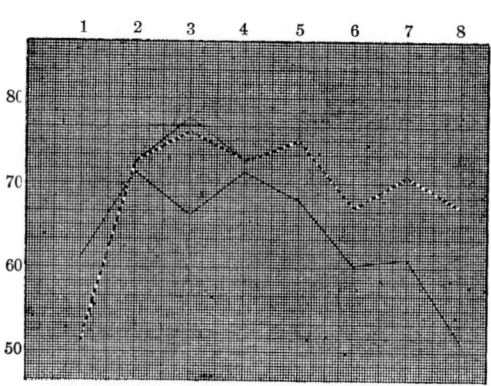

Per cent. of attendance in Grand Forks County, North Dakota, rural schools by sex, 1910-1911.

Dotted line represents girls. Straight line represents boys.
Numerals at top indicate grades. Numerals at side indicate per cent.

The attendance graph denotes the average attendance of those enrolled in the successive grades. It is evident that in the country the distance from school and the cold winters make the first year more uncertain than later years. After the second grade two things appear. First, there is a general downward trend on the part of both boys and girls in attendance. Second, there is a greater general decrease in the attendance of boys as compared with that of girls. The influence of farm work in drawing boys away from school registers its increasing strength after the fourth grade, leaving an average attendance of but 50 per cent. of the 146 school days which constitute the legal school year.

Variations in population, death, sickness and retardation naturally exercise an influence on the attendance and enrollment, but it is impossible to get a line on the most of those items in the country schools. The reports from these schools are not well kept nor are the records of other matters available, save on the item of population. Hence, while these statements must be regarded as only approximate they are as good as we may expect until better methods of reporting are established.

The rural districts of Grand Forks County have lost population during the last ten years. The last Federal census gives it as 8.3 per cent. This includes several cities of less than 2500 inhabitants, but an inspection of their population numbers for 1890 and 1900 indicates no material change. This loss would be applicable to the school population and would influence the enrollment in a small measure.

It is probable that Grand Forks County is quite typical of rural regions generally. It has been settled for thirty or forty years, and its population and civilization have become the established and conservative sort. It does not represent frontier conditions therefore. The western part of the State of North Dakota is frontier. Observation in that region and conversation with school officers indicate that the boys of the rural districts, and it is almost wholly rural, are largely kept out of school to do work about the farms and ranches as soon as they reach a working age. Herding stock is something which boys may easily do and there is much of this to be done. Moreover successive crop failures have impoverished farmers so that they are actually unable to hire farm labor. In many cases the boys are really needed to carry on farm operations.

It is often said that compulsory education laws will eliminate rural child labor. North Dakota has had such a law for many years. But it is not rigidly enforced. I have heard county superintendents advise rural school directors that the compulsory attendance laws would be leniently executed. Since the farmers' vote is responsible for the incumbency of superintendents it is readily seen why they must be cautious in exercising their duties in this direction. Rural school inspectors and truancy officers would undoubtedly be more successful in securing a better attendance.

SYMPOSIUM

UNREASONABLE INDUSTRIAL BURDENS ON WOMEN AND CHILDREN:—EFFECT ON EDUCATION

I

By Mrs. Florence Kelley

Some beginnings have at last been made in the way of lifting the unreasonable burdens upon women and children of the working class. In four States we deal a little mercifully with widows who have children required by the law to attend school. In Ohio, in Oklahoma, and very recently in Illinois and Michigan, and in those four States alone, so far as I have been able to learn, there is now provision made to lift the burden from the widowed mother by giving her, as her right and not as the dole of a private charity (and not by taking her children from her as we do cruelly in New York and putting them in institutions away from their mother), an allowance out of public funds on condition that she stay in her home and keep her children at home and in school as the State requires. In those four States the burden has been lifted somewhat from the shoulders of the widowed mother in the working class.

In a few States, in sadly few we have lifted the burden a little from the children who are handicapped, who are mentally deficient. Ten years ago when we proposed to require that before a child should go out into the world of industry it must first finish a few years' work in the schools, we used to be bitterly reproached, particularly in the great cities where the schools are in a chronic state of overcrowding, that we were requiring the dull children to fill throughout long years school seats which could be more usefully, more profitably filled by the talented children, that we were wasting school money and wasting the years and the earning capacities of the dull children by requiring them to do what nature had incapacitated them for doing.

We know better now. In the schools of the City of New York we have nearly 3,000 mentally deficient children, and those children we know now are thus kept out of the juvenile courts. They are kept from becoming in their childhood the dull tools of scheming and cruel people, who ten years ago would have been free to exploit them. But we do not yet lift as effectually as we shall do five and twenty years from now, the whole burden of industry from the shoulders of the mentally deficient children.

Just before I left New York, a boy was tried in the court in Brooklyn, and convicted of setting fire to three crowded tenement houses. The explanation that he gave the court was that he longed to see the fire engines run, and that he could not restrain himself from setting fire to these buildings, one of which was occupied by fifty **families**.

We know now that the mentally deficient children are best off when they are in school under the care of the principal, the teacher, the doctor, and the nurse, since we are not yet humane enough to provide for all, as we provide for a few, in villages in which they can live very simply, free from the temptation to burn up their **neighbors.**

Educational Standards Too Low

Few States, however, require that children shall stay in school until they finish the work even of the first five years. There are States in which there is no requirement of any educational accomplishment before the child may go to work. I fear that the number of such States far exceeds the number of States which require some educational accomplishment. But is there any other way in which the burden—the unreasonable burden—of industry can be lifted from the subnormal children, than this of requiring that they shall finish at least the work that a normal child would finish by the time it is eleven or twelve years old, or else stay in school until they reach their sixteenth birthday? So much, at least, we do in our sinful metropolis.

Then we have begun in a few places to lift the burden of industry from the youngest children. It was as recently as 1876 that the first State, Massachusetts, required a child to be as old as ten years before it could work in a cotton mill. It was a revolutionary step when Massachusetts, after the fire in the Granite Mill in Fall River, which had cost the lives of several children eight and nine years old, established ten years as the earliest age at which a child might work in that enlightened commonwealth. And all the restrictions upon the working age of children in force in this republic to-day date back no further than that.

It seems dreadfully slow that in all the years since 1876 we have only reached the fourteenth birthday as the lowest limit for work for children in the Northern States, with the single exception of New Hampshire. So far as I am aware, no other Northern State provides that a child may work in a factory or work-shop, aside from some canneries, even during vacation, before the fourteenth birthday.

In the South, so far as I know, it is only in Kentucky, Tennessee, Louisiana and Virginia that the children are not permitted to work until the fourteenth birthday. As I understand it, the working age shades off from fourteen in these enlightened States to thirteen in North Carolina, and twelve in a number of States, and to no workable restriction in Georgia, while a provision in South Carolina that the children should not work so early, was rendered illusory by a stroke of the pen of Governor Blease when he struck out the appropriation for the salaries of factory inspectors, which would at least have made the law in part effective.

We have lifted a little the burden from the youngest children who used to be free to work in the streets, but we have lifted it sadly little. The age proposed in our first bill for beginning to work in the streets was lowered from the twelfth birthday to the tenth, the hour for stopping work was deferred from eight o'clock at night until ten, and the penalty clause was made non-enforcible. To this day, therefore, we have an army of pitiably little boys in the streets of New York working legally in selling papers, which we know now as the occupation that is the vestibule to the juvenile court first, and to the criminal courts later on.

Progress Made

We have lifted a little the burden from the children who carry our messages in four of our States. We provide now in Massachusetts, New York, New Jersey and Wisconsin that telegraph and messenger boys shall not work below the age of 21 years, between the hours of 10 o'clock at night and 5 o'clock in the morning. But in many States there is no restriction upon this work, which is not less dangerous, from the moral point of view, than the selling of papers in the streets. This also is a street trade. This also is done in the absence of supervision. The difference is that, whereas a newsboy is on the streets and can in a measure determine where he will go, the messenger boy must go withersoever he is sent, and no place in any city is too evil for the admission of these boys.

Until the enactment of the provision that boys under 21 years of age should not work between 10 at night and 5 in the morning in this service, we had in force this strange provision of the penal code in New York, that a boy under the age of 16 years could not be sent to any saloon or gambling house or to a long list of forbidden places, "Provided, however, that nothing herein contained shall be construed to prevent the delivery of merchandise and messages at the doors of such places." If anything could spur on a lad it would be permission to go to the door but not enter in, and that stands to-day in our penal code, so far as it is not overriden by the other provision, that only *between* 10 *at night and* 5 *in the morning,* boys under 21 shall not work in this service.

We are leaving the burden, all the unreasonable burden upon the children; only the corners of it have been lifted, not the real burden. We have dealt with specified, particular, spectacular horrors, and we have virtually done only that. If, as a nation, we really valued our children, we should, in the first place, care passionately to know how many are born, and how many die. But judged by our registration of births and deaths, we do not rank among the civilized nations. Only a part of our country is within the registration area. Only a part of our country keeps any record of what child is born and what child has died. The rest of us do not rank even with some of the better republics of South America in this respect.

Burdens Are Unreasonable

We do not really value the health of our children or we should not let little girls just fourteen years of age leave school, turn away forever from all preparation for home life, and go into mills and stores to work as many hours as may suit the convenience of employers who have the children there for the sake of profits and dividends and not for the sake of this Republic, certainly not for the sake of the souls of the children. It is not in reverence for the soul of any little girl that we let her go into a department store or a cotton mill, or a tobacco warehouse, or into any of these wholly unfit occupations into which we let little girls go, 20,000 of them every year in the single city of New York.

The real burden of industry for women and children is the perfect unfitness of industry, as it is carried on to-day, for women and children. Industry is carried on for profits and dividends, and for no other consideration. How else should we find large bodies of young people working 10 hours a day, watching for instance, as my young neighbors do, in thousands of cases, machines carrying from one to twelve needles setting three thousand stitches a minute, lighted by a crude electric ray, so that those young eyes are focused seven, eight, nine, ten hours—twelve hours in the rush season—on a gleam of steel lighted by a crude electric ray? Is it any wonder that a certain young oculist had under his care in one month last winter from a single factory, nine girls whose eyes were ruined by their work before they were four and twenty years old? That is the real burden of industry upon women and children, that the women and children exist for the industry and not the industry for the people of this Republic.

I am thankful that other speakers to-night will have more cheerful discourse than mine. I had simply to state what some of the burdens are that we have tried to lighten a little during the past eight years.

II

By Mrs. Millie R. Trumbull,
Secretary, Oregon Child Labor Commission, Portland.

In any discussion of industrial conditions as they affect women and children, one is naturally influenced by the character of one's contact with the problem. If an employer, the viewpoint is mainly that of getting as much service for as little money as possible; if an employee, the question is answered according to the varying degrees of economic pressure under which each worker is driven. It remains for the man or woman, either paid or volunteer, whose work brings contact with both employer and employed, to name the failures or the weak spots in the uniformly wretched conditions under which our women and children earn their living.

One of the speakers at last evening's meeting said that the solution of this problem was in the hands of the educators and philanthropists. To this group I would add a third factor—the factory inspector. It is he who interprets into action, the result of the labors of the educator and the philanthropist—he deals directly with the child when he has passed through the educator's hands and notes the degree of efficiency or failure that marks his industrial career. For a satisfactory working out of the problem, the educator, the philanthropist and the factory inspector must work together.

In this present time of crowding into industrial life of all available material, we look jealously at any system which would prolong the period of childhood. Certain forces will gasp at the idea of excluding all children under the age of 18 from industry. But we bar all youths from participation in civic duties until 21 years of age—no boy can contract a debt until he is 21 for which his parents are not responsible—a girl is hardly a social possibility until she is 18, neither attains full physical stature until older than 18, and yet we gasp at the suggestion I have just made. We allow these children who have no legal, or social status at the age of 16 years, to decide the most important question of their lives—in most states, children of the age of 14 years may decide for themselves their industrial status. In Oregon the age is 15.

Educators and Philanthropists

From my own point of view, that of factory inspector, all children under the age of 18 should be taken out of the industrial field entirely. It is a disgrace to our much-vaunted civilization that an organization like the National Child Labor Committee, that an audience like this, that a nation like ours should find it necessary to even consider the industrial burdens of children under the age of 18 years. Is it not an arraignment against every phase of our development that our progress has been attended by such an alarming waste of human life, that the United States ranks so low in the list of nations in her care of her workers, that we have failed to profit by the experience of older nations in their exploitation of their women and children? Year after year our army of unemployed grows larger, the degree of efficiency of the worker is rated lower, and we are just beginning to see the relation between the mass of human driftwood and our reckless indifference to the whole problem of conservation of human wealth.

Is it not disgraceful that we as a nation should find it necessary to maintain an organization—under business management—under the leadership of some of the brightest intellects in the country—whose whole thought and energies are devoted to devising ways and means for the abolition of a slavery that is worse than any black slavery that ever existed—the economic slavery of women and children? It would be a sufficiently evil indictment against our national development if, to the tremendous cost of the reckless waste in men's lives, in our mad pursuit of wealth, we added the sacrifice of mothers and future mothers of the race which factory, sweatshop and department store carry on with increasing toll each year. But are there any words in our language strong enough to use in condemnation of the system which thoughtless America has permitted to grow up and which we call Child Labor? There are no words strong enough for condemnation and no methods yet devised equal to the task of eradication, so long as we maintain as a nation the slavish devotion to wealth and abject deference to the accumulators of wealth.

Some believe this state of affairs can be reached through legislation. I believe regulation of the exploitation of our women and children is all that can be accomplished. We can make the burden less unreasonable, but it will be a burden just as long as the day nursery takes the place of the mother in the home and just as long as the play time of the child is spent in the factory. It will be an unreasonable burden, just so long as we set aside in a class by themselves the working woman and the child laborer—just as long as we hold the perverted social view held to-day that a woman who earns her living with her hands is not in the same social class with the woman who is being supported by some one else, no matter what relationship. I paid but little attention to this view, superficial as it may seem, until I found it was a serious factor in the choice of their life work among children I questioned in their application for working permits. The stenographer feels herself a shade finer than the girl behind the counter. The girl behind the counter holds herself a grade higher than the girl who works in the laundry. The organizers in the labor unions tell me that this feeling is one they encounter in a serious degree in their work among the different groups of women workers. The children in the schools are affected by it. They are not taught in the schools that one's value to society is determined, not by social position, but by work, no matter what that work may be. More of the dignity of labor should be taught our children and less of the superficial, servile truckling to fine clothes and idleness. Thoughtless and superficial, again, as the whole question may seem, it is still too serious to be passed over lightly. Too many boys and girls have started life wrong because of it. Is there not some way we can get rid of it?

In Oregon

The burden which presses heaviest upon our working women and children is the low wage. I believe that to be the worst of all the abuses that attend their employment. Next come long hours. And I have traveled for five days from western Oregon to tell you as much as I can in twenty minutes what we are doing in Oregon to clear our State of its share in our national disgrace. We do not pretend we are better than the East in this respect. We may not be quite so bad, but it is simply a question of degree. We have not as many factories, not as many women and children employed as in some of the Eastern States, but that we have women working in laundries at an average wage of $1.25 a day and in our rope, bag, cracker, candy and box factories at an average wage of $1.20 and $1.40 a day, and the fact that we have had a child labor law since 1903 would indicate that we are guilty of the violation of the principles, just the same as New York, Pennsylvania or any Eastern State that holds a blacker record.

We have begun the campaign with our 10-hour law, and at the next session will amend it to eight hours a day. But as to wages, we are still hopelessly in the rear. Sanitary conditions may be bad, the work may be hard, the environment disagreeable; but if good wages are paid, a woman may provide herself with some of the comforts, the necessities, the care and recreation that keep life sweet and wholesome. With a low, inadequate wage, her whole life is below grade. The whole social life becomes an artificial structure with its poorly paid, ill-fed, miserably clad, wretchedly housed, half-educated women and children workers for a foundation which carries the beautiful, the wonderful, the ease, the luxury, that can be secured through the wealth of the exploiters. With adequate—please note that I say "adequate," not "good" only—with adequate wages we would have less need of jails and reformatories, industrial homes, places to put girls who were not paid enough wages to keep themselves decent, day nurseries, charity organization societies, visiting nurse associations, baby homes and children's aid societies, miserable palliatives of the modern industrial system.

Inefficient School System

Low wages I believe to be the most unreasonable, unjust burden of the working woman and child; but the latter carries an additional burden, that of an inefficient public school system; a school system which is slowly and painfully waking to its own inadequacy and is trying to adjust itself to the needs of our future workers. After nine years of experience with the working child, I am ready to confess that the school systems of the nation have been obstructive rather than constructive forces. The whole program offered at this meeting is proof of my assertion. The average boy or girl who leaves school at 14 or 15 years has reached but a halfway place. There is no well-developed power of application, of concentration, of intensity of purpose, and no power of initiative, all of which are needed in these strenuous days. He is a product of school routine and of school books, but not of his own powers of development. He wants to do, to be, to grow, to work, himself. And what is offered him after he escapes the school system? The burden of a dead-end industry, cash boy in a department store, tending a machine in a factory, the blind alley of the messenger service. What we need in place of the cramming institution we call the public school, which grinds out children whose school cards show varying percentages but whose hands are listless and helpless, what we need in place of these machines, are laboratories which will hold the child until 18 years of age and then give him to the world a worker with head and hands harmonious and to whom work is a joy and not a disgrace.

Oregon's Remedy

It would ill become me to scold if my own State were not doing something to rid herself of her share in these iniquities. To begin with, we find it much easier in Oregon to wipe out stains, to cure our social diseases, to consign bad legislators and bad legislation to oblivion. Under Oregon's initiative and referendum her workers are coming into a knowledge of their own power and a belief in their own integrity. If the legislature refuses to pass a law in the interest of the common good, the same law appears on the ballot at the next election under the initiative, and without any mutilation in committee rooms or any trading of votes in either Senate or House of Representatives, the people vote the measure into law. This was the case with our employers' liability act. When it came to a vote in the legislature of 1909 it was so torn and mutilated its own father did not know it, and even then it was lost. But on the ballot in 1910 appeared an employers' liability act, much more stringent than its crippled relative of 1909, and it became law by an overwhelming majority. Under our referendum, obnoxious ordinances and laws are wiped off the books and our recall serves as a sword of Damocles over the heads of evil disposed officials. Neither do we seem to have any faith in the theory that because a lawyer happens to be elected a judge he has begun to sprout wings; we still believe him a human being and he is compelled to maintain an even balance of the scales of justice or out he goes.

In this way we propose to deal with the problem of low wages and long hours. We are preparing for the next legislature a bill establishing minimum wage boards for women and children workers. If our legislators refuse to vote it into law the people of the State will do so themselves. We are planning a careful investigation into wages and cost of living of women in industry so that we shall have an array of facts from which they cannot escape. There are times when I wish that instead of always legislating for the poor, we could sometimes pass a law strictly confined to the other end of the economic line. Instead of asking for a law establishing a minimum wage board for the poor women workers, we could go to the legislature with a law to establish a maximum percentage on the investment scale for the exploiters. Do you think it would pass?

The school burdens of the working child we are trying to reach through trade schools for the city and through classes in agriculture in the rural school. Oregon is tired of the school-machine child.

We oppose segregation of working children because we believe creation of class distinction fatal to democracy. But we plan to specialize after an all-around development has been provided and the special bent is developed.

III

By Rev. John A. Ryan, D.D.,
Professor, Moral Theology and Economics, St. Paul Seminary, St. Paul, Minn.

We can divide the unreasonable burdens upon women and children in industry into two classes, first, burdens which have to do with the conditions in which the work is performed, second, burdens which have to do with the return received by the worker for his work.

Under the first head come the hours of labor for both women and children, the time of labor—whether night or day,—age at which children go to work, kind of labor—whether too hard, too dangerous, or too hurtful to the morals of the workers—and, in general, safety and sanitation of the place of work.

Now, with that class of burdens, we have made sufficient progress, I think, to justify the hope that we shall continue along the same lines until most of the unreasonable burdens—not all, because we do not attain perfection in this world, which have to do with conditions in which work is done, shall be removed; for a start has been made with every one of them, the public has become accustomed to the principles involved, and to the reasonableness of that legislation which aims to remove one or the other of these burdens.

I believe, for example, that if I live to man's allotted age, three score and ten, I shall see throughout this country the minimum age of labor for children in urban occupations, at least during the school term, fixed at sixteen years. I do not know that I am ready to go as far as Mrs. Trumbull, to the eighteen-year limit, but I believe the time is coming when no child will be employed during the school year at any kind of wage-earning occupation under the age of sixteen. There may be continuation schools and perhaps some work done part of the day, between fourteen and sixteen, especially if that labor be in harmony with and a carrying out of school training.

Industrial Training

That naturally calls up the question of industrial training, which has been discussed so fully at this Conference that I do not intend to go into it; but I think it necessary not merely for the child but for the whole wage-earning population. I say in the interests of the wage-earning classes generally, for one of the causes of low wages is the fact that there are too many unskilled workers. Furthermore, I hope to see the time when no woman will be employed for more than eight hours a day in any industrial or commercial occupation, and I think there is no doubt that that time is not far off. And so with the other burdens which have to do with conditions in which work is done.

The Need for a Minimum Wage

But with regard to the second kind of burdens, namely, insufficient wages of women and children, the problem is more difficult, because we have not made even a beginning toward dealing with it. We have begun and made some progress with all the other problems, through legislation. We have not done anything through legislation to solve the problem of the underpaid worker, whether man, woman or child. We are talking to-night of women and children merely, and I will confine myself to these because they bear the heaviest burdens, and because the means of lessening these burdens in our legislative, political and legal system, the means of lifting them by legislation can be obtained with less difficulty than in the case of men workers.

We have no very up-to-date statistics on wages of women and children, particularly on wages of children. But we have some not very old, and that will be sufficient to give some idea of the situation with regard to the earnings of women.

The Census of 1905 made a pretty thorough investigation of wages paid in manufacturing industries of the United States. I think it actually investigated one-half of all manufacturing establishments. The result showed about one-half the women 16 years old and over employed in manufacturing industries were getting less than $6 a week. Professor Nearing, of the University of Pennsylvania, has lately published a book entitled "Wages in the United States," in which he used all the latest statistics available, and he comes to the conclusion that, making allowances for lost time, three-fifths of the women employed in this country receive less than $6.25 a week.

The report of the Massachusetts Commission on Minimum Wage Boards, based on investigation of four industries in the State, corresponds in general with the estimates just stated.

Those who have investigated, or made any attempt to investigate, the cost of living—the cost of properly supporting a working woman in this country—vary, I think, in their estimates as to such cost in cities from $7 to $10 a week. Probably in most cities of considerable size, the amount needed would be between $7.50 and $10. Yet three-fifths of the women, according to Professor Nearing, get less than $6.25 a week.

Try to figure what it means, that so many women—we do not know just how many, but I should say roughly between two and three million—are getting so much less than enough to maintain them decently!

And there is no hope of a change for the better except through legislation. The improvement cannot be brought about by organization. Organization has done much for women in many trades, but no one who realizes the problem and its different elements would want to wait for improvement until these women are able to organize and get higher wages through that means. It is practically impossible, and the proportion of women in industry is increasing faster than the proportion of men. There is not any indication from any direction that things are going to be improved in the case of women workers, or child workers either, except through legislation.

Effect of the Insufficient Wage

I do not intend to attempt to show the evil, to the State and Nation, of such a large number of women working for less than decent wages. The evils are, of course, physical and moral to themselves, and evils to the succeeding generations.

Lieutenant Governor McDermott mentioned the statement that the fourth generation of the London cockney does not exist, that the tribe is wiped out after the third generation. I think no one who visits England and observes the population even casually in the great cities, can help feeling that the population there is degenerating—physically, at any rate. And we do not need to rely upon general observations. We know that during the Boer war the English army authorities found the average height of the recruits was three inches less than the average height of the recruits in the Crimean war, less than half a century before; that the average weight of these recruits for the Boer war was 30 pounds less than it had been during the Crimean war; and that in Manchester, the great centre of the modern industrial system, with its *laissez faire* policy, and all of the rest of it—in Manchester, 8,000 out of 12,000 recruits were rejected, and of the 4,000 selected, only 1,200 were really fit. They stretched a point to take in the other 2,800.

We have not yet come to anything like that in this country, but our women have not been in industry nearly as long.

To give the statement a little more concreteness, I quote the following:

Speaking of the almost 200,000 women employed in Pennsylvania factories, Dr. Peter Roberts says that the textile industries are not self-supporting, since 50 per cent. of their employees expend an amount of energy which the wages do not replace. In other words, the workers are degenerating and the next generation will naturally be worse.

One aspect is put thus by the Wisconsin Bureau of Labor—and in Wisconsin industrial conditions are not so bad as in some of the older States:

"Unless we change the present demoralizing conditions we will continue to see women worn out by the work of their youth, unable to do their part in making happy and successful homes; their children, if not given better opportunities, go through the same course and keep up the circle of vicious inefficiency."

Minimum Wage Boards

I say there is no way of remedying this except by legislation, and it is one of the most important acts of legislation that can be enacted. Some, I presume, are startled at this suggestion, or perhaps were when Mrs. Trumbull mentioned it, but there is no more reason why the State should hesitate to make laws regulating wages, at least by placing a minimum below which no one should be permitted to work, than that it should hesitate to protect a person's pocketbook against a thief, or his life or limb against an assassin. All these things, all these goods, have to do with human life and welfare.

Shylock says: "You take my life when you do take the means whereby I live." Why should the State pass a law protecting life and limb and property, and not have laws for the protection of the means of livelihood? They had such legislation throughout European history up to a hundred years ago—regulation of wages by law. Generally they were regulated in the interest of employer rather than of employee, but the principle was recognized. And in at least two countries a beginning has been made in regulating wages by law. Victoria, Australia, has had since 1896, wage boards composed of representatives of employers and employees in a trade and representatives of the government which fix wages throughout the trade. Two or three years ago about 39 of these boards were in existence. Some had been asked for by employers, some by employees. The law has worked so well that it has been adopted by three of the other States in Australia. And if I mistake not, there is only one State in Australia without such a law to-day —the State of Western Australia, in which there are not many industries. These wage boards fix the rate of wages for men as well as for women and children.

England, about two years ago, enacted a similar law for fixing the wages of the "home-workers." These are women workers, and the most exploited in England, the most helpless. In fact, the decision of the Parliamentary Commission which was appointed to investigate the conditions and possible means of relief for these workers, seems to have recommended as a sort of counsel of despair these Australian minimum wage boards because they had worked well in Australia. That was for four trades. In three trades the boards have been in operation some time. They were established the other day in the fourth trade, which takes in a very much larger number of workers than exist in the other three together. In the first three trades there has been already a marked improvement in the conditions of workers and wages.

IV

By Jean M. Gordon,
Formerly City Factory Inspector, New Orleans, La.

The whole question of unreasonable industrial burdens upon women and children resolves itself into a question of legislation. We have not had better legislation in regard to employment of women and children because women and children have not been represented in our legislative halls, and this knowledge was very forcibly borne in upon me at the three last sessions I attended of our Louisiana Legislature.

The Oyster Over the Child

When we went in 1908 to Baton Rouge with our child labor bill we found everything represented at that legislature but the interests of working women and children. One of the first interests we met was the shrimp and oyster commission. They were there to protect the young oyster and shrimp so they could grow unmolested by the fisherman into juicy, succulent, toothsome morsels which the manufacturer could put into tin cans later on! Why, it is a crime, punishable by heavy fine, for any one to dig from its natural home on the oyster reef an oyster that has not attained a certain number of inches. The same with that most delicious of shellfish, the shrimp! But I did not see anybody there worrying about those little Bohemian children who are brought from Maryland and Delaware to the Gulf coast to be employed during the winter season in the shrimp and oyster industry and then returned to the Northern States during the summer to work for the fruit and vegetable packers. Nobody was at that legislature worrying that they should first reach a certain age and measure a certain number of inches. On the contrary, the shrimp and oyster people thought us sentimental because we were there to object to little children 6, 7 and 8 years of age being dragged from their beds at half-past four or five o'clock in the morning to open oysters and pick shrimp.

The economic value of those little boys and girls was right then and there, and the manufacturer intended utilizing it to the fullest extent. We women of the Era Club watched the different interests at that legislature, the lumber mills, the grocers, the furskin animal agents, the doctors. They all took precedence of the child interests. And to show of how little importance they thought our child labor bill, when we would ask the leader of the bill to bring it up he would say: "I would not risk it to-day. There are some very important measures before the House, and the friends of the bill will not have time to give to it." On one occasion, when urged, he said: "Why, the question of the division of the parish of Calcasieu is to come up to-day, and the members are in no humor to listen to any child labor proposition. We have to consider this very important question." Now, Calcasieu parish has more square miles than all New England put together, and some of the politicians saw a chance for more court houses, sheriffs, etc., if it was divided into four parishes, and of course to their minds that was much more important than that children should be protected. So you can readily see why it is impossible for me to make an address on child labor and not talk woman suffrage at the same time. The two are so indissolubly united in my mind, I cannot separate them. The care of the child has always been given over to the woman, hence it is a subject which very seldom enters man's thought, while the building of court houses, appointing sheriffs and canning oysters have been man's work; and naturally that which we have always done we do best.

Injury to Health

We are going to have this unnecessary industrial burden placed upon women and children just as long as they remain unrepresented in our legislative halls, and as long as society permits this just so long will little girls of 12 and 14 work all day long in stocking factories, laundries, bag mills, and cracker mills, doing over and over again, throughout the long, long day, the same old wearying thing.

Have you ever been in a stocking mill? They weave the stocking leg in long lengths, and cut it to the required size for No. 7, 8 or 9. It is then passed on to children, whose duty it is to take each leg and catch each stitch on a very fine needle. It requires very keen sight to get each stitch on to its corresponding needle, and the deftness with which the little fingers run around the machine and place each stitch is marvelous. If a stitch is not properly caught, then you have what is called a "drop stitch," and the stocking is rejected and the child loses the wage.

The average child can manage four or five of these machines. After she puts the stitches on she starts up the machine and it automatically knits on the foot. Meantime she has put the legs on the other machines, and returns to the first to remove the finished stocking, which is passed on to the girl who is to pull it inside out.

Can you imagine any work more deadly, unless it is that of the girl who stands before the mangle in a laundry? It is generally the new applicant, the youngest girl, who is put at the mangle —a great, heavy rolling machine, from which the moisture rises and over which she stands all day in a highly heated (I have taken the temperature with my own thermometer and often found it register 104 degrees), moist atmosphere, a most salubrious ground for developing consumption. It does look as if man's mechanical genius had taken a fiendish delight in making all places where young people work regular hot-beds for consumption.

Effect on Education

How can we expect the child who has been allowed to leave school with barely a knowledge of the A, B, C's, and worked under such conditions, to feel any interest in education? There may be some great souls in these little bodies, who, after such a day's work, want to go to night school. I think there is no more cruel sight than to see those poor little tired bodies and brains trying to cram themselves with arithmetic and geography and spelling. I sincerely hope that the American people will soon be educated to the point of legislating against night schools for children under 16 years of age.

Organization of Women Workers

Sometimes I feel hopeless about benefiting the condition of young working girls and women, particularly young girls. When I first went into the factory inspection work in New Orleans, I knew very little of the actual conditions, except what I had gathered from girls on the outside. I thought that it would be very easy to get the girls to form unions. But when I looked at them, talked with them, and came to understand how immature they were both mentally and physically, I realized it was an almost impossible task to unionize this fluctuating, moving, eternally changing mass of girls in the factories. The men have realized this and do not take in the boys under 21, but long before that age the majority of girls have left to get married, and though a large percentage return later as widows, or deserted wives, or wives trying to eke out the family purse, they come with broken spirits and it is very hard to do anything for them. Then a great many are very ignorant—I am speaking of the unskilled trades—and it is hard to make them understand the advantages of standing together, hard to overcome centuries of training along individualistic lines. And then, too, they are afraid to do anything to displease the "boss." If they become what the foreman considers agitators, they are soon dismissed, their names are passed along from one manufacturer to another, and they find themselves shut out of any chance to get another job.

The Awakening

But I feel my spirits braced up when I come to a meeting like this and realize the two great forces which are going ahead with such terrific momentum—the demand for the ballot for women and the great social awakening that is spreading all over the world by the people who insist upon knowing how and where and under what conditions the commodities they use every day are made.

The public can no longer plead ignorance on this question. There have been too many millions of acres of trees turned into wood pulp to be printed upon by the National Child Labor Committee and the Consumers' League for the American public to dare declare itself ignorant of conditions.

Another hopeful sign has been given at this splendid conference—the awakening of the schools and that greatest laggard of all, the great Christian Church which has done less than any other organization to lighten the industrial burden put upon women and children. It is realizing that good wages and healthy bodies and clean environment will do more to save souls than singing psalms. And with all these forces at work I feel we are making great headway and the fight against us will become stronger.

Needed: Proof of Age and Adequate Factory Inspection

In the past the manufacturer has not objected to a child labor bill provided it did not have any teeth in it. But the minute a bill was presented that provided for genuine proof of age and real factory inspection, just that minute the manufacturer arrived with his lobby at the State capitol.

Those are the two points upon which the protection of the child depends, and the sooner we all turn our attention to the question of factory inspection the sooner will conditions for women and children be improved.

And this brings me to my annual appeal, for I have vowed never to come before a gathering great or small without making my appeal to educated, independent women to take up the work of factory inspection, women who can meet the manufacturer on his own heath, at his own table and bring home to his own people the conditions as they exist. When the factory inspector can meet the manufacturer's wife or sisters at lunch or teas and tell the conditions as found in his factory, the manufacturer does not like it. I am hoping America will yet require of her young girls who have been so splendidly trained by the State that they give to the State two or three years at least of service. Our girls do not marry as early as they did and between the close of the school period and the average marriage there are several years in which to pay back to the State the debt they owe for the splendid training offered by the State from the kindergarten through the university.

Pensioning the Widow

The question has been asked what are we going to do with parents who need the wage of the child? This is a very important question, because we have all found cases in which the family is dependent upon the labor of the child. But none of us believes such responsibility should be placed upon undeveloped shoulders, and I contend it is just as much the duty of the State to pension dependent mothers as dependent veterans. Certainly the mother does as much for the country in rearing her children as the veterans did in killing her sons!

I think our Child Labor Committees should make this pension for deserving mothers one of our slogans. Of course, it would have to be more judiciously administered than our present pension law.

Our Responsibility

The responsibility for our national disgrace, child labor, rests upon you and me, not upon our legislators. It is because of our indifference that these conditions exist. I have associated for a number of years with politicians, and the sensitive plant is as hard as an oak in comparison with them as regards public opinion. They are a mass of little tentacles reaching here and there to learn how the community stands on this or that subject, and just as soon as those little feelers bring back the report that the community is awake and demanding a certain law, you have an ardent advocate for any measure. Let us hope some of the waves from this conference will reach to the powers that be and make them realize that America has awakened to the enormous social cost of child labor and has signed its death warrant.

REJUVENATION OF THE RURAL SCHOOL

By Ernest Burnham,
Western State Normal School, Kalamazoo, Michigan.

The problem of child welfare is in part at least an agricultural problem. It concerns country schools and farmers. We should have it discussed in every farmers' institute, where last year alone it would have come to the attention to three million people. Yet before we can handle such a subject intelligently, we must have definite statistics on which to base our work. We must not only know how many children are of school age, and how many children are attending school, but we must know what the others are doing who stay away. Such facts as these, secured through the Bureau of Education and the local schools, will be of as great importance as any information now at hand.

The problem of rural education is causing widespread interest and discussion. The President of our State Bankers' Association the other day showed me a copy of their proceedings, which read, "First Conference of the Committee on the Development of Agricultural Education, First Day, Morning Session." There are many such "first sessions" being held now to consider rural education. I know of one—a gathering of rural school teachers in St. Louis, teachers who believe that they have the most concentrated opportunity for public service that exists anywhere in America.

The subject of rural education is too large a topic to be hastily treated. In our effort to provide a directly practical training for the boy or girl, we must see to it that we do not rob him of the poetry and the beauty which are childhood's right. Our system of education has been built up by the wisest men of this nation, and we should pause somewhat before declaring it a failure.

If the rural school is to be rejuvenated, its opportunities must be recognized. We must secure the highest grade of teachers, well-trained men and women who see in this a worthy field for their ambition, who are willing to rise up and declare that in the country is the finest field of education, the greatest opportunity for social service. In my class the other day we were asking some young girls who are going to teach next year, "When you go to apply for your school, if you drive by your school house what do you want to see?" Finally one young girl with all of a soul's dawning in her face spoke out and said, "I could see more chance to work where everything had not already been done." It was the pioneer spirit moving within her.

The first frontier which attracted men by its rude splendor and its physical challenge has for the most part passed away. The second frontier has just been discovered. The first was rich in opportunities for individual sacrifice, attainments, and easy social adjustments; the second is incomparably richer in intellectual problems and compelling social necessities. We are face to face with the economic demand for efficiency in rural life. A survey of several townships in Tompkins County, New York, completed in March, 1911, furnishes some significant statistics as to what it means economically to deprive prospective farmers of educational preparation. I quote:

PROFITS AND EDUCATION OF 573 OWNERS AND 137 TENANTS.

Education	Farms Operated by Owners		Farms Operated by Tenants	
	Number	Income	Number	Income
District School	398	$318	113	$407
High School	165	622	24	473
Above High School	10	847	0	0

Besides an appreciation of the inner meaning—the philosophy of this movement to rejuvenate the rural schools, we need what Dean L. H. Bailey calls "the survey idea." We must be able to see things in their true perspective; and in order to do that we need a mass of carefully prepared data. In a local investigation by the Carnegie Institution five years ago, an attempt was made to see if there were any direct relation between child labor on the farms and school attendance. The reasons given for absence in one locality showed 12 per cent. lack of interest, 23 per cent. sickness, and 51 per cent. farm work. An investigation of this kind on a national scale would throw light on our entire problem. The Massachusetts Commissioner of Education says that we want definite projects that can be carried out in rural education, and he is seeking to work out some formula that may be applied. Suggestions are coming in from all sides. We must combine philosophy and imagination with an intelligence which shall direct our work along the wisest paths.

And if we are really to understand the significance of our work, we must look at it from the view of the happiness of childhood. You remember Mrs. Browning's lines:

> "But the child's sob in the silence curseth deeper
> Than the strong man in his wrath!"

We must feel that, and appreciate these lines from the *Outlook* on "The Joy of Life.":

> "It speaks in the throat of the woodland bird
> In the rose-flushed hush of the morn;
> It gleams in the gold of the billowing wheat,
> In the tasseled pride of the corn.
> It follows the feet of Beauty and Love;
> It stirs in the strength of the Strong;
> Its light leads up on the trampling fields
> Where Bravery battles with Wrong.
> It shines in each deed that is nobly done;
> But sweetest, most undefiled,
> It sings to the world, in the world-old way,
> From the face of each little child."

We must find inspiration for our work in the service of children, preparing them for useful citizenship, preserving life and liberty. We must make the school a place to which the children's feet will turn in the pursuit of happiness.

In our normal schools and teachers' colleges and universities we are giving rich opportunities to hundreds of young students. They have received their training at the hands of the State. Shall they not feel called upon to make some return? Let the graduates of our higher institutions of learning show their appreciation for the privileges bestowed upon them by devoting their energy and talent to leading country children toward the goals which they have attained. When will they do this? They will do it as soon as they come to a realization of the present problems and future possibilities of rural education. We are all working toward a common happiness. Unity must be the ideal, power the motive, and service the satisfaction.

Seventh Annual Report

For the fiscal year ending September 30, 1911

By OWEN R. LOVEJOY

General Secretary

NATIONAL CHILD LABOR COMMITTEE

I. Legislation

The Seventh Fiscal Year of the National Child Labor Committee has been notable in two respects. First, in the number and importance of legislative changes. Second, in the formal adoption of a Uniform Child Labor Law by the Commission on Uniform Laws of the American Bar Association.

A summary of legislative changes, reported in pamphlet 167, shows improvement in the laws of thirty states. The more important of these are:

1. The eight-hour day in Colorado, Missouri and Wisconsin; in California and Washington for women and girls.

2. Prohibition of night work in California, Colorado, Indiana, Missouri, New Hampshire, New Jersey, South Carolina and Wisconsin.

3. Regulation of the night messenger service by prohibition to 21 years in Massachusetts, New Jersey, Utah, Wisconsin; and to 18 years in California, Michigan, New Hampshire, Oregon, Tennessee and in New Jersey outside of first-class cities.

4. The prohibition of employment of any child under 16 years in coal mines in Pennsylvania.

5. The regulation of street trades. Perhaps more serious attention was given to the regulation of street trades than in any former year. Attention is especially called to Colorado, Missouri, Nevada, New Hampshire, Utah and Wisconsin.

II. Investigation

In preparation for the regulation sought, this Committee has continued its policy of collecting and reporting first hand information.

Investigations during the year have been chiefly of glass factories, textile mills, sea-food canneries, truck gardens and berry fields, the stage and the night messenger service. The amount of field study devoted to the various investigations expressed in units of one worker for one month are as follows:

Glass factories 13
Textile mills 15
Sea-food canneries 7
Truck gardens and berry fields.......................... 10
Night messenger service................................. 11
The stage 13
General 10

Total 79

The principal investigations have been conducted in the following states:
Glass industry..................Illinois, Indiana, Ohio, Pennsylvania, West Virginia.
Textile mills...................Alabama, Georgia, Massachusetts, Mississippi, Tennessee, Vermont, Virginia.
Sea-food canneries..............Alabama, Florida, Louisiana, Maine, Mississippi.
Truck gardens and berry fields..Delaware, Massachusetts, New Jersey, New York.
Night messenger service.........Connecticut, Illinois, Massachusetts, Michigan, Missouri, Pennsylvania, Rhode Island, Tennessee, Wisconsin.
Stage...........................Illinois, Massachusetts, New Jersey, New York, Pennsylvania.

III. DISTRICT WORK AND STATE COMMITTEES

THE SOUTH

Dr. A. J. McKelway has been engaged in legislative campaigns in Alabama, Arkansas, Georgia, Tennessee and Texas.

In Georgia the principal child labor bill was postponed, a sixty-hour week was prescribed, and a bill providing for a department of labor was enacted, which leaves only North Carolina, Arkansas and Florida without some kind of factory inspection. In Alabama a bill was introduced to raise the age limit from 12 to 14 years, but could not be reached on the calendar. The legislature, however, made a marked improvement in the factory inspection law and under the direction of enterprising factory inspectors real progress should be made.

In Tennessee two important bills were passed—a factory inspection bill, and a child labor bill fixing a 14-year age limit with more rigorous restrictions in certain occupations. The area of compulsory school attendance was also increased. This removes from importance the old law which was declared unconstitutional by the Supreme Court of Tennessee within the past year.

Dr. McKelway directed the organization of the Arkansas Child Labor Committee, but was unable to remain for legislative work on account of his duties in Washington, and no advance was made in child labor legislation. The compulsory education law, however, was applied to a large number of new counties, making the present law cover about two-thirds of the state.

In Texas a Child Labor Committee was organized which led the campaign for a better law. The original bill followed closely the model of the uniform law, but was so amended that, as it finally became law, it provides a 15-year age limit for work about machinery in factories, and a 17-year age limit for work in mines. The chief significance of the Texas law is that it fixes a higher age limit for employment than is found in any other state where cotton is extensively manufactured. A factory inspector was also appointed in Texas and at present much activity is indicated.

Dr. McKelway was also present at the constitutional conventions of New Mexico and Arizona, inducing both to make ample provision for good child labor laws when their first legislatures meet.

The campaigns in North and South Carolina were conducted by the State Committees, assisted by our agent, John Porter Hollis, under Dr. McKelway's direction.

In North Carolina the child labor bill was defeated, but a bill reducing the hours from 66 to 60 per week was passed. In South Carolina a bill passed striking out the former exemption of children of widows and fixing a straight 12-year age limit. The effort to fix a 14-year age for employment was defeated by opposition of the cotton manufacturers, and the appropriation for two factory inspectors was vetoed by the governor.

In Florida an effort was made to secure a good child labor law, the Committee being represented by your Secretary, Mr. Hollis, and Mr. Lewis W. Hine. Valuable assistance was rendered by local workers, but the bill was entirely defeated, principally through the opposition of a prominent oyster packer.

OHIO VALLEY STATES

Important legislation was secured in West Virginia, Indiana and Missouri, campaigns being chiefly under the direction of Mr. E. N. Clopper.

The most important success was in Indiana, where night work of children in the glass factories was abolished, and in Missouri, which improved and extended its law to the entire state.

In West Virginia the age limit was advanced from 12 to 14 years, Mr. Charles L. Chute assisting in the legislative work. Mr. Clopper also assisted in legislative work in Ohio, Illinois, Tennessee and Alabama.

In order to strengthen the forces in the Southern Field, Mr. Clopper has been asked to direct the work next year in such Mississippi Valley

States as will hold legislative sessions. Mr. Clopper's title has been changed to Secretary of the Mississippi Valley States, and he will represent the Committee next winter in legislative work in Mississippi and Louisiana.

Aside from the states covered by these districts, the legislative work of the Committee has been carried on chiefly through coöperation with state and local committees. Among the principal activities have been the following:

OTHER STATES

New York.—The New York Committee has led the effort to secure from the state legislature the establishment of a commission to investigate conditions of tenement home workers in New York City, but thus far without success. The effort to restrict child labor in cannery sheds was also unsuccessful.

Pennsylvania.—The Pennsylvania Committee led a lively campaign for the regulation of child labor in glass factories, coal mines and night messenger service. Three separate bills were introduced, but only the one relating to child labor in coal mines was passed. This was secured through coöperation of representatives of the coal industry and prohibits employment of children under 16 years of age inside all coal mines. The other bills were prevented from being considered, by opposition of the political leaders.

On August 1st Fred S. Hall resigned the secretaryship of the Pennsylvania Association to enter other work and the association is at present without a secretary.*

New Jersey.—The New Jersey Committee coöperated with us in the enactment of laws regulating the night messenger service and improving the compulsory education law.

Massachusetts.—We provided the evidence on which the Massachusetts Committee was able this year to secure a good night messenger law and have coöperated in investigations of other industries.

The financial arrangement with the Massachusetts Committee, begun in April, 1910, was terminated by mutual agreement April, 1911. During the year the Massachusetts Committee collected and placed in our treasury $1,250. We have contributed to the Massachusetts Committee the services of Mr. Hine, photographer, in investigations of mills and cranberry bogs.

Vermont.—The Vermont Child Labor Committee, organized in September, 1910, through its chairman, introduced a bill before the state legislature which was passed and makes some slight improvement in law, but is still far from a satisfactory standard.

Delaware.—The Delaware Child Labor Committee has rendered excellent service in helping to defray the expenses of investigation and in directing the legislative campaign at Dover. All child labor bills introduced were defeated and the only substantial gain was the appointment of a commission of five to investigate and advise upon necessary legislation.

* Charles L. Chute became Secretary Feb. 1, 1912.

Other state and local committees have been active during the year, as indicated in the report of the Seventh Annual Conference and in the record of legislative advances shown in pamphlet 167. Particular attention should be called to the federation of organizations in Missouri under the name of "Committee on Social Legislation." Their plan of pushing the interests of reform legislation was eminently fruitful.

IV. CHILD LABOR IN AGRICULTURE

Pursuing the policy outlined by this Committee last year of attempting to dislodge from the popular mind the tradition that all child labor in agriculture is good for the child, with a view to securing legislation at a later date, an investigation was conducted last October in the cranberry bogs of New Jersey and in other fruit and vegetable fields. The report of conditions in the cranberry bogs, presented in the *Survey* in November, 1910, was bitterly attacked by representatives of the industry. To substantiate the report of our agents last year, a further study has been made this year covering the principal cranberry bogs of Massachusetts and practically all those in New Jersey. Your Secretary has spent a number of days personally in this investigation and has seen enough to corroborate the reports made by our agents. Children as young as four and five years work regularly during the picking season; hundreds of children are deprived of the first five or six weeks of schooling; the housing conditions on many bogs are unspeakably indecent and unsanitary; and the whole situation calls for careful attention. Conditions as to child labor, wages, housing, etc., are far inferior in New Jersey to those found in Massachusetts.

V. THE STAGE

The attitude of this Committee in relation to child labor on the stage has been a conservative one. Our policy as outlined by the Trustees in various meetings is:

1st. To gather all available information as to the extent and effects of child labor on the stage.

2d. To assist state and local committees in Massachusetts, Illinois, Louisiana and Oregon to maintain their existing laws for the prohibition of child labor on the stage.

3d. To advocate in general the enactment of laws that shall forbid child labor under 16 years of age at night, whether in theaters or elsewhere unless evidence shall be gathered showing that an exemption should be made in favor of the stage.

We have made a transcript of all records relating to stage children in the Mayor's office—the New York Society for the Prevention of Cruelty to Children having closed its doors against us on account of criticisms made in the Illinois campaign of the New York stage license law. We have also investigated many stage children in New York and in nearby seashore cities.

VI. FEDERAL CHILDREN'S BUREAU

The Sixth Annual Report recorded the bill on the calendar of both Houses. In the short session the bill was brought forward in the Senate by Senator Flint, of California, and passed. In the House, in charge of Hon. Washington Gardner, of Michigan, the bill received a favorable report, and efforts were made during the closing days of the session to press it to vote. These efforts were unsuccessful because of the opposition of certain leaders in the House. The bill was again introduced at the extra session by Senator Borah, of Idaho, and Hon. Andrew J. Peters, of Massachusetts, and the campaign in its behalf has been urged by this Committee throughout the year. On August 16, 1911, the bill was favorably reported by the Senate Committee and is on the calendar for the regular session of Congress. A hearing was given by the House Committee, at which the chief arguments in favor of the bill were advanced and no opposition was expressed. Dr. McKelway has been continued in charge of the work in Washington and the Committee hopes to have the matter brought to vote in the early days of the next Congressional session.*

VII. UNIFORM CHILD LABOR LAW

At the twenty-first annual meeting of the Commission on Uniform Laws of the American Bar Association, the Report of the Special Committee presented at the Chattanooga Meeting last year was again taken up for action. At the invitation of the Commission your Secretary was present to explain the various provisions of the bill, and after careful consideration the draft prepared by the National Child Labor Committee was adopted on August 26th. A copy of the bill as adopted is issued as pamphlet 147 of the Committee publications.

VIII. OFFICIAL MEETINGS

The Annual Business Meeting of the Corporation was held at the office of the Committee on November 2, 1910, seven members and your Secretary being present. Following the provisions of the Constitution, the membership of the Board of Trustees was divided into five groups by lot and elected to serve as follows:

* Bill approved April 9, and Julia C. Lathrop appointed chief April 17, 1912.

Term expiring in:—

1911	1912	1913
Felix Adler	James H. Kirkland	Edward T. Devine
Samuel M. Lindsay	Lillian D. Wald	Robert W. de Forest
V. Everit Macy	Paul M. Warburg	Florence Kelley
1914		1915
Francis G. Caffey		Homer Folks
William E. Harman		Isaac N. Seligman
————————*		John W. Wood

Four meetings of the Board of Trustees, three meetings of the Field Work Committee, one meeting of the Program Committee and two meetings of the Finance Committee have been held.

IX. ANNUAL CONFERENCE

The Seventh Annual Conference was held in Birmingham, Alabama, March 9-12, 1911. The discussion of the general topic, "Uniform Child Labor Laws," brought from various parts of the country the rapidly growing demand for a more uniform standard of regulation and for the adoption in various states of measures already found successful in the more advanced states. Ten sessions were held, at which all important phases of the child labor problem were presented to large audiences, and it was the judgment of those in attendance that this was the most important meeting in the history of the Committee. The people of Birmingham, through their special committees, gave excellent coöperation, and the newspapers of the city devoted approximately fifty pages of space to the Conference. On Sunday the subject was presented in the local churches either by pastors or visiting delegates. A full report of the meeting and addresses was published as a Supplement to "The Annals of the American Academy of Political and Social Science" for July, 1911, and reprinted by this Committee in a volume of 232 pages, under the title, "Uniform Child Labor Laws."

X. PUBLICITY

The publications issued during the year number 252,400; total pages, 3,310,400. In addition, we have utilized newspapers and magazines for the discussion of timely topics and have kept in circulation sets of slides with descriptive lectures; thirty-five sets of slides have been rented in twenty-nine cities in fifteen states in addition to the use made by our own representatives. Letters regarding the work of the Committee, written for the purpose of adding financial support, also constitute an important part of our publicity

* Successor to John S. Huyler. Jane Addams, elected October 26, 1911.

campaign, as these letters are always designed to be constructive and educational. Of such letters 107,790 were sent out during the year.

XI. Exhibits

The charts, photographs and other exhibit material have been placed in charge of Miss Elizabeth M. Dinwiddie and offered for use in various cities. The exhibit covers approximately 150 x 8 feet of wall space, and has been shown in:

Birmingham, Ala.	Boston, Mass.	Louisville, Ky.
Chicago, Ill.	Memphis, Tenn.	Montgomery, Ala.
Madison, Wis.	New York City, N. Y.	Providence, R. I.
Nashville, Tenn.	St. Louis, Mo.	Washington, D. C.
Raleigh, N. C.	Charlottesville, Va.	

Less extensive exhibits have been prepared in the office and used by the Membership Secretary, Mrs. Frederick Crane, and other representatives of the Committee.

XII. Addresses and Conferences

Lectures and Addresses by Mr. Lovejoy

1910.
Oct. 11	Public School No. 169, Manhattan	New York City
" 25	Indiana Child Labor Committee	Indianapolis, Ind.
" 26	Wednesday Club	St. Louis, Mo.
" 27	Ferris Institute	Big Rapids, Mich.
Nov. 1	Free Synagogue	New York City
" 7	Monday Afternoon Club	Plainfield, N. J.
" 9	Evening School of Philanthropy	New York City
" 10	Colony Club	New York City
" 16	Unitarian Church	Watertown, Mass.
" 18	Maryland Conference Charities and Correction	Frederick, Md.
" 20	Young Men's Christian Association	Elizabeth, N. J.
" 21	Mt. Morris Baptist Church Missionary Society	New York City
" 21	Civic Club	Arlington, N. J.
" 27	Congregational Church	Brattleboro, Vt.
Dec. 4	Universalist Church	Stamford, Conn.
" 5	Public School No. 101, Manhattan	New York City
" 8	Young Men's Christian Association	Newark, N. J.
" 11	Congregational Church	Upper Montclair, N. J.

1911.
Jan. 11	State Federation of Women's Clubs	Dover, Del.
" 20	Congregational Brotherhood	Chicago, Ill.

The National Child Labor Committee

Jan. 23	Public School No. 5, Manhattan	New York City
" 24	Bennett School	Meadow Brook, N. Y.
" 26	Church Club Diocese of Connecticut	Waterbury, Conn.
Feb. 1	Child Welfare Exhibit	New York City
" 6	Public School No. 51, Manhattan	New York City
" 11	Child Welfare Exhibit	New York City
" 12	Hudson Theater (Union Service, three churches)	New York City
" 16	Philadelphia Training School for Social Workers	Philadelphia, Pa.
" 17	Parlor Meeting, Mrs. Harold Brown	Newport, R. I.
Mar. 7	Jacksonville Woman's Club	Jacksonville, Fla.
" 9-12	Seventh Annual Conference National Child Labor Committee	Birmingham, Ala.
" 13	Young Men's Christian Association	Pensacola, Fla.
" 24	Children's Conference	Jacksonville, Fla.
" 27	Public School No. 164, Brooklyn	Brooklyn, N. Y.
" 28	School of Philanthropy	New York City
" 29	East Side House Settlement	New York City
Apr. 3	Trinity Church	Mt. Vernon, N. Y.
" 4	School of Philanthropy	New York City
" 5	Young Women's Christian Association Training School,	New York City
" 10	Civic Forum	New York City
" 11	School of Philanthropy	New York City
May 1	Ministers' Conference	Sanford, Fla.
" 11	New York Conference of Charities and Correction,	Chappaqua, N. Y.
" 12	House Committee on Federal Children's Bureau	Washington, D. C.
" 16	Churchmen's Club	Providence, R. I.
" 17	Consumers' League	Providence, R. I.
" 17	Consumers' League	Westerly, R. I.
" 25	Woman's Christian Temperance Union	Whitestone, N. Y.
June 2	School of Philanthropy	New York City
" 7-14	National Conference of Charities and Correction	Boston, Mass.
" 11	Second Church	West Newton, Mass.
" 20	Social Workers' Conference	Yonkers, N. Y.
July 9	Open Forum	Ridgewood Park, N. J.
" 18	School of Philanthropy	New York City
" 20	School of Philanthropy	New York City
Aug. 25	Commissioners on Uniform Laws	Boston, Mass.

LECTURES AND ADDRESSES BY DR. MCKELWAY

1910.

Oct. 7	Woman's Club	Richmond, Va.
" 18	Lexington Church	Lexington, Va.
" 20	Meeting Social Service Club	Baltimore, Md.

Oct. 28 Committee on Woman's Clubs..................Baltimore, Md.
Nov. 11-30 Southwestern Trip:
    Presbyterian Church ....Little Rock, Ark.
    Committee on Revision of Constitution......Sante Fé, N. M.
    St. Michael's College.......................Sante Fé, N. M.
    State Conference of Charities and Correction....Houston, Tex.
    Child Welfare Conference...................Memphis, Tenn.
Dec. 25 Southern Educational Association ....Chattanooga, Tenn.
" 25 Methodist Training School ....Nashville, Tenn.
" 25 Presbyterian Church ....Clarksville, Tenn.
1911.
Jan. Child Welfare Conference......................Richmond, Va.
Feb. 1 Child Welfare Exhibit.........................New York City
" 10 Child Welfare Exhibit ....New York City
Mar. 9-12 Seventh Annual Conference National Child Labor Committee
    (three addresses) ....Birmingham, Ala.
" 20 Lenten Parlor Meeting on Child Labor..........New York City
" 21 Lenten Parlor Meeting on Child Labor..........Brooklyn, N. Y.
" Three Committee Meetings, Tennessee Legislature,
    ....Nashville, Tenn.
Apr. Southern Conference on Child Labor................Atlanta, Ga.
June Second Presbyterian Church ....Washington, D. C.
" 7-14 National Conference of Charities and Correction....Boston, Mass.
July 7-14 Four addresses Legislative Committee ....Atlanta, Ga.

LECTURES AND ADDRESSES BY MR. CLOPPER

1910.
Oct. 15 Ohio Conference Charities and Correction........Newark, Ohio
" 27 Convention Indiana Federation of Women's Clubs (morning)
    ....Richmond, Ind.
" 27 Convention Indiana Federation of Women's Clubs (afternoon)
    ....Richmond, Ind.
Nov. 2 Christ Church Parish House.....................Cincinnati, O.
" 9 Middle States Juvenile Court Conference......Indianapolis, Ind.
" 13 Young Men's Christian Association..................Toledo, O.
Dec. 8 West Virginia Child Labor Committee..........Wheeling, W. Va.
1911.
Jan. 16 House Committee ....Indianapolis, Ind.
" 23 House Committee ....Indianapolis, Ind.
Feb. 10 Senate Committee ....Charleston, W. Va.
" 20 Senate Committee ....Indianapolis, Ind.
Mar. 1 Aldermen Committee ....Louisville, Ky.
" 2 House Committee ....Columbus, O.
" 9-12 Seventh Annual Conference National Child Labor Committee,
    ....Birmingham, Ala.

The National Child Labor Committee

Mar. 12	Baptist Church, Morning Service	Birmingham, Ala.
" 12	Baptist Church, Evening Service	Birmingham, Ala.
" 21	Public School Teachers	Cincinnati, O.
" 28	Consumers' League	Cincinnati, O.
Apr. 11	Assembly Hearing	Madison, Wis.
" 17	University of Cincinnati	Cincinnati, O.
" 26	Students from Miami University	Cincinnati, O.
May 9	Susan B. Anthony Club	Cincinnati, O.
" 19	Mothers' Club	Carthage, O.

LECTURES AND ADDRESSES BY MR. HOLLIS

1910.

Oct. 25	Convention Mill Superintendents and Overseers	Charlotte, S. C.
Nov. 16	South Carolina Child Labor Committee	Columbia, S. C.
" 30	South Carolina Baptist Convention	Laurens, S. C.
Dec. 9	South Carolina Conference Charities and Correction,	Florence, S. C.
" 10	South Carolina Conference M. E. Church South	Charleston, S. C.
" 16	South Carolina Child Labor Committee	Columbia, S. C.

1911.

Jan. 18	South Carolina House and Senate Committees	Columbia, S. C.
Feb. 3	North Carolina House and Senate Committees	Raleigh, N. C.
Apr. 15	Women's College of Florida	Tallahassee, Fla.
" 25	Southern Child Labor Conference	Atlanta, Ga.
May 3	South Carolina Federation of Women's Clubs	Columbia, S. C.
June 7-14	National Conference of Charities and Correction	Boston, Mass.
July 4	Educational Rally	Leslie, S. C.
" 13	Convention South Carolina County Superintendents of Education	Rock Hill, S. C.
" 21	Educational Rally	Mt. Holly, S. C.

LECTURES AND ADDRESSES BY MISS ESCHENBRENNER

1911.

Jan. 20	Girls' Department of the House of Refuge	Darling, Pa.
Mar. 2	St. Michael's Protestant Episcopal Church	New York City
" 10	Birmingham Seminary	Birmingham, Ala.
" 11	College Club	Birmingham, Ala.
" 12	Norwood Methodist Episcopal Church	Birmingham, Ala.
May 12	Flatbush Congregational Church, Social Service Club,	Flatbush, L. I.

LECTURES AND ADDRESSES BY MRS. CRANE

Jan. 13	Presbyterian Church, Mothers' Club	New Rochelle, N. Y.
" 27	Mothers' Congress of Atlantic City	Atlantic City, N. J.

Mar. 2 St. Michael's Protestant Episcopal Church........New York City
" 14 Lenten Parlor Meeting ....Brooklyn, N. Y.
" 21 Ladies' Guild, Christ Protestant Episcopal Church..Jamaica, N. Y.
Apr. 7 Young Woman's Educational Association....Asbury Park, N. J.
May 6 Ladies' Home Missionary Society, Westminster Presbyterian
 Church ....Bloomfield, N. J.

IMPORTANT CONFERENCES AT WHICH THIS COMMITTEE HAS BEEN OFFICIALLY REPRESENTED

1910.
Oct. 10-15 First American International Humane Conference,
 ....Washington, D. C.
" 10 Meeting of Representatives of National Organizations
 ....Washington, D. C.
Nov. Tennessee Child Labor Committee............Nashville, Tenn.
" Arkansas Child Labor Committee.............Little Rock, Ark.
" 15 Boston, 1915 ....Boston, Mass.
" 15-18 New York Conference of Charities and Correction
 ....Rochester, N. Y.
" 15-16 Conference on Vocational Guidance..............Boston, Mass.
" 18 Maryland Conference of Charities and Correction
 ....Frederick, Md.
" New Mexico Constitutional Convention........Sante Fé, N. M.
" Arizona Constitutional Convention...............Phoenix, Ariz.
" Arkansas Child Labor Committee...............Little Rock, Ark.
Dec. Local Committee, Birmingham Conference......Birmingham, Ala.
1911.
Jan. 10 Maryland Child Welfare Committee..............Baltimore, Md.
" 10 Conference West Virginia Child Labor Committee
 ....Wheeling, W. Va.
" 11 Conference West Virginia Child Labor Committee
 ....Fairmont, W. Va.
" 16 Conference Indiana Child Labor Committee.....Indianapolis, Ind.
" 19 Milwaukee Children's Conference...............Milwaukee, Wis.
" 20, 24 Conference Indiana Child Labor Committee....Indianapolis, Ind.
" 24 Council of the Churches of Christ............Washington, D. C.
Feb. 1 Child Welfare Exhibit.........................New York City
" 1 Conference with Indiana Child Labor Committee..Indianapolis, Ind.
" 2 Maryland Children's Conference.................Baltimore, Md.
" 6, 16, 20, Mar. 3 Conference Indiana Child Labor Committee
 ....Indianapolis, Ind.
Apr. 2-4 New Jersey Conference of Charities and Correction.Princeton, N. J.
" 3 Conference with Illinois Child Labor Committee......Chicago, Ill.
" 19-21 Southern Educational Conference ....Jacksonville, Fla.

Apr. 25   Southern Conference on Woman and Child Labor....Atlanta, Ga.
May 12   Congressional Hearing on Federal Children's Bureau
          ....Washington, D. C.
" 16   Senate Committee on Education.............Washington, D. C.
"   Meeting North Carolina Child Labor Committee....Raleigh, N. C.
" 24   Child Welfare Exhibit ....Chicago, Ill.
June 7-14 National Conference of Charities and Correction....Boston, Mass.
"   Meeting Social Service Commission of Protestant Churches
          ....Boston, Mass.
"   Georgia Child Labor Committee....................Atlanta, Ga.
Aug. 26   Conference on Uniform State Laws ....Boston, Mass.
Sept. 8   Ohio Commission on Laws Relating to Children
          ....City Club, New York
" 12   Governors' Conference ....Spring Lake, N. J.

Our Secretaries and Agents have also represented the Committee before Legislatures in:

Alabama,	Illinois,	New Mexico,	South Carolina,
Arizona,	Indiana,	New York,	Tennessee,
Connecticut,	Massachusetts,	North Carolina,	Vermont,
Delaware,	Michigan,	Ohio,	Wisconsin.
Florida,	Missouri,	Pennsylvania,	
Georgia,	New Jersey,	Rhode Island,	

XIII. Travel

The Secretaries and Agents of the Committee have traveled:

Owen R. Lovejoy,	22,885	miles
A. J. McKelway,	25,769	"
E. N. Clopper,	15,650	"
J. J. Eschenbrenner,	2,778	"
John Porter Hollis,	7,129	"
Lewis W. Hine,	19,000	"
Edward F. Brown,	10,650	"
Charles L. Chute,	12,200	"
E. M. Dinwiddie,	7,450	"

XIV. Coöperation

The Trustees carefully considered whether the National Child Labor Committee should take the lead in an effort to have the subject of Federal Aid to Education taken up for general national discussion. It was finally decided that we should stand ready to participate in any such movement, but could not undertake to organize or direct it.

A number of Trustees and your Secretary served on Committees of the New York Child Welfare Exhibit, and under our direction the culminating meeting was devoted to the Federal Children's Bureau, with an address by Senator Robert L. Owen, of Oklahoma.

We have also, as heretofore, coöperated with the National Consumers' League, the Association for Promoting Industrial Education, the American Association for Labor Legislation, the American Federation of Labor, the Women's Trade Union League and other bodies engaged in kindred work.

We may fairly claim a large share of responsibility for the Government Report on Condition of Woman and Child Wage-Earners, which is now being issued in nineteen volumes as Senate Document 645. We promoted the bill which secured the appropriation for this investigation and have placed all our available information at the disposal of the United States Bureau of Labor.

XV. MEMBERSHIP

The Trustees have sustained the loss of one of their number and the Committee one of its loyal supporters in the death of Mr. John S. Huyler on October 1, 1910. The vacancy on the Board has not yet been filled.*

Two other Guarantors lost through death are Mr. Samuel W. Bowne and Miss Carola Woerishoffer.

Mr. Adolph Lewisohn was elected to membership in the Committee on February 8, 1911, and has become the largest single contributor to the Treasury.

The Contributing Membership compared with the Sixth Fiscal Year is as follows:

	SIXTH YEAR.		SEVENTH YEAR.	
Guarantors	41	$10,118.76	57	$17,600.00
Sustaining members	536	13,458.00	454	11,720.00
Associate members	4,136	16,968.41	5,330	21,894.31
Contributors	293	2,020.87	253	729.57
Total	5,006	$42,566.04	6,094	$51,943.88

The above table shows an increase of 1,088 members and contributors and $9,377.84 over the Sixth Year.

In September a special appeal was sent out to meet a threatened deficit, to which 562 members responded up to October 10th with $4,095.08, making the total receipts for the year $56,038.96.

Miss Eschenbrenner, the Membership Secretary, has received gratifying results to appeals for new members and the renewal of former members.

*Jane Addams, Hull House, Chicago, elected October 26, 1911, to fill vacancy.

The responses of former members have been especially encouraging; 15,213 letters were sent to delinquent members at a cost of $520.88, netting 749 subscriptions of $4,251.32, a cost of 12.5 per cent. The total renewal of members was 81.3 per cent.

XVI. FINANCES

The complete record of the year is presented in the following Treasurer's Report:

TREASURER'S ANNUAL REPORT

[*As examined, audited and found correct by Haskins & Sells, New York, Certified Public Accountants.*]

The Treasurer's report for the year ending September 30, 1911

DEBITS.

Cash on deposit, October 1, 1910.............................. $973.71

Receipts.

Paid subscriptions	$55,278.55	
On account of New York Child Labor Committee from joint appeal	208.00	
Special fund, investigations in southern states	3,750.00	
Loan account	1,500.00	
Sales of publications	105.88	
Sales of photographs and slides	157.20	
Rental of slides	95.30	
Interest on bank deposits	32.43	
Refund, account investigations	438.54	
Miscellaneous	334.50	61,900.40
Total debits		$62,874.11

CREDITS.

Expenses.

Salaries: Administrative, $9,529.17; clerks and stenographers, $6,430.64; total $15,959.81
Stationery and office supplies......................... 903.91

Postage	$4,145.49
Investigations	17,858.79
Special fund, investigations in southern states	5,425.82
Exhibit expenses	3,175.35
Rent	2,128.04
Travel	1,775.87
Printing	4,300.57
General expenses	226.23
Telephone and telegraph	406.68
Purchase of material on Child Labor	198.44
Loan account	1,500.00
	$58,005.00

Miscellaneous.

Office furniture and fixtures	183.35
Exhibits	57.00
Reserve expenses sixth fiscal year	921.53
New York Child Labor Account	208.00
	$1,369.88

Total credits	$59,374.88
Cash on deposit, September 30, 1911	*3,499.23
	$62,874.11

E. & O. E.,

V. EVERIT MACY, *Treasurer.*

New York, October 19, 1911.

XVII. WORK AHEAD

The work of the Committee has been especially fruitful in bringing to public notice the actual conditions in which children work and the need for better laws. Better legislative standards in nearly all states have followed with gratifying promptness, especially in the year just closed. The adoption of a model form of law by the Commission on Uniform Laws of the American Bar Association also helped to fix in the public mind a standard toward which the states will tend.

But our own investigations as well as reports from other sources indicate that often these laws are not taken seriously and that a favorite method by which legislatures render child labor laws ineffective is by passing them in response to public demand and then declining to make appropriation of

* Unpaid bills outstanding, $718.71.

public funds sufficient to equip a state department for their enforcement. In addition, therefore, to our efforts to promote better knowledge of child labor conditions and secure better laws, we must devote more direct attention than heretofore to the proper administration of child labor laws and to constructive suggestions for the education of children with whose labor our activities interfere.

Respectfully submitted,

OWEN R. LOVEJOY,
General Secretary.

October 1, 1911.

II

PROGRAM EIGHTH ANNUAL CONFERENCE ON CHILD LABOR

UNDER THE AUSPICES OF THE

NATIONAL CHILD LABOR COMMITTEE

LOUISVILLE, KENTUCKY, JANUARY 25, 26, 27, 28, 1912.

By Invitation of the Kentucky Child Labor Association and the Louisville Convention and Publicity League.

All State and local Child Labor Committees urged to send representatives. Members of all National and local organizations interested in Child Welfare invited to attend and participate in the proceedings of the Conference. The general public also invited.

Sunday mass-meeting at Macauley's Theater; all other sessions at the Seelbach Hotel. Headquarters at Seelbach Hotel.

General topic: CHILD LABOR AND EDUCATION.

Note.—All papers limited to 20 minutes. Speakers were asked to discuss educational problems only in so far as they relate to Child Labor.

First session, Thursday evening, January 25th, 8 o'clock.

Topic: "An Efficient Elementary School the Foe of Child Labor."

Greetings from Judge J. W. Clements, representing the Mayor of Louisville.

Conference opened by Lafon Allen, Esq., President of Kentucky Child Labor Association, introducing Dr. Felix Adler, Chairman of the National Child Labor Committee, who presided.

1. "Vocational Work in the Public School."
    By E. O. Holland, Superintendent of Schools, Louisville, Ky.
2. "Future Development of the School."
    By Carroll G. Pearse, Superintendent of Schools, Milwaukee, Wis., and President National Education Association.
3. "Education a National Obligation."
    By Samuel McCune Lindsay, Director New York School of Philanthropy.

Second session, Friday, January 26th, 9 o'clock.

Topic: "Street Trades and the Public School."
Presiding Officer: Edward W. Frost, Esq., Milwaukee, Chairman Wisconsin Child Labor Committee.
Symposium—Ten minute addresses:
1. "Need for Regulation of Street Trades."
    By the Chairman.
2. "Connection Between Street Trading and the School."
    By Z. L. Potter, Buffalo, Field Secretary New York Child Labor Committee.
3. "The Proper Standard for Street Trades Regulation—Ways and Means to Secure It."
    By E. N. Clopper, Cincinnati, Secretary for the Mississippi Valley States, National Child Labor Committee.
4. "Enforcement of Street Trades Regulation."
    By Lillian A. Quinn, Pittsburgh, Pa., Secretary Allegheny County Child Labor Committee.

Third session, Friday, January 26th, 11 o'clock.

Topic: "Industrial Training and Vocational Guidance."
Presiding Officer: Dr. Helen T. Woolley, Cincinnati, Director of Survey of Children at Work.
1. "Relation of Industrial Training to Child Labor."
    By William H. Elson, formerly superintendent of schools, Cleveland, Ohio.
2. "Possibilities and Dangers of Vocational Guidance."
    By Alice P. Barrows, New York, Director Vocational Guidance Survey.
3. "Social Uses of the School."
    By Pauline Witherspoon, Louisville Girls' High School.
4. Round Table Discussion: "What the School Can Do to Solve the Child Labor Problem."
    Led by the Chairman.

The National Child Labor Committee

Fourth session, Friday afternoon, January 26th, 2:30 o'clock.

Conference of State Committees.

Presiding Officer: Owen R. Lovejoy, General Secretary National Child Labor Committee.

Chairmen, Secretaries and other members of State Committees discuss under 5-minute rule:
- "Regulation of Street Trades."
- "Night Messenger Service."
- "Tenement Home Work."
- "Relation of State Committees to Factory Inspectors and School Officials."
- "Practical Measures for Arousing the Public."

Address: "How to Interest Young People."
   By Mrs. Frederick Crane, New York.

Address: "The Educational Test for Working Children."
   By Richard K. Conant, Boston, Secretary Massachusetts Child Labor Committee.

Fifth session, Friday afternoon, January 26th, 5 o'clock.

Reception by the Woman's Club of Louisville.

"The Woman's Club of Louisville asks the privilege of being hostess at an informal reception on Friday, January 26th, at 5 o'clock, at the Woman's Club House, in honor of the officers, delegates and guests attending the Conference of the National Child Labor Committee."

Addresses by Dr. Felix Adler, Chairman National Child Labor Committee, and Jean M. Gordon, New Orleans, La.

Sixth session, Friday evening, January 26th, 8 o'clock.

Topic: "Unreasonable Industrial Burdens on Women and Children, and the Effect on Education."

Presiding Officer: Hon. Edward J. McDermott, Lieut.-Governor of Kentucky.

Addresses by:
- Mrs. Florence Kelley, General Secretary National Consumers' League, New York.
- Mrs. Millie R. Trumbull, Secretary Oregon Child Labor Commission, Portland.
- Rev. John A. Ryan, D. D., Professor Moral Theology and Economics, St. Paul Seminary, St. Paul, Minn.
- Jean M. Gordon, formerly State Factory Inspector, New Orleans, La.

Seventh session, Saturday, January 27th, 9 o'clock.

Topic: "Relation of Rural Schools to Child Labor Reform."
Presiding Officer: Owen R. Lovejoy.
1. "Economic Value of Education."
   By Edith Campbell, Director Schmidlapp Fund, Cincinnati, O.
2. "Child Labor in Canneries."
   By Z. L. Potter, Buffalo, N. Y.
3. "Rejuvenating the Rural School."
   By Prof. Ernest Burnham, Western Normal College, Kalamazoo, Mich.
4. "Rural Child Labor."
   By Prof. J. M. Gillette, University of North Dakota.

Eighth session, Saturday, January 27th, 11 o'clock.

Topic: "Child Labor and Compulsory Education."
Presiding Officer: Edward N. Clopper.
1. "Need of Compulsory Education in the South."
   By Prof. W. H. Hand, State High School Inspector, Columbia, S. C.
2. "Administration of Child Labor Laws."
   By Charles L. Chute, New York, Special Agent, National Child Labor Committee.
3. "Difficulties of Enforcement Without Compulsory Education."
   By Hon. Geo. Kennedy, Chief Factory Inspector, Memphis, Tenn.
4. "A Legislative Program for South Carolina."
   By John Porter Hollis, Rock Hill, S. C., Special Agent, National Child Labor Committee.

Ninth session, Saturday evening, January 27th, 8 o'clock.

Topic: "Federal Aid to Education."
Annual Address by the Chairman of the National Child Labor Committee, Dr. Felix Adler, New York, Founder Society for Ethical Culture.
"Part Time Schooling."
   By Mrs. Florence Kelley.
"Child Labor and Democracy."
   By Dr. A. J. McKelway, Washington, D. C., Secretary for Southern States, National Child Labor Committee.
"Extending Medical Inspection from Schools to Mills."
   By George F. Ross, M. D., Superintendent of Health, Guilford County, North Carolina.

Tenth session, Sunday afternoon, January 28th, 3 o'clock, mass-meeting, in Macauley's Theater.
Topic: "The American Child—Exploitation *vs.* Education."
Presiding Officer: Hon. Augustus E. Willson, Ex-Governor of Kentucky.
1. "The Federal Children's Bureau."
     By Congressman Andrew J. Peters, of Massachusetts.
2. "Social Cost of Child Labor."
     By John P. Frey, Editor of *Moulders' Journal*, Cincinnati.
3. "An Educational Substitute for Child Labor."
     By Hon. P. P. Claxton, United States Commissioner of Education.

CHILD LABOR DAY

Sunday morning and evening, January 28.—Child labor addresses delivered by pastors and delegates in the churches of Louisville and vicinity.

CONFERENCE NOTES

Exhibit.—An exhibit of photographs, charts and tables illustrating child labor in various industries throughout the country, open to the public during the conference, in charge of Elizabeth M. Dinwiddie, at the Seelbach Hotel, adjoining auditorium.

Registration.—All persons attending the sessions of this Conference invited to register at the Committee Headquarters, Mezzanine Floor, Seelbach Hotel. Registration office in charge of Josephine J. Eschenbrenner, Membership Secretary.

Membership.—All persons are invited to join in the campaign against child labor by becoming members of the National Child Labor Committee. Associate members pay $2 or more. Sustaining members $25 or more. Guarantors $100 or more. All members are entitled to the publications of the Committee for one year, including the proceedings of this Conference.

Louisville Committee on Arrangements and Reception.—Lafon Allen, *Chairman*, President Kentucky Child Labor Association; George L. Danforth, President Louisville Board of Trade; Thomas C. Timberlake, President Commercial Club; Fred. W. Keisker, President Louisville Convention and Publicity League; Harry I. Perkins, President Merchants' and Manufacturers' Association; Lee Lewis, President Retail Merchants' Association; W. Hume Logan, President Employers' Association; M. H. Barker, President Associated Charities; Edward Sachs, President Federation of Jewish Charities; J. J. Caffery, President St. Vincent de Paul Society; Mrs. Pattie B. Semple, Mrs. R. P. Halleck, Mrs. John Little, Charles F. Huhlein, Arthur D. Allen, Miss Frances Ingram, Mrs. Charles Bonnycastle Robinson, H. G. Enelow, Mrs. Morris B. Belknap, Mrs. Robert Horner, Mrs. Bernard Selligman.

III

EIGHTH ANNUAL CONFERENCE ON CHILD LABOR

Session I

The Eighth Annual Conference on Child Labor, under the auspices of the National Child Labor Committee, was held in Louisville, Kentucky, January 25-28, 1912, and opened at the Seelbach Hotel, Thursday evening, January 25th, with Dr. Felix Adler, Chairman of the Committee, presiding. The general topic for discussion was "An Efficient Elementary School the Foe of Child Labor." Lafon Allen, Esq., President of the Kentucky Child Labor Association, opened the meeting with a few appropriate remarks, and introduced Judge J. W. Clements, Representative of the Mayor, and Dr. Adler, Chairman of the meeting.

After a brief address by Judge Clements, Mr. Allen said: "The public nowadays is from Missouri and wants to be shown. It wants to see, before it will support an organization of this kind, that it can offer something in the way of practical results, or—to use a suggestive slang expression—to see that the organization can 'deliver the goods.' This organization can and does deliver the goods. I am persuaded of this, not only by the character of the men and women who manage its affairs, but by the very purpose it has in view, and the means it proposes for effecting that purpose.

"The declared purpose of these child labor organizations is to give to children who start life under the handicap of poverty a fair chance of success through a sound mind in a sound body. To say that you are taking a child out of a mill or factory in order that his body may not be maimed or destroyed by a burden of labor too heavy for his strength is only to state half the benefit. The other half is that you will deliver him to school, and give in him the habit of sound and temperate thinking. That object ought to appeal to all right-thinking and right-feeling people, irrespective of any selfish consideration, just out of a broader sympathy for their fellow men, and a desire to touch the lives of countless men and women who perhaps will never hear of this organization, and will know as little about it and its influence in their lives as the dweller on the shores of the Shetland Islands knows about the Gulf Stream, which makes his garden bloom in summer, where otherwise there would be but desolation."

In opening the meeting, Dr. Adler said: "Child labor work makes a special and incisive appeal to us for three reasons; first, because of the enormity of the thing. It is profound sorrow that such work should be necessary, profound humiliation that in our American civilization there should be 10,000 children in 150 mills, under sixteen years of age; in 150 factory establishments there should be more than 4,000 children thirteen and under, and of those more than 2,000 twelve and under, down to eight, and even in some instances to seven and six. The appeal of the movement for the abolition of child labor comes to us because it seems simply intolerable that these things should go on. This humiliating condition, this blemish upon our American civilization, should be removed. We must use our power and our influence to bring this result to pass.

"There are other kinds of philanthropy which we approve. There are good things we like to see blossom, but possibly civilization can stand without them. The appeal is not so piercing as that of the 4,000 and more children in 150 establishments, thirteen years and younger, working 60 to 64 hours a week, as a rule, and some of them doing night work from six o'clock in the evening to six o'clock in the morning, when your little ones are tucked safely in their beds. Why is it that American mothers do not rise up in protest and say, 'This thing must cease.'

"This is the first reason, because the thing is so impossible, so horrible. If you read the reports of our field workers, you will find other data quite as incredible—work in the canneries, for instance, where 125 young children, baby children, one three years old, had been found at work.

"The second reason is that, unlike most social evils, this is an evil that can be abated at once. Child labor can be abolished in a day if the American people so decree. 'Let my people go, my little people.' That is all you need to say, 'Let them depart out of the house of bondage, and the chains will fall from them.'

"And the third reason why we are so tremendously interested in it is because of the great, positive results that will come when we have taken these children out of the mills and put them into the schools, because every little child, as has been said, is an asset for humanity.

"Now, we have in this conference to touch chiefly upon the relation of child labor to education. We have been constantly met with the objection that it is useless to take the child out of the mill. I say it is not useless. Take a child that works from six o'clock at night until six o'clock in the morning, or any child that works in the mills 60 to 64 hours a week, free it, send it out into the streets into God's sunshine; and you have done far better than to keep it where it is. But we realize the obligation, that if we take the child out of the mill we ought to send it to school, and we want to discuss the kind of school, the kind of great, beneficient, new American school we are planning—the vocational school with industrial and agricultural training that will fit the child for its task—for citizenship; the school that will make the child in his own humble way the Messianic influence in the world. This is the reason we have selected education for our special topic."

Addresses were then delivered by E. O. Holland, Superintendent of Schools, Louisville, Kentucky, on "Vocational Work in the Public Schools";*

* All the articles thus marked are printed separately in this number.

by Carroll G. Pearse, Superintendent of Milwaukee Public Schools, President of the National Education Association, on "Child Labor and the Future Development of the School";* and by Dr. Samuel McCune Lindsay of Columbia University, on "Education, a National Obligation." *

The Chairman then referred to the bill pending in Congress for the establishment of a Children's Bureau, which, he reported, was to be voted upon in the Senate on the following Tuesday, and called on the General Secretary of the National Child Labor Committee, who read the following resolution:

"*Resolved,* That the National Child Labor Committee, in annual meeting at Louisville, Kentucky, and representatives of State Committees and other child welfare organizations, also delegates appointed by the governors of twenty-two states, and citizens of Louisville, in mass-meeting here assembled, unanimously indorse Senator Borah's Bill for a National Children's Bureau now pending and to be voted on in the United States Senate next Tuesday, and earnestly urge their senators and representatives in Congress to vote for this highly important measure which will secure for the people of all the states the needful information on which to base wise state legislation and thereby abolish the evils of child labor and promote other reforms for the health and education of children."

The resolution was adopted by acclamation, and after announcements for the next day's session the meeting adjourned.

Session II

The second session was devoted to "Street Trades and the Public School." Edward W. Frost, Esq., Milwaukee, Chairman of the Wisconsin Child Labor Committee, presided. He discussed the need for juvenile courts, more practical educational methods, and the coöperation of all agencies interested in child welfare, in order to make child labor laws effective, especially those regulating street trades. He called attention to the fact that the development of interest in the eight-hour day and in the exclusion of children from certain forms of manufacturing and mercantile life would tend to bring heavier pressure upon street trades, and to turn children toward labor in sweatshops, unless statesmanlike policy can be adopted which will include these occupations. He referred to the new street trades law in Wisconsin, and to the coöperation of the state industrial commission with the school authorities; and asked the members of the Conference to watch the operation of the law which had just passed.

The Chairman then introduced the following addresses, which were delivered and will appear in the next Bulletin: "Connection Between Street Trading and the School," Z. L. Potter; "The Proper Standard for Street Trades Regulation, Ways and Means to Secure It," Edward N. Clopper; "Enforcement of Street Trades Regulation," Lillian A. Quinn. Following these addresses, the subject was discussed by Mrs. Millie R. Trumbull,

Secretary of the Oregon Child Labor Commission, Portland, Oregon; Mrs. Esther Faulkenstein, Head Resident of the Esther Faulkenstein Settlement, Chicago; Edward N. Clopper; Mrs. Florence Kelley, and others.

Session III

The third session was devoted to "Industrial Training and Vocational Guidance"; Dr. Helen T. Woolley, Cincinnati, Director of the Survey of Children at Work, presiding. William H. Elson, formerly Superintendent of Schools, Cleveland, Ohio, spoke of the "Relation of Industrial Training to Child Labor."* A paper by Alice P. Barrows, New York, Director of the Vocational Guidance Survey, on "Possibilities and Dangers of Vocational Guidance"* was read by the Secretary of the Conference, and an address on "Social Uses of the School" was given by Miss Pauline Witherspoon, of the Louisville Girls' High School. Miss Witherspoon said:

"There are many reasons for using the schoolhouse as a recreation center. The simplest, and the one which seems to appeal to most people, is that of economy. We are using our schools for regular instruction four or five hours a day, five days a week, twenty days a month and eight months a year—that is, about 800 hours annually. Now, if we reckon from eight o'clock in the morning until ten in the evening, the possible number of hours the school buildings might be used, we find that instead of 800 only the same building might be used 5,000 hours every year; that is, five-sixths of the time our school plant is lying idle.

"A greater reason than economy for the use of the school building as a social center is to give the people of the community an opportunity to come in touch with the great questions of to-day. Our ordinary school course does not give a broad viewpoint and understanding; and we owe it to the people to supplement their earlier training with public lectures and discussions. All around our school buildings are commercialized amusements; and these amusements are very easy to get. They do not require dressing up or carfare; and therefore people who are tired from the day's work drop into them naturally. It must be our aim to make the free recreation center in the local school as attractive and as easy to attend as the commercialized center, and in this free recreation center we must give opportunities for self-culture.

"The third use of the schoolhouse is for the prevention of lawlessness. In Rochester they found that when a social center was fully in operation, the juvenile court record for the district around the schoolhouse dropped fifty per cent. Our taxpayers are building schools, juvenile courts, jails and reformatories; but, as prevention is always better than correction, let us put our money into the schoolhouses, and as a natural result the expense at the other end will be cut off.

"Finally, one of the highest reasons for the social center is the need of city people to know each other. We need to get together, to make acquaintances, to form friendships.

"A little over a year ago the social center movement was started by the Woman's Club in Louisville. There are three general methods of starting such movements: by public lectures, civic clubs and political discussions, and recreation. We tried all three. Before opening the center we called mass-meetings in the district, and explained the idea to the people. We sent out circulars and personally visited different families to enlist their coöperation. Then we opened one center with public illustrated lectures on art, literature, travel, and current events. We added dances in the kindergarten room, a Housekeepers' Conference, a young men's civic club, a girls' class in folk dancing, games for the children, and a public reading room. It did not seem advisable to admit persons under 14 in the evening, since that tended to keep older boys and girls away, and we, therefore, opened the building to the children after school hours. In one schoolhouse we have a large gymnasium, in which interest largely centers. In that same school, also, is a civic club of about 60 men, who meet in one of the rooms in the basement, where they talk and smoke.

"The social center idea will materially affect plans for the building of schoolhouses. In the future, I believe, no school building will be erected without an auditorium opening on the street and capable of being shut off from the rest of the building. There will be some rooms with movable desks and comfortable chairs in which a grown person may sit. Of course, the primary use of the school building is for the instruction of children, but these changes need not interfere.

"The problem of running a social center comes down to two things: equipment and helpers. The equipment is what is found in the school building, applied with a little ingenuity. As to helpers, we find it wisest to call upon the people themselves for most of the work. They are very willing—sometimes willing in proportion to their inability to handle the situation—but if you can make them feel that they are put in charge, not because they are better than other people in the neighborhood, but because they are able to promote the use of the building, they make very efficient helpers. You must have one person—or more than one—who is able to put his whole time into the scheme, to gather up workers, direct their energies, decrease friction, and take general charge. If such a person is found, I see no reason why you cannot start a social center anywhere."

These papers were followed by the Chairman's address, "What the School Can Do to Solve the Child Labor Problem." *

SESSION IV

The fourth session on Friday afternoon was devoted to a conference of state committees, Owen R. Lovejoy, General Secretary of the National Committee, presiding. In the general discussion Dr. Helen T. Woolley, of Cincinnati; Dr. Hubert W. Wells, of Wilmington, Chairman of the Delaware Child Labor Committee; Dr. John C. Granbery, Barboursville, W. Va., Chairman of the West Virginia Child Labor Committee; Hon. Edgar T. Davies, Chicago, Chief Factory Inspector of Illinois, and Mrs. Millie R. Trumbull, Portland, Oregon, Secretary of the Oregon Child Labor Commission, discussed the problem of street trades, night messenger service, and tenement house industries.

The Chairman called upon Edward F. Brown, Special Agent of the National Child Labor Committee, to report briefly his investigation of the night messenger service, based upon original study of this problem in about 25 states. Mr. Brown said in part:

"Broadly speaking, the messenger service is an organization which supplies laborers for indiscriminate light work. The necessity for inviolable secrecy regarding the messenger's work is apparent, and the possibilities of a dishonest and illegal exploitation of this necessary secrecy become obvious to any keen observer. It is not the character of the office which settles the educational value of the night messenger's work, but it is the character rather of the service his employer solicits and caters to.

"In such a study we are struck at the outset by the difference in the character of American cities by day and by night. Aften ten o'clock at night most of the calls come from those who move in the circle of the underworld. It may be the demand of the inmate of the brothel for food; or the saloon may have an order of drink to be delivered to a bawdy house; the prostitute may seek to send a note to her lover; or the patron of a resort may wish to make an assignation, and a messenger is to carry the message. The opium or cocaine victim is in need of the drug, and the messenger can get it. These and numerous other errands fall to those boys unfortunate enough to engage in this occupation.

"Obviously such a round of duties performed by boys in the midst of the most susceptible period conduces to an abnormal impression of life, and a perverted sense of morality. The lure of the night shift is twofold—the tips at night are large and numerous; the glamor of the night life offers everything the youthful instincts crave. It is only necessary to offer the night messenger liberal largess, and he will attempt almost anything the moral or legal code prohibits.

"The contact of day messengers with professional and business offices spurs boys on to some ambition, and the likely boy is quickly taken up. The night service offers nothing. There is little or no promotion. No attempt is made to instruct the boys in any useful trade. The havoc wrought by the unnatural hours of sleep, irregularity of meals, exposure to the inclemencies of the night, the absence of supervision is added to the danger of permitting adolescent boys to come in intimate contact with unfortunate women.

"The result of this investigation has been as follows: In New York, where the campaign was started, a law was secured prohibiting the employment of boys under 21 years of age as messengers between 10 o'clock at night and 5 o'clock in the morning. Massachusetts followed with a similar law.

Utah and Wisconsin have 21-year-age limit, as well as New Jersey, in cities of the first and second class. The 18-year-age limit prevails in Ohio, Oregon, California, Michigan, Tennessee and New Hampshire. The following states have 16-year-age limit: Idaho, North Dakota, Minnesota, Nebraska, Kansas, Missouri, Kentucky, Indiana, Louisiana, Vermont, Delaware and Georgia. The remaining have no restriction on the night messenger service."

Following Mr. Brown, the Chairman introduced a discussion of the problem of tenement home work, and referred especially to the abuses of this kind of child labor in New York City, reporting the investigation in progress for the purpose of securing remedial legislation in New York. He explained that there is practically no age limit for child labor in New York tenement house work, except an age limit for school children. No child of school age can be at work in a tenement during school hours without disobeying the compulsory school law. As a result children of school age are ordinarily found at work only in the morning and after school hours at night. There are, however, many little children under age, and the Committee reported having found boys and girls of four, five, six and seven years "who do not violate the compulsory school law, and therefore can be worked as many hours as they can keep their little eyes open."

The session was then briefly addressed by Judge Howard Kennedy, of Omaha, Chairman of the Nebraska Child Labor Committee; Hon. W. W. Williams, Chief Factory Inspector of Missouri, who urged that one of the chief defects in the enforcement of child labor laws is the inadequate appropriation from state funds to employ sufficient inspectors to cover the field; and Hon. C. L. Daugherty, Labor Commissioner of Oklahoma, who reported that Oklahoma had been saved from the great abuses of child labor partly because of the law passed in the second state legislative session; and explained the operation of the compulsory education law and the relief of indigent parents, saying: "If there is a widowed mother or parents who are dependent upon the earnings of their children, while they are complying with the compulsory education law, the Commissioners of the County must appropriate from county funds an amount sufficient to support the parents while their children are at school." Hon. James A. Starling, Labor Commissioner of Texas, reported the recent legislative campaign and the purpose of the Department to see the law still further amended and supplemented by compulsory school laws; Hon. J. Ellery Hudson, Chief Factory Inspector of Rhode Island, urged upon the Committee and its friends the importance of coöperation with the Factory Inspection Departments, saying, "As a rule the factory inspection departments in all states are in far greater need of coöperation than criticism, and where criticism should come, coöperation should always precede." The discussion was closed by the Chairman, who urged the importance of organized public sentiment to coördinate and reinforce the activities of all constituted authorities. Addresses were then delivered by Mrs. Frederick Crane, New York, on "How to Interest Young People"; * and by Richard K. Conant, Boston, Secretary of the Massachusetts Child Labor Committee, on "The Educational Test for Working Children." *

Session V

The fifth session, Friday afternoon, was a reception by the Women's Clubs of Louisville, at which Mrs. Pattie B. Semple, President of the Woman's Club, presided, and brief addresses were made by Dr. Felix Adler, Chairman of the National Child Labor Committee, and Miss Jean M. Gordon, formerly Factory Inspector of New Orleans.

Session VI

The sixth session, Friday evening, at the First Christian Church, was devoted to the subject "Unreasonable Industrial Burdens on Women and Children and the Effect on Education." Hon. Edward J. McDermott, Lieutenant-Governor of Kentucky, presided; urged the importance of improving state affairs as well as those of national significance, and expressed the belief that the child labor laws of Kentucky would be still further improved as the people came to understand their importance.

The Lieutenant-Governor quoted from a letter he wrote to the Labor Inspector when the child labor law of 1902 was passed in Kentucky, in which he said: "If we want to get intelligent citizens, vigorous in mind and body, and with sufficient education for the performance of the duties of citizenship, we must guard the young in their tender years from injurious and dangerous occupations. . . . We must protect our children from their own ignorance and helplessness, and also from the ignorance and brutality of their parents. Too often they are made the support and the victims of lazy, thriftless, or degraded parents, and the law for the punishment of all parents guilty of such criminal conduct should be applied in all its might." He also spoke in favor of the pending bill to regulate the hours of employment of women, and introduced as the speakers of the evening on the general topic Mrs. Florence Kelley,* of New York, General Secretary of the National Consumers' League; Mrs. Millie R. Trumbull,* Portland, Oregon, Secretary Oregon Child Labor Commission; Rev. John A. Ryan, D. D.,* St. Paul, Minn., Professor of Moral Theology and Economics, St. Paul Seminary; and Miss Jean M. Gordon,* formerly State Factory Inspector of New Orleans.

Session VII

This session was devoted to "The Relation of Rural Schools to Child Labor Reform," the General Secretary of the National Child Labor Committee presiding in the absence of Dr. A. J. McKelway, of the Southern office, who was called to Washington by the pending Children's Bureau Bill. Addresses were delivered by Miss M. Edith Campbell, Cincinnati, Director of the Schmidlapp Fund, on "The Economic Value of Education";* and Mr. Zenas L. Potter, Buffalo, New York, Field Secretary of the New York Child Labor Committee, on "Child Labor in the Canneries of New York State." *

In discussing the administration of laws in many of the agricultural communities, where child labor abounds, Mr. Edward F. Brown said: "Two years ago in Delaware we found a little girl of eight years working at the capping machines in a corn cannery, while 60 cans passed before her eyes every minute for nine hours. We found that the principal of the local high school was the paymaster in this cannery. When we objected the owner said there was nothing harmful in having the local superintendent subsidized in his cannery, and he thought there was nothing harmful in the employment of young children in this industry, especially at the capping machine, which, I believe, is considered hazardous by all who know what it is."

Chief Factory Inspector W. W. Williams, of Missouri, said the canning industry was not of great consequence in Missouri, but that however important it was, his department had no jurisdiction over it; that the law in Missouri not only exempted agricultural pursuits and domestic service, but all cities under 10,000 inhabitants. He said a few canneries were located in the small towns, "and I know positively they are working all kinds of time because there is no one to enforce the law. The same is true with the strawberry season. We run train after train out of Missouri with strawberries, and if the industry grows to any alarming extent in our state we may have a decision something similar to the New York decision, declaring that the entire canning industry is an agricultural pursuit."

The paper of Miss Campbell raised a number of important questions about the economic value of education, and the discussion turned upon the kinds of industry in which children engage and the difficulty of getting adults to perform the simpler industrial processes. The Chairman of the meeting said: "Many people believe that when our inventions, the products of the genius of our race, come to be regarded by Society as labor-saving machinery instead of profit-making machinery, we shall then understand that there is no reason why a full grown man or woman should not operate an almost automatic machine. There is no reason why we should put a machine in the hands of a baby simply because it is almost automatic, except that we can get the baby to do it for less money than it costs to get a man or woman."

The Chairman called on Professor Leavitt, of the University of Chicago, who urged that our educational institutions should be more fully adapted to the needs of the larger number of children. He said: "Our educational institutions are shaped primarily for those who go through, who go to the top, and very little attention is paid to the boy, and still less to the girl, who must drop out very near the bottom." He referred to the intense interest of the child entering the adolescent stage in industrial problems—a very proper interest—and urged that our schools give a variety of opportunities so as to meet the needs of different tastes and desires. He said: "It seems to me our schools are a very excellent example of the factory system of production; machines where we are trying to turn out people exactly alike. Our schools should turn out children, either by graduation or otherwise, as different as nature intended them to be, and as their future positions in life shall demand that they be. Everyone should be equally well prepared for the particular place in life which he must or will occupy. The one thing our schools ought to do, if they fail in everything else, is to turn children out of school eventually loving it, not hating it, as is the case with a majority of the children who now leave school." He referred to the desire of children for activity and for work, saying: "The trouble with our industrial arrangement is that people are being worked," and cited the words of Booker T. Washington, "There's a heap of difference between working and being worked." He urged that under proper conditions children might be taught the dignity of labor, and be taught to love labor, but it must be in such a spirit as to be entirely free from the element of exploitation. He referred to successful efforts being made in a number of cities to introduce practical features into the higher grades.

The Chairman approved the suggestion of Professor Leavitt and said that, having discovered in reformatories and in similar institutions that physical activity and the ability to produce things tend to the happiness and development of children confined there, our educators ought to learn "either to revolutionize our whole school system or do something that will give these opportunities to the boy or girl who does not commit an offense against society, and thus receive them as punishment."

In discussing industrial opportunities Mr. Wells, of Delaware, asked what advantage high school or college graduates show in industry above those with lesser educational opportunity, and Miss Campbell expressed the belief that employers did not demand high school or college graduates for particular positions; that there was very little evidence of the higher economic value of these advanced grades. Mrs. Trumbull, Portland, Oregon, said: "My dream of keeping children out of the industrial field until they are eighteen has been referred to so often I must explain it a little more definitely. I mean that children should be kept out of paid service. I think we are adapting our schools and our whole system of dealing with the child to the profit-making system. We are not considering the child as a child, we are considering him as a part of the great industrial machine and trying to adapt our schools to a process that will make him a more efficient cog in that machine. If we want to make a prize animal of any kind, we adapt the whole condition to that animal. We are not doing this with our children; we are attempting to turn out that child as a bit of machinery. A millionaire manufacturer in my state said to me the other day: 'The mistake of the present day civilization is that we are allowing individuals to capture the life of the nation, instead of making the life of the nation the property of the whole community; and we are turning our children, we are turning everything, into that one ideal, so that man can level down instead of taking the child and leveling up.' I believe our child labor reform should attempt to make the child a wonderful man or woman, and not a wonderful invention of this industrial age."

Professor Ernest Burnham of the Western Normal College, Kalamazoo, Michigan, spoke of "Rejuvenating the Rural School," * and Professor John M. Gillette, of North Dakota State University, spoke on "Rural Child Labor." *

The Chairman then called on Mr. Chute, who recited briefly the results of the Committee's investigation of child labor in the cranberry bogs of New Jersey, and urged the importance of such legislation as would protect the child and its family by proper housing conditions, and protect the child from loss of schooling at the beginning and end of the school year.

At the close of the meeting the Chairman read a letter from W. O. Hart, Esq., of New Orleans, one of the Commissioners on Uniform Laws of the American Bar Association, and said: "Last year at Boston at the twenty-first annual meeting of the Commissioners, a uniform bill was indorsed by the Association, to be presented to the legislatures of all states. The bill was drafted in coöperation with the National Child Labor Committee. It is compiled of the best features of these laws. Since the American Bar Association has indorsed this and recommended it to the country it has had the indorsement of several other national organizations. It seems to me fitting that this assembly should respond affirmatively to the request of Mr. Hart, and give the American Bar Association whatever influence we may exert in getting it before the legislatures of the various states." Thereupon Mr. E. N. Clopper, of Cincinnati, presented the following resolution, which was adopted:

"*Whereas,* The lack of uniformity in the laws of our states for the protection of children in industry and the great difference in the standards of enforcement have been most strikingly shown by the reports of delegates to this conference from every part of this country,

"Therefore, *Be It Resolved* by this Eighth Annual Conference on Child Labor, That it heartily indorses the Uniform Child Labor Law recently drafted by the United States Commissioners on Uniform State Laws in connection with the American Bar Association, and that all state officials, social workers, school authorities, religious organizations, women's clubs, and all other associations interested in the welfare of the children of this country be urged to familiarize themselves with the provisions of this proposed law, and to work for its passage in their own states, so that the evil of child labor may thus through a great national movement be brought under control by the same standard in all our states.

"And *Be It Further Resolved,* That copies of these resolutions be sent to all state child labor committees, including copies of the proposed law, for the purpose of propaganda."

Session VIII

The eighth session, on Saturday morning, was for the discussion of "Child Labor and Compulsory Education," Edward N. Clopper, Cincinnati, presiding. Papers were read by Professor W. H. Hand, State High School Inspector, Columbia, South Carolina, on "Need of Compulsory Education in the South," * and by John Porter Hollis, of Rock Hill, South Carolina, Special Agent of the National Child Labor Committee, on "A Legislative Program for South Carolina." *

The chairman then called upon William R. Collicotte, of Colorado, Vice-President of the National Farmers' Union, who discussed the need for the passage of the pending Federal Children's Bureau Bill. Commissioner James A. Starling, of the Texas Bureau of Labor, urged the importance of compulsory education laws for the state, but suggested the possibility of securing local option in compulsory education where state laws could not be passed.

Luncheon Meeting

Luncheon at Neighborhood House, Saturday, January 27, 2 p. m. The members of the Conference were entertained at luncheon at Neighborhood House on the invitation of Miss Frances Ingram, Head Worker, and the Board of Directors, and addresses were given by Mrs. Millie R. Trumbull, Owen R. Lovejoy, and Hon. P. P. Claxton, United States Commissioner of Education. These addresses were devoted to a discussion of "The Relation of Industrial Education to the Child Labor Problem."

Saturday Afternoon Session

On Saturday afternoon, January 27th, at 3 o'clock, a special session was held for the purpose of discussing such topics as had been crowded out, and especially for giving factory inspectors an opportunity to discuss the technical problems of their official work. Mr. Snyder, of the State Federation of Labor, referred to the fact that the entire movement against child labor in this country had its birth in the ranks of organized labor. He urged the importance of equal pay for equal work when women are employed, and referred to the standards established by the typographical union, where the principle holds. Mr. Clopper, the Chairman, said: "I can say from personal experience that much of our child labor legislation would not be upon the statute books to-day had it not been for the earnest efforts of labor unions."

Others who spoke at the session were: Mrs. Trumbull, of Portland,

Oregon; Hon. George Kennedy, Chief Factory Inspector of Tennessee, who discussed the difficulties of factory inspection with so small a force; Mrs. V. H. Lockwood, of the Indiana Child Labor Committee, who spoke of the recent development of a good child labor law in that State; Hon. Edgar T. Davies, Chief Factory Inspector of Illinois; Judge Kennedy, of Omaha; Mrs. W. L. Murdoch, of Birmingham, Alabama; and Commissioner W. W. Williams, of Missouri. Charles L. Chute, of New York, read a paper on "The Administration of Child Labor Laws." This will appear in the July issue of the Child Labor Bulletin.

Session IX

The session on Saturday evening was devoted to "Federal Aid to Education." Dr. Felix Adler, Chairman of the National Child Labor Committee, delivered his annual address;* Mrs. Florence Kelley, Secretary of the National Consumers' League, spoke on "Part Time Schools,"* and George F. Ross, M. D., of Greensburg, North Carolina, Superintendent of Health for Guilford County, spoke on "Extending Medical Inspection From Schools to Mills."* An address by Dr. A. J. McKelway on "Child Labor and Democracy"* was read by title.

Session X

The closing session of the Conference was held at Macauley's Theater on Sunday afternoon, January 28, at 3 o'clock, Hon. Augustus E. Willson, Ex-Governor of Kentucky, presiding. Addresses were delivered by Congressman Andrew J. Peters, of Massachusetts, on "The Federal Children's Bureau";* John P. Frey, of Cincinnati, Editor of the *Molders' Journal*, on "The Social Cost of Child Labor,"* and Hon. P. P. Claxton, United States Commissioner of Education, on "An Educational Substitute for Child Labor."*

In commenting upon the address of Congressman Peters, Ex-Governor Willson said: "State rights do not interfere with this proposition. Of course, the care of the children of the state is the business of the state, and the laws about it must be made by the state. But we must have information about so important a subject. Whether this should be done by law or by philanthropic organizations like this, it is the business of the people to get whatever information they can. Congressman Peters has put the idea correctly that the National Children's Bureau will establish a standard by which everything must be measured; and it will be a very valuable thing."

Mr. Lovejoy, General Secretary of the National Child Labor Committee, then introduced the following resolution, which was adopted unanimously:

"*Whereas,* Our federal government does not at present provide any agency for gathering and distributing such information relative to the welfare of children as is efficiently supplied by government bureaus in relation to other less valuable forms of life, and,

"*Whereas*, There is before Congress a bill introduced by Senator William E. Borah, of Idaho, and Congressman Andrew J. Peters, of Massachusetts, for the establishment in the Department of Commerce and Labor of a Children's Bureau, to gather and publish to the people of the United States information relating to the welfare of child life, and,

"*Whereas*, This bill has been favorably reported by committees in both houses of Congress, and has been indorsed by nearly every national organization engaged in studying and improving the conditions of childhood, as affording the only means of securing authoritative information,

"Therefore, *Be It Resolved*, That the National Child Labor Committee, in Eighth Annual Conference, together with state child labor committees, delegates appointed by governors of twenty-two states, and citizens of Kentucky here assembled, indorse the Children's Bureau Bill and especially urge favorable action on this bill in the United States Senate on Tuesday, January 30th, when by agreement the bill comes to vote, and in the House of Representatives at the earliest possible date.

"*Resolved*, That copies of this resolution be forwarded to Senator Borah and Congressman Peters, with expressions of our appreciation for their active interest in this meritorious measure."[1]

Introducing Mr. Frey, Ex-Governor Willson said: "The working people of this country compose the majority of the strength, the bone, the sinew, and the conscience of the people. There are more working people's children than any other kind; and therefore there is greatest sense in having every workingman's influence, and the influence of every workingman's organization, and the influence of all who are trusted to act for the workingmen in behalf of all these movements to better the condition of children and improve their chances for citizenship."

Following Commissioner Claxton's address, the General Secretary of the National Child Labor Committee introduced the following resolution, which, at the request of Ex-Governor Willson, he submitted to vote, and the resolution was adopted unanimously:

"*Whereas*, This, the Eighth Annual Conference on Child Labor, has been the most successful in the experience of the National Child Labor Committee as to the extent of interest aroused and the securing of the effective coöperation of the people in this movement for the protection of children in industry,

"Therefore, *Be It Resolved* by the National Child Labor Committee, That its sincere thanks be tendered the Kentucky Child Labor Association, the Louisville Convention and Publicity League, all local members, the Woman's Club, the churches, the Neighborhood House, and the people of Louisville generally, for their cordial reception and entertainment, their hearty coöpera-

[1] See footnote, Mr. Peters' address, p. 85.

tion both before and during the conference, and their earnest and successful efforts, making it of real educational value to the state and nation."

The meeting closed with a brief address by the Chairman of the National Child Labor Committee, Dr. Adler. Dr. Adler said, in reference to the suggestion of one of the speakers that children should be taught to work with a view to adding to the family revenue, "To my mind that is a moral idea that applies to the adult; but for the blessed little child, I wish to say that in my opinion the child should receive freely. 'Freely ye have received,' He said to us parents, 'and freely give.' I believe the child should return only with its beaming little eyes and its heart brimful of recognition of love. I should not like the child to work for revenue. As soon as you introduce the idea of raising articles for the purpose of selling, even at the rate of $3,000 an acre, you cannot avoid the impetus to drive the child.

"My thought in conclusion of this great meeting is this: I have been stirred by a good many addresses, but the thing that pained me as well as caught my heart strings was the address by Mr. Frey. I had never seen the advertisement which he put before us,[1] and as an American citizen I feel profoundly humiliated that one of these United States should offer as an inducement for capitalists to invest within its borders the savage booty of freedom—absolute freedom—to exploit the child. When we speak of the need of education I would say that it seems to me perhaps there is something even more pitiful than that the child is exploited, that the child of whom Dr. Claxton has spoken spurs itself by drinking strong coffee in the night so as to get through its shift by four or five in the morning; there is something more pitiful to my mind than its pinched features, its colorless face, its lack-luster eye, and that is the state of mind of the man who exploits it. That American democracy should have produced this type, that here as no where else in the world, not in monarchies, not in aristocracies, here as the fruit of democracy we should have this boundless, unscrupulous exploitation of children—that is the thought that should give us pause.

"We speak of building up the great democracy, and preparing its children for citizenship. Reflect upon the condition of democracy in America as evidenced by child exploitation. When I attend such conventions as this, when I see such facts as this, I say to myself, 'America, *quo vadis?*' 'America, whither art thou drifting?' Is that what we have a right to expect as the fruit of free institutions? When I was in Europe a few years ago men sneered at democracy. They said that our democracy was a failure; that we were dollar-mad, that we were so conceited we strutted on the stage of the world as if we were the admiration of other nations and did not perceive that others hissed at us; that we were the scorn of the enlightened of other nations because our vaunted free institutions had turned into dollar-

[1] See page 118.

democracy; everything—even our children—sacrificed to the dollar. That is what they say of us.

"We do not feel that they are right; we do not believe that democracy has failed. We know we are going to do better, we are going to change all this; but we need your help. We want you to feel how serious the problem is. We hope we have left some stimulating influence with you; and that we have your support in this great work which concerns not only the children and not only the future, but the good name, the honor, the fair fame, the decent reputation of the country to which we belong, and to which we are devoted.

"I thank you on behalf of our committee for the support you have given us. I assure you we shall go away from Louisville freshly stimulated and encouraged."

In closing the meeting Ex-Governor Willson said: "I want to take a vote of our people in recognition of the very graceful thanks and the generous resolutions adopted by our visitors. All who feel that we are a thousand times more benefited by their visit than they have been by coming here, I ask all of you Kentuckians to prove it by a rising vote." The suggestion was unanimously adopted by a rising vote, whereupon the Eighth Annual Conference of the National Child Labor Committee was adjourned.

What the National Child Labor Committee is Doing to Combat Abusive Child Labor

THIRTY-NINE states have improved or enacted new child labor or compulsory education laws since its organization in 1904.

It drafted the Uniform Child Labor Law adopted in 1911 by the Commission on Uniform Laws of the American Bar Association.

It secured the establishment of the Children's Bureau in the Federal Government by a bill signed by the President, April 9, 1912.

It publishes literature on all phases of child labor; has a corps of expert investigators to study and photograph conditions throughout the country; has prepared for rental at nominal charge a set of stereopticon slides, with typewritten lecture, showing children at work, home environment, and the constructive features of its campaign; has prepared a traveling exhibit of photographs, charts, diagrams and actual samples of materials on which children work; provides public lecturers; provides legislative experts to draft and help secure improved laws.

It co-operates with physicians, officials and educators in order to provide to children excluded from prohibited work, physical, mental and moral opportunities needed to develop efficient citizenship.

It co-operates with relief societies to provide "Scholarships" for children of poor families forbidden work.

Six thousand contributing members supplied $55,000 to carry on the work of 1910–11. Sixty-four thousand dollars are needed this year.

To V. EVERIT MACY, Treasurer
  National Child Labor Committee
    105 East 22d Street, New York

I enclose $ for the help of little children at work in tenement sweatshops, coal breakers and coal mines, cotton mills and glass factories.

Enroll me in your membership and send me your literature for the coming year.

Signed..

  Address...

Membership Enrolment
Associate—Persons contributing annually $2 to $24
Sustaining   "   "   " $25 " $99
Guarantors   "   "   " $100 or more

National Child Labor Committee
INCORPORATED

ORGANIZED APRIL 15, 1904

105 East 22d Street	New York City
204 Bond Building	Washington, D. C.
803 Union Trust Building	Cincinnati, Ohio

OFFICERS

FELIX ADLER, Chairman
V. EVERIT MACY, Treasurer
SAMUEL McCUNE LINDSAY,
HOMER FOLKS, Vice-Chairmen

OWEN R. LOVEJOY, . . . General Secretary
A. J. McKELWAY, . Secretary for the Southern States
JOSEPHINE J. ESCHENBRENNER, Membership Secretary

BOARD OF TRUSTEES

FELIX ADLER, Chairman
JANE ADDAMS
FRANCIS G. CAFFEY
ROBERT W. DE FOREST
EDWARD T. DEVINE
HOMER FOLKS
WILLIAM E. HARMON
MRS. FLORENCE KELLEY
JAMES H. KIRKLAND
SAMUEL McCUNE LINDSAY
V. EVERIT MACY
ISAAC N. SELIGMAN
LILLIAN D. WALD
PAUL M. WARBURG
JOHN W. WOOD

OBJECTS

To PROMOTE THE WELFARE OF SOCIETY, WITH RESPECT TO THE EMPLOYMENT OF CHILDREN IN GAINFUL OCCUPATIONS.

To INVESTIGATE AND REPORT THE FACTS CONCERNING CHILD LABOR.

To RAISE THE STANDARD OF PUBLIC OPINION AND PARENTAL RESPONSIBILITY WITH RESPECT TO THE EMPLOYMENT OF CHILDREN.

To ASSIST IN PROTECTING CHILDREN BY SUITABLE LEGISLATION AGAINST PREMATURE OR OTHERWISE INJURIOUS EMPLOYMENT, AND THUS TO AID IN SECURING FOR THEM AN OPPORTUNITY FOR ELEMENTARY EDUCATION AND PHYSICAL DEVELOPMENT SUFFICIENT FOR THE DEMANDS OF CITIZENSHIP AND THE REQUIREMENTS OF INDUSTRIAL EFFICIENCY.

To AID IN PROMOTING THE ENFORCEMENT OF LAWS RELATING TO CHILD LABOR.

To CO-ORDINATE, UNIFY, AND SUPPLEMENT THE WORK OF STATE OR LOCAL CHILD LABOR COMMITTEES, AND ENCOURAGE THE FORMATION OF SUCH COMMITTEES WHERE THEY DO NOT EXIST.

Persons who contribute $2 or more annually toward the support of the child labor campaign are enrolled as associate members, $25 or more as sustaining members and $100 or more as guarantors of the Committee. Members receive the "Child Labor Bulletin" and other publications of the Committee and are thus kept in touch with the child labor movement throughout the country. Remittances may be sent to V. Everit Macy, Treasurer, 105 East 22d Street, New York City.

CHILD LABOR AND POVERTY

THE NORTH CAROLINA LEGISLATURE IN 1913 DECLARED THAT THE COMMERCIAL INTERESTS OF THE STATE REQUIRED SUCH AS THESE IN THE COTTON MILLS.

The Child Labor Bulletin

| Volume Two Number One | MAY, 1913 | Issued Quarterly |

CHILD LABOR AND POVERTY

The papers and addresses and discussions of the Ninth National Conference on Child Labor, held at Jacksonville, Fla., March 13-17, 1913, under the auspices of the National Child Labor Committee

PUBLISHED BY

National Child Labor Committee
INCORPORATED

105 East 22d Street, New York City

Press of
CLARENCE S. NATHAN
New York

CONTENTS

	PAGE
THE CHILD BREADWINNER AND THE DEPENDENT PARENT................................*Mrs. Florence Kelley*	1
CHILD WAGES IN THE COTTON MILLS: OUR MODERN FEUDALISM................................*Dr. A. J. McKelway*	7
CHILD LABOR AND NEED........................*M. Louise Boswell*	17
CHILD LABOR AND POVERTY: BOTH CAUSE AND EFFECT....................................*John A. Kingsbury*	27
SHALL CHARITABLE SOCIETIES RELIEVE FAMILY DISTRESS BY FINDING WORK FOR CHILDREN.—A SYMPOSIUM,	
I. *R. T. Solensten*	35
II. *Mary H. Newell*	39
ANCIENT STANDARDS OF CHILD PROTECTION.........*Rabbi David Marx*	42
CHILD LABOR AND LOW WAGES........................*Jerome Jones*	52
THE FEDERAL CHILDREN'S BUREAU..................*Julia C. Lathrop*	56
HOW TO MAKE CHILD LABOR LEGISLATION MORE EFFECTIVE....................*Dr. Samuel McCune Lindsay*	63
FROM MOUNTAIN CABIN TO COTTON MILL...........*John C. Campbell*	74
SOCIAL WELFARE AND CHILD LABOR IN SOUTHERN COTTON MILLS..............................*Rev. C. E. Weltner*	85
THE TEXTILE INDUSTRY AND CHILD LABOR.........*Richard K. Conant*	91
THE CAMPAIGN IN NORTH CAROLINA. THE MOUNTAIN WHITES—BY ONE OF THEM........................*W. H. Swift*	96
THE BURDEN ON CHILDREN IN SHRIMP AND OYSTER CANNERIES...*Lewis W. Hine*	105
NEGLECTED HUMAN RESOURCES OF GULF COAST STATES......................................*Edward F. Brown*	112
CHILD LABOR AND HEALTH........................*Dr. W. H. Oates*	117
DEVELOPING NORMAL MEN AND WOMEN..............*Jean M. Gordon*	121
CONDITIONS IN CHILD EMPLOYING INDUSTRIES IN THE SOUTH.—A SYMPOSIUM......... I. *Mrs. W. L. Murdoch*	124
II. *Mrs. E. L. Bailey*	128
III. *J. A. McCullough*	133
IV. *Edward F. Brown*	138
AN EIGHT HOUR DAY IN A TEN HOUR STATE...........*Henry Nichol*	142
PROCEEDINGS OF THE NINTH NATIONAL CONFERENCE ON CHILD LABOR...	145

THE CHILD BREADWINNER AND THE DEPENDENT PARENT.

Mrs. Florence Kelley,
General Secretary, National Consumers' League, New York.

We are confronted by the question, why have we so many child breadwinners, so many dependent parents, and who are the dependent parents?

Many children are at work because their fathers have deserted. We suffer particularly from desertion in the great port of entry of the State of New York. Fathers who cannot endure the strain of family life with precarious work leave, trusting to charity to care for their dependent children and wives better than they have been able to do. And so foolish has been much of our charity that that calculation has not by any means always been an error. It is, however, cheering, that exactly the people in the state in which desertion is a more serious problem than elsewhere, in relation to child labor, the people who are under the sorest temptation to desert, the poorest of the immigrants, the Russian-Jewish exiles, have themselves taken the initiative for bringing back recreant fathers. It is extraordinary to see in the Yiddish papers in New York City photographs of deserters and exact descriptions of them, and a request that the Garment Workers' Unions or the Cigar Makers' Unions—or whatever the trade of the fellow workers may be of these particular fathers—will send them home. In more than one state it has now been made a felony to desert minor children. It should be a felony everywhere—an extraditable offence. A cowardly father who leaves his children should be sent back to face his own community. That is one set of working children for whom surely pity, the deepest pity, must arise in the human heart—the children upon whom our ruthless society puts the burden of earning support which should be borne by the deserting father.

Industrial Accidents Produce Child Breadwinners.

Then there are the orphan children whose fathers have been killed in industry. We have an undue number of them because, for instance, in the second greatest manufacturing state in this Union, in Pennsylvania, for many years, the highest court of the state held that, where a working man who was killed was an alien whose family lived abroad, no claim could be made through any representative for any damages payable to that alien family living abroad. The consequence of that was the employment in Pennsylvania industries of so great a mass of detached alien men, who could be killed and maimed without claims for damages being brought against the employers, that the court's decision constituted a premium upon neglect of necessary safe-guards. In our second greatest state, thousands of men were hurt, were killed or permanently disabled without danger to the employer of claims pressed in behalf of their dependents. The inevitable consequence of that was a generally prevailing recklessness, through which our own working people have suffered with the alien employes. Hence we have in Pennsylvania so great a body of working children in dangerous employments as I believe cannot be found in a like population anywhere else in the world to-day. I think no other state has had so sinister a decision of its highest court, putting a premium on cruelty and recklessness.

We have no adequate workmen's compensation law sustained by any court in this country. And until we have adequate workmen's compensation laws sustained by the Supreme Court of the United States and the highest courts in the states, we shall always be having communities attempting to lay the burden of self-support, and the support of dependent mothers and dependent younger brothers and sisters, upon the too slender shoulders of the eldest child in such families, and of younger children, too.

Preventable Industrial Disease, a Cause.

Besides the children of deserting fathers, and the children of widows, and the children of men disabled by industrial injuries, we have another set of boys and girls upon whom industry, through ruthlessness towards the parents, places an undue burden. Those are the children whose fathers have been disabled by preventable industrial diseases. We have heard at this conference of the bad air which is characteristic of cotton mills from Georgia to Maine.

We have no good breathable air in spinning rooms that ever I have visited; and I have never heard of one where precautions for ventilation were taken with such interest in the lungs of the workers, as in the quality of the cotton spun, and the moisture and heat that are good for cotton. What is true of the cotton industry is true all the way down. We have nowhere any adequate premium put by any insurance, or by any compensation laws, on protecting the health of the breadwinner and keeping the breadwinner really the head of the family, alive and in the field of industry at his maximum earning power. We are far behind Germany and England in that respect. Even the most enlightened and advanced of our manufacturing states, even Massachusetts, which takes the lead in the medical inspection of the workers at their work, is still far behind Germany in this.

Multitudes of children work whose parents are dependent because their pay is too little. Here in Jacksonville I have been horrified at the spectacle of newsboys in the streets with no badges on their arms to show that they are allowed to sell papers as a premium on good behavior in school; with no indication that they are looked after by any official as future citizens of importance in the community. Of course, boys who are neglected, who are allowed to sell papers at any age, are going to be important citizens, for they are going to be very expensive convicts later on. When I asked about this, my attention was called to one particular boy as suggesting a complicated difficulty—a barefoot little chap who cannot go to school because he has no proper clothes, and has to sell papers in order to get what insufficient clothes he has. I asked whether his father was dead. "No, his father is living." "Is his father a drunkard?" "No, he is a working man." "Is he a lazy working man?" "No, he is a very hard working man." "What is the matter? That is a sinister thing if both father and son work, and the boy is out of shoes, and out of school for lack of shoes." "The City of Jacksonville pays the father only $1.35 a day for hard laboring work, and since he has a wife and seven children he cannot keep his oldest boy in shoes to be in school." There we have a dependent father with a vengeance, made dependent by the employer, which is the community in which he lives. And that kind of dependent parents we have all over our Republic—parents who are made dependent by their employers, whether public or private.

The Dependent Parent.

The dependent parent is usually the mother, for the reasons that I have suggested. The father deserts, or he becomes ill by reason of his occupation, or he is maimed by his occupation, or he is killed by his occupation. Ordinarily the dependent parent, so far as the child breadwinner is concerned, is the mother; because the tuberculous father is (or, should be) taken care of as a charity patient in the sanatorium. Then what about the dependent mothers? They usually work. But they receive such insufficient wage for their work that they usually, even in the more enlightened industrial states, have both to work taking care of the children in the home and then for the employer.

They may take goods into the home, or may go out of the home. And whichever they do, sooner or later they suffer a physical breakdown. That is what ordinarily happens when the mother of four, five or six children tries to be both mother and breadwinner, however much she may be helped by the child breadwinners in the families. There could not be a worse investment for any community in this age, than boys engaged in the messenger service and newspaper selling. There could not be a worse investment for the community than letting the widowed mother and her breadwinning children stagger along alone, as we do ordinarily, with doles from charity, but no adequate substitute for the wages which the departed or disabled father no longer affords.

In other words, dependent parents are, as a rule, dependent because we do not make Industry pay its way, and we try to make the unhappy children pay the bills due to the family from Industry. I think that is one of the very blackest spots of the whole black child labor stain upon this Republic, that we have gone on doing this as our industry has developed for the last sixty years. We have gone on letting the children pitifully try to make up in some small measure for the bills which industry has not paid.

For twenty years I have been urging that we should take care of the school children who are now by thousands out of the public schools, the children whose fathers are dead or disabled; and I am profoundly thankful that that subject has been forced upon the attention of charitable societies all over this country. The charitable societies have never efficiently and adequately met the needs of the children who are either forced into industry cruelly or forced out of industry and into the school by compulsory education laws, equally cruelly if no financial provision is made for their physical welfare. But now that we are getting mothers' pensions—they exist already in Missouri and Utah and Oklahoma and Oregon and California and Illinois—I am not altogether pleased at the way we are getting them, because we are now discussing charity, whereas we ought to be discussing the immeasurably more important question how to make industry pay its debts to these children. There ought not to be any suggestion of charity in relation to a child who has been deprived of his breadwinner, because industry has killed or disabled or sickened or tempted beyond his powers of resistance that breadwinner. The bill ought to be sent in to the Steel Trust if it has killed the breadwinner; or it ought to be sent in to the railway if that is responsible for the child's loss; and it ought to be sent in continuously as long as the period of the natural dependence of the child runs, or the period of statutory school attendance in states where, as in New York State, for instance, the period of enforced attendance continues until the child is sixteen years old, unless it has met a fairly rigid educational and physical test. And besides that we ought to send in the bill to industry for an adequate wage for the father who is working, when he has not been killed or disabled or sickened or tempted beyond his powers of resistance. We should not forget that.

So it seems to me that we are taking the third class first; that we ought first to get workmen's compensation laws effective for collecting the needed money for the child's education to the sixteenth birthday, and we ought to get minimum wages boards. They have begun in Massachusetts and Oregon and Washington and Utah already. There are already laws providing for minimum wages boards in those states. But they are very poor laws; they apply only to women and the great essential thing is that they should apply to men also, that they should apply to all the underpaid people in all the underpaid industries, and the underpaid industry is the industry which does not enable a man and woman to bring up a family of at least four children according to the standard that is set in the state in which the industry is carried on. Then, after we have collected from industry the bill for the necessaries of life for the children who have lost their breadwinners, or whose breadwinners are not now, under the competitive system, able to support those children according to our standards, then the remnant of widows would be a much more manageable portion of the population than the whole body of mothers now dependent upon the state or the community bids fair to be.

It is idle for us to pretend that money taken out of the taxes and given to widows who have been deprived of their breadwinners is not charity. Of course, it is charity; it is public charity. If we take it by begging from the pockets of philanthropists that is private charity. But if we collect it from the industry that has wrought the havoc, that is not charity; that is the merest justice. It is giving the children and families compensation for the loss of their breadwinner, not for the loss of their father as a father.

I am sorry that my own favorite measure which I have been advocating for twenty years has been dislocated from its relation to workmen's compensation and minimum wages boards, so that it gets discussed without regard to these. However, until we get them, I think the more we push the subject of education by means of public funds the better it is for the children.

The Remedy.

Most of these dependent parents, as I have said, are mothers. We think of them, sometimes, perhaps, with pity, but mostly we do not think of them at all. And I believe the reason that they are there is that society has not been compelled to think of them at all. They themselves have had nothing whatever to say about the laws surrounding industry—industrial insurance laws, or the absence of insurance laws, employer's liability laws, workmen's compensation laws, child labor laws, compulsory education laws. In all the states in which the conditions are worst for the children—in Pennsylvania and in all the southern states, the mothers do not have to be consulted about the children or about the laws. They simply provide the children and take the consequences. I believe that this will continue until, throughout our whole Republic, the responsibility for dealing with this complicated problem, this whole child labor problem, including the child breadwinner and the deserting father and the disabled father, is shared by the mothers, and they cease to be as politically dependent as their breadwinning children.

CHILD WAGES IN THE COTTON MILLS: OUR MODERN FEUDALISM.

A. J. McKelway, Washington, D. C.,
Southern Secretary, National Child Labor Committee.

"We work in *his* mill. We live in *his* houses. Our children go to *his* school. And on Sunday we go to hear *his* preacher." This is the pathetic plaint of the cotton mill workers of North Carolina, spoken more than once to our agent in North Carolina. It is refreshing to observe that at least the system of feudalism is recognized by the workers themselves. The expression we have quoted might be amplified with regard to some twenty or twenty-five mills in the South that are invariably advertised for their betterment work, with a significant silence as to the 700 other cotton mills that merely bask in the reflected glory of the "show mills." "We also go to *his* Y. M. C. A. when he has built one. We spend our leisure time, after the eleven-hour day, those of us who can read, in *his* reading room. Our children play in *his* streets. Our cow sleeps in *his* stable. We are sent to *his* store to buy our goods. When we are sick, or hurt in the mill, we go to *his* hospital. We are arrested by *his* constable, and tried by *his* magistrate. And when we die we are buried in *his* cemetery."

I have been assigned the discussion of two apparently unrelated subjects: Child Wages in the Cotton Mill, and Our Modern Feudalism. As a matter of fact, the two themes are as closely related as cause and effect, as I shall undertake to prove.

The children of the cotton mills whom we undertake to bring within the operation of the law prohibiting their employment are the children under fourteen years of age. They are employed mainly in the spinning rooms, and are principally spinners, doffers, band boys and sweepers. Children under fourteen have been found in other operations of the cotton mills, girl spinners sometimes graduating into weavers and boys occasionally found at the warping machine. The doffer boys work intermittently and much has been made of the fact that when they have replaced the empty spools with full ones, they can go out into the mill yard and play marbles. Nothing is said of the eleven-hour day, preventing all attendance at school by day, and making the night school oftentimes an added cruelty to tired and sleepy children. And nothing is ever said of the girl spinners who do not work intermittently but must ever be on the alert to watch the spinning frames and tie the broken threads.

Mr. R. M. Miller, Jr., of Charlotte, N. C., who recently appeared before the Ways and Means Committee of the House of Representatives to plead for protection against the competition of the "pauper labor of Europe" in the manufacture of cotton goods, once went into print to say, in opposition to a child labor bill which proposed the raising of the age-limit for girls only, from twelve to fourteen years of age, that 75 per cent. of the spinners of North Carolina were fourteen years old or under. It is one of the traditions of the cotton mill in the South, that spinning is work for girls, not for boys or women. And that tradition of the industry is directly in the face of all the teachings of medical science, as to the necessity for the especial care and protection of young girls at that period of life. Think of your own girls, fathers and mothers, standing at a spinning frame for eleven hours a day, or sometimes a night! Of 295 spinners found under 12 in Southern mills, 246 were girls.

Children's Wages High.

Now the wages which these children get, the doffers and spinners, are not low, considering the fact that it is child's work. The wages are comparatively high, considering the ages of the children. The Federal Bureau of Labor found in 1908-9, in the Southern mills that were investigated, the agents being required to prove the ages of the children, 17 children 7 years of age, 48 of eight years, 107 of nine, 283 of ten and 494 of eleven years of age. There is not much remunerative work that children from seven to eleven years can do in the South, not very much that children 12 to 14 years can do.

In a representative South Carolina cotton mill,
    doffers of 12 years were paid $3.54 per week
    doffers of 13 years were paid 3.92 per week
    doffers of 14 years were paid 5.04 per week
    doffers of 15 years were paid 4.75 per week

and doffers of 20 years and over were paid $2.52 per week, while the earnings of the spinners in 151 Southern mills were $4.54 a week and scrubbers and sweepers $2.96 a week. These are actual wages paid, not the wages computed for full time, which was an average of 62.7 hours per week.

Adult Wages Low.

But here is the impressive thing about the comparative wage of children and adults per week: 251 children under 12 years of age earned less than $2 per week and 731 children of twelve and thirteen earned less than $2 per week. But there were 1,700 workers from 14 to 20 years of age who earned less than $2 per week. And 1,085 operatives twenty-one years of age and over who earned less than $2 a week. There were more girls from 18 to 20 years of age earning less than $2 per week than there were of girls from 14 to 15 earning less than $2. There were 1,733 children under 16 who made from two to three dollars a week and there was almost an equal number, 1,712 workers, sixteen years and over, who earned the same wages. Children under 16 earning from three to four dollars a week numbered 2,426, and those from 16 to 21 and over earning from three to four dollars a week numbered 2,597.

Out of 32,409 workers in the cotton mills, whose actual wages per week were copied from the pay rolls, only 1,444 earned from $8.00 to $9.00 a week, and one of these was a boy and one a girl under 12 years of age. And when we come to the $12 limit, only 54 women out of 17,066 earned from $11 to $12 a week, and one of these was a girl under 16 years of age, while 241 men out of 14,000 reached that wage and one of these was a boy under 16.

I know of no employment in the South for girls under 14 that pays so well as work in the cotton mill, and only one employment for boys, the demoralizing messenger service which is vile for the night shift and bad for the day shift from association with the boys who work at night. And their wages are increased by the tips they get for serving the denizens of the underworld. But the facts driven home by these unquestioned figures is that the wages of children are high as compared with the wages of the adult workers. The same general result is shown, though with higher ages for children and a slightly higher scale of wages, for the New England mills.

Here is the temptation which the cotton mill in its long child-enslaving history, in Old England, in New England, in Pennsylvania and the South has set in the way of ignorant, indifferent or poverty-stricken parents. And who are mainly responsible for this—the employers, enlightened and educated men, able to read and to appreciate the full consequences of the child-labor system to the children, to the country and to democracy itself? Or the parent who supplies the demand which the cotton manufacturer creates? Whom does the enlightened conscience of mankind hold responsible for the introduction of African slavery into America and the British possessions to-day? The African chief who sold his people, already slaves to his lordly will, or the British or New England slave-trader who bought them and transported them?

And now perhaps we begin to see the relation between the comparatively high wages that the children receive and our modern system of feudalism. Why is it that a thousand workers 21 years and over out of 3,700 earn less than $2 a week in the cotton mills? It is because a thousand children under 14 can earn just as much. When the child can do the man's job or the woman's job, the man or woman must lose the job or take the wages that are paid the child. There is no escape from that conclusion. If there is anything the matter with the logic of the argument, I should like to have it pointed out.

When 17,517, more than half the employes whose wages were reported, earn less than $5.00 a week, I know they earn that small sum because out of the 17,517, there are 7,825 children under 16 who earn the same wages. In any child-employing industry the wages of the adult are measured by the wages of the child.

The children are offered wages that are high for a child and the children are employed, 40,000 of them in the cotton mill industry according to the manufacturers' own figures in 1909, as reported by the Census Bureau. The labor unions have known for a long time that child labor depresses wages. They are charged with selfishness in their advocacy of child labor reform. Even if that be true, I had rather see a man selfishly on the right side of a humane question than selfishly on the wrong side of it. I pay the cotton manufacturer the compliment of supposing that he is as intelligent as the trade unionist. Then he knows that child labor depresses wages and he holds on to the children whom he employs for a double purpose. First, because in the cotton mill, the child can do the work required. It is even claimed that the child can do it better than the adult, the work of spinning in particular. Then because he can get the children at children's wages, he naturally believes in equal pay for equal work, and the employment of children keeps down the wage-scale for all his employes. The children are members of the family. The family requires a certain amount of wages to live at all. The wages for the support of life can be obtained by the employment of several members of the family and large families of adult workers are rare. Therefore let the children work or let the family try starving for a while. So the cotton mill workers go to work as children. They get married as children. They become parents of other children while they are children themselves. Their illiteracy ranges from 44 per cent. in Georgia to 48 and 50 per cent. in the two Carolinas—children 10 to 14 years of age. Often they forget the little they have learned, and, as a South Carolina manufacturer recently confessed to me, there are practically no mill children over 12 in school. They have been condemned for life, with few exceptions, to an unskilled trade, in which there is not hope for advancement for 1 per cent. of the workers, while for 99 per cent. the maximum of efficiency is reached before manhood or womanhood is reached.

Feudalism.

Meantime, while the employes have become thus helpless the employers have grown more powerful. Forbidding their employes to organize in labor unions, the manufacturers are themselves organized in State and National Associations. And as the employes keep poor the employer grows rich and becomes independent enough to run his mill regardless of a temporary shut-down. Since the employer owns the house in which the operative lives he is landlord as well as employer. The only freedom yet retained by these helpless people is the liberty of changing their feudal lords, and there has been such bitter complaint of the migratory character of the cotton mill workers that I look to see some baronial edict put forth that no family will be employed at one mill that moves from another without the employer's consent. As for other employment, the operatives have often told me that after a few years or even months in the confinement and monotony of mill work they were unfitted for work on the farms from which they had come, requiring the exercise of muscle and brawn.

I have spoken at this conference my individual views, for which I alone am responsible, on the tariff question as related to child labor. At a meeting on February 13, last, in Charlotte, N. C., the Hard Yarn Spinners Association passed the following resolutions: "We are opposed to any material reduction in the present tariff that would place us in competition with the mills of Europe employing pauper labor." The same manufacturers passed resolutions against any advance in the protection of the working children. Now, disregarding the fact that with a tariff that is practically prohibitive on cotton goods the American consumer must pay a price for those goods made artificially high, the fact stands out that no part of that added profit finds its way into the pay-envelope. If the report of the tariff board is to be believed, the American cotton manufacturer, without any protection, has the advantage now against his English and German competitors. But the point I have often made is one which was recently endorsed by Miss Ida M. Tarbell in a personal letter, namely, that to make the employer more powerful through excessive profits is simply to make the employe more dependent. If the Southern manufacturer were obliged to accept the dividends that content his English or German rival, then there would be less of a sense of power over his employes. A few years ago, there was an attempt in a certain Southern mill district to organize the employes into a labor union. Some progress was made and the mills simply shut down and remained in masterly inactivity until the employes were scattered and the effort to organize them was given up. At the last meeting of the Virginia legislature the cotton mill men opposed a very slight advance in the child labor law and a manufacturer from Danville took a solid hour to tell of his benevolence and philanthropy, so far as his beloved employes were concerned, while I held in my hand a letter with the names of several girls in his mill who had been discharged because they had tried to form a union.

A book has recently been published with the help of cotton manufacturers defending child labor in the cotton mills. I do not regard it as an authority on any phase of the problem, but as one chapter of the book is devoted to the Pelzer Mill, and it seems to have been so pleasing to the manufacturer, who is called "the King of Pelzer," that he bought 140 copies of it to present to the members of the South Carolina Legislature, I may perhaps quote a paragraph as either history, or fiction, which the manufacturer seems to have approved and enjoyed.

Says the author: "I was told a story about these people that not only aptly illustrates their spirit of independence (*sic*), but also the tyranny of the King of Pelzer. The labor unions of the North had determined to organize the down-trodden mill operatives of the South, and they sent one of their delegates to Pelzer. . . . But he had scarcely arrived in the place, when his plans and movements were reported to the King. The King, seated at his office desk, listened to the report, and then quietly looking up at the clock said: 'The next train leaves at eleven; have the constable put him on that train.'" And the veracious historian comments with approval: "The order was obeyed as effectively as though it had been a royal or presidential decree with a Swiss Guard or a company of Mexican Rurales to enforce it." This is treated as a great joke. But the point is, that the man was probably a trespasser if he set foot in that village of more than a thousand souls, and the constable, though presumably an officer of the state, was only carrying out, in rather summary fashion, the law against trespass on one's private estate.

One of our agents, a lovable and gentle Christian minister, went to a cotton mill in Georgia, two miles from the railroad. He engaged a room at the hotel. Going first to the school he took some photographs of the children. Then the president of the mill learned of his presence (he had told his name and his errand), and ordered him not to trespass further, saying that the school as well as the mill, and even the streets of the mill were his property. Further investigation was impossible, and the minister then found that his room at the hotel was forbidden him, he was warned that it would be unsafe for him to remain in the village that night, and he had to return to the railroad station.

A mill just on the outskirts of Atlanta then, within the corporate limits now, after I had made some rather searching investigations and published the results, put up signs in the streets, forbidding anyone to enter the mill community without permission. This position, however, was too absurd to be maintained long. Another of our agents wrote a little sketch once entitled, "A Little Kingdom in Cotton-Land." He described a North Carolina cotton mill town where the whole mill community stood in awe of the superintendent, who was also magistrate and exercised all the functions of landlord, employer, and officer of the law.

I remember seeing a sign on the fence of a New England mill in Georgia, to the effect that if a boy were found with an air-rifle, the family must leave the mill as soon as the lease on their house expired, and the houses of the operatives were leased for a term of two weeks. It may have been a good thing to discourage the air-rifle and even to hold the parents responsible for the child's misdoings, but one would rather see that done by the law and the officers of the law than by the employer and landlord.

Perhaps the most pitiful example of this sort of feudalism is the petitions which are brought to the Legislature from the operatives against the enactment of laws for their own benefit. I have seen these petitions, some of them signed by one hand, as if they were simply copied from the pay-roll. But others are signed by those of the operatives who can read and write, while the majority make their mark. They petition the Legislature not to shorten the hours, not to prevent night work, not to abolish the child labor which keeps their wages down, not to authorize inspectors who will see that their limbs and lives are guarded from accident, or their buildings from unescapable flames.

Two years ago in Georgia we attempted to change the limit of 66 hours a week, 12 a day, to a 10-hour day for children. The Legislature began to receive petitions from the mill operatives protesting against any shortening of the hours. Then the manufacturers thought they had better compromise on a 60-hour week and the 11-hour day, and thereafter the operatives petitioned for a 60-hour week, but sought to be saved from the dire distress of working less than 60 hours a week. On the other hand, the only organized mill I know in the South recently petitioned a legislature for a nine-hour day for women and an eight-hour day for children.

The same feudalism existed in New England cotton mills not many years since. Eight and a half years ago I took a trip through the New England mill cities. We learned that at Lowell any operative who was found even attending a labor union meeting was discharged. Last fall, eight years afterward, I went to Lowell again. I found that the Industrial Workers of the World, generally styled the I. W. W., had called a strike at one mill, because, having about 90 per cent. of the operatives members of that organization, they insisted that the mill should discharge those who would not join them. And now the New England mills are falling over themselves in the effort to get the American Federation of Labor to organize them and thus deliver them from the I. W. W.

This feudalism is sometimes called a benevolent feudalism, because it occasionally builds, out of the surplus made by the labor at low wages of the workers, schools, hospitals, libraries and so forth. But there is no benevolent feudalism. The expression is a contradiction in terms. The best benevolence would be to increase the pay-roll, so that the employes might do some of these things for themselves.

Yet no people of this stock has ever remained long in bondage. It is American stock, with the English and Scotch instincts against every form of tyranny. In South Carolina the manufacturers have lost the political control of their employes. In State elections the employers vote one way and the employes the other and whatever else we may say about this, the employes have recently been on the winning side. The State should and will incorporate the mill towns and the people will begin to learn the first principles of local self-government and will again be free men. Then they will organize sooner or later, if not in the regular labor unions then in the irregular. They will slowly learn that their interests lie on the side of the reform of conditions of labor for children and women. They come of the stock that fought at Kings Mountain and at New Orleans, at Gettysburg and Chickamauga. There is hardly a child of the cotton mills in the South who cannot claim descent from some soldier of the wars of the Republic. They will not always remain helpless. Compulsory school attendance laws will soon begin to influence the education of the next generation, at least, and when they learn their rights, they are of the breed that has always dared maintain them, and they will demand more hours for rest and recreation, and a fairer share of the profits of industry.

The Danger.

Nor can a democracy encourage a feudalism within itself save to its everlasting hurt. In a democracy the people all rule. Also, the people are ruled. And when it comes to the people's ruling us by their votes, electing our governors and presidents, initiating and vetoing legislation, taxing our incomes, we grow mightily concerned over the intelligence and independence of the electorate. We do not like to trust our interests now and the lives and fortunes of our children to a mass of voters who have been deprived of all opportunity for an education, who have been held in feudalistic bondage, who have been embittered by the robbery of their childhood, who are the material for the agitator, and the prey of the demagogue. Patriotism is partly an enlightened instinct of self-preservation, and patriotism demands that we abolish the system under which large and continually increasing masses of our people are led into a bondage from which there may be no escape, save by way of a social revolution.

Abolish child labor and the child can go to school. We shall never have compulsory education in the cotton manufacturing states of the South until we abolish child labor first. Then the wage-scale will rise to the point where a man or woman can support the family, when educated and intelligent workers can make their own terms as to hours and wages and the conditions of labor. This is not theory, but history. In England, after a century of struggle, these things have happened in the cotton mill industry, and the industry itself stands on a high plane with the others. There is no reason under heaven, save that of unenlightened greed, why the same industry in the South should not be put upon a better basis than anywhere else in the world, so that it shall become one of which we may all be proud, rather than one whose profits smell of blood.

CHILD LABOR AND NEED.[1]

M. LOUISE BOSWELL,
Visitor, Cincinnati Bureau of Vocational Guidance.

In the consideration of this report of the economic necessity for child labor, the most important point to be noted is that it is purely a report of an *impression* on that subject, and by no means a report of conclusions that could be, in any sense, considered final.

It is not based on a systematic compilation of data gathered *to show or not show* economic need of child's work, but is merely an *impression* derived from the consideration of certain statistics, gathered as an incidental part of the child study inaugurated by Miss Edith Campbell and Mr. E. N. Clopper and carried on by Dr. Helen T. Woolley, in Cincinnati, in connection with the issuance of the work certificates. The estimates upon which the report is based are from two main sources:

1. Statements given by 14-year-old children at the office when applying for certificates to work.
2. Estimates formulated by visitors to the homes of the children.

The term *Economic Necessity* refers, throughout this report, to the necessity of the 14-year-old child's leaving school in order to give financial assistance to the family. The term is concerned in no way with "desirability"—the question is not one of securing greater comforts, but rather whether there would be suffering or need of assistance from the city if the child did not work. More stress is laid upon the probable number of persons working than upon the conditions under which they live, concluding for example, that when a family with several children of working age are crowded, say, into two rooms, the problem, in the average case is not so much an economic as a moral one.

[1]NOTE.—A special study made for the National Child Labor Committee from the records of the Cincinnati Bureau of Vocational Guidance.

The question of just how far women should be viewed as economic factors or older children held responsible for family support, does not pertain to this discussion. As a matter of fact, 27 per cent. of the mothers are working—and in a large majority of the families there are older children contributing to the general support. In other words, cases where there is sufficient "earning capacity" have been classified under *No Economic Need*.

The home visitors, whose estimates are taken for the second part of this study, have found that good management and mismanagement in the home have an important bearing on the question of the economic need of child labor. In certain cases listed as No Economic Need it is undeniably true that there would be serious Economic Need, were it not for the exceptionally good management of the mother.

For example, the extent to which good management can offset a wholly inadequate income may be seen in the case of one family of six (father, mother and four children). The father, a driver, made $13.50 a week. They owned their home and paid about $2.50 a month taxes, paid 65 to 70 cents a week insurance, and had a good, comfortable home. The mother acknowledged there was no need of the child's leaving school for work.

In another family of ten (father, mother and eight children), the father as janitor was making about $20 a week. They paid $2.25 a week for rent and about $14 a week for food. This home was not so good as in the former case, but the boy was working only during vacation and returned to high school where his parents expected him to finish the course.

Conclusions from Children's Statements.

In the part of the study based on the children's statements, the data have been grouped under three heads.
1. The *child's* statement regarding the Economic Necessity for his work.
2. The child's preference for work or school—at the time of going to work and after his first job.
3. The judgment of the office in the question of Economic Necessity—this being a personal estimate based upon various information given by the child.

Under the first head—the child's statement regarding the economic necessity for work—such statements as "Mother needs help,"

"Father not able to earn enough," "Large family, mother not able to work," etc., are taken to indicate Economic Need; while such statements as "Finished school," "Too big," "Don't like to study in evening," "Made first Communion," "Mother wanted me to work," "Wanted to help pay for house," "Wanted to buy own clothes," "Father may desert," are classed under No Economic Need.

The second group—the child's preference for school or work—contains definite statements and needs no explanation.

In the third group—the judgment of the office in the question of Economic Need—more explanation is necessary. Here consideration is given to the child's statements, regarding the kind of occupation of father, whether or not mother is working, health of parents, size of family, number of older children, number of rooms and amount of child's spending money.

From these, a personal estimate is made for each individual case, for example:

From one set of cards we find that father is a laborer, mother is not working, there are seven children, the oldest 14 years, they live in two rooms.

The inference here is that there is Economic Need of the child's work.

In another instance father is not well and only works part time, mother is well and does cleaning, uncle boards with family, there are two younger children, and the 14-year-old child spends all her money for clothes and spending money.

The conclusion is that there is No Economic Need of the child's assistance.

Obstacles to accurate estimate occur in such cases as those where no indication is given of how many of the older children are still at home and assisting the family, nor whether if any have died, they were older or younger—and in cases of step-parents and their children (if the number of the latter is not known). Also, in a number of cases, children have made uncertain statements or no statements. Moreover, there is no information as to whether the wage-earners are unreliable or what their earnings are. These uncertainties necessitate a number of questionable cases; yet, if from the statements that are given, a rough estimate can be formed and the figures therefrom bear strongly one way or the other, they will carry some *significance*, even though they bear no actual proof.

In forming the judgment of the office as to Economic Necessity, the estimates were made independently by more than one person (M. Louise Boswell, Olive G. McMillan and Mrs. Martin Fisher), the results compared and careful reconsideration given to doubtful cases. The weight of evidence in doubtful cases was thrown to the weaker side. No standard of estimation could be made to cover all cases, but an attempt to tabulate the results roughly was made. In this the child in question is the 14-year-old child applying for the first time for his certificate to work.

Tabulation of Estimates.

A. *General Factors*
   1. Estimates made accepting living conditions as they are, *i.e.*, without allowance for desire for improved conditions.
   2. Questions of sentiment ruled out. Guardians viewed in the same light as parents (unless there are exceptional determining factors).
   3. Temporary unemployment not taken as economic need.
   4. Responsibility of support not laid on mother if she is not well, nor if there are more than 2 younger children (or in some cases if there are only 2 younger children).
   5. Minor determining factors are:
      a. Number of persons to a room.
      b. Percentage of child's spending money to his earnings (reported at second visit to office).
      c. Ownership of home.

B. *Cases of No Economic Need*
   I. Self-evident, self-determining factors.
      1. Child gives up school (or work after a few weeks), to remain at home.
      2. Child uses all earnings for self (clothes or spending money or savings).
      3. Child intends to work during vacation only.
      4. Child earning $1 to $2 after school-hours, several older children.
   II. Father working, mother not working.
      (a) skilled trade, family small or only typical size.
      (b) skilled trade, 1 or 2 older than 14-year-old, 1 to 4 younger children.
      (c) not highly skilled trade, small family; 14 years, oldest; large percentage of spending money.
      (d) unskilled work.
         (a) 1 older child, 1 or 2 younger, not more than one person to a room (or else other determining factors).

(b) 2 or 3 older, 1 younger, not more than 2 persons to a room.
(c) 3 or 4 older, as many as 3 younger (other determining factors).
III. Father and mother both working.
(a) 14 years, youngest; or not more than one younger.
(b) 14 years, oldest; 2 or 3 younger; more than 6 rooms.
IV. Father dead, deserted or disabled.
1. Mother working.
(a) skilled trade, 1 child; especially if more than 2 rooms.
(b) skilled or unskilled, good health (1 or more older children, 14 years, youngest).
(c) grandparents some assistance, 14 years, oldest; small family.
(d) several adult relatives with family, and working; other boarders.
2. Mother not working.
(a) 3 or 4 older children, no younger.
(b) at least 3 older children, not more than 2 younger (determining factors).
(c) 1 or 2 older children (such determining factors as skilled work for one, large amount of spending money, etc.).

C. *Cases of Economic Need*
I. Father working but mother *not* working.
(a) unskilled work; 14 years, oldest, 3 or 4 younger children (influenced by determining factors).
(b) unskilled work; mother ill; 14 years, oldest; 1 younger (influenced by determining factors).
(c) unskilled work; 1 or 2 older; 3 or more younger; determining factors such as 3 or more to a room; little or no spending money.
II. Father and mother both working.
(a) 14 years oldest; 1 or 2 younger; (2 rooms and little spending money).
(b) 1 older, 5 or more younger.
III. Father dead, deserted, disabled; or cases of prolonged unemployment.
1. Mother working.
(a) good health.
1. unskilled work; only child 14 years (determining factors).
2. unskilled work; 14 years, oldest; 1 younger (determining factors).
3. unskilled work; 1 older; 1 or more younger (determining factors).
4. 2 to 6 younger children.
(b) not well; only child, 14 years.

2. Mother *not* working. Ill health, or 2 or more younger children.
   (a) 14 years oldest.
   (b) not more than one older, one younger.
   (c) not more than 2 older, several younger (determining factors).
V. father disabled, working part time.
   1 older, several younger, possibly grandparents to support.

Or to put it briefly, there may, or may not, be economic need when the father is dead and when he is living; the older children at work have an important bearing on the economic need; the mother's health and whether she does or does not have a number of young children to care for are important factors. In other words, there is held to be no economic need when there is a sufficient number of persons working, although the percentage of spending money and the number of rooms are significant modifying factors. In the later estimates from the Home Visiting cards, irregular employment and low pay may be found causing economic need.

Very questionable cases are sometimes caused: by insufficient, or *no* determining factors; when mothers and fathers both work, despite three younger and one or more older children; when father is dead, mother not working, more younger than older children. For example, in one case, the father was dead; mother doing unskilled work; only one child; no determining factors of health, rooms or spending money; again, a family of six people; father, paper cleaner, in poor health; mother not working; three younger children; three rooms; child has 50 cents a week spending money. In instances such as these, no estimate of economic necessity was possible, and the cases were classed as questionable.

During this study it has been necessary also in the classification of certain cases to depart from standard, for example: in a family of four, living in two rooms; father a stationary fireman; one older child, 14-year-old child, youngest; the mother had been ill for six months, and the debts, doctor bills, etc., were heavy. The judgment of the office in this case was that there was Economic Necessity. Or again, a family of three; father dead; mother not working; 14-year-old child oldest, one younger; they lived in *six* rooms, and the child received 75 cents a week spending money.

The inference here was that the mother must have other means of support, and that there was no need of assistance from the child.

Final Result.

Of the 648 estimates made by the office, 475 or 73 per cent. did not show Economic Necessity for the child's work, and 145 or 22 per cent. recognized Economic Necessity. Twenty-eight cases or 4+ per cent. were left as questionable.

In thus stating its judgment of Economic Need, the office has been obliged to depart many times from the judgment of the child, there being considerable evidence that the child's statement of Economic Need was largely influenced by his desire to go to work or by some external cause. Out of 395 cases where the child stated there was Economic Need, the office judged 130 or about 33 per cent. of the cases had such need.

That the child's own inclination has greatly modified his statements can be inferred from the fact that of the 475 cases where, according to the office estimates, Economic Need of the child's work was not shown, 265 or 56 per cent. of the children stated a *preference* for work. Of all the children (419) of whom the preference for school or work is recorded, 76 per cent. preferred to go to work. Here indications seem to point, regardless of the Economic Necessity, to a strong desire on the part of the child to go to work. Of all the children who at the end of their first job state a preference for either school or work, a rough estimate shows that about 74 per cent. still prefer work to school. Here again the indications are that work holds the child's interest more than school, despite the fact that his wages, in the majority of cases, are poured into the family budget and that he expects to reap only the reward of a few cents' spending money.

The Estimates Compared.

The degree of accuracy or inaccuracy in the office estimate of Economic Need may be gauged somewhat by comparison with the estimates of visitors to the homes of the children. Over 300 of the 648 homes have been visited. In a number of cases the results were unsatisfactory and little or no information was gained that is of value in this study. In others very definite statements of the family budget were given. Comparing the estimates of the home visitor with the estimates of the office, it appears that out of 270 cases there was an agreement of 203, or *about 75 per cent.* If we base much weight on the estimate of the home visitor, this would make a 75 per cent. estimate of accuracy for the office estimate of Economic Necessity.

Examining the figures a little more closely, it is seen that in so far as the home-visit estimates are available to supplement the conclusions of the office data, when Economic Necessity was shown by the latter, the visiting data agreed with the office to the extent of 53 per cent., and disagreed to the extent of 47 per cent. Whereas, in cases in which it was concluded that Economic Necessity did *not* exist, the home-visit estimates corroborated those from the office data to an extent of *84 per cent.* and differed to the extent of 16 per cent. From this it is evident that the percentage of disagreement is greater in cases where Economic Need was stated, or, in other words, the home-visiting cards uphold more strongly the conclusions of the office judgment where there was No Economic Need, and the greater error, therefore, is on the side where there is statement of Economic Necessity.

Turning from the study of the child's statements as gathered at office, to a somewhat similar study based upon visits to the home, the information—as before—may be grouped under three heads.

1. *Parents' statements* regarding the necessity of the child's going to work.
2. *Parents' attitude* toward education, *i.e.,* indifference or interest in the child's continuing school; if not now, possibly later in night school.
3. *Visitor's own estimate* regarding the Economic Necessity for child's work.

This estimate is made:
1. From the visitor's general impression of the home, interior conditions, etc.
2. From the parents' own statements to the visitor, which affect but do not always determine the estimate.
3. From family budgets—when possible to obtain them.

In a few cases of unsatisfactory visits, the information from the homes has been supplemented by such data as was used in forming the judgment of the office; for example, when the mother would give no information, but the visitor received the impression of a very poor home, and the child's statement at the office gave lengthy unemployment, or a large number of young children, the home visitor's estimate was made for Economic Need.

In making the estimates of necessity for the child's work the standard taken is low, but in all cases where there are budgets some margin is allowed beyond the sum scheduled by the Cincinnati Associated Charities as necessary for the support of families of corresponding size.

No Economic Need.

The results of the estimates indicate, first, a larger proportion of cases where there is not *Economic Necessity* for the children's going to work. Of 279 cases examined 197 (or 71 per cent.) were for No Economic Need, and 82 (or 29 per cent.) seemed to indicate Economic Need. (A possible source of error in the percentage must be admitted here—in that a number of poor districts in the city have not yet been visited.)

Second, a large percentage of mothers themselves state there is No Economic Necessity for the children going to work. Of the 197 cases where the visitor estimates no need, 116 have the mothers' acknowledgment of no need. In only 39 of the cases did she claim there was need (in 42 no statement was recorded). This would seem to indicate a willingness on the part of the parent to let the child work and unwillingness or indifference about keeping him in school. In general there seemed to be marked indifference on the part of the mother toward education. In 133 of the 279 cases, the mother seemed to take no interest in it. In some of these instances the mother explained that she considered the child old enough to begin to learn a trade; in a few health was used as an argument against continuing school. Some mothers had never felt the need of education themselves, and in a number of cases were concerned not in how much education could be given the child but how much money could be got out of him. As one mother said: "The law won't let a child work until he is 14 years old and he gets married when he is 17 and there ain't no good to be had out of children these days, no how."

Of the 116 cases where the mothers acknowledged no need, 48 of the mothers, or 41 per cent., exhibited an interest in education. This seems to indicate a considerable percentage of parents who simply yield to the child's desire to stop school for work.

Some parents attempted to explain their sending children to work by such reasons as: "To keep them off the streets," or "they get lazy and never will work unless they work before they are 16 years," etc.

No study of economic need based solely on family budgets has been attempted, as the number of budgets thus far collected is inadequate.

Throughout the report, two points seem to stand out conspicuously:

1st. In the greater number of cases, the call that takes the children into work is not suffering need. The cry of the people seems to be more for relief from strain—for a chance to live—than for the chance to exist.

2nd. Whatever may be the cause, there seems to be something which draws the child more strongly toward work than toward school.

It must be mentioned, however, in closing, as in the opening of this report, that it is a report of impressions only, and is not intended to express any final conclusions.

ACKNOWLEDGMENTS.

In the preparation of this paper, valuable assistance was given by Mrs. Woolley in outlining the *method* of study of the children's statements; helpful co-operation was given by members of the office staff; advice and encouragement by Prof. F. C. Hicks of the Economics Department of the University of Cincinnati.

CHILD LABOR AND POVERTY: BOTH CAUSE AND EFFECT.

John A. Kingsbury, New York,
General Agent, New York Association for Improving the Condition of the Poor.

There is a popular misconception about the relation between child labor and poverty. The popular notion seems to be that child labor is the result of poverty, or at any rate, that it is due to the economic status of the parents of the child laborer, and there the matter ends. It is admitted that there is a measure of truth in this proposition. Most of the truth, however, lies in the converse to it, viz., that poverty is the effect of child labor. Of course, it is not claimed that all poverty is the result of child labor, but it is asserted that child labor, as it is understood to-day, almost invariably results in a condition of poverty. To those familiar with the subject it is axiomatic to say that child labor causes poverty, but the general public is slow to grasp this self-evident proposition.

The American nation is only just beginning to feel the baneful effects of child labor. The English nation, however, is staggering under a weight of poverty, much of which is due to child labor; England has come to realize that a very considerable amount of its vast army of paupers has been produced by the pernicious system of child labor which has prevailed there for nearly a century.

At the beginning of the industrial revolution in England over a century ago, factories and mills sprang up on every available site in the British Isles; the demand for labor was so great that the owners of factories, by permission of the government, emptied the orphan asylums of its boys and girls who were strong enough to labor. These little orphans were "apprenticed" until the boys were twenty-one, the girls eighteen. Among these orphans put to work in the mills at a tender age were the father and mother of Dr. Robert Collyer, for many years the beloved minister of the Church of the Messiah in New York City.

Deprived of training, even for moderate remunerative labor, stunted by the cruel racking of child labor, Robert Collyer's father, even in good times, was able to earn only $4.50 a week. Therefore, at the early age of eight, little Robert began his sad and painful period of child labor. His father's scant earnings and the increasing family forced the child into the mills to labor for a living. Dr. Collyer has left a pitiful picture of his awful experience as a child slave.

The hours were from six o'clock in the morning until eight o'clock in the evening; on Saturday from six to six, with an hour off each day for dinner. Still worse, the little children were never allowed to sit down at their work and if they were caught by the overseer resting themselves for a moment upon some stray box or barrel they were speedily brought to their feet by the stinging lash of a heavy leather strap across their shoulders. "The result of this," says Dr. Collyer, "was that the weaker children were so crippled that the memory of their crooked limbs still casts a sinister light for me on the Scripture, 'The Lord regardeth not the legs of a man.'" "I was tired beyond all telling," he continues, "and thought the bell would never ring to let me out, and home at last, and to bed. And it seemed as if I had only just got to sleep when it rang again to call me to work."

Rev. John Haynes Holmes, the present minister of the Church of the Messiah, from whom I borrow this illustration, says that one day when he "chanced to ask Dr. Collyer if he would like to live his life all over again Dr. Collyer instantly replied with great good cheer that he would. Then his face darkened for a moment and he said, 'But not those years in the mill. I wouldn't live those over again, not for all the blessings that might be given me in compensation.'"

At fourteen years of age Robert Collyer was rescued from this slavery by the necessity of learning a trade. "There was one article in our home creed," he tells us, "that would admit of no doubt or denial; 'the boys must learn some craft better than we were taught in the factory.'"

Fortunate Robert Collyer! Happily the age of apprenticeship had not completely passed in England; otherwise, in all probability, the world would have been deprived of a multitude of blessings brought to it through the life of this "Saint and Seer." To-day chances are hundreds to one that Robert Collyer—even so strong a character as he—would not have escaped the terrible consequences of child labor. Instead, he would have lived to complete the remaining segment of the vicious circle in which his life started to move. Moreover, the chances are that he would have lived only to start the next vicious circle on its monotonous round.

The Vicious Circle.

In this illustration you have my subject fully developed. The poverty of these orphans forced them into the factories to become child laborers. The long hours of confining labor must have broken most of them in body and in spirit. "The intensity of modern methods of labor, made possible by the machine, sets a pace so fast and uninterrupted as to tax the strength of the strongest men, and naturally therefore, to rack the weaker bodies of the children." Only a small fraction of these little laborers could have been so fortunate as Robert Collyer. Most of them must have brought forth a generation of weak and wretched children condemned at birth to a life of child slavery, deprived of education, denied the wholesome development of play; at best, nothing to look forward to but a miserable existence at hard labor; at worst, a life of poverty, pauperism and probably a career of crime. They must live the same lives their fathers have lived and in turn beget a generation similarly condemned at birth.

Statistics Cannot Show All.

England is notoriously a land of paupers. A third of its last generation lies at rest in a Potter's Field. If the life histories of these poor wretches could be traced, how many of them would lead back to the poor little tired bodies, to the crooked limbs of the Robert Collyers who were dragged out from the barren walls of orphan asylums to be bound to the racking machines in the factories and mills—the Collyers who never escaped? The question cannot be answered. We haven't the figures. But who will doubt that they would be most illuminating if they could be obtained? If we could show accurately the extent of the poverty under which England staggers to-day, which is the result of child labor, the statistics would be invaluable to us in securing proper child labor legislation.

But after all, as someone has strikingly put it, "You cannot put tired eyes, pallid cheeks and languid little limbs into statistics."

But Robert Collyer escaped the common fate of a child laborer. In 1850, when about twenty-five years of age, he and his bride reached the bright shores of this Land of Opportunity. It *was* a land of opportunity then. No child labor to speak of, as it was then known in England, as it is known here to-day. No poverty such as England was then beginning to struggle with, such as we now see in our large cities. A half century has passed since Robert Collyer landed. We have recruited a standing army of child laborers, 1,700,000 strong. It is quite impossible to visualize this appalling number of little tots at labor, but as Robert Hunter says: "We could never forget the sight of a hundred of these little ones if they were marched out of the mills, mines and factories, before our eyes, or if we saw them together toiling for ten or twelve hours a day or night for a pittance of a wage; but that we do not see. What we see are the figures, and we forget figures."

One million seven hundred thousand child slaves! "New York City has not so many children," asserts Hunter; "all the thousands in the streets are not so many as those children of the workshops; even the massed crowds in the evening at Brooklyn Bridge are few compared with this 1,700,000; but it is all figures again and not tired eyes, pallid cheeks and languid little limbs, and we forget figures."

Preventing Development of Genius.

Among these 1,700,000 children there are hundreds, perhaps thousands, of Robert Collyers, doomed in this land of opportunity to a life of hard labor and poverty, destined to be the forebears of generations of paupers and criminals.

Prof. Lester F. Ward, the dean of American sociologists, as a result of a careful study of the subject of genius, has reached the conclusion that it is possible to increase the supply of our geniuses two hundredfold by removing the social and economic obstacles which now prevent their development; and perhaps the greatest among these obstacles is child labor. In other words, in Dr. Ward's opinion, society is teeming with potential Collyers. It should have two hundred dynamic Collyers where now it has but one.

Eugenics is a valuable science, and by its practical application we shall undoubtedly greatly strengthen the race; but let us not forget the paramount importance of so improving the social and economic condition as to make it possible for all our geniuses to develop. If we do not put a stop to this national crime of child labor an American Lloyd-George will be struggling with a great American nation of paupers. And undoubtedly the historian will convict our employers of child labor of a vast amount of this crime.

Poverty Both Cause and Effect.

In America we have been anxiously watching the growth and extension of child labor. We shall provide the historian with a full record of thousands upon thousands of cases from which he can generalize.

In New York City alone we have the records of many thousands of families receiving charity, public and private. I cannot say what proportion, but undoubtedly a very large proportion of these families are dependent chiefly because of child labor. Last year eleven thousand families were under the care of the Association for Improving the Condition of the Poor. This is but one of the large private charitable organizations in that city. I personally have looked over the histories of many of these families and I can assure you it is difficult to find a single case in which the father or the mother, and usually both, did not go to work at an early age. Here are a few typical cases:

1. Man and woman practically illiterate; both worked at an early age—do not know how young they were when they began. The man kept a coal and ice cellar; worked very hard, contracted pneumonia, tuberculosis developed, and he died of this disease. At the tender age of nine the eldest boy was forced to work to help support the family. Thus he was deprived of education, and hard labor undermined his health. When the father died the family was brought to the attention of the Association. The boy was found to have incipient tuberculosis. If he lives and marries, unless someone continues to help, it is easy to imagine his children repeating this history.

2. A widow with five bright and ambitious children. The eldest girl graduated from public school at the age of thirteen. Anxious to complete a commercial course, she attended high school. But her mother needed her help to support the family. If the assistance the mother is now receiving from private charity is continued, these children, or some of them, may be fortunate enough to escape, and may live to be useful citizens, like Robert Collyer.

3. George graduated from public school and got his working papers. He is a bright boy and his mother was anxious to send him to high school, but she needed his support. Unless George is the one boy in a thousand who subdues his environment, instead of being subdued by it, it is not difficult to tell the sequel to this story.

4. The father worked until he became the victim of an industrial disease, of which he died. Frank, the 18-year-old boy, then became the main support of his mother and four brothers and sisters. Since he was fourteen, Frank has worked in an electrical shop earning $6.00 to $9.00 a week. Bright, industrious and ambitious, he attended night school regularly to fit himself for a better position. He, too, would be a Robert Collyer. But in December, 1912, Frank's tired body broke under the strain. It was tuberculosis again. The family was then referred to the Association for assistance. Frank is now in a hospital, his wage loss is being paid to his mother, and arrangements have been made with the employer to take Frank back to work when discharged from the hospital. There is more to this story. Rosie got her working papers last April and her mother immediately placed her in a garment factory at $3.00 a week. The mother was finally persuaded to let her attend the Manhattan Trade School on condition that the wage loss be paid her. Rosie's progress there was very satisfactory until August, 1912, when it was found that both she and her six-year-old sister had developed tuberculosis. There is a possibility that these three children may be saved, but they will be saved only for a life of child labor, unless the family is kept under care and receives wise treatment.

5. The father of this family became a rock-driller in his youth. There are three grown sons, but not one is working regularly. The mother and the 16-year-old girl, who has never been at school though born in New York City, work at home on feathers; their earnings constitute the only visible income for a family of twelve. As the older children of this family do not know their ages, it needs no fortune-teller to forecast the next generation sprung from this man who began to drill rock while a mere child.

In most of the cases cited above, poverty may be said to be both cause and effect of child labor. As stated at the outset, most anyone will grant that child labor is frequently brought about by poverty.

Actual Family Need Not General.

Comparatively few people in this day of free schools would deny their offspring a good education if they did not feel that the child's labor was needed to keep the wolf from the door, or at least to help provide more of the common comforts of life. As a matter of fact, however, it has been shown by the child labor scholarship plan that the instances are rare in which the child's earnings are required to prevent actual suffering.

Mr. Homer Folks first brought this to the attention of the National Child Labor Committee Annual Meeting in Cincinnati in 1906. He showed that in the greater City of New York a little less than thirty per cent. of the applications for scholarship were granted. After fifteen months of publicity in that city, whose population was then 4,250,000, only ninety-five cases were found to be in actual need of such assistance as the child labor scholarship of $2 to $3 a week would provide. Mr. Folks found that a similar condition obtained in every other city in which the plan was in operation. Although I have not the figures at hand, I am informed that the recent statistics substantially confirm Mr. Folks' findings that, if deprived of their children's earnings, only a small percentage of families would be made to actually suffer.

But while poverty is given as an excuse for much child labor, and while, no doubt, it is true that practically all child laborers are children of parents who are living close to the poverty line, the statement that poverty itself requires that these children labor to prevent real suffering is usually quite unwarranted. It is not denied, however, that poverty is the cause of a considerable amount of the child labor of the world; but the important proposition which I wish to emphasize is that poverty is generally the inevitable effect of child labor. I believe it no overstatement to say that in ninety-nine cases out of every hundred, where the child is put to work at the tender age of five or six and kept steadily at it until fifteen or sixteen, when he may be old enough to rebel, poverty is the result.

Robert Hunter tells us of a vagrant he once knew who "had for years—from the day he was eleven until the day he was sixteen—made two movements of his hands each second, or 23,760,000 mechanical movements each year, and was at the time I knew him,' says Hunter, "at the age of thirty-five, broken down, drunken and diseased, but he still remembered this period of slavery sufficiently well to tell me that he had 'paid up' for all the sins he had ever committed 'by those five years in hell.' "

I maintain that where you have one Robert Collyer making his escape from the deadening effects of child labor, you will have ninety-nine vagrants and paupers. But that is not all. The undermined health, the broken spirit of the child, the incipient vagrant and pauper, are not the only pauperizing effects of child labor.

Child labor causes poverty, in so far as it lowers the scale of wages below the minimum living wage, and likewise to the extent to which the child displaces the adult laborer. The child can take his father's place in the factory at a wage of about one-third of what the father was getting. All this means more poverty. It would be a most valuable contribution to the statistics of child labor to determine the poverty due to unemployed men and women, whose places have been taken by children, or due to a starvation wage which has been cut and kept down by child labor.

"Child labor in any state lowers manhood labor in every state," says Senator Beveridge, "because the product of child labor in any state competes with the product of manhood labor in every state. Child laborers at the loom in South Carolina mean bayonets at the breasts of men and women workers in Massachusetts, who strike for a living wage.

"Child labor in factories, mills, mines and sweat shops must be ended throughout this republic. Such labor is a crime against childhood, because it prevents the growth of normal manhood and womanhood. It is a crime against the nation because it prevents the growth of a host of children into strong, patriotic and intelligent citizens."

In closing I want again to quote Robert Hunter and join him in saying: "There is to my mind nothing more astonishing in modern society than the way in which the state seems ever willing to support as paupers and at public expense, the men, women and children who are brought to poverty and misery by the parasitic industries."

SHALL CHARITABLE SOCIETIES RELIEVE FAMILY DISTRESS BY FINDING WORK FOR CHILDREN?

A SYMPOSIUM.

I.

R. T. SOLENSTEN,

Secretary, Associated Charities, Jacksonville, Fla.

It is the aim and purpose of modern charity to effect such family rehabilitation and to help bring about such social and economic adjustment as will insure a normal standard of living for every family.

We conceive a normal standard of living to be one "which permits each individual of a social unit to exist as a healthy human being, morally, mentally and physically." We recognize the essential elements of a normal standard to be: Nourishing food in sufficient quantity to maintain physical efficiency; a sanitary house including light, heat and modest household furnishings, which shall provide shelter for the family group in an environment free from moral contamination; clothing for work and for holiday dress adapted to seasonal changes in climate; some leisure time for education and recreation for all members of the family; regular school attendance for all children between the ages of six and fourteen years; provision for dental, surgical and other care necessary for the attainment and preservation of health; insurance against sickness, accident and death, and savings of not less than five per cent. of the income, for contingencies and extraordinary expenses.

A normal standard implies an income sufficient to provide the necessaries briefly described above, and to carry the family through the ordinary vicissitudes of life without charitable assistance. It also presupposes that its requirements be met from the earnings of the father, unsupplemented by any earnings of the mother or children under proper working age. Wherever a family fails to provide for its members the necessities and advantages accepted as requirements of a normal standard, the explanation of the failure is usually a condition, the chief characteristic of which is death or desertion of the breadwinner, or the disability, inefficiency, unemployment or underpaid employment of the breadwinner. The causes producing this condition may be social or personal or both.

Any family which for any reason lacks one or more of the essentials included in the standard, is a proper object for the attention of our charitable forces. The treatment applied by them must be in the form of individualized care, personal service and oversight, because the conditions and circumstances leading up to and producing this want will vary among different families who fail to maintain the proper standard.

Encouraging Child Labor Inconsistent.

I have introduced these remarks on the subject of relief of family distress by an outline of the principle of the standard of living, because it represents the lowest plane upon which a family can live and hope safely to maintain social efficiency, and because without it no charitable agency can have a proper working basis for administering adequate or constructive relief. If we now examine, in the light of this principle, the question whether charitable societies shall relieve distress by finding work for children under proper working age, and if it be granted that charitable agencies should seek to help families to reach and maintain a normal standard of living, an important element of which is the regular attendance at school of all children under working age, it remains quite clear that any society attempting to relieve distress by encouraging the labor of children defeats its own purpose.

Constructive charity finds its chief opportunity for effective work among families of widows with young children, and among families in which the normal breadwinner, because of disability or other reasons, is not contributing the necessary income. Work with such families, where it is not a question of disciplinary treatment of the parents or of increasing the earning power of the normal breadwinner, consists largely of securing a suitable substitute for the lost breadwinner's income and of administering this aid to the family in a manner which shall insure the mental, moral and physical development of the children. One of the fundamental tenets of all charity organization society doctrines is that kind, helpful supervision and adequate relief should be given every needy, fatherless family, so that the children may have the chance to grow up to become useful citizens, able to maintain for themselves and families a normal independent life.

The history of the administration of charity is replete with illustrations of the fact that this opportunity is not afforded in the vast majority of cases where children are obliged to enter the ranks of competitive industrial life at a tender age. Deprived of the privilege of obtaining even a rudimentary education, stunted in mind and body from the strain of toil for which their young and undeveloped bodies were never intended, weakened in will and with moral training neglected or misguided by enforced association in improper environments, they reach maturity and middle age and are found altogether too frequently adrift upon society, swelling the ranks of the inefficient, the unemployable, the dependent, the delinquent and the socially unfit.

Special Substitutes.

All thinking people, all who have the best interests of our great country at heart, and who are not dominated by an insatiable spirit of greed or self-interest, agree that the employment of young children in industrial pursuits, as a social policy, is utter folly. The obstacles arise when we begin to consider the ways and means of providing adequate relief for families who have been deprived of the normal income of the breadwinner. Private charity has attempted this through pensions and scholarships, but it has not been extensively successful because of inability to raise the necessary funds for adequate relief and adequate treatment. However, it is fair to say that the possibilities of private charity in this direction have not yet been exhausted.

The recent movement in favor of widows' pensions, mothers' compensation, funds to parents, etc., aims at a solution of this problem. These methods are now being tried out in Illinois, Colorado, California and Missouri, and it will be interesting to watch the results of the experiments. Undoubtedly, until we reach the stage where that kind of poverty which means lack of essentials for a decent living shall have been eliminated, the solution of this problem will be found in some form of public aid. The objections to most of the public relief and pension measures now advocated so extensively, seem to be related largely to the difficulty of mastering the methods and principles of proper administration. With these objections overcome by the perfected methods which will surely be worked out very soon by our wise statesmen and social experts, it will be only a question of time before the public will follow the lines of advance which they have opened up. In the meantime charitable societies will do best to wait for a satisfactory conclusion of the experiments now being conducted, and endeavor to meet local situations by securing adequate relief for families on the "case-fund" or "scholarship plan," and by providing adequate treatment through personal service and individualized care of a high grade.

The question whether charitable societies should relieve family distress by finding employment for children cannot be answered without considering what those children would be doing if not at work. Presumably they would be at school. But if, as in Florida, there is no compulsory education law or other legal machinery to make indifferent parents keep the children at school, the case is further complicated. It then becomes the duty of the charitable agency to secure such co-operation of the home, the child and the school, as will accomplish the result desired. If it be impossible, after all means have been tried, to keep the children in school, it would be better to withdraw the pension or scholarship and let the children earn support for the family. The charitable society would then, of course, endeavor to find the least objectionable work for the children. Organized charity, however, should remember that upon it, to a large extent, rests the responsibility for paving the way for new and higher standards of social service in its community, and it should vigorously and continuously resist compromise.

In answer to the argument that families would prefer to have the children work and not receive charity, we must have the courage to insist that the child has rights which the parent must not violate, and that the family owes to society of which it is the unit, the obligation that its children and future citizens shall be in every sense, free men and women, equipped, according to the social will, to take their places as useful and efficient members of our social order.

Conservation and Prevention.

Even though we solve, for the time being, the problem of providing adequate relief by charitable funds or public aid, in the form of widows' pensions, we yet have before us the larger problem of the conservation of human life, the problem of preventing disease and accidents which cause widowhood, of securing adequate compensation for the human risks in industry; we have, in fact, before us still the real problem of correcting the whole wide range of conditions and circumstances which tend to keep families below the economic level at which they can safely maintain social efficiency. The ideal of constructive charity demands that we give our attention also to this greater problem of prevention.

This Conference represents one effort in that direction. We shall have made a great advance toward social justice when we have successfully eliminated the evils of child labor. Charitable societies should not encourage child labor by taking children out of school and placing them at work in order to relieve distress. They should provide adequate relief for needy families. They should aim to help families reach and maintain a normal standard of living, one of the most essential elements of which is the education and unrestricted development of every child, mentally, morally and physically.

II.

Mary H. Newell.
Secretary, Associated Charities, Columbus, Ga.

In choosing one of these topics for this afternoon, I do not know whether it was because I was the last to lead in the discussions or not, but I just naturally took the last question: "Shall charitable societies relieve family distress by finding work for children?" I feel that we should just say No, in great big letters. I am awfully proud I am from Georgia, but I am not a bid proud of Georgia's child labor laws. We have not even a compulsory school law over there where I live; the only compulsory school law in Columbus is the fact that in helping families I try to make it a rule, if a family applies to me for aid, to sound around and find out how much it is going to take that family to live on and then tell them: "Provided you have every child of working age in school, we will do this for you." And we find that it has worked like a charm. It is the best substitute I know of for a good state law.

I am not only secretary of the Associated Charities, but I live in a school in a mill district and breathe the atmosphere. It is a city organization in Columbus and has been arranged for the children who carry the dinners and come back in the afternoon. It is very hard to get the children to attend regularly, but when they get so hard up that they have to come to me, I am just as good as a truant officer. And this is the way I do it: every morning at the breakfast table when they are passing by—I do not have to teach, so I am eating breakfast when they come to school at eight o'clock—I say, "If I see you in the line it keeps up, but if I do not there is something doing." So that is our compulsory school law.

I want to tell you about one family I was called in to see in the neighborhood. I found the father with a chronic case of Bright's disease, absolutely no hope for him, the doctor said. The mother had just a little wee one a few days old, and where do you suppose the support of that family came from? There were twins, a boy and a girl, twelve years old, and a boy of nine, and those three children were supporting that family. I wish I could show you a picture that I had of them. I would let you see the difference. We just couldn't stand for that; so we found out how much it would take for that family to live on and we are putting that much into it, and the children are all of them in school. Each and every one of them pass by and say, "Good morning, Miss Newell." They are at school regularly and very enthusiastic about it. And where do you suppose those twelve-year-old children are? In the first grade.

Now someone said: "What are you hoping to do by this? What good is coming from it?" I am afraid if there are many secretaries of associated charities here and they should look over my records they would be disappointed if they could see the small amount of help we get from relatives. But I will tell you why We deal with a mill population entirely. We go to an uncle and what is his answer? "Clarence is twelve years old. I started work at nine." And they are not going to pay a cent into that family because they see no reason why every one of those children should not be working. In Georgia they can work at six. The law does not say so, but they do. Ten is the lowest age; they are not supposed under any circumstances to work under that age. We hope that we are going to have those children when they grow up feel that their children must not go to work until they are fourteen, and gradually we hope to raise it higher.

A Dead-end Occupation.

There is another thing we are hoping to gain by it. You know when these children start in the cotton mills somehow they are cotton mill workers for life. We have in Columbus iron foundries and huge railroad shops, and my ambition was to see if I could not get two of our night club boys apprenticeships. Through one of the directors of the board I succeeded. The boys were elated and the next morning they reported to work and what do you suppose? The boss in the iron foundry found out that they were cotton mill workers and had been for two or three years. He didn't want them; wouldn't have them. And the reason of that is this: it is typical of that class that they do not work any more than it takes money for them to live. If a boy of that class has no family to support, if he can live by working four days a week, he is not going to work any more; he is not going to put up that money or spend it. If the four days give him money enough to go to all the moving picture shows that he wants to, that is all that he will work. So this machinist thinks that it is a shiftless class and will not give them work. And we are hoping that if we can keep these children in school until they are fourteen, then they can get into the iron foundries and machine shops and not have to go into the cotton mills at all.

SOME ANCIENT STANDARDS OF CHILD PROTECTION.

Rabbi David Marx, Atlanta, Ga.

Within the past half-century, the welfare of the child has received more attention and consideration than at any time in the known scope of authentic history. His right to a healthy birth, to happiness, to normal physical development, to education and the opportunities that make for home building and good citizenship are of such intimate concern that almost daily some new thought is advanced, some new law enacted to insure to childhood the right to laugh and play and grow strong physically and develop mentally and morally.

A newer ideal combats an ancient thought that the child is the concern of only the parent or the state. This ideal makes for a dual responsibility. In this making, it meets with law. Custom precedes law; law becomes in turn custom, with all the implications of tradition and precedent. Law rests on conceptions of the past; it embodies ancient form and usage. Nor is it always mindful of the origin of the usage or the form. It is this loyalty to the past, which, while it affords stability, presents obstacles to advanced legislation for child welfare.

The idea of parental right as guardian, judge, arbiter of the child's life, is ancient. His property right in his children goes back to prehistoric times. That the children are his and he can use them as he sees fit, work them if he will, sell the labor of their young lives, receive their wages, yea, demand again of the employer the wages already paid to the child without parental authorization,—goes back into the hoariest of times before Rome had sunk the foundations for the walls that were to enclose the people that in so large a measure gave laws to the world.

In the ancient world, in general, the standards of child protection were most limited. The father was supreme within his home. He was the priest who kept alive the sacred fire. He was the judge with unquestioned authority. Wife, child and slave were his property. When the city grew and began to frame laws, the lawmakers found the father entrenched behind the barriers of his home. He, personally, might be answerable to the city authorities and the law, but not so his family. They were answerable to him, and he dare do with them that which was good in his own eyes. At least this was so in very ancient Rome. As priest and family head, to become, after death, deified, religion gave him his imperious position, yet it acted as a check upon him at least in so far as his male children were concerned. Through them lay not only the succession but also the religion of the family. Their death would entail the extinction of the hearth-fire, and would deprive the Manes of the father of the veneration and offerings which ought to be given, and could be given only by the son. Thus it was that even the severe law, originally a custom, which gave the father right to kill or to sell his children, had somewhat of a check upon it. *(De Coulanges: Ancient City, Bk. II., Ch. 7 and 8. Henry Sumner Maine: Ancient Law, Ch. V.).*

Similar parental authority, "Patria potestas," seems to have been an almost universal custom in the early days. As Sir Henry Maine remarks: "The unit of an ancient society was the family; of a modern society, the individual." *(Anc. Law, p. 126.)*

The patriarchal system of government naturally simplified the application of external laws, and this to so great an extent, that except in questions involving property succession, it is rare that the child is even considered by the ancient legislators.

To ascertain then what were the standards of protection would be almost impossible, were it not that the literature of the past occasionally throws some light upon the attitude of parents and public towards the children.

It is not just to infer that the child was not an object of solicitude to parents, watched over and cared for, merely because no law stands on the statute book prohibiting the exploitation of the child. Industrial conditions such as obtain to-day, were unknown and undreamed of then. It is true that many of the customs of that past, relative to children, were brutal. It is so even to-day.

Child Life in Ancient Israel.

The limitations placed upon this paper compel us to direct our attention, and that somewhat hurriedly and not entirely satisfactorily, to child life among the people that gave us the Bible. Of all ancient nations (for reasons into which it is not necessary to go at present) we are the most closely interested in this one whose literature we esteem.

There can be no doubt that in the earliest stage of the Semite Beduin life, the sacifice of the first-born son was an established custom for insuring a large progeny *(Rob. Smith: Religion of the Semites)*. This custom was later changed to that of redeeming the child with an animal sacrifice or with money. According to the primitive thought, such sacrifice, as an act of religious reverence, was essential for securing a family.

Likewise it was customary, for a long time, to immolate a child and rear the structure of a house or of a city-wall on such a foundation-sacrifice. Thus in the time of King Ahab, "did Chiel, the Bethelite, build Jericho. With Abiram, his first-born, he laid the foundation thereof, and with Segub, his youngest son, set he up the gates thereof" *(I. K., xvi. 34; Josh., vi., 26)*.

So, too, in these days with less religious reverence and with a finer cruelty, we rear the foundation of our industrial success upon the attenuated forms of infants and children.

Such acts of stamping out child life must not, however, be taken as typical of the attitude of Ancient Israel towards its children. The genius of Biblical custom and law, as reflected in the pages of Sacred Writ, shows a brighter side.

The attitude of mind, rather than the legal expression, the sentiment of the people, more than the compression of that sentiment into the form of compulsory enactment, is, after all, the better gauge and the truer measure of the ideals and practices for which that people stands.

What then was this attitude as reflected in Biblical thought and usage? What laws served as standards? What were the principles employed in the post-Biblical, in the Talmudic periods, and to what extent were such principles converted into laws?

Biblical Times.

The assumption that man is created in the image of his Maker, and that the children are likewise so formed, permeates the Bible. Love, affection, sympathy, devotion towards those who have come into being, is fundamental thought.

Children are desired. They are prayed for. What beautiful sentiments cluster around the very thought of the little ones' advent; for are they not a "heritage from God"? *(Ps. cxxvii., 3, 4)*. Abraham pleads, "What wilt Thou give me, seeing I go childless?" *(Gen. xv. 2)*. Sarah rejoices at the thought of motherhood *(Gen. xviii. 10)*; Isaac is entreated of his wife for children *(Gen. xxiv. 21)*; Rachel demands children lest she die *(Gen. xxx.)*; Hannah beseeches God to bless her *(I. Sam. i.)*, Noah is hailed as a comforter by his parents *(Gen. v. 29)*. The life of Jacob "is bound up with that of the lad," Benjamin *(Gen. xliv. 30)*; he grieves over the loss of Joseph, refuses to be comforted; he will "go down mourning to the grave" *(Gen. xxxvii. 5)*; the news that Joseph is alive revives him; he will go even into Egypt to see his son *(Gen. xlv.)*. Esau is told by his brother, "these are the children whom God hath graciously given me" *(Gen. xxxiii.)*; Miriam is placed by her mother to watch over the frail craft in which lies her brother *(Ex. ii.)*; Israel refuses freedom from bondage unless the children can go *(Ex. v.-x.)*; aye, the "crown of old men is their children's children" *(Prov. xvii.)*; while the classic epitomes of parental affection are the heart cries of David for treacherous Absalom: "O my son Absalom, my son, my son Absalom; would that I had died in thy stead, O Absalom, my son, my son" *(II. S. xix. 1)*; and the tragic figure of Rachel, weeping for her children and refusing to be comforted *(Jer. xxxi. 15)*. The Prophets, in ecstatic vision, see the Messianic time when the streets will resound with the shouts of laughing children *(Zech. viii. 5)*; or, "when the hearts of the fathers shall be turned to the children and the hearts of the children to the fathers" *(Mal. iii. 24)*. Moreover, "The Lord chasteneth as a man does his son" *(Deut. viii. 5)*; "He bore thee in the wilderness as a father carries his child" *(Deut. i. 31)*. Nor was it only in poetic imagery that human relationship was likened to that of God towards His children.

Parental responsibility was real, even as was the obligation on the part of the child "to honor thy father and thy mother." If, on the one hand, the child was often admonished "to hear the instruction of parents and conform thereto" *(Prov. i. 8; iv. 1, vi. 20)*, to remember that aged parents must not be despised *(Prov. xxiii. 22)*, that to despoil the parental home brought disgrace and dishonor *(Prov. xix. 26)*, the parent, on the other hand, was repeatedly cautioned "that a son becometh wise through correction" *(Prov. xix. 18)*, "that folly can be best removed from the heart of the child by discipline" *(Prov. xxii. 15)*, "that a lad should be brought up with a view to the way in which he shall be expected to go in the future" *(Prov. xxiii. 6)*. There were certain positive, legal commandments in force regarding the child. It was obligatory upon the parent to instruct the child, to teach him the laws of religion *(Deut. vi. 7)*, to give such instruction daily, for Israel was to be "a kingdom of priests and a holy people" and the *entire* people must be holy unto the Eternal. Education was the right of every child under the law. Nor did the father hold the power of life and death over his children as in Rome. Life was sacred. The law was explicit. He dare not decree sentence of death on his children, no matter what the offence. Severe as was the law, with its death penalty, in the case of a stubborn and rebellious son, the power of "patria potestas" was denied the father. The offending son might be brought before the judges if the parents so willed, but the judges must decide the gravity of the offence. *(Ex. xxi. 15, 17; Lev. xx. 9; Deut. xxi. 18-21)*. Neither dare the parent sacrifice his child as was the custom of the neighboring people: "Thou shalt not let thy son pass through the fire" *(Lev. xviii. 21; Deut. xviii. 10)*. So, too, the chasity of the home must be preserved: "Thou shalt not profane thy daughter to cause her to be a prostitute" *(Lev. xix. 3)*. Seduction of a virgin made marriage compulsory *(Ex. xxii. 16)*. In an age when the conception of woman was rather that of a possession than a being with rights; when it was quite customary to sell children into slavery, the daughter was protected to the extent that she might be sold as maid-servant but dare not go out as a man-servant *(Ex. xxi. 7)*. If she pleased not the master he could not re-sell her; she must be redeemed. If he or his son married her and then dealt treacherously with her, she became free. Neither could daughters be disinherited as in Rome. They were entitled to their patrimony when otherwise left unsupported *(Nu. xxxvi.)*.

But perhaps the finest expression of sympathy and law was enunciated innumerable times in regard to the stranger and the widow, likewise the orphan. "Do justice to the fatherless" *(Is. i. 17)* was a positive command. For them, also, the corners of the field, the forgotten grapes, the overlooked and dropped corn remained not as a gift, but as a right under the law *(Deut. xiv. 28, 29; xxiv. 19f; xxvi. 12f)*. Their support was a matter of solicitude. Anathema rested upon him who dared violate the law.

Post Biblical.

When we consider the attitude towards the child as expressed in the later, the post Biblical writings, the Talmud and the Codes, we find that the position of the child has advanced. Here, also, there is a wealth of sentiment favorable to conserving the rights of childhood. There is in evidence here, as in the Bible, great love for children.

The childless are as dead *(Mid. Rab. Gen. 45; M. K. 27)*; who leaves a godly son does not die *(Ibid. 49)*; no man hates his child *(Tal. San. 105)*; will a father witness against his son *(Arvood. Zorah 3)*; children are an adornment of parents; they should be nurtured and cared for *(Kes. 3, 8)*.

That the care and education of the child was taken for granted as an obligation and duty, springing out of parental love and affection, is patent from the aphorisms of the Rabbis of old. The Temple at Jerusalem was certainly near and dear to their hearts. Its destruction was a source of national grief, the greatest sorrow that had befallen the people. Severe as was the affliction, and most commendable as was the spirit which prompted the people to labor zealously to raise again the Sanctuary of the Most High, they that sorrowed and bemoaned its fate, were reminded that Jerusalem had been overthrown because the proper training of the children had been neglected. Furthermore, they were told that the maintenance of the schools was of greater moment than the building of the Temple; that the work for the latter must not interfere with the former; that study was more meritorious than sacrifice; that the salvation of the world is in the breath of school children; that a scholar is greater than a prophet, and that a teacher is more to be revered than even a parent. *(See The Talmud, Eman. Deutsch.)*

Although education was rather religious than secular, it was not wholly so. The dictum of the wise Rabbi Yehudah Hanassi, "He who teaches his son no trade is as one who teaches him theft" *(Kid. 29, 30)*, and the injunction to "add a trade to study, you will then be free of sin," for, "great is the dignity of labor, it honors the man" *(Git. 67a, Ned. 49a)*, had the binding force of law. The Rabbis themselves considered it neither disgraceful nor exceptional to ply even the humblest of trades, recognizing "that the man at his work need not rise up to honor the most learned." There was dignity in work as there was in study. It was a common thing for men renowned for wisdom to earn a livelihood through manual employment.

In such an atmosphere the children grew up. The standards for their welfare were set high. The child was safeguarded from infancy. First and foremost, the Rabbinical law made no distinction as to inheritance between children born in lawful or unlawful wedlock. The shamefulness of birth must not be held against the child. The parents are responsible and the child must not suffer further wrong *(Mielziner: Jewish Laws of Marriage and Divorce, p. 95).* The paternity of children must, however, be protected. A widow or divorcee could not marry within three months after the death of the husband or the annulment of the marriage, nor could a widow with infant marry before the child was two years old *(Ibid.)*

In the event of a separation of parents, the girls remained with the mother, the boys with the father *(Ket. 102b),* although at the request of the mother the boys remained with her until they were six years old, the father, however, supporting them *(Ket. 68b).*

Although the power of chastisement is given the father during the minority of his children, he is not permitted to provoke the child to defend himself, nor shall the character of the punishment be such as to destroy the child's self-respect *(M. K. 17a; Ketub. 50a).* As in modern law, the child's earnings belonged to the parent, but only as long as the parent supported the child *(Chos. Mishp. 270, 2),* and under no circumstances could the parent demand anything unlawful of his child *(B. M.).*

Within the father's house, the child had certain rights which sprang out of parental obligation. In addition to certain religious duties which were expected to be performed by the father for his children, he must provide teachers; failing to do this, he can be compelled *(B. B. 21a; Y. D. 245, 4).* He must teach his son a trade. He must provide for the wants of his minor children, and do for them whatever is necessary for their future welfare. Some authorities add that he must teach his children swimming *(Kid. 29a).*

Among the praises accorded women, is that mothers encourage the education of their sons *(Ber. 17a).* The daughters rarely came into the schools. Their education was within the home, learning in the best manner from the best of teachers, the mothers, the science of housewifery.

It is a significant fact that the Talmud, when it refers to children, usually does so as "children of the house of the teacher," or as "children going from school." That a child could be elsewhere than in school was unthinkable.

Already as early as the first prechristian century, Simon B. Shetach, head of the Sanhedrin, established high schools for boys of 16 years and older. Joshua B. Gamala, who was High-priest in the first century, opened schools for boys in the small towns *(B. B. 21a)*, while in the second century, Judah, the Prince, made education broadcast. He sent out overseers to visit the towns and establish schools. Upon coming to a certain town and asking to see the guardians of the place, they rebuked the leaders who presented to them the soldiers. "These," said they, "are not its protectors. Show us the children and the teachers." Still other protective methods shielded the child from labor.

Whereas in Biblical times and in the period coming close thereafter, it seemed to have been taken for granted that parents need not be compelled to protect their children, in the course of time violation of the rights of children arose. The severe persecutions that befell the Jews in Palestine during the life of Hadrian beggared the people, and as is the case under such circumstances, the children suffered. At a meeting of the Rabbis held in Usha in Galilee about 140 C. E., it was decreed that a father must support his child until the child be grown up (thirteen years of age in the Orient) *(Ket. 49b; E. Ho. 71, 1)*. It is recorded that when at a later time one of the Rabbis, Raba by name, was confronted by a father who failed in his duty, he admonished the parent. "Is it right," said he "in your opinion that your children should be supported by the charities?" Rabbi Chisda (2nd half 3rd cent.) advanced the opinion in a similar case that "We should proclaim against such parents that they are like the wild ass in that they do not care for their young but throw them upon the community." We infer from these cases that the community or charities provided for those children who were neglected by the parents. That the children were not expected to earn their livelihood might best be instanced from the interpretation which was given to the law which is stated in Exodus xxi. 2 relative to the slave with wife and family. The Talmud

(Kid. 22a) explains that the master must support the children "because the children cannot be expected to work and earn their living." If the child of a slave was so protected, how much the more so the children of the freeman?

"If," says Rabbi Meir (2nd cent.), "the law teaches us to have regard for a man's property and not damage it, how much the more regard must we have for his children, his boys and girls, not to cause them harm?"

Another example of advanced legislation might be mentioned here. We have already referred to the Biblical law *(Ex. xxi. 7)* which gave the father the right to hire out his daughter. This right is limited in the Talmud only to cases where there is the prospect of the employer marrying the girl.

Such, in a measure, was the attitude of Israel towards its children; an attitude that reaches down to the present time when changed conditions, resulting from causes which have borne upon the immigrant Jew with peculiar force, have worked serious harm. The deprivation of natural rights in the land of his birth, his compulsory migration, his inability to speedily adjust himself to a changed economic condition, his exploitation on coming to America by those economic factors that continuously operate to scale wages and hold cost of production down, at any cost to human life and morals—these things have produced a lowering of his traditions and standards. Compulsion, necessity, not desire nor longing to exploit the child, have weakened the binding power of the law under which he lived. He and his children adjust themselves under the inefficient laws of a new land in the struggle to keep body and soul together. The lessening of parental authority because the child has now become a bread-winner still further breaks the potency of the ancient relationship of fatherhood as support and nourisher, and childhood as apprenticeship for life within the school room. This relationship once disrupted, the spirit of commercialism gains ascendancy with all the attendant evils with which we are familiar; the sacrifice of the child rather than for the child; the wooing of the law to protect commerce rather than to build character; the breaking of homes instead of the making of homes.

But here I trespass. These are modern conditions, made acute by industrial evolution and human greed. To these particular problems modern standard makers will address themselves. Incomplete and exploratory as this paper is, it may perhaps encourage others to a more thorough investigation. Whatever the past can tell us to aid in solving the problems that perplex men, will not be lightly regarded.

REFERENCES:
    Jewish Encyclopedia, sundry articles.
    Graetz: History of the Jews.
    Emanuel Deutsch: Essay on the Talmud.
    W. Robertson Smith: The Religion of the Semites.
    Karl Budde: Religion of Israel to the Exile.
    Sir Henry Maine: Ancient Law.
    Fustel de Coulanges: The Ancient City.
    Moses Mielziner: Jewish Law of Marriage and Divorce.
    Talmud Babli.
    Jewish Codes.
    The Bible.

CHILD LABOR AND LOW WAGES.

JEROME JONES, Atlanta, Ga.
Editor, the Journal of Labor; President The Southern Labor Congress.

When men, women and children are steeped in ignorance, they are more completely at the mercy (?) of brutal taskmasters of the world. Not knowing their rights, they dare not or cannot maintain them unorganized—like "dumb driven cattle" they are pitilessly exploited, plundered and profaned.

It has been so all through the ages. History shows that where there was the densest ignorance and most galling poverty of the masses, there was also enormous wealth in the hands of a few. When the artisans and peasants of France received but a few cents per day and lived on black, unsalted bread (salt was too great a luxury), Louis XIV. built the palaces of Versailles at a cost of seventy million dollars. To-day over 85 per cent. of the population of Mexico are wholly illiterate, living on less than ten cents per day, and yet the few landed proprietors and other large employers for the past 30 years have become enormously wealthy, some families owning several million acres of land.

Current news dispatches tell that in Chicago many thousand women and girls work for less than $5 per week. The president of one of the great department stores which employs thousands of them admits, under oath, that his company cleared over seven million dollars the past year—and that the company could easily pay a minimum wage of $9 per week without appreciably lessening dividends.

The United States Steel Corporation, which employs several hundred thousand men, pays handsome dividends on its twelve hundred million dollars of capital stock—including, confessedly, over $450,000 of "water," and the wages of many of its employes are beggarly, entailing bitter privations upon their families. The cotton mills of the South generally pay enormous dividends—some as high as thirty and forty per cent. per annum. And yet cotton mill employes, both in the South and in the East, are the poorest paid of all skilled and semi-skilled labor of the country.

The peons of Mexico, the women and girls in department stores and sweatshops of our large cities, the steel workers, the cotton mill operatives—mere samples of the evils of low wages—are blinded by ignorance, lack initiative, courage and method, else they would make a brave effort to obtain living wages.

I do not protest against the "rights of property"—and other "vested rights." I simply assert the superior rights of those whose sweat and brawn largely create such property. I do not indulge in Utopian dreams and demand the immediate abolition of the wage system; I simply demand that the wage system be made fairer and juster to the other partner in the common enterprise—the employe.

I do not ask that the impossible be performed, that the employer pay more wages than the business will legitimately justify; I simply demand that the employer shall not declare hundreds of thousands and millions of dollars in dividends when his employes are in the midst of poverty and surrounded by nameless tragedies, which come too often to the wretchedly paid women and girls of our land.

I have no sympathy with him who would break down all the barriers of law and order and bring on anarchy in its worst form. But I respect less the coldly calculating, grasping employer who, day after day, witnesses the hopeless struggle of his adult male employe trying so hard, but vainly, to furnish the necessaries of life to his hapless family; the grim tragedy which follows the footsteps of girls who receive absolutely too small wages to exist in decency; the children in the mills and sweatshops who work from dawn to dark upon wages which would not properly feed and house a respectable dog or horse.

I did not come here to exploit the cause of organized labor, knowing that this conference is made up of many excellent people of divergent views, and, in my crude way, I would be pleased to observe all the proprieties of the occasion. But, from many years of study and practical experience in my vocation as journeyman printer, I have never yet discovered any other practical way to measurably obtain better wages, shorter hours of labor and safe and sanitary environment. Perhaps, some day, other, better means or methods will be devised. God speed that day!

Next in importance and practical benefit are such associations as yours, composed of men and women of broad views and brave and sympathetic hearts, who labor without other reward than that which comes to noble souls when they help

"A worn and weary brother,
Pulling hard against the stream."

It is you who prick the public conscience, stir the sluggish waters of indifference and neglect, challenge, with mailed hand, the barons of greed and plead with the tongues of angels with those otherwise kind employers, who are not innately grasping and cruel, but whose point of view is sadly warped.

It is such as you who give rise to such investigations as are now going on in Chicago, where vast good will speedily come from exposing the sordid conduct of many employers. Your noble association has come to the assistance of organized labor and helped to strike the shackles from the limbs of thousands of factory child slaves.

A Living Wage.

My friends, in this country of magnificent natural resources, blessed above all other lands in soil and climate, richer than any other country in the world in its agricultural and industrial wealth, there is no real basic reason why any industrious, law-abiding man or woman should work for less wages than will pay for decent shelter and raiment and food.

THAT should be the *irreducible minimum* in our industrial life.

The public conscience should be so aroused that, when it becomes known that any employer hires children under 16 years of age, or pays any older employe less wages than will buy such unstinted necessaries of life, while he, himself, is arrayed in fine linen and fares sumptuously every day, the finger of Scorn should be pointed at him and he should be denied the association of honorable, right-thinking men.

Public opinion, properly aroused and set in motion along these lines, will do more substantial good than statute laws.

WORK is the primal law of the Universe. Idleness blights mentally, morally and physically. But there should be no aristocracy in one form of labor over against another; no gross inequalities, no oppression and cruelty. I think it was Browning who said:

"All service is the same with God,
With God whose puppets, best and worst,
Are we: There is no last nor first."

Low Wages Related to Child Labor.

There is a strong connection between child labor and low wages. I speak particularly of cotton mill labor, with which I am more familiar.

There is not a doubt in my mind but that if the mills had to pay as much for child labor as for adult labor there would be no child labor problem. The child is thus brought into competition with adult labor and what is the result? Both child and adult get starvation wages. As long as the men and women have to compete with children they cannot struggle effectually for a fairer wage. And as long as their own earnings are pitifully small, the children cannot expect to receive more than they now do. One reacts upon the other, the sum total of which horrible condition is, that the mill operatives remain, as a class, largely illiterate and poor, without hope or courage.

Shall such conditions ever be?
Shall we always see
"Truth forever on the scaffold,
Wrong forever on the throne?"

No, thank God! there are throughout this broad land new forces at work. As declared by President Wilson in his inaugural address, the old, old indifference, cruelty and neglect shown towards the masses, is disappearing under a new dispensation of brotherly love. Thousands of good men and women are doing more, at this hour, to better conditions of their more unfortunate brothers and sisters, than at any previous stage of the world's history. This fact should urge us on!

THE FEDERAL CHILDREN'S BUREAU.

JULIA C. LATHROP, Washington, D. C., CHIEF.

A Scotchman once said it was a good thing not to have things in order, because if you did not have things in order, when you were hunting for one thing, you were always finding another thing, too. Now, Nature, to our dull eye, seems not to have got things in very good order; and so, when we are hunting for one good thing, like the abolition of child labor, we are always finding another thing, too,—it was in this way that the National Child Labor Committee found the Children's Bureau.

I take it that I am here, even if I seem to depart a little from the direct program of the evening, to render to you who really created the Bureau some account of my stewardship, and to state as well as I can what I understand to be the functions of this Bureau which you have made.

Now, while you kept to a very easily defined and perfectly straight path in deciding that you would work all your lives, if necessary, to prevent child labor, you set up a very different task for the Children's Bureau, in that it was "to investigate and to report upon all matters pertaining to the welfare of children and child life among all classes of our people." It would be hard to write a broader charter in as many words. Then, after this charter was written, a staff of fifteen people and an appropriation of about $30,000 a year were provided with which to carry out your orders. On the whole, it is probably an advantage to the Bureau to have been obliged to begin in a small way, as its first work must necessarily be experimental and tentative. It was however peculiarly necessary to secure a high degree of efficiency in the staff. The very title "The Children's Bureau" constitutes a touching human appeal. It is only just to the public, never deaf to this appeal, that it be based always upon absolutely scientific work.

Forty years ago, when the standards of public service were not so well established, a scientific bureau of this type would have been unthinkable. Yet now, it was easily possible to discover in the governmental service, by the regular methods of inquiry, persons who had had the best university training, together with special experience in governmental methods of inquiry and statistical research, glad to cast their fortunes in with a new and untried bureau, whose avowed purpose is to aid and protect American childhood. Not a person on this staff who was not chosen for special qualifications; not a person whose appointment cannot be justified under the strictest interpretation of the merit system.

After the general organization of the office was effected, it was necessary to decide what piece of work should be undertaken first, and after careful discussion, it was determined that a series of studies of infant mortality, undertaken in some of the smaller cities, which could be made rapidly and published as collected, was the most practicable subject for an original inquiry. As you know, the term "infant mortality" means the deaths of children under one year of age, and we are challenged by being told that in this country the infant mortality is twice what it should be, since at least half those deaths could be prevented by methods of sanitation, hygiene and wholesome living with which we are perfectly acquainted, but which, as individuals or as communities, we neglect.

In view of the limited funds of the Bureau, it was obviously impossible to enter the great urban areas,—and, indeed, since Booth's "Life and Labor of the English People," the great cities have received an amount of study and ameliorative work which has shown their needs fairly clearly and which has already resulted in a high degree of sanitary improvement. The efforts of the cities themselves to lessen infant mortality, in Boston, Philadelphia, New York and Chicago, are familiar instances in this country.

It was determined to confine the first work to a series of small industrial communities. Moreover, it was to be conducted on a new plan,—instead of examining the record of deaths and compiling statistics therefrom, the birth records were to be first studied, the homes of all the babies born within a certain year visited, and each child traced through his first year, or through so much of the first year as he survived. This was not to be a medical inquiry, but one which should endeavor to present a view of the social and economic status of the family and its civic surroundings. It was to be an entirely democratic inquiry, since the only basis for including any family within it was the fact that a child had been born within that family during the selected year, thus giving a picture, not of a favorable or an unfavorable segment of the community, but of the whole community.

Birth Registration in Only Eight States.

An inquiry has accordingly been started in one small city in Pennsylvania, selected because of its typical industrial conditions as well as because it is within the registration area. In choosing the first city, we were restricted to states in which public records of births and deaths are kept. Curiously enough, with all our democracy, as a nation we have been very careless about giving this recognition to every life. In only eight states at the present time can we find such records as will allow us to carry on our inquiries. This limits the type of towns into which we can go, and limits the usefulness of the Bureau in this first investigation.

The Bureau has therefore been obliged to enter the campaign which the Census Bureau, the Bureau of Public Health and many volunteer societies are carrying on, to awaken America to its responsibility for publicly recording the birthdays of its children, so that the children can be given better care from the moment they are born.

Someone has said that a birth certificate is a real asset to a child, and I believe it is. In the first place, there can be no doubt that if the birth of children can be promptly recorded in every city like Jacksonville, as well as in the great cities of the country, the city health department and the volunteer associations, or better still, the city nurses, can at once go to every family in which it is not certain that the child will have all the care he needs. They can at once apply the standard methods to make sure that the child shall not be blind, and especially can look after the health of the mother. The birth certificate means that we can preserve health and keep many children from dying. Then when the child begins to go to school, it means that the child shall go for as long as the law allows. It means that no child shall be defrauded of a single day of school because there is uncertainty as to his age. It means that no parent shall be tempted to make a false statement as to a child's age.

There is an odd story of the reversal of the parental practice of exaggerating a child's age so that he may go to work earlier, which was told by Mrs. Ella Flagg Young, Superintendent of Schools in Chicago, at a birth registration dinner last winter. (I may boast, in passing, that Chicago is the first city on the planet to have a birth registration dinner. We did feel very proud that we had got the subject up to that degree of elegant and popular interest.) Mrs. Young told of a recent experience in which a principal was dealing with a woman who came with a little child. The woman said: "Well, now, Miss Principal, here is Johnnie. He was six years old on the last day of December, and now the January term is beginning and I want you to take him." And the teacher said gently, "You must be mistaken, because you know you brought brother *Joey* the 1st day of September, and he was just six years old then. Don't you think it is too soon for Johnnie to be six years old?" "Well," said the woman, "you are too smart. If you are as smart as that, you are smart enough to take Johnnie and take care of him anyhow. I have got too much to do."

We want to get birth registration in the state of Florida; to make it possible for our investigators to come to this town, or to some other good town in Florida, to study the social, industrial and economic conditions of every family into which a child is born in a given year, so as to give you a picture of that community. Then you can determine what it needs.

The Bureau's Larger Field.

We believe we shall find the greatest mortality rate among the poorest people and in the poorest quarters in the city, where the city pays less attention to its own housekeeping and where that very fact paralyzes the humble housekeeper who lives there. We want to find out how many of the budgets of these humble families are helped along by older brothers and sisters; how far they are defrauded of school. We want to know about the mothers themselves; what relation there is to early work, to early training for family life, to the burdens of their own home life. We want to know how far the family budget means that older children must go out as younger children come into the family, crowded out before they ought to be crowded out. An inquiry of this sort, tending to make plain what ought to be the standard of care for the American child in his parents' home, cannot but illuminate the whole problem, just as you are making clear the facts of child labor. There were two ways, you remember, of avoiding the call of the siren. One way was to put wax in the ears of the sailors. That is the first way to deal with a thing—to get a law against it. But there was another way, and that was to teach the sailors themselves to make more excellent music. We want to stop everything that stultifies the children and youth of our land, but we are only beginning the task when we do that—we must make certain for every child that it is better for him to come into our schools, for those schools to equip him for the richer and happier industrial future; and must invent the ways to do it. If you will read the Report of the United States Bureau of Labor, "Why Children Leave School," you will be astounded to learn that a very large proportion leave school and go to work because they are bored by school, and because their parents have no confidence that the schools are really going to be a help to the children when they go to work.

Compulsory education and the prohibition of child labor are all very well as temporary expedients, but the task for us is to make the schools so attractive, so manifestly serviceable to the child, that the school compels by its own advantages. This is a sort of compulsory education which will truly dovetail the prohibition of child labor. The readjustment of education to the needs of to-day must match the abolition of child labor. The readjustment is coming, but it presents baffling difficulties. For instance, children leaving school at the age of 14 seem destined to go largely into what the English call the "blind-alley" industries, whether they have industrial training or not, and we may well decide that, with all that vocational guidance can do for children of 14, nothing can displace their need for further education. It is hateful and preposterous to plan upon a system of night schools and day labor as a way of educating young people, with muscles still tender and with the whole process of growth still undetermined, a double strain at the very period at which there ought to be no strain.

If we could satisfy our consciences as to the education and the improvement afforded young people, we are still confronted by the fact that our youth have a right to demand some guarantee of safety in their pleasures, just as we have a right to demand from the city some guarantee of safety on the highways. There is now a subtly arranged series of temptations and dangers, with dancing halls whose occasion of profit rests not so much in the dancing as in the drinking connected with it; with shows and entertainments which city policing should rescue from darkness and indecency. It is encouraging to see that there is in Jacksonville an interest in creating playgrounds, to make a start towards that civic care for the amusements of a city which is as legitimate and proper a part of its service as to make sure that we are protected against fire or against contagious diseases, and just as dignified—amusements that will satisfy the youth of the city, which they will consider pleasant, and not the imposition of goody-goody people, whom certainly children never did like and never could bear.

Examination of the letters which come constantly into the office, show that the subjects about which the public is most stirred are, first, child labor, and then the questions of wayward children, feeble-minded children, the pensioning of mothers, infant mortality and infant care, vocational training and the special protection of girls; and there is an increasing sense of the human value of such abstractions as birth registration. If the daily press publishes some tale of punishment of a child which is not in accord with the newer view of protection rather than penalty, the Bureau receives letters of inquiry and protest from all over the country, notwithstanding the fact that the Bureau has no authority to go beyond investigating and reporting.

It is the business of the Bureau to know what is going on in the world concerning children, and hence, a library has been established which consists largely of clippings and pamphlets, and which, as rapidly as possible, is securing through translations from the current literature of the world, information as to the world progress of all movements affecting children.

It is an indication of the wisdom of those of you who created this Bureau that you desired it to be larger than the compelling title of this Committee and larger than the topics on which I have touched. You have undertaken by the very scope of the charter of this law, to create a bureau which slowly and painstakingly shall devote itself to ascertaining and setting forth the essential conditions under which the Childhood of America is to secure its constitutional birthright.

HOW TO MAKE CHILD LABOR LEGISLATION MORE EFFECTIVE.

SAMUEL McCUNE LINDSAY,
Vice-Chairman, National Child Labor Committee; Professor of Social Legislation, Columbia University, New York.

The past decade has witnessed very considerable progress in the *standards* of child labor legislation, respecting age limits, working hours, night work and in the elimination of children from some of the more hazardous occupations. In common with other labor laws and with nearly all social legislation, child labor laws have often failed or broken down in their enforcement because of defects in form or legal phraseology, bad drafting of statutes, and poor or inadequate administrative machinery.

What a witty district attorney once called "the moral yearnings and aspirations of the community" have too often been enacted hastily into legislation of this kind, and no one has thought out in advance the full consequences of the problems involved in the application of the general principles or decisions with respect to policy which had been agreed upon. The proper legislative language was not found to express the exact purposes desired and none other. It is, therefore, necessary and desirable to give more attention in these national conferences of the workers for child labor reform, than has been customary in the past, to questions of how to perfect and enforce the child labor legislation already on the statute books, if future legislation is to be improved both in form and substance and if the continuing advance in standards is to be assured.

The National Child Labor Committee has rendered recently a great public service by co-operating with the Commissioners on Uniform Laws, the American Bar Association and others in the preparation and recommendation of a uniform child labor law for adoption in all the states. This uniform law, however, is in the nature of the case little more than a skeleton giving an enumeration of a great many kinds of child labor which must be regulated in accordance with different standards. This skeleton must be filled in somewhat differently in different states, adapted to their local needs and especially made really effective by adaptation to the local means or machinery of enforcement. This work requires great skill and patient effort. There is a technique of child labor reform and a basis of experience attained by the various child labor committees in different parts of the country that has not yet been fully utilized in the improvement of child labor legislation. The child labor committees have been thus far, and will for some time to come, continue to be engaged in a work that is largely negative and prohibitive in character. They must point out the evils as rapidly as diligent and faithful investigation reveal them in a system of industry that permits of the employment of children for wages and their consequent and inevitable exploitation. They must condemn these evils and present sound standards of regulation or prohibition of child labor in all of its harmful ramifications. This repressive work will go on long after we have entered a second stage of evolution in child labor reform.

The second stage of progress in legislation has already been entered upon in a few communities and the time is ripe in all. This is the stage of constructive statesmanship which will take our prohibitive statutes relating to child labor which we find happily to some extent in every state of the Union, and will unite them into one strong and effectual force, not only forbidding child labor, but also making provision in a constructive and practical way to guarantee the newer freedom for the child. This new freedom, which is the positive and real side of child labor reform, will never be fully realized until our child labor laws are carefully co-ordinated with the school laws, the public health laws and all laws and ordinances that aim to protect the home and guard the health and morals of the community. To co-ordinate properly this body of law, so as to secure in the not too distant future what many have long wished to see, a veritable children's code, will be no easy task. The vast amount of work imposed upon the average state legislature in this progressive age makes it increasingly difficult for the legislatures themselves to prepare legislation with that care and precision which this task demands. The legislatures are developing gradually through legislative reference bureaus and the beginnings of legislative drafting bureaus a machinery of their own which may in time provide for the kind of legislative work which I hope our child labor committees will insist upon. But until much more is done in this direction by Congress and the state legislatures, I believe the National Child Labor Committee could render the greatest service to the cause we represent by devoting a good share of its time and resources to the better preparation and to the more scientific study of the problems involved in our legislative proposals.

I. *A National Child Labor Legislation Drafting Service.*

It would be a fine contribution for all child labor committees of America to make to the cause of better government, if the purely voluntary organizations represented in this National Child Labor Conference were to set a new standard of real reform in legislative expression. I am sure it would result in economy both in the cost to the state and to those who voluntarily support the efforts of the various child labor committees. It would focus attention more and more on the results obtained from legislation rather than upon the struggle to get legislation. From such a movement we might expect not only the unification and co-ordination of child labor laws with school and health laws and other similar or allied branches of legislation, but also the detailed study of the administrative organization of the community, both the official and that of private societies which can be relied upon to help enforce such regulations. The uncertainties of poor legislation lead to litigation, to adverse decisions from the courts, to the annoyance of honorable employers and to evasion on the part of dishonorable employers. A precise and exact statute stands a far better chance of acceptance by a legislature, even when it is not entirely friendly, and will have back of it from the start the support of the best employers whose business is regulated by it.

It seems to me a fair question to ask, at least in many of the states that have had complicated child labor laws on their statute books for years, whether sufficient attention has been paid to the daily experiences of factory inspectors or others charged with the detailed work of inspection and enforcement. It was from the reports of such pioneer factory inspectors as Horner and Taylor in England, who carefully recorded their personal experiences and freely drew upon them in their recommendations to the government and to Parliament, that much of the best that is found in English factory legislation came. Various devices will suggest themselves to an intelligent chief factory inspector or labor commissioner who has an intellectual grasp of his work as he looks over, day by day, the reports of his field staff, which ought to be embodied at once in the law and could not have been foreseen by the original draftsman. Thus, for example, the Commissioner of Labor in New York found several years ago that children much under the age of sixteen in some factories were taught to say that they were sixteen years of age in order to keep out of the jurisdiction of the factory inspector. A simple change in the law was recommended by that commissioner whereby thereafter the factory inspectors were empowered to challenge any child found at work who was apparently under the age of sixteen and require the employer to furnish at once the legal proofs of age required of children fourteen to sixteen years of age in securing their working papers, or discharge the child so challenged. The burden of proof of age was thus shifted from the inspector to the employer, where it more properly belonged, and that particular kind of evasion of the law ceased to exist. There are probably hundreds of equally valuable bits of experience which nobody in this country has collected and made available for the draftsmen of future legislation.

It might well be considered the special province and duty of the National Child Labor Committee, in its relations to the various state and local committees, to act as a clearing house in such matters. I would advocate a further and still more important step. The National Committee might, with profit, organize a drafting service which could be used by all other organizations in the preparation of child labor legislation. Such an arrangement would not deprive any state or local committee of its right to decide questions of policy nor would it make any other organization or state or local committee necessarily subject to the control of the National Committee. On the contrary the necessity would devolve on the local committee to gather the material for its legislation and to decide all questions of policy and of standards in accordance with its own desires, while the drafting service of the National Committee would simply put the policies decided upon into precise and exact legislative language and advise on questions of law, constitutionality and administrative procedure.

A legislative drafting service for child labor legislation in all parts of the country would be an expensive undertaking for the National Committee if it alone had to do all of the work involved. Fortunately, even for the actual drafting work apart from preliminary investigations, there are other agencies which would gladly co-operate. Columbia University has a department or bureau of legal research and legislative drafting in which men are being trained professionally for this work. While its financial resources are not sufficient to meet all of the demands that are made upon it for free service, it could and would probably develop a special division for child labor legislation as it has already done for labor legislation in general, provided a very modest sum of money was available to meet the additional expenses incurred. In any event, whether the National Committee decided to turn this drafting work over to some other organization or to organize its own staff, it would find it easy to secure at little cost some valuable assistance from the Columbia University Bureau and from the existing legislative reference and drafting bureaus already established by several state governments.

The problems of child labor will always vary greatly in the different sections of a country as large and diverse in its population and industries as the United States, and the variations will often be equally great within the boundaries of a single large industrial state like New York or Pennsylvania. We have, however, had our attention fixed too long upon the differences in conditions and standards, and we have not reaped the advantage which I see immediately before us, which will come from a realization and knowledge of the greater and more important field of administrative experience in which there is greater uniformity. Unfortunately this uniformity has until very recently been largely in the break-down and in the lack of enforcement of child labor legislation. The possibilities in the uniformity of administrative experience that will make child labor laws effectual and rally to their support all of the official agencies of government, have not been realized and will not be until a more exact and painstaking study of legislative draftsmanship and the problems therein involved has been made. The day when a bill was ready for introduction into the legislature after it had received the hasty glance of an experienced but busy lawyer engaged in active practice, or even after it had been more or less carefully drafted by such a lawyer, is now past. Some legal knowledge is, of course, necessary for the proper drafting of any legislative proposal and a great deal of legal knowledge is sometimes needed to determine difficult constitutional questions involved in the preparation of all social legislation. A much more important requisite, however, is the painstaking historical research and the actual field investigation of the problems involved in dealing with the regulation of industry and labor. The National Child Labor Committee is already carrying on intensive investigations of industrial conditions in different parts of the country, and therefore the extension and utilization of such work in a department of legislative drafting ought not to be very difficult. Nothing that could be suggested, I feel sure, will make the National Child Labor Committee more alive to its chosen task and tend to keep it at the high mark of efficiency than to face continuously the real problems involved in drafting scientifically the legislation on child labor that is needed in all parts of the country.

Mr. Thomas I. Parkinson of Columbia University has seen the vision of what better legislative drafting would mean in the service of social reforms and has illuminated the discussion of the essentials of good drafting in a recent article entitled *Legislative Drafting* (Proceedings of the New York Academy of Political Science, Vol. III, p. 190, New York, 1912), from which I quote: "The need for better drafted legislation has been presented frequently and forcibly by prominent lawyers and political scientists. The quantity and quality of our statute law, federal and state, has been the subject of vigorous criticism for many years. There exists a well-founded belief, which found frequent expression at the recent meeting of the American Bar Association, that the popular discontent arising from the tendency of our courts to declare unconstitutional or render ineffective by interpretation legislation enacted to remedy existing social and industrial evils can be traced directly to the fact that much of our so-called social legislation is hastily prepared, ill-considered, and thrown on the statute book without careful study of constitutional limitations, existing statutes, or the phraseology of the principles and rules necessary to give effect to the intentions of its proponents. . . . The scientific preparation of a statute involves (1) Knowledge of conditions proposed to be regulated and determination of the exact evils requiring regulation; (2) Determination of the nature of the regulation required and the precise principles or rules which will effect such regulation; (3) Phraseology of the new principles or rules and of necessary administrative provisions in apt and precise language which will fit them into existing principles of constitutional and statute law and make them reasonably clear to the executive and judicial officers who are to enforce them."

Such is the philosophy and the practical advantages of a new movement in legislation that promises a new and better way of doing old tasks. I am sure that an organization like the National Child Labor Committee, whose work necessarily lies so largely in the field of legislation and whose leadership in new and forceful methods in social reform has contributed as much as the great humane cause it represents to its enviable reputation, will not be slow to heed the message: Draft better child labor laws.

II. Better Means of Enforcement of Child Labor Legislation.

There is another aspect of the improvement of child labor legislation besides the need for better drafting of child labor statutes, to which I wish also to call attention. A great deal is said, in the discussion of other social problems, of their interrelations. A few weeks ago a prominent economist, in advocating minimum wage legislation, was asked: "What are you going to do with the people who cannot earn the minimum wage you propose?" He replied: "The adoption of a minimum wage law will make us face, more clearly than now, a whole program of social reconstruction, and will make it necessary for us to do something to train people of small earning power and develop their latent capacity, and to care for, either by state aid or by private philanthropy, those who are hopelessly handicapped and cannot be trained to earn a living wage. We will not know exactly how many such people there are, nor how great is this problem, and perhaps others like it, until we segregate the people who cannot earn living wages." In like manner, when we enact child labor laws, if we really mean to make them work, we will face many of the real difficulties for the first time only when we begin to enforce them.

The improvement of legislation, therefore, involves the discovery and development of adequate means to carry out such laws.

The ordinary machinery for the enforcement of the criminal law, such as that providing for fines and imprisonment of persons found guilty of burglary, manslaughter and the general crimes and misdemeanors against property and persons, does not always apply to legislation which has back of it only the more intelligent and only a fraction, at best, of the total population of a community. We must provide ways and means for utilizing new agencies and creating new machinery for this work.

Experience has proven that labor legislation generally has no power of self-enforcement, but, on the contrary, is apt to be used as a means of greater exploitation on the part of unscrupulous persons, when it is not rigidly and uniformly enforced. The good suffer who voluntarily obey its precepts, and the evil make the greater gains. This is a total loss to the community. It is deceived in thinking that it has security, when in reality the evils complained of grow greater. For this reason it has been said that a child labor law without provision for enforcement is worse than useless. There is no community so poor in resources that it cannot afford to make some provision for enforcing officers for any law which has aroused sufficient interest to secure its enactment. It is primarily the business of every child labor committee to hold the public authorities to this fundamental duty inherent in government itself.

We have not done all that can be done to develop efficient factory inspection and, first of all, to secure, in connection with every child labor law, some provision for factory inspectors (by whatever name they are called), whose sole official duties shall be to inspect continuously and report fully the results of their observations. The state or the public authority must be held to full responsibility and should not be encouraged to expect this work from private agencies. There is, of course, a great deal that the individual citizen, as well as a private society, can do to co-operate with the public authority.

It is fundamentally wrong in principle, however, to expect private societies or individuals to organize and pay the cost of the machinery to enforce child labor laws or any other kind of social legislation. The public has a right to expect another kind of service from such societies as ours and from groups of citizens who enjoy superior educational advantages. This other kind of service is the study and investigation of the facts underlying social evils and the education of the public mind and conscience with respect to decisions on questions of public policy in dealing with them. All government, however, becomes ineffectual, and social justice a meaningless concept, unless the decrees of law are enforced and the authority of government established through the acts of public officials who represent it in its abstract relations to all the people, rather than by the agents of groups of citizens who advocate particular policies. It seems clear, therefore, that it is our duty as a child labor committee, whether national or local, to spend whatever money and effort is necessary to hold government and its responsible officials up to the highest measure of duty and efficiency in the enforcement of child labor laws. Where a legislature merely passes a child labor law and makes no provision for factory inspectors to see that it is obeyed, it has failed in a part of its duty. The child labor law as passed is incomplete and imperfect and we should continue to point out this fact and to agitate for the completion of its work in the same manner and with the same insistence that we would do for new legislation. Have we not been somewhat remiss in this matter, and is it not also incumbent upon us to do likewise where some factory inspection has been provided but is ineffectual by reason of the incompetency or the mal-administration of factory inspectors? Would not greater improvement of child labor legislation be accomplished in many quarters if the organized efforts of its friends were directed in greater measure to its enforcement, rather than so exclusively as at present to the extension of its scope or to new legislation?

III. Federal Child Labor Legislation.

There is still a third aspect to the improvement of child labor legislation, to which I can only very briefly refer here. With the growth of industries organized nationally, with plants or factories located in several states but under one central management or direction, the difficulties of securing reasonable regulation of labor conditions have been greatly enhanced. The opposition that is made to the most moderate demands for the protection of working children at the various state capitols has become stronger, because of the effect of any action of the state legislature upon large business interests, powerful within the state but operating as well in other states which do not have the same regulations. We may recognize, on the one hand, the difficulties of securing uniform regulation through the adoption of our Uniform Child Labor Law, and, on the other hand, the difficulties and limitations both constitutional and political in securing any regulation by Congress that would not fall below the standards already adopted in many of the industrially more advanced states. It does seem to me, however, that we are far enough advanced to propose a minimum national standard which would not go as far possibly as that of the Uniform Child Labor Law, but would give us the basis of a more substantial, effective and reasonable regulation of all industries operating and organized to operate in more than one state. The industrial situation increasingly demands national action of this character in justice to those engaged in interstate transactions. Such regulation is within the spirit of the Constitution of the United States, and it is the opinion of well-informed consitutional lawyers and publicists that Congress is not without power to accomplish this result. James Wilson, a signer of the Declaration of Independence and one of the really great leaders in the constitutional convention of 1787, as well as a justice of the Supreme Court of the United States, who exerted an influence second only to that of Marshall in the formulation of the principles of interpretation laid down at the outset of the government in determining what the Constitution means, has well said: "Whatever object of government is confined in its operation and effects within the bounds of a particular state should be considered as belonging to the government of that state; whatever object of government extends in its operation or effects beyond the bounds of a particular state should be considered as belonging to the Government of the United States."

I do not contend that all, or even a very large part, of the necessary regulation of the manifold forms of child labor throughout the country could be or should be contained in a national law. I do believe that a minimum standard could be formulated and should be established by national authority to affect those forms of child labor that we find in great interstate industries engaged in interstate traffic and competition which cannot be adequately reached through any mere state regulation. That this would stimulate and strengthen the further regulation of other forms of child labor that are local in character and confined within the boundaries of particular states, and therefore make necessary greater activity, rather than less, on behalf of the states themselves in dealing with child labor matters, I have not the slightest doubt. The National Child Labor Committee, if it is to go forward and continue to hold a position of supremacy in leadership, must undertake the delicate and difficult task of determining what national legislation is needed and how it can be secured without doing violence to our traditions, or to the constitutional system of government under which we live.

FROM MOUNTAIN CABIN TO COTTON MILL.

JOHN C. CAMPBELL, Asheville, N. C.
Russell Sage Foundation.

The subject assigned me is too large for discussion in the time allotted. In reality, my theme consists of two subjects to be compared.

Careful comparison requires well-established facts. Such facts are lacking for the most part and the comparison of mountain and mill conditions is, as yet, in the main, a weighing of probabilities and a balancing of the opinions of investigators.

It is a difficult matter to get facts relating to the lives of men, women and little children. One's feelings enter into such an effort and opinions are therefore likely to be advanced as facts. Many honest investigators have a natural bias induced by feeling on the subject under investigation, and also a bias that arises from the influences of experiences in intimate personal matters entirely disassociated, seemingly, from the question at issue. Personal experience generally brings one to his view-point and places before his eyes the glass through which he looks. That glass may be clear or clouded, in or out of focus, or such as outlines even the defects in things looked upon, in the glowing colors of the rainbow.

To judge fairly the findings of any investigator, in sociological matters especially, it would therefore seem highly important to know what influences and experiences have affected the investigator. Lest you be alarmed, let me say I do not intend to give you my life history. It is fair, however, that you should know before I begin that I have been somewhat intimately in touch with mountain questions and conditions as a resident of the mountain country of the South for nearly twenty years, five of which were spent in a more or less comprehensive and comparative study of different mountain areas.

This study led to a secondary and incidental study of mill questions and a weighing of some of the claims made by the advocates of the mills.

In this secondary study, in the effort to ascertain how many mountain people really came to the mills, letters were sent to five hundred or more mills of the South, interviews were held with mill men—especially with those noted for their interest in their employes—and inasmuch as comparatively little time could be given to this secondary study, the better mills were visited for the most part. It was felt that with a knowledge of conditions existing in these better mills, together with a knowledge of the response made by the mountain people when they went to these mills, and a general knowledge of mountain conditions, conclusions more nearly just could be reached.

In this mountain-mill discussion there is yet more of heat than of light, and it is with something of hesitancy that I seek to make my contribution to the discussion, for an unguarded statement or a statement that cannot be viewed from all sides in the time at our disposal, may add to the heat rather than to the light. It is in the hope, however, that something may be offered to help in reaching ultimate right conclusions, that I venture upon a discussion of this much discussed question.

The Mountain Country and the Mountain People Who Go to the Mill.

It would seem that some of the resentment aroused might be avoided if there were a clear definition of terms.

What is the mountain country? Who are the mountain people? What mountain people go to the mills?

We may regard, I think, as approximately the mountain section of the South the upland regions of the Virginias, the Carolinas, Kentucky, Tennessee, Georgia and Alabama—or that portion of these eight states included between the front of the Blue Ridge on the East and the more or less indefinite western escarpment of the Cumberland Plateau and its northern extension.

A cross section of this highland region would reveal a central depression, much fluted by numerous minor and elevated valley ridges and bordered on the east and on the west by lofty mountains and plateaus. The central depression in its entirety is called the Greater Appalachian Valley; the upland belt to the east, the Blue Ridge section, and that to the west, the Allegheny Cumberland Mountains and Plateaus.

Within these Southern Highlands—in an area of approximately 100,000 square miles—live over 5,000,000 people. Although the United States Census uses as its urban minimum an incorporated community of 2,500, let us use less than one-half of that or 1,000 as our urban minimum and we shall find then that we have 1,000,000 of the 5,000,000 as our urban and near-urban population—and 4,000,000 in round numbers as our more or less remote rural group, living in unorganized communities, in incorporated villages of less than 1,000 inhabitants and on small farms and scattered holdings.

We find, however, that the cotton mills do not draw equally upon the mountain areas of the eight states under consideration. Virginia has a few cotton mills and also Kentucky, but practically the pull of the cotton mill is felt most in the mountains of the Carolinas, Georgia, Alabama and in Tennessee. In discussing the mountain-mill question, therefore, we must consider chiefly the mountain population of these five states, which numbers 533,248 in its urban and near-urban group, and 1,922,832 in its rural group.

But what mountain people of these five states go to the mills? Are they from the urban group, or the rural group, or from both? We would naturally suppose, from the arguments advanced by mill advocates, that they are from that group which is so isolated and so poverty-stricken that their only hope for well-being—almost for preservation—is in being taken to the cotton mills. Surely the argument, based on such disinterested consideration, is not meant to apply to our urban group nor to many even in the rural group.

Those who know the mountain country know that while life is hard for many in the rural group, and that life will grow harder for many with the passing of pioneer conditions, without the training to meet new conditions—there are hundreds, yes thousands, who live a wholesome rural life. There are also many of this rural group in unorganized communities, and in the ever-increasing number of industrial nuclei that are springing up, who might properly, so far as attainment is concerned, be included in our urban group. It would seem, then, that this unselfish effort of mill men for the uplift of the mountain people must refer merely to the most needy of our intensely rural group.

When I review the arguments advanced to justify taking these people from the mountains (presumably from the sub-rural group) I find myself in perplexity. On the one hand, I hear and read the claim that the sturdy mountaineer and his children, inured to toil and bowed down by the excess of it in their mountain environment, should be taken to the mills where they may have release from excessive labor and may live in comparative ease with only moderate effort; on the other hand, the argument is advanced (and sometimes by those who advanced the argument just given) that these mountain people are so debased, so criminal, so shiftless and indolent, that it is a mercy to take them to the mills to better their morals and to teach them how to labor. In either case, one notices that the mill agent is pictured as an altruist.

Every reasonable person at all acquainted with the situation knows, however, that mill men are not angelic messengers seeking out the over-worked, the lonely and the criminal to help them or to reclaim them. Let us be frank. When the mill emissaries go to the mountains, they are after operatives and they do not waste their time in searching only for the dwellers in the little isolated cabins. They go to organized and unorganized communities alike, to fertile valleys and coves if need be, and not alone to areas of so-called barren soil. They go wherever the people are and they take the best they can get, regardless of the possible effect. In times of scarcity of labor they want many operatives, and they always want cheap operatives, and the song they sing in praise of the cotton mill is as sweet as the siren song of old. In the minds of those best able to judge, there is little doubt that that siren song means shipwreck to many mountain lives; both to those who are induced to leave their mountain homes from a desire for a change, or because of the increasing stress of life.

The comparative method of treating this whole subject has obscured the main issues. I use it only in order that the other side of some of the arguments advanced by mill advocates may be presented.

Better Health?

Prominent among the arguments put forward by the mill advocates are those that have to do with health, wage, morals and schooling for the children.

It is impossible as yet to get accurate data on all of these subjects. In the matter of health there are special difficulties and we must await a much needed registration of births, deaths, disease, etc., before any definite conclusions based on vital statistics can be drawn.

We cannot mention the matter of health in this connection without having the hookworm wriggle into the foreground. Earlier we were led to suppose that in all of the mountain country the percentage of hookworm infection was higher than in the region in which the cotton mills are situated. More careful investigation shows this to be true in certain mountain counties and areas, and not in others. We have been urged to allow women and little children to work long hours in the cotton mills in order that the mountain population may be cured of hookworm infection. On paper we have seen established within the cotton mill belt a veritable Eden for the mountaineer and his children. Labor there is, to be sure, but of such a beneficent nature that the whir of the wheel and the hum of the spindle are drowned in the happy laughter of children making play of work, when they are not crowding the beautiful school buildings to their utmost capacity; and when the day of playing-at-work is over, they troop to their cheerful and sanitary homes furnished tastefully by father's savings. We are asked to hear the sounds of innocent revelry at eventime, when the fascinations of night school do not hold the young enthralled, and on the Sabbath we are called to listen to the music of matin and vesper bells—and all because the hookworm has not entered this Eden (at least, to any great extent).

That there is such a disease and that it has worked and is working sad havoc in mountain and lowland areas, men of scientific standing have demonstrated beyond a doubt. But is the cure of hookworm or typhoid or tuberculosis in the mountains to be found in taking an out-of-door, liberty-loving people, putting them to work indoors for long hours day and night and forcing them to live in congested villages made up largely of people who have hitherto known little of organized community life? Is not a conclusive answer given by the splendid work being done jointly by the various state boards of health and the Rockefeller Sanitary Commission, whose officers think it eminently worth while to send their physicians and place their dispensaries far back in remote mountain areas in order that the people may be cured of their ailments speedily in their own environment?

Is it not a sufficient answer to those who argue from a better diet and results obtained by patients who have submitted themselves to hospital or laboratory tests, to say that we are not dealing with laboratory tests or with results obtained in hospitals, but with self-directing human beings with established food habits? The mountain people would prove themselves a remarkable people, indeed, if with more money to spend than they had in their mountain homes they should spend it for food that they did not like, but which was said to be good for them, in preference to food which they did like and of whose wholesomeness they had no doubt. As a matter of fact, experience in mountain schools has proved that the food habit is as difficult to change in mountain people as in others, and the food which in the open air of the country and in out-of-door occupations is sufficient, at least for a modicum of health, in indoor life and occupations may often become an active source of ill health. In this matter of health, as in all others, we face the problem that we face everywhere, of inducing people to choose of their own accord what is best for them.

A Better Wage?

In the discussion of wage, if by "better wage" is meant a larger money earning, there is little question that such wage is better in the mills for most adults and children than in the mountains. And yet it is difficult to compare the returns made for labor in mills with those made in the mountains, for in the mountains service rendered is often paid for by an equivalent in labor or in commodities whose monetary value would be hard to estimate. There remain also the difficulties of finding the relation of wage to the cost of living.

If, however, in this question of a better wage there be estimated the actual return in benefits to the individual or family for services rendered, the whole question is put into the larger question of family condition.

Those who lay stress on the mill wage as being better, emphasize the benefits derived from the savings resulting. From government reports we learn that mill operatives who had remained a long time in one locality and had been industrious, had accumulated something, but the class of families who moved frequently from one mill to another was without savings. If we accept this statement, and I think we must, and hold that the mountain families as a whole have saved, we must class the mountain operatives among the industrious, among those who have enjoyed good health and who have remained in one place. A better wage is a better wage only if it be properly earned, well-spent or wisely saved.

Better Morals?

I cannot enter into the many questions that bear upon morals and moral codes, but if the arguments as to the degradation and the criminality of the mountain people be based upon facts, or if the mountain people be unmoral rather than immoral, I would ask you if it is not likely that active immorality will become more active, and an unmoral state pass into an immoral one more readily where many people of the same social grade are closely grouped together?

It is seen in certain industrial communities that are more justly noted for fostering a right environment for their employes than are the great majority of those we are now considering, that the employes find in the neighborhood the level to which they are predisposed. Must there not be a low level in the envioronment of the mills as well? Or why do we hear so often the argument by mill advocates that it is better to keep even very young children employed in the mills than to subject them to the temptations of idleness in the mill village or nearby city? Possibly by night the young employes are too tired to seek any influence, good or bad, or if not, they go out to seek only the good to which, we are told, they were formerly unaccustomed.

Social service workers in the mountains appear, after all, not to enjoy a monopoly of delightful inconsistency, as some would have us believe.

Better Schooling?

Exceptional stress has been laid upon the school advantages open to mountain children when they go to the mills. In several of the mill villages are modern school buildings amply equipped, presided over by trained teachers of ability and of personal charm. This, however, is an exceptional condition, and for the mountain children at least, even in such mills, school opportunities are limited to those under or near the legal age of employment. Most of the mill teachers that were seen were desirous of having the children remain at school. One of the mill men, justly famous for the educational equipment he had provided for mill children, told me in all frankness that his teachers needed to be reminded continually that the schools were run for the mills—not the mills for the schools. With equal frankness, he admitted that when the mills were running at full time every hand over legal age was needed, and when mills were running on short schedule the families, usually large, needed to put as many members of the family as possible in the mills in order to have a weekly living wage.

Much is made of night school, but how many of you, were you children of the class of people alleged to come from the mountains, would seek a night school after a day of labor—or if you were on the night shift, how many of you would be drawn to the day school?

Educational equipment in the mountains is far from what it should be and does not compare with that in the few exceptional mill villages; and yet while in the mountains, if the mountain child wishes, he can attend for from three to six months in the year such schools as there are, but when he goes to the mill and becomes a wage-earner with wages payable to his parents, indolent acquiescence to schooling on the part of the parents passes often into active opposition.

All Southern Mills Together Could Accomodate Only a Fraction of Mountain Population.

But enough of this comparative method. Anything can be proved by it if one picks his mill and picks his mountain cabin—or makes generalizations from local instances.

I sometimes wonder if those who are so sure that the mills are solving mountain problems can realize what the mill men should know: that operatives from the mountains are, after all, but a small fraction of the total number of operatives, even in the group of mills accessible to the mountain people. The maximum estimate given me of the total number of mill operatives in all the southern cotton mills (not merely those near the mountains, but in all the

Southland) is 250,000 and the total population dependent on the mills 585,000. Assuming this mill population to be 600,000, there remain 1,300,000 in the rural group of the mountain areas of the five mountain states under discusssion, the total rural population of these states (as I have used the term rural) being in round numbers 1,900,000.

Why defend the mills, then, by putting forward the limitations of mountain life when *all* the mills of the South, if manned entirely by mountain operatives, would affect less than one-third of all the rural mountain population in only five of the eight mountain states, and when in point of fact only a small fraction of the total 250,000 operatives are mountain people?

It is not a question primarily of the mountains. It is an industrial and a rural question and the people whom it is affecting chiefly are the people of the piedmont section and the lowland section, who come from a fertile soil and to whom the arguments based on isolation do not apply to the extent applicable to the mountain people.

The Questions at Issue.

The real question, therefore, is not whether the mountain fraction of operatives is better off in the mills than in the mountain environment. The questions at issue are these: Are the conditions now existing in the mills all they ought to be under the present laws? Are the present laws all they ought to be? Is the employment of children in gainful occupations right? Ought the unrestricted employment of women in such industries as the cotton textile industry to be allowed?

Those of us who believe in the mountain country and the mountain people resent the imputations that have been placed upon them in this discussion. If the worst be true that has been charged against some mountain people, an indictment ought not to be brought against all the mountain people, and surely a charge, whether false or true, against one people ought not to be used to conceal the wrongs in an industrial system working harm to other people.

There are mill men who admit that the mountain people in their mountain environment can earn a better living more easily than in the cotton mills, even under present conditions.

If we all will but open our eyes we shall see that there is a nation-wide rural question in this land of ours and not one pertaining to the highland section of the South alone. The Southern highlanders have been held up as a peculiar people with peculiar needs, requiring peculiar treatment. The urban highlander can take care of himself and the remote rural highlander needs only what rural people need everywhere. Poor roads and other disadvantages in the mountains are offset to an extent by the fact that the urban pull of the South has not been strong enough as yet to drain the rural sections of the mountains of their virile stock a statement which cannot be made of all rural areas in our country.

We should thank our friends and temporary enemies of the opposition for calling to our attention the defects of our rural education, and we should face the facts that they bring forth, even though we are forced to disagree with their remedies for the present limitations of rural life in the mountains. Did time permit, I think it could be proved to you conclusively, from the findings of men of scientific attainment, that the mountain country, whether viewed in its entirety or by its regional belts, is a land of resources and a land of promise in which the soils are not barren but need only the adaptation of method and crop to soil, slope and elevation.

There is need for us to ally ourselves actively with all movements for rural betterment—to uphold the hands of our national and state educational and agricultural authorities in their efforts to promote farm schools and rural life schools, of our state boards of health and their federal and privately endowed allies. Is there not significance and promise in the announcement of the Red Cross Society that it is to take up rural nursing as a part of its activities? Who will make the promise possible of full realization by properly endowing this movement—and other rural movements?

In our zeal for rural welfare, we ought not, however, to ignore our industrial life. It must not be assumed that all mill men are primarily selfish. Some probably would gladly break from the shackles of a competitive system and the insistent calls of stockholders, North and South alike, for larger dividends.

What we all need is a larger social vision, a deeper sense of brotherhood. If there be industrial leaders bound in selfishness and blinded by greed, they must be forced by an awakened public opinion to acquiescence in righteous popular demands. Their children and our children must not be allowed to climb to luxury and ease upon the labor-bent backs of other children. It is futile to attempt to make smooth the way of industrial progress by using any group of laborers as road material. Ours is the task to force by legislation, made operative by public opinion, recognition of the fact that men's bodies are worth more than the machines they operate, that the welfare and happiness of women are of more value than increased dividends, and the soul of a little child of infinitely more value than the saving on a spool of cotton or on a bolt of cotton cloth.

SOCIAL WELFARE AND CHILD LABOR IN SOUTH CAROLINA COTTON MILL COMMUNITIES.

REV. C. E. WELTNER, D.D.,
Welfare Worker, Olympia Mills, Columbia, S. C.

You remember the time when the kaleidoscope afforded amusement. How delighted we were when at the slightest turn of the hand the little pieces of glass fell into different positions, forming new designs, and new color combinations as we held the little tube up to the light. We are still deeply interested in the kaleidoscope, though it is no longer a toy; the great kaleidoscope of life has become to us all a matter of observation, study, and vital concern. Its pictures are larger—the pieces of glass have become men, women and children; at each turn from day to day the designs make deep impressions which change with wonderful rapidity from humor to pathos, from joy to sorrow, from pleasant surprise to bewildering perplexity. The kaleidoscope of the South Carolina cotton mill communities presents ever changing pictures of perplexing problems.

What We Wrestle With.

There are 164 mill communities in this state with 47,000 operatives, and a population of 110,000—about one-fifth of the white population of the state. The purest American white stock has been drawn together from the mountains and the rural districts. They are fast being welded into a new class of industrial workers. The chief barrier to their development is absolute illiteracy and near illiteracy. The last United States Census states that ten per cent. of the white males of this state between the ages of 14 and 21 are illiterate; other estimates of the illiteracy among the whites range from 5 to 20 per cent. A conservative estimate of the illiteracy of the cotton mill operatives is 12 per cent.; to this must be added a large percentage of near illiterates. This is the fundamental problem to which all the lesser problems point.

Another phase of the perplexing problem is the shifting about from one mill community to another of a considerable part of the population. Work is easily secured in any mill, transportation readily advanced by the new employer, the scant furniture quickly packed on a dray.

Results: loss of money, loss of time at both ends of the line, wear and tear of moving, a debt to work off in the new place, interruption of school work and religious training, hindrance to effective church development.

That bulwark of our Christian civilization, the Home, is gradually crumbling all over the land, but nowhere are conditions more serious than in our mill communities. Many conditions conspire to bring this about: the long hours of work, the early period at which children leave school to enter the mill, the inability of many to fill out the little leisure they have with reading, writing, and various kinds of needlework—these and many other causes help to make the home life unattractive, to the young people especially.

Closely connected with this is the evil of early and ill-advised marriages. Many girls and boys of seventeen and sixteen marry for no other reason than to get away from home with its misery and monotony and most of such early marriages that have come under my notice have become new centres of more misery. These child-wives, know little, if anything, about cooking or other household work, the boy-husbands as a rule have not learned to save, and thus it is not difficult to fortell their future.

There is in the state of South Carolina no registration of births, and this fact adds greatly to the difficulties in the way of those engaged in welfare work among the operatives.

One of the most serious phases of this perplexing problem is the low age limit for child labor. In spite of persistent endeavor to raise the age limit to 14, children in South Carolina cotton mills are allowed to go to work at 12 years of age.

An additional twist in the already badly knotted problem is the fact that lazy and drunken fathers are allowed to draw the earnings of their children under age. Many instances could be cited where young people not quite twenty-one years of age are compelled to work, only to see their hard earned money spent for liquor. The only course open to such young people is to run away from home.

The lack of strong, educated leaders in the various mill communities and especially in the isolated rural ones, is one of the principal reasons for the slow progress in uplift work. Often the pastors of the various mill churches lack leadership, initiative and executive ability, or else change so frequently, that no work of any permanent kind can be done. Wherever good leaders are found, the people are eager to follow and there are a number of mill communities in South Carolina where this has been demonstrated.

The careful student of mill conditions asks himself this question: Why are not these people organized? There are upwards of two hundred thousand people engaged in the same industry throughout the South and yet no labor organization among them. It is safe to predict that the new South will ere long have a Union of Cotton Mill Operatives.

Welfare Work Wins Welcome.

Having so far pointed out some of the perplexities of this problem, let us now turn our attention to the earnest and efficient endeavors at social welfare work among the operatives. The writing of this chapter affords genuine pleasure because it brings into focus two bright and hopeful spots, a class of mill owners who spend much time, thought, talent, and money in bettering the conditions of their employes, and the remarkable capability of development on the part of the operatives. There are in this state several groups of mills, mostly located in and near larger towns and cities, whose managements are courageously blazing the way in efficient social welfare work. One of these groups, controlling sixteen mills, has a well organized Welfare Department directing the operations of sixty paid welfare workers. This department helps to establish churches and supplements the salaries of its ministers, furnishes equipment and salaries for Y. M. and Y. W. C. A., employs trained nurses and domestic science teachers, opens kindergartens, day and night schools, furnishes circulating libraries, provides village parks, pastures, land for corn and tomato clubs, well kept and lighted streets, substantially-built three, four, six or eight room houses, always in good condition, detached, with garden in front and large yard in rear and rented at fifty cents a month per room.

When Miss d'Aubigné, daughter of the famous French Huguenot historian, and herself a welfare worker in one of the cotton mill centres of France, visited one of these South Carolina cotton mill communities about a year ago, she was surprised beyond measure at the comfortable condition of our people as compared with the same class in her native land.

The operatives as a rule appreciate what is being done for the improvement of their condition and an ever increasing number of the young people are making good use of these opportunities for self-help. Nor are practical results wanting. One of these night schools has established a scholarship fund—entirely apart from the mill interests—for higher education, which in the past three years has enabled nearly one dozen young people to take full or partial college courses.

Now here are other results, tangible results. I am trying my best to get the boys and girls to leave the mill, and I tell the owner of the mill frankly that I am doing so. He says, "You are right. You ought to do it. I consider my mill a stepping stone to higher points, and I just want the people to pass through and use the mill for the time being as a crutch." He is a philanthropic man. So in the last year or two there have been passed out of that night school—out of the mill into the larger life—thirty-five young people who are filling positions as nurses, teachers, stenographers, typewriters, bookkeepers, electricians, motormen, carpenters, ironworkers, clerks, etc.

But I must put another dash back of all this lest you get too good a taste in your mouth. The fact is that four-fifths of the mills in South Carolina do not have these opportunities—four-fifths of them. I speak whereof I know. They are rural mills, far away from centres of population, without close observation, and they practically do as they please.

What We Want.

Intelligent men and women, engaged in uplift work in various cotton mill communities and giving the study of conditions much time and thought, as a rule agree upon certain things we want. Foremost among these is a *state-wide compulsory school attendance law*. When one considers that the illiteracy among the whites of the state is at least twelve per cent.; that out of the 143,000 white children between the ages of 6 and 14 years, fully 40,000, or almost thirty per cent. are out of school; that the leading educational, commercial, benevolent, and industrial organizations of the state are in favor of such a law; that the mill owners have declared in favor of such a law, provided it be coupled with raising the age limit for child labor; that most of the states, East, North and West, have by such laws reduced their illiteracy to less than four per cent.; and that repeated efforts to pass such a law in this state have failed, it is no wonder that South Carolinians are sorely disappointed and mortified.

Next in importance among the things we want is a *child labor law* raising the age limit to fourteen years. For the past fifteen years, state officials, private individuals and committees have persistently brought this crying need to the attention of the legislature. In 1903 a law was passed raising the age limit for child labor gradually from ten to twelve years. In 1905 the age limit was twelve years, but there were so many exemptions, and evasions were so easy, that this law was of little value. In January, 1912, this law was so changed as to cut out all exemptions. There is satisfactory evidence that this law is honestly obeyed, with possibly a few isolated cases where parents deliberately lie about the age of their children and where inspectors are unable to get at the truth.

Some of the mill owners have voluntarily established the 14-year age limit; others have no objection to such a law on the ground that the labor of children under fourteen years is no longer profitable, especially in the larger mills located in or near larger towns or cities. As a body, the mill owners of the state have gone on record that they are in favor of such a law, provided it be coupled with a state-wide compulsory school attendance law. The serious side of the situation is that the principal opposition to the raising of the age limit comes from the operatives themselves; this was clearly brought out during the session of the legislature just adjourned, when the South Carolina Child Labor Committee urged the passage of the fourteen year age limit law, and stacks of petitions, signed by hundreds of operatives, were presented against the bill. An attempt was even made to introduce a bill reducing the age limit to ten years. Does not this clearly show that those who would help the children of South Carolina must concentrate their endeavor upon a state-wide compulsory school attendance law?

We want a *birth registration law* in order to enable factory inspectors and other officials in the future to enforce the laws regulating the labor of children.

We want a *vagrancy law* equally enforced among whites and blacks. Every mill community has a number of white loafers, spending their days in idleness, hunting or fishing, and supported by the earnings of women and children. This nuisance is responsible for much of the misery and for the otherwise unnecessary child and woman labor. I can point out case after case of the most abject poverty where the lazy or drunken father regularly twice a month draws the money earned by his sons and daughters under 21. On remonstrating with the mill authorities I was told that they regret this but the law leaves them no alternative. We want that law changed to remedy this abuse which is to be found in every mill community.

We want the cotton-mill operatives of the South organized so that they may not be obliged to depend upon the mill owners for churches and for all these conveniences and comforts, so that they may be able to help themselves. They are now being helped, plentifully, wonderfully, marvelously, extensively, expensively. I sometimes say to these men, "If that money which you now spend on welfare work, thousands of dollars and tens of thousands of dollars, could be put to the point of raising the wages of your people a little bit, I think it would be better." We feel that under the leadership of Southern men who understand local conditions, and who have heads, hearts, and consciences, these people, thoroughly organized, could do more for their all-around improvement than can be done for them by others.

THE TEXTILE INDUSTRY AND CHILD LABOR.

RICHARD K. CONANT, Boston,
Secretary, Massachusetts Child Labor Committee.

A friend from South Carolina, visiting cotton mills in Massachusetts, was astounded to discover that the operations of doffing and spinning were so frequently performed by adults, and that the stories he had heard about the need for deft and pliable fingers of little children were myths. The study of the Condition of Woman and Child Wage-earners in the United States, made by the Bureau of Labor, is sufficient evidence that child labor in the textile industry is unnecessary. In the mills studied in the states of Maine, Massachusetts, Rhode Island and New Hampshire, practically one-half of all the doffers reported were men, slightly more than one-fourth were women and slightly less than one-fourth were children. The ages of all employes were tabulated in that report and there was ascertained for each department of the mill the age at which the largest number were employed. For ring spinners this age was 18, for speeder tenders 19, spoolers 18, weavers 20, doffers 16, back boys 15. In every New England state more than 50 per cent. of the back boys were 16 years of age or over, and in Massachusetts more than 75 per cent. A few men of 21 years were engaged in the occupation and occasionally a man over forty years old. The study of the Bureau of Labor showed only 120 children under 14 in the 46 New England mills studied.

There is little chance to argue, after these figures, that the industry depends, for its mechanical or financial success, upon the labor of little children. Mills with one or two thousand employes frequently use as few as 40 or 60 children under 16, and none under 14. When a mill uses a larger proportion of children, it makes the same kind of goods and competes directly with one that uses only a few children.

I am especially anxious not to be understood as boasting of Massachusetts. Because Massachusetts has been at work on the problem for three-quarters of a century, she ought to have progressed as far as this. The first law, in 1836, provided that children under 15 must attend school three months every year. In 1842, children under 12 were given a ten-hour day. In 1866, children under ten were prohibited from work. In 1867, came the 60-hour week up to 15, in 1874 up to 18, in 1888 an absolute prohibition to 13, in 1898 an absolute prohibition to 14, in 1907 the prohibition of work for women and minors in textile factories after 6 P. M., and in 1911 the 54-hour week. Massachusetts should have progressed further than this; by this time she should have secured the eight-hour day for children between 14 and 16, which has been attained by fourteen states and the District of Columbia. It is for the eight-hour day that we at present strive.

Experience of Eight-Hour Day.

There is some strength behind a movement for a five-hour day for these children, and the outlook for at most an eight-hour day seems very hopeful. Under existing laws, children under 16 years of age may work 58 hours a week, without a daily limit, in mercantile establishments. In manufacturing and mechanical establishments, they may work 10 hours a day or 54 hours a week. Ten hours is considered too long for almost every kind of worker, except one who digs in the ditch or works in a factory. The carpenter, stone-cutter, painter, paperhanger, printer and plumber have an eight-hour day. The little child of 14, toiling in the cotton or woolen mill, must stay at his monotonous, high-speed machine for ten hours a day. That a child of 14, as soon as he begins work, should be denied the time for development which is accorded to every skilled worker, is a clear injustice. The stupefying effect of the ten-hour day, on children who are expected to attend evening school, has been brought out at our hearings in previous years. The evil of the 10-hour day has not been disputed. If you watch the day's work of a child of 14 in a textile factory—watch him go in at a quarter of seven in the morning and come out at twelve, go in at one and come out at five-thirty—you will see that he has little of the sunlight, little of the fresh air, no chance for play, that he is too tired to care for study and that a future civilization based on such foundations cannot be the best.

The opposition to the eight-hour day has come from a few textile manufacturers. Presumably these manufacturers would oppose such a bill for the reason that they will be financially affected by it. The textile manufacturers who appeared before the Committee on Labor last year were closely questioned by the members of that committee upon this point. Not one was able to show convincingly how the passage of the law would increase materially the cost of his labor or decrease his dividends. The manufacturers stated that they would not pay any more for the work if it took more people to do it or if it took older people to do it; the amount paid for the work would be at the same rate, no matter how it was done. One of the manufacturers, when hard pressed by questions of the committee, stated there would be a decrease in the supply of labor because of the eight-hour provision and that a decrease in the supply would raise the cost to the manufacturer, would increase the wages which he would have to pay. He stated that the supply of labor in Fall River is small and that the scarcity of labor would raise wages. When further questioned, however, he was unable to show any considerable scarcity of labor in Fall River. The manufacturers then took the stand that is reported of a Pennsylvania manufacturer as early as 1837, who said that although he personally was in favor of a child labor law, he objected to it because it would work hardship on the families and the parents would oppose it. And it has not been very difficult for the manufacturers to persuade the parents that it will work hardship to have the children's wages reduced. Only occasionally has it been seen that abolishing child labor increases the total wage paid to labor because older labor demands more.

Family Need?

An investigation of the need of families for the earnings of their 14 to 16-year-old children, was recently made by our committee. We examined the family income and expenditure in the cases of 100 children who obtained working papers in December and January last, in Fall River. As the families were interviewed within two months after the child first went to work, the reasons for putting the child at work were obtained while they were still fresh. 22 of the 100 families answered that they needed the earnings of the children. Only 6 of the 100 were poor widows.

The statement of the families themselves is not, of course, the best means of judging their need for the wages. For that reason their income and expenditures were studied in detail. In 67 of the 100 families there was no doubt, after a study of the earnings and expenditures, that the families were perfectly well able to get along without the support of the children. The 33 cases where there was some doubt in the mind of the investigator were analyzed in accordance with two standards of living set up in the report of the United States Bureau of Labor above referred to, the two standards being (1) a fair standard of living, and (2) a minimum standard of living. 14 of the 33 families were found to be able to live, without the earnings of their 14 to 16-year-old workers, above the fair standard of living. 10 more of the families were found to be able to live, without the earnings of their 14 to 16-year-old workers, above the minimum standard of living—leaving nine of the 33 doubtful families, 9 of the entire 100 cases studied who would be forced below the minimum standard of living if they were deprived of the earnings of their 14 to 16-year-old workers.

The results of this study accord in some measure with other conclusions. The Douglas Commission of 1905 on Industrial Education found that 23 per cent. of the families interviewed stood considerably in need of the wages of their 14 to 16-year-old children. The Bureau of Labor in its later study found that 32 of 226, or about 14 per cent., had a per capita income of less than $5 a week. None of the studies shows an enormous need on the part of families for the wages of the 14 to 16-year-old children. All show a slight need, varying according to different standards from 9 to 20 per cent. of the cases. The economic value of the years between 14 and 16 has again and again proved to be much less than the educational value. It was proved by the Commission on Industrial Education in 1905, that education for children between 14 and 16 is more profitable than the 10 cents an hour which they get in wages. But these facts we have found to be of little use in convincing people who are afraid that the children will lose their jobs. This year, however, we are not compelled to use these arguments because we can show conclusively that there is absolutely no danger that the eight-hour law will result in turning children between 14 and 16 out of their jobs.

The eight-hour law for children under 16 has been passed and has been in force for some time in fourteen states. Among them are the great industrial states of Ohio, Illinois, New York, and Wisconsin in which there is invested in manufacturing pursuits many times as much capital as there is in Massachusetts. In Ohio, a special agent of the National Child Labor Committe, Mr. H. H. Jones, made detailed investigation of the operation of the eight-hour law passed in 1908, by visiting factories, interviewing employers and by correspondence. The factories selected were of the kind that made most use of child labor, and an attempt was made in each city to include the largest employers of children and the most representative factories of the industry; 80 factories in thirteen cities and towns were investigated. In every case the hours of adults were over 48, in most cases they were 54 or 60 per week. 3,025 children were found at work eight hours a day. Of the 21 textile mills covered by the investigaton, 14 employ as many children under 16 as they did before, one employs more, and only two of those who answered employ fewer children.

The experience of other states, then, shows that the eight-hour day is practicable, the experience of workers in all trades shows that for children between 14 and 16 the eight-hour day is humane. We are asking this amount of protection for the children of Massachusetts. We hope that Massachusetts can again show the way to make the textile industry more wholesome and more valuable to the community. We hope that the human output of the mill will be given this small amount of care and forethought.

THE CAMPAIGN IN NORTH CAROLINA.
THE MOUNTAIN WHITES—BY ONE OF THEM.

W. H. SWIFT, Greensboro, N. C.,
Special Agent, National Child Labor Committee.

On the first of January, 1913, the laws of our state permitted the employment of children twelve years of age at day work, and of fourteen years of age at night work. We are supposed to be working our people sixty hours a week. We had no inspectors, and as a result, frequent violations of our very poor laws. During the past year—and I do not mean to reflect upon my State—I have seen many violations of the law. There are children twelve years of age working ten hours every night and six mills reported that instead of working ten they work twelve hours a night.

On the first of January, 1914—our new law will go into effect on that date—the law will not be much different. We will have an age limit of sixteen for night work—an increase from fourteen to sixteen—and we will have our County Superintendents of Public Instruction charged with the duty of investigating violations of the law. That is about all we have accomplished.

There may be other results not now revealed, but these must await the future; and it is very questionable whether progressive or even modern humane ideas shall soon prevail. It may be that we shall continue for some time to be dominated by the old-time conceptions. It is certain that every step yet to be made will be met with determined opposition. Men who are interested stand dead against any legal reforms. We have even had a teacher and two or three preachers pleading that things be left alone. It reminds one of the days of slavery. Manufacturers stand, as they say, upon their rights. I think it likely that they may be able to control for some time. They *will* control just as long as they can.

I have found this one fact: that there is in North Carolina one business which, as a body, with exceptions here and there, is determined to resist any and all attempts on the part of the citizens of the state to have anything to say in regard to the employment of child wage-earners. We do not have to hunt for these men. As soon as the question is up they come to the front. I refer—and I do not think they will object—to the cotton manufacturers of my state. Generally, they have always opposed and are now opposed to any suggestions about this matter.

Attitude of Manufacturers.

I have learned not a few things in this campaign dealing exclusively with cotton manufacturers. They are the ones we have to deal with.

1. There are a few manufacturers who recognize that reforms must come and who will enter into our agreement upon this subject, standing just as true to it as men do in any other business of life. It has been one of the good things to come to know these men. They give to one a new and richer conception of the big business man.

2. There are others who aspire to be considered benefactors, who tell you of all that they have done and are doing—who make themselves into a distinct class of straddlers. They will enter into a definite agreement and then go back on it as completely as the public will permit. This has been a great disappointment to me. They have taught me that not a few of these big captains of industry, these builders of churches and schools, are made of plain common dirt, just like the rest of us. They will do nothing except as they think public opinion will shout their names for the doing, or rebuke them if they do not. They are not open fighters. Action on the part of their help will put them into a panic. They are afraid of public opinion, and if we can arouse it, we will take care of them.

3. There is another class of manufacturers who believe that a man who can build a mill shall be left to run it as he pleases, employing whomever he pleases on such terms as he pleases, without let or hindrance from any source whatsoever. These men stand on their rights, questioning all legal suggestions and resisting any and all state regulation. It is refreshing to fight with these.

State Organization.

To handle these two latter classes in North Carolina we had a state organization of good men. These men came from different walks of life. They are in earnest. They are willing to spend time, money and energy.

Back of them stood the woman's clubs of the state and what in my opinion are the two strongest organizations for progressive legislation in North Carolina—the Farmers' Union and the Junior Order of American Mechanics. Back of them is a large body of men and women who are beginning to think upon *these matters* and to insist that something be done; and finally, back of them is a still greater body of people who have not yet come into the realm of serious thought about these things. These are content, not because things are all right, but because they have never thought much about there being anything better. I should also mention the State Conference for Social Service—five hundred strong the day of its birth.

We undertook to get everybody thinking upon this question. This is about all that I have done during the past year. They sent me from one end of the state to the other; from the mountains to the sea. They told me simply to ask the people whether or not it is right to work children as they are being worked. Whether or not it is right to work women and children all night long? I was then to let the people say. Our trouble was that we were not able to reach all. If we had been able to put the question squarely before every citizen in North Carolina it would have been settled. Our people know what is right. We think along progressive lines. We do want to take care of our children, but somehow we have never been made to think much about it.

Progress Slow.

Of course, too much must not be expected. It was only yesterday that we learned that one can't keep on dragging everything off a field and keep it fertile. It was only yesterday that we began to learn how to keep our lands from washing away, that disease may be prevented and that flies are not altogether helpful. It was only yesterday we learned that it pays to raise good pigs, good calves and good cattle. Things must come in order. You could hardly expect us to know yet that it pays a state to grow strong men and women—that work hurts a child just the same as a colt. Not a few of our business men doubt this proposition. They fear, actually fear, the development of strong men and women. Above all, they fear any independence of action on the part of this working people. This is our position and I think you should understand it.

Consult the Operatives.

We made one mistake in North Carolina, a very serious mistake. There was a sort of gentleman's understanding that neither I nor any one else should go to the mill operatives themselves to put the matter square up to them. The owners were consulted. The workers were not. I do not think that a man who runs a factory ought to be consulted about child labor laws any more than a man who runs a store or a farm or a school. He should be consulted as a citizen, and not as an employer of children. A violator of child labor laws has no more right to dictate child labor laws than a pot-hunter has to make the game laws.

But there is one class that should be consulted: the operatives. They cannot be wisely consulted except by going into a full economic discussion. You must sit down with pencil and paper and show the absolute loss which comes from working children. When this is done in my State, a most terrible row will break loose. It will be labor agitation. But this question will not be solved in North Carolina until it is done, and if I can do it I will do it.

Defective Principle.

The arguments offered for this present state of affairs are most interesting. They are stock arguments.

Take any man who opposes legislation for the protection of children; if he be a North Carolinian, I can outline his speech.

First, there will be a glowing reference to his churches and his schools. He wants you to know of them. So often have I heard it that I have begun to doubt the good of it all. I am made to think that he offers them to conceal other facts. Would it not be much better to have a people able to build their own churches and support their own schools? A local tax, such as our farmers vote upon themselves, would, if levied upon mill property, give more money than most of them, and perhaps, than any of them are giving. The fact is, that this giving is all wrong and is the most sure, as well as the most seductive method of destroying the manhood of any race. Not much will be done till these people do for themselves and quit having it all done for them. The very fact that it has to be done for them shows a most vital defect. You have heard all about their fine schools. These schools are for children under twelve years of age. The children are not in school after the age of 11 to 12 in mill communities, and anybody at all familiar with conditions knows it. What is the good of the school if the children are in the mill?

The second stock argument is that mill people are so much better off than they were before coming to the mill. In other words, the same argument is handed out to the public as is given to the family, for all employment is of the family; namely, that the family is so much better off at the mill than on the farm.

This presupposes that all the children down to the legal age of 12 work all the time.

Which had you rather be, a farmer living on fifty acres of land, making an independent living, or one of a family of operatives in a mill? The farmer, by moving to the mill, would gain just as much in village life, in churches, in schools, in electric lights, as any other operative. If he worked himself and worked his children just as much on the farm as he will have to work in the mill he would be far better off. The same is true of the tenant.

But there was one argument not used—that the operatives must need work their children, often at night, in order to live. I thank God that these men felt it best to touch lightly upon this. It shows that we are going forward. No more in North Carolina will we hear this. Mountain men do not have to hire out their girls at night in order to live, and many of them will not much longer be drawn into a system where this is a necessity.

But the fact is that in some cases it seems almost needful. A cotton mill is no place for a man who seeks to support his family by his labor. With three or four small children and a wife dependent upon him things would go hard; if he should try to leave the mother at home with the little ones while he earned food and clothing, it would go hard with that family. With all these small children being fed into competition with him, he will be lucky not to be forced to the wall.

A cotton mill, as it is generally run in my state, is an institution designed for a man of a family of three to six boys and girls, twelve to eighteen years of age. He can put them to work and rest the balance of his life. Often, too often, this is what he does.

I have hastily run over the defense. This has been a hard fight. It will be harder. Slowly our people are being aroused. There is just one more job awaiting somebody—that of shaking up the mill operatives. This is a man's job. The sooner these people are made to realize that all is not well with them, the better. They must learn this lesson. It should have been taught them long ago.

Somehow, I feel that the mountain man can help in this. Back there he is learning to do it. Amidst stern problems, and often in dire poverty, he has learned, and knows well that a child was never born to support the family during infancy. It is only when he is lured away by deceptive stories of much money to be had by family work that he loses his mountain independence. It is a shame for him to be thus tempted.

In a valley between the Blue Ridge and the mountains further to the west, there lie one hundred acres of mountain land. A man, now old, walks daily over this mountain farm. He is the father of ten children. As earners of money in a mill, this family, working as mill families work, at any time during the past twenty years would have given him an average income of fifty to a hundred dollars a month, even if he himself became a mill vagrant. Instead, he with his good wife have fought it out on his own little farm, counting no sacrifice for their children great. Their children are all strong, every one of them has a fair education. One son owns his mountain farm. Two others are living out strong lives in Western Canada. One sister is married and has her own home in Tennessee. Another sister is a skilled nurse in a leading hospital. Still another will be graduated from one of our educational institutions this year. The younger boys are on the farm, while I, the oldest son of this plain mountaineer, am pleading with the people of my state to see to it that every boy and girl has his or her chance in life and gets at least an opportunity to grow as boys and girls should grow. Think you, thinks any man, that my father had better have gone to the mill? He and his people are the plain mountain folk.

I know the man with a house of one room. I have grown up with his boys. I know the hardships of that life. Many of us are poor. There are worse things than poverty. It would give me great sorrow to see my people begin to move from their mountain homes to our mills. Before any man starts, he must have already made up his mind to throw the burden of family support upon the shoulders of his wife or his children. When a mountain man decides to do this, he has lost the best part of him. Men don't hire out their children in my mountain county, and the average of intelligence is better than that of any mill village known to me.

I can recall now men and women, children of a widow left with nothing. They fought it out. They are excellent citizens. They are proud of their own progress.

I tell you that in my native county no farmer would be suffered to put his children and his wife out to work all night long. His neighbors would not allow such a thing to be. Nor would any man stand well if he made his crop by working women and children.

The average mountain renter raises his family, gives them plenty of food and clothing, and rarely ever hires one out under fourteen. The mother stays at home with the little ones. They grow to be strong men and women.

If in any state there is a necessity for violating these principles which the average mountaineer knows to be wrong, it is evidence of the need of reformation. If men are thus undermining the ideals of family responsibility—and these mill men are—it is time now to investigate, and investigate fully. There is something wrong.

Perhaps I can make it clear by making it personal. I have three boys. Under our present laws six years from now I could have two of these working in a mill. Now suppose, in the turn of the wheel of fortune, I should find myself forced to live by the daily work of my hands. I would have no land and would be forced to rent. Understand that I know the mountains and the life, and I know the best side of the mill life. I live next to the best cotton mill in North Carolina.

There would be no question with me. I'd go directly to the

hills where my boys would have some chance to grow. Before I'd put my boys of 12 to 14 at work in a mill either day or night, before we would put our boys there to work, depriving them of all opportunity and destroying our own ambitions for them, my wife and I will build us a cabin by the side of a mountain spring and I'll plow a brindle-bull on the Ivy-Bluffs of the barrens of the Pick-Breeches. I am sure that it would be much better for my boys. Before God, we should seek no better things for our own boy than we try to get for the other man's boy; no better things for our girl than for the other woman's girl. There should be no line drawn here.

Fallacy of Mill Benefits.

And yet we are told that we must not legislate for the protection of children, because the mills have done so much for the mountain people. The school and the church is sneered at and a cotton mill is offered as the cure for all social disease. We mountain people do have our problems. We have had them since first our sturdy ancestors felled the trees of the forest. We do have our poor, and even our almost worthless families; but I cannot believe that it is a good thing to teach any body of people that they should hail an opportunity to make their women and children the supporters of the family a blessing.

Granting all the good that the mills have done us, does that furnish any reason for violating an instinct that even the birds have? Your farm girl who goes wrong and drifts to the city generally wears much finer clothes, has costly fittings in her room, rides in a carriage and, for a time, has money to burn. Does any sensible person offer these as a plea for the conditions in which she lives? There is just about as much reason for the latter as for the former. Neither ought to be.

And yet, these arguments have had a great influence with our people, especially with our legislators. Of all states in the American Union, North Carolina changes perhaps most slowly. That certain conditions have been is proof to many of our people that they ought to be. Many of our leaders stand firm upon this proposition. This makes all reform up-hill pulling.

But I want to promise you one thing, and this whether the National Child Labor Committee feels it wise to help longer in North

Carolina or not: these reforms are going to come. Many of us recognize that there has to be some fighting done. Our men and our women, many of them, are ready for the fray. We are anxious to get into it. And we are going to win. God has given us everything that makes for a good life. It is possible for all of us to live without making beasts of burden of our women and children. The only reason why we do make these work is because one part of our people are getting too much, and others too little. It is up to us to change this, and we will change it. It may take years to force the change, but the change will be made.

THE CHILD'S BURDEN IN OYSTER AND SHRIMP CANNERIES.

LEWIS W. HINE, New York,
Staff Photographer, National Child Labor Committee.

I wish to present to you a phase of child labor, serious in the extreme, and I hope a little careful consideration will give you an accurate, sympathetic view of the situation.

The two chief sections engaged in the work of canning oysters and shrimp are first the Gulf Coast from New Orleans eastward to Florida, and second the Atlantic Coast of Maryland, the Carolinas, and Georgia. Maryland was the pioneer state, but it has already been outstripped by Mississippi, and several other states are following close in the annual output.

When we speak of child labor in oyster canning, we refer to the cooked or "cove" oysters, not to the raw ones. Children are not used in opening raw oysters for the sole reason that their fingers are not strong enough. Occasionally one finds young boys at work on the boats dredging for oysters, but not many children work on the boats; for that is a man's job.

Every year, about October, hundreds (some authorities say thousands) of Polish and Bohemian people are herded together by various bosses or "padrones" and shipped over to the southern coasts by train and by boat. You may imagine that the long ride in the crowded day coach or on the boats is not without its hardships, and every day of the long six months of their stay is crowded with discomfort, hardship and peril.

First they move into the shacks provided by the company. We are told by one of the canners, "We give these people all the modern conveniences. They have an artesian well. What more can we do?" But one becomes skeptical when inconveniences and insanitary conditions are so much in the majority. If there were no cold or wet weather in these parts, if waste and sewage were carried off, and if there were no crowding, these temporary quarters would be endurable; but in cold, or hot, or wet weather they are positively dangerous, especially to children.

A row of dilapidated shacks that I found in South Carolina housed 50 workers in single-room homes. One room sheltered 8 persons. The shacks were located on an old shell pile within a few rods of the factory, and a few feet from the tidal marsh; odors, mosquitoes, and sand flies making life intolerable, especially in hot weather.

There is a prevailing impression that in the matter of child labor the emphasis on the labor must be very slight; but let me tell you that these processes are *work—hard work*—deadening in its monotony, exhausting physically, irregular—its only joy being the closing hour. We might even say of these children that they are condemned to work.

Come out with me to one of these canneries at 3 o'clock some morning. Here is the crude, shed-like building, with a long dock at which the oyster boats unload their cargoes. Near the dock is the ever-present shell pile, a monument of mute testimony to the patient toil of little fingers. It is cold, damp, dark. The whistle blew some time ago, and the weary workers dressed themselves, slipped into their meagre garments, snatched a bite to eat (there is no time for breakfast now), and hurried to the shucking shed. The padrone told me "Ef day don't git up, I go and *git 'em up*." See those little ones over there stumbling through the dark over the shell-piles, munching a piece of bread, and rubbing their heavy eyes! Work has already begun—little ones of 6, 7, and 8 years of age take their places with the adults, and are at work all day.

The dreary cars are ready for them with their loads of dirty, rough clusters of shells, and as these shells accumulate under foot in irregular piles, they soon make the question of mere standing one of extreme physical strain. Note the uncertain footing, and the dilapidated foot-wear of that little girl; and opposite is one with cloth fingers to protect herself from the jagged shells ("finger-stalls" they call them) and their fingers are often sore in spite of this precaution. When they are picking shrimp, their fingers and even their shoes are attacked by a corrosive substance in the shrimp that is strong enough to eat the tin cans into which they are packed.

Naturally, the day's work on shrimp is much shorter—as the fingers of the worker give out in spite of the fact that they are compelled to harden them in an alum solution at the end of the day. The shrimp are packed in ice, and a few hours' handling of these icy things is dangerous for any child. Then, too, the mornings, and many of the days, are cold, foggy and damp. The workers are thinly clad, but (like the fabled ostrich), cover their heads and imagine they are warm. If a child is sick, it gets a vacation, and wanders around to kill time.

They are left to shift for themselves at a very early age. One young father told me with pride that they brought their baby, 2 months old, down to the shucking-shed at 4 o'clock every morning, and kept it there all day. Another told me that they locked a baby of 6 months in the shack when they went away in the morning, and left it until noon—then it stayed alone all the afternoon. A baby carriage with its occupant half smothered under piles of blankets is a common sight. Snuggled up against a steam box you find many a youngster asleep on a cold morning. As soon as they can toddle, they hang around the older members of the family—something of a nuisance, of course, and very early they learn to amuse themselves. For hours at a time they will play with the dirty shells, imitating the work of the grown-ups, and toddle around in the shed, and out onto the dock at the risk of their lives.

Work for All Ages.

Then they learn to "tend the baby." As a substitute for real recreation, this baby-tending is pathetic—simply an extra burden dumped onto these little ones, who cannot work, or who work part of the time. Mary said, "I shucks 6 pots if I don't got the baby—2 pots if I got him." So there is not much care wasted on these little ones. As soon as they can handle the oysters and the shrimp, they are "allowed to help." The mother often says: "Sure, I'm learnin' her de trade;" and you see many youngsters beginning to help at a very early age. Standing on a box in order to reach the table, little Olga, 5 years old, was picking shrimp for her mother at a cannery I visited. Later in the day, I found her at home worn out with the work she had been doing, but the mother complained that Olga was "ugly." (Little sympathy they get when they most need it.) Four-year-old Mary was working irregularly through the day shucking about 2 pots of oysters. The mother is the fastest shucker in the place, and the boss said, "Mary will work *steady* next year." The most excitement many of them get from one month to another is that of being dressed up in their Sunday best to spend the day seeing the sights of the settlement.

We all know that the amount of *work* these little ones can do is not much, yet I have been surprised and horrified at the number of hours a day a 6 or 7-year-old will stay at work, and to find so many parents willing and eager to keep them working. Freckled Bill, a bright lad of 5 years, told me that he worked—and his mother added reproachfully: "He kin make *15 cents* any day he wants to work, but he won't do it steady." Think of a mother urging a boy of his age on to more work. Annie, 7 years old, is a steady worker. The mother said (for her benefit, of course): "She kin beat me shuckin,'—an' she's mighty good at housework too—but I mustn't praise her too much right before her." This is only one of the means used to keep the children at work. Another method is to tell the neighbors that Annie can shuck 8 pots a day. Then some other child gets the record, and so the interest is kept up, and (incidentally) the work is done, and the income enlarged. Can we call that motherhood? Compared with real maternity, it is a distorted perversion, a travesty. The babe at Ellis Island little dreams what is in store for him.

Hundreds of these children from 4 to 12 years of age are regularly employed (often as helpers) for the greater part of the six months, if it is a good season. At 3 and 4 years of age they play around and help a little, "learnin' de trade." At 5 and 6 years of age they work more regularly, and at 7 and 8 years, they put in every working day for long hours. This is the regular program for these children day after day, week after week, for the six months of their (alleged) "outing down South." I remarked to one of the village people, "It's a wonder that these youngsters live through it all." "Yes," she replied, "and when they don't live through it, there is a corner over in a little cemetery waiting for them, and many of them go there." (You see, "They're only Hickeys.") I suppose the cemetery is one of the "conveniences" that the Company doesn't boast about.

Wages Small.

The wages of these workers vary according to their locality, and the kind of season they find. The work on the shrimp is better paid, but it is much more irregular than oyster-shucking. On the latter, families frequently earn 10, 15 or 20 dollars a week, so you see when there are several children, and the work is steady, there is a great temptation to make them all help. Children of 7 years earn about 25 cents a day, and at 8 and 10 years of age often 50 cents a day, or more. At 12 and 14 years they frequently make a dollar a day. There is, however, a great discrepancy between the earnings of a child and those of an adult. The fastest adult shucker seldom earns much more than a dollar a day, after years of experience. What, then, is the outlook for children beginning this industry?

"What is your name, little girl?" "Dunno." "How old are you?" "Dunno." "How many pots do you shuck in a day?" "Dunno." And the pity of it is that they do not know. What then do they know? Enough to stand patiently with the rest, picking up the hard, dirty clusters of shells, deftly prying them open, dropping the meat into the pot; and then to go through this process with another and another and another, until after many minutes the pot is full; a relief—she can carry it over to the weigher and rest, doing nothing, a minute, and walk back,—such a change from the dreary standing, reaching, prying and dropping—minute upon minute, hour upon hour, day upon day, month after month. Or perchance, for variety, the catch might have been shrimp, and then the hours of work are shorter; but the shrimp are icy cold, and the blood in one's fingers congeals, and the fingers become so sore that they welcome the oysters again.

Their Education.

Are you surprised then to find that many children seem dumb and cannot understand our language? "But we educate them," some canners tell us—and this is the way they do it (in the few places where I found any pretence to education) : for four hours before school these children shucked oysters. Then they went to school for half a day. Returning at 1 o'clock for a hurried lunch, they worked for four hours more—this for the five school days.

On Saturday they put in an (alleged) half day, consisting of 8 or 9 hours' work. Is it any marvel that the school principal told me "It isn't satisfactory, but at least we are giving them some help in learning the language"—and they need the help. At another place, with two canneries, two of their children went to school, and the illiteracy of both adults and children was appalling. "There is no compulsion about schooling here," the principal said.

The vocational guidance that most of them receive, year in and year out, is seen in the sheds, where under the eagle eye of the boss, who watches that they do not shirk, and under the pressure of parental authority, they put in their time where it will bring tangible returns. One padrone told me, "I keep 'em a-working all the year. In winter, bring 'em down here to the Gulf. In summer, take 'em to the berry fields of Maryland and Delaware. They don't lose many weeks' time, but I have a hard time to get 'em sometimes. Have to tell 'em all kinds of lies." So here we have a certain kind of "Scientific Management" by means of which even the vacation time of the children is utilized.

"Why do they do it?"—That question comes to one over and over—what keeps these little ones at their uninteresting task? In the first place, these imigrants are frugal, even parsimonious; every little helps. Then they think it keeps the children out of trouble—little realizing they are storing up trouble when these little ones grow up (handicapped by lack of education, broken physically, and with a distaste for work), they drift into the *industrial maelstrom* of *cheap, inefficient labor* and float on as *industrial misfits*.

Would that we could convince these parents that it is an *industrial mortgage* they are loading onto the shoulders of these recruits—one that draws a *high interest* and insures an *early foreclosure*.

"*The Goods Are Perishable.*"

If we look at it from the employer's point of view we find his chief justification is that children are needed because the goods are perishable, and must be put up immediately. You ask him if the children are not perishable and he says he can't see that they are spoiled. "It doesn't hurt 'em. They're tough. I began myself at their age," etc.—and it will be long years before they can all look at it with a long-range finder—a problem to be met along with those of improved machinery, housing, etc. The children themselves are docile; they do as they are told; they are imitative, like to do what the rest are doing; they are easily stimulated by the idea of competing with other children; and they are very susceptible to criticism and ridicule. (I do not, however, recall a single case of a child being whipped for not working.) It can easily be seen that with the parents, the employers, and the children against us, our task of liberation is not an easy one.

The chief difference between the canneries on the Gulf Coast and those on the Atlantic Coast is that in the latter more negroes are employed, and they do not work the children very much, except where they have come under the influence of the immigrant workers. In almost every case, the bosses and padrones agreed that the Baltimore workers are much more satisfactory than the negroes. They said, "There is no comparing them. The whites work harder, longer hours, are more easily driven, and use the children much more." The chief advantage of negro help is that it saves the cost of transportation; but where it is necessary to get the work done promptly the immigrants are imported.

That this exploitation of the children is absolutely unnecessary is proven by the canneries that get along without them. It needs merely more efficient planning on the part of the managers and better supervision on the part of the state. It is certainly a condition not to be endured when we consider the hardships involved—the long hours, the monotonous and tiring work, the irregular conditions of work and of life, the exposure, the insanitary conditions, the moral dangers, the lack of education and the double exploitation in summer and winter.

One morning I found little Rose working away on the endless job. At the end of the day she asked me to photograph her dolly too; and as I did it the question overwhelmed me: Shall we condemn these other children of yours and of mine to this early toil, or shall we open to them all the resources of recreation and education that go to build up the family?

THE NEGLECTED HUMAN RESOURCES OF THE GULF COAST STATES.

EDWARD F. BROWN, New York,
Special Agent, National Child Labor Committee.

Oyster and shrimp packing is an important industry in Louisiana, Mississippi, Alabama and Florida, four states bordering the gulf coast. These states, except Mississippi, permit unrestricted employment of children of any age in the processes of canning oysters and shrimp. Mississippi prohibits employment of children in canneries and other industries.

In 1911 the National Child Labor Committee conducted an investigation of child labor on the gulf coast and found that children, some as young as five years, were gainfully employed in canning factories. Mr. Hine has described the results of that inquiry. During the past three months I have made a tour of the gulf coast canneries and found that the employment of young children prevails as generally now as it did at the time of Mr. Hine's study.

In Mississippi, where the statute prohibits child labor in canneries, more children were found illegally employed than in any other gulf state visited. The ages at which these children were found actually at work range from five years up. The shucking of oysters or plucking of shrimp, the process in which children are used, commences usually at three or four o'clock in the morning, and continues, the supply permitting, until late in the afternoon.

This paper purposes to show the comparative esteem in which the gulf states hold children and shellfish.

In Louisiana game has been the subject of protective legislation as early as 1857, and amendatory legislation has continued to the present day. It was not until nearly half a century after the first game protective statute that Louisiana saw the need of a child labor law. When, after a most discouraging fight, a child labor law was finally enacted, the machinery provided was, and is now, so inadequate as to render almost ineffectual the legislative intent which sought to preserve children from premature toil.

From August, 1910, to June, 1911, the Louisiana Board of Commissioners for the Protection of Game, Birds and Fish spent in its work of conservation and culture approximately $128,180. During the same period of time only $900 was spent for factory inspection, and that only in the Parish of New Orleans. This niggardly grant of $900 could hardly serve the health, safety and comfort of upwards of 76,165 wage earners—a sum equivalent to twice as much as the Louisiana Oyster Commission spent for postage in one year.

The annual report of the Louisiana Oyster Commission for 1911, in its foreword, says:

"Almost everyone admits the necessity of laws for the conservation of our natural resources in the way of game, fish, oysters, shrimp and water sites."

And, believing in this principle, the state passed an elaborate code for the protection of its shellfish supply. Yet Louisiana has not apparently reached the point when it recognizes the propriety, economy and right of the child to legal protection and the enforcement of that right by an adequate staff of competent officials.

Mississippi Law Ignored.

Mississippi considers her human resources even less significant than her sister state Louisiana. The high regard in which the oyster is held in Mississippi is manifest in the generous provision the legislature makes for the proper propagation of its life. As early as 1904 the legislature made large grants to the Mississippi Oyster Commission. In five years the state spent approximately $187,855.55 to replant depleted oyster reefs and to see that they are not exploited except in accordance with the elaborate code the legislature adopted in 1902. Still, Mississippi with 2,600 manufacturing establishments alone, and an average of nearly 51,000 factory wage earners alone, has not provided a single penny for factory inspection. The child labor law in Mississippi provides that no girl under 14, no boy under 12, shall be employed in canning establishments, but there is no one in the state whose sole business it is to see that the law is enforced. The sheriff is empowered to do so, but it is not known that he ever officially visited a single factory for the purpose of enforcing the labor laws of the state. If he has, he surely missed the 93 children between six and fourteen years of age whom I found actually at work in four Mississippi oyster canneries.

These little children work from three or four o'clock in the morning until late in the afternoon. It can hardly be said that the sheriff who is empowered to enforce the child labor law has no knowledge of these plants. Only a few weeks ago the Dunbar, Lopez & Dukate Company, oyster packers, pleaded guilty to a charge of violating the Sherman anti-trust law and paid a fine of $10,000. Within the past month two other Mississippi oyster packers were fined for violating the federal pure food act. Still another oyster packing firm was complained of before the United States Commissioner of the District of New Orleans for peonage. It was alleged that this firm at its isolated canning factory held in virtual slavery seventeen men, women and children, whom they had brought from Baltimore to work in their factories.

More Money for Paper Clips Than for Children.

Mississippi, like many other states, has adopted the favorite method of nullifying a good child labor law by passing one in response to an indignant public demand, and neglecting to provide machinery for its enforcement. In other words, Mississippi has spent more money on paper clips for the office of the Oyster Commission than it spent on the protection of the children who toil in the state.

Now we will pass to the neighboring state of Alabama. So solicitous is Alabama of the oyster that in the foreword appearing on the reprint of its elaborate code for the protection of the oyster family, the Oyster Commission advertises:

"Liberal laws for the protection and promotion of every feature of the industry."

May we assume that Alabama's neglect to protect the child who toils in the cannery is one of those liberal laws to protect and promote the oyster industry? It must be conceded that the law is most liberal in the freedom it gives the canners to exploit the helpless child of industry.

The Game and Fish Protection fund in Alabama is so richly endowed that it has not been able to spend its revenues and grants. After disbursing $5,337.69 to protect game and fish in 1911, the fund had an unexpended balance of $25,285.88 to its credit, or nearly $2,000 more than it had the year previous.

In 1910 Alabama spent $907,648.30 for the relief of needy Confederate soldiers. For its history and archives Alabama spent in one year $11,243.97. We hope the historian has not failed to record Alabama's shameful acts of omission, as well as her glorious achievements. Alabama spent $40,266.81 for armory rents and military expenses, $24,000 of this sum going for an encampment alone.

Florida's Ancient Standards.

Florida, following in the footsteps of her sisters, has now before its legislature a proposed code to protect the oysters and fish of the state. While most progressives admit the necessity of laws to conserve our natural resources, it does seem that some legislation to protect the human resources of this state might justly precede this attempt to protect the oysters.

In the South, Florida stands alone in the shame of making no provision to enforce its body of labor laws. It cannot be that Florida's economy has rendered possible this legislative omission which leaves over 60,000 factory wage-earners alone in the state without any legal protection. The expenditure of $15,505.52 for a national guard encampment refutes this. And if it were necessary to retrench, surely Florida could spare some of the $307,132.48 she received from the hire of her convicts for private profits for the machinery to protect the employed of the state against industrial diseases and accidents and the enforcement of its ancient child labor standard.

No Closed Season for Children.

It is a high crime in Louisiana, Mississippi, Alabama, and soon will be in Florida, to gather oysters or catch shrimp out of season, because of the legally-enacted principle that to do so is to endanger the preservation of this precious family. There is no closed season for children. These states through their acts of omission permit unscrupulous industrial poachers to track down the little children during all seasons, stunt their growth by exhausting toil, blunt their sensibilities by monotonous activity and stifle their mentality by taking them from the school room and placing the unnatural burdens of industry on their weak shoulders.

As we cast these little crumbs of humanity on our turbulent industrial waters, unlettered, not strong, and with their ideals shattered, so are they returned to us by way of the almshouse, the hospital, the prison and the street. Can it be that the protected child of the north is more dear to them than the fair children of the South who toil in your canneries and mills?

The states of Florida, Louisiana, Mississippi and Alabama spent millions annually in pensioning the needy Confederate veterans. It is but right that those who baptized the nation in blood that it might be saved, be justly rewarded for their sacrifices. But the children of those whose valor won them the admiration of the world—they are being sacrificed on the altar of industrial greed.

The states of Louisiana, Mississippi and Alabama maintain elaborate nd expensive water patrols to prevent pirates from exploiting the oyster beds. These states, so anxious of the life of the oyster and shrimp, have provided no adequate machinery to stop the wanton waste of childhood in the gulf coast canneries. There is no fleet to prevent the industrial pirates of our day from swooping down on the reefs of childhood and robbing them of their choicest possessions and the inherent right to normal lives.

CHILD LABOR AND HEALTH.

W. H. OATES, B.Sc., M.D., Montgomery, Ala.,
Alabama Factory Inspector.

The fact that children have to labor is in itself deplorable. It is an economic question, however, which is far from being solved and in my opinion will be settled eventually only by interstate cooperation, uniformity of regulation and compulsory education.

I will not discuss deleterious occupational diseases, as they were to be assigned to another paper. As State Factory Inspector of Alabama, my attention has been called very forcibly to the child labor conditions in that state and, as a vast majority of the child laborers are in the cotton mills and textile manufactories, I will confine my remarks to the cotton mill children.

The health of the mill operatives is what one would expect. It varies in different mills. In certain localities the hookworm is pictured on the faces of nearly all the children. Red blood is conspicuous by its absence. The trained eye of the inspector is often unable to tell whether the age of a weazened, dried-up, anæmic specimen of the *genus homo* is twelve or eighteen.

Children between the ages of twelve and fourteen are prohibited from working more than sixty hours in any one week. The manufacturers throughout the state, in most cases, are working the children eleven hours a day for five days, and five hours on Saturdays.

Picture a little child, a girl just twelve years of age—and the data in this office shows that in numerous cases they are started to work the day they reach the age of twelve. Imagine this little girl, in the winter months, arising at five o'clock in the morning, eating a poorly cooked meal (and in most instances their food is hastily and improperly prepared) wending her way in the darkness to a mill, working not for one hour or two hours, but for six hours steadily at one continuous task (a task which does not in any way elevate), a monotonous, invariable, nearly incessant, grind before two or three machines, amid the rattle of spindles and the roar of pulleys; surrounded by the incessant deafening noise and constant motion of machinery; deprived of the pleasure of conversation on account of the noise and oftentimes breathing an atmosphere vitiated by lack of ventilation and by artificial humidity and the presence of dust and cotton fibre. Fancy this child, with only half an hour for dinner, continuing at her labor until the eleven hours of required toil are completed. Tired and worn out she goes home in the darkness to such a home as she has, rarely seeing the sunshine. This picture causes me to wonder, as a physician, what kind of a mother can this child make; what kind of offspring can she bring forth? Has this child no rights? Is it humane to make a machine out of this illiterate, helpless, maltreated human? Is it not entitled to the same consideration the farmer gives his colt or his calf? The idea of working a colt or a calf in harness would seem preposterous to the average farmer. Can we not put our children of the laboring classes in the same category as the farmer puts his beasts of burden?

This is a plea for the children between the ages of twelve and fourteen; that vital period in a girl's life when she changes from girlhood to womanhood.

Sixty hours' application a week at any vocation is certainly not conducive to good health, particularly during this period of life, and I want to go unqualifiedly on record as being heartily in favor of changing the age limit in Alabama to fourteen in the case of boys and sixteen in the case of girls, and regulating the hours so as not to exceed ten in any one day for children of these ages.

Remedial Methods.

My subject has, in my opinion, not so much to do with criticism as it has to do with pointing out conditions as they exist and suggesting means and methods of remedying, or at least mitigating, these conditions.

Ventilation, or rather lack of ventilation, is to me one of the most noticeable conditions in cotton mills. The architects have almost invariably ignored the rudimentary principles of ventilation. No means of ingress or egress of air is provided, other than the windows, and in a vast majority of cases these windows are closed and at times nailed down.

This could easily be remedied by the installation of ventilator tubes from each floor through the roof. In the case of very large mills, these ventilators could be actuated by exhaust fans.

A pernicious disease-spreading habit, nearly universal among cotton mill operatives, is spitting. They are nearly all tobacco and snuff users. I am not converted to the theory that tobacco and snuff will kill the tubercle bacilli. The installation of paper cuspidors, changed at frequent intervals, the prohibition of spitting on the floors and a little education on the spread of tuberculosis, would soon become a potent factor in preventing the spread of this scourge.

The hookworm will be discussed in another paper. Incidentally, however, I would state that the mere treating of people for hookworm is not sufficient. They should be taught how the disease is carried from one person to another and the precautions necessary to prevent this spreading.

Various diseases, noticeably syphilis and tuberculosis, are spread by the common drinking cup, the causative germ being transmitted from one mouth to another by this means. The recent abolition of public drinking vessels on all common carriers by the Interstate Commerce Commission is of far-reaching effect, its chief benefit being educational in its nature. It has started the unthinking to ask questions. Why does not the railroad give us glasses to drink out of? I am advocating and urging the installation of sanitary drinking fountains in all Alabama manufacturing establishments.

In cotton mill villages the operators frequently furnish nice houses, adequate drinking water—and stop at that, thinking that they have furnished modern homes for these people. They have, however, ignored the most vital of all sanitary problems, namely, the disposal of sewage.

This is a local question at any given point. Where a sanitary sewerage system exists or can be installed, the question is easily solved; but where the topography of the land is such that drainage is not feasible, I find in nearly all cases the antiquated, open, disease-spreading, privy. The medical world has demonstrated conclusively that typhoid fever, hookworm, various dysenteries, cholera, diarrhœa and other diseases are spread, or rather communicated, from one person to another through sewage. It is true that flies may be the intermediate carrier from the sewage to the food and thence to another person, but often water is a conveyor. This problem has been solved in numerous places by the installation of septic tanks. If this is not feasible the sanitary privy should be installed.

Malaria, that disease which is nearly universally disseminated throughout the South, is known to be carried from one person to another by means of the mosquito. Mosquitoes breed in stagnant water, frequently found in tin cans, old bottles, barrels, buckets and similar receptacles, which receptacles could be easily removed. In ponds and such places where stagnant water is found, the propagation of the mosquito can be stopped by a small quantity of oil placed at intervals on the surface of the ponds. The larvæ of the mosquito breathes air and comes to the surface of the water to breathe. It cannot penetrate the thin film of oil and hence is soon asphyxiated.

Physical Examination.

I have briefly outlined a few methods of preventing the spread of diseases. In conclusion, I urge the physical examination, by a competent physician, of all children prior to employment in any manufacturing establishment. It is due the child. If its eyes are abnormal, means should be adopted to remedy the abnormality. If it has incipient tuberculosis, the parent should know it and should be taught how to care for it. When any physical unfitness is evidenced, it should be attended to. A thorough physical examination should take in account general health, family history, whether the child is fully matured or not, any physical or mental defect, and means should be adopted to remedy, if possible, any deficiency.

Our public schools are excluding children suffering from the various acute, infectious or communicable diseases, likewise, pediculosis, scabies, trachoma, etc. Why not the factory and the mill? If these diseases are communicable in schools they are certainly communicable in mills. The installation of the system of medical examination cannot possibly work adversely to the interests of anyone. Primarily, the children are benefited and, secondarily, the manufacturer or owner of the business enterprise will soon find it to his interest.

In view of the fact that the conditions of life drive some children to the necessity of toiling for their livelihood, let us one and all use every effort to see that they get the benefits of modern sanitation, hygiene, ventilation and the full benefit of the application of modern preventive medicine.

DEVELOPING NORMAL MEN AND WOMEN.

JEAN GORDON, New Orleans, La.,
Former Factory Inspector, Parish of Orleans.

A Child Labor Conference always puts me in a bad humor. Child labor is such a blot on our Christian civilization, it is such a waste of economic values, that it seems to me it should be so recognized by every one. That it is not so recognized is proved by the fact that a few of us travel up and down this fair land every year, trying to educate men and women to the very evident fact that little boys and girls are just little human animals, and like every other kind of young animal, need plenty of sleep, play and schooling so as to grow into normal men and women. Evidently we are not very convincing speakers, because we have yet a very strong opposition to overcome—an opposition entrenched behind selfishness, greed and ignorance. And this trinity does not mean only the manufacturer—not that I am here to defend the manufacturer—there are some good manufacturers and there are plenty of bad; for this child labor problem has three angles—the manufacturer, the parent and the child. Many parents, through ignorance and indifference, are just as anxious to get the child to work as the manufacturer is anxious to work the child; and the child is just as anxious for the work as are the manufacturer and the parent to put it to work.

And here is where the state's responsibility comes in: to pass and enforce such laws as will prevent greedy employers, ignorant parents and undeveloped children from permitting child labor that hinders the development of future citizens.

It seems so stupid for me to have to come to Florida to tell you that ten, twelve and fourteen hours' work, opening oysters and picking shrimp, is not good work for little boys and girls; that those same little boys are going to come back on you and me in a few years, as worn-out men and women at twenty-five or thirty years of age, to be cared for by relief associations for a much longer period of years than they were of value to the manufacturers.

Short Work Day Means Greater Efficiency.

As to the question of the economic value of the eight-hour day, that is also a self-evident fact. Some of the most successful factories I know have an eight-hour day. Josephine Goldmark's wonderful book, "Fatigue and Efficiency," has proven that the greater the fatigue the longer rest required to restore the exhausted nerves and muscles.

It does not require a very wonderful mind to be able to reason out that the child who works twelve hours in a factory, which means it has been at that factory from 5.30 a. m. to 6.30 p. m.—for the hour for dinner is never considered part of the working day—is deprived of necessary rest and has no time for play.

Under our present industrial system I tremble with fear for the home of the future working men and women of America. In one breath men tell us the home is the place for women, that the whole future of the country depends upon the stability of the home, and with that argument played through every possible key, we, suffragists, are advised to go back to our homes and let the men run things. And then, when we agree with them and say "All right; but those thousands of young girls who are out of their homes from early dawn till dewy eve—we want to get *them* back to the home, give them a shorter work day, an eight-hour day, so they will have some time to learn the home-making arts!" Do we get it? Not yet, in this chivalrous South; the nearest to it is Texas—she has just passed a nine-hour day in certain industries. It has taken those cold, calculating, ungallant western and eastern states like Ohio, New York and a few others, to give the eight-hour day. And what has been the effect? Greater efficiency, a quality which every one recognizes as the greatest need of our young Americans, better machines, better workers, so as to get the best possible work out of the eight hours.

It also makes the older workers wonder why they cannot have a little more time to sleep and play, why work, work, work only should be their portion. And the wave is beginning to gather such momentum that soon the entire country will be putting its working women and children on an eight-hour day, just as men in most industries have gained for themselves a short day.

Personally, I think the greatest impetus to shorter hours will be given when the votes of the working women will be cast in favor of such candidates for the legislatures as will heed their pleas for better conditions for the future mothers and homes of the country, instead of, as now, having candidates who look only to the arguments of business men that this present condition is inevitable because the country depends upon its business interests, and any disturbance of tariffs, or hours, or wages, means destruction to commerce, etc. The country does not solely depend upon business; the most important factor in any country's development is the kind of men and women it is developing. You are not going to develop a strong manhood and womanhood from a lot of weaklings, and you are bound to get weaklings from over-worked, under-fed boys and girls!

CONDITIONS OF CHILD EMPLOYING INDUSTRIES IN THE SOUTH.

A SYMPOSIUM.

I. ALABAMA.

Mrs. W. L. Murdoch, Birmingham, Ala.
Chairman, Alabama Child Labor Committee.

If the workers in the National Child Labor Committee believe the old saying of Talleyrand, "Public opinion is mightier than any monarch who ever lived," then it seems to me the wonderful awakening of public opinion shown the length and breadth of our land should be most encouraging and should make it possible almost to begin to discern that day when no child in any state will be exploited for gain and when each commonwealth shall insure to its children the right not only to be well born and to grow up, but also to a prolonged playtime and joy of youth and to a useful education.

In spite of the fact that more children are working to-day than ever before, in spite of the fact that more occupations are open to children each year, nevertheless a force of public opinion is being openly displayed which is sure to put an end to these evils. Articles on the evils of premature labor for children are no longer confined to the *Survey* and kindred magazines, but *Life,* the *Saturday Evening Post* and many others are revealing conditions so shocking that the reading public has awakened from its lethargy and an interest has been created which will surely kindle into action. Even the grossly exaggerated and rather silly articles in *Life* have served a purpose in Alabama, for inquiries have come from all over the state about the truth of these reports and a protest that such conditions should obtain in the state.

The problem of child labor was slow in coming to the South, and very slow has she been in awakening to the evil of it. Even now we occasionally meet that old argument that the cotton mill is a blessing to the South, as it takes the children out of the rural districts where life is on a plane little better than that of animals, and gives them the civilizing influences of schools and churches. They do not explain how much this helps children who are at work ten hours a day nor do they mention that where the family all work in the mill, home conditions are not exactly ideal. It is hard to be patient longer with arguments like this.

The Present Law.

Alabama was the first Southern state to pass a child labor bill. In 1887 a bill was passed and was in operation for seven years. As no inspection was provided we can be sure it was of no great value. In 1894 this law was repealed and the history of legislation on child labor since then is not unlike that of other states—a series of unsuccessful attempts to get adequate protection for the children, resulting in the present law, one of the poorest in the country.

Our law applies only to mills, factories and manufactories, and is absolutely silent about all other forms of occupation for children, so that we have actually in the state children as young as nine years legally at work 12 or 14 hours a day.

The child-employing industries of Alabama differ in the large cities and small towns, but may be taken in general to mean agricultural pursuits, cotton mills and the newspaper and telegraph offices. As the state is largely agricultural, by far the largest number are to be found on the farms. We think, too, that the large percentage of illiteracy given to Alabama by the recent report of the Russell Sage Foundation is to be found on these farms. The farmer employing these children would probably deny any condition of child labor, contesting that this was wholesome occupation. Well, compared to ten hours a day in a cotton mill or factory, it is—but the absolute disregard for the necessity of education for these children makes it a very great evil; it is going to take a vigorous campaign of education for the farmer, himself, to change this situation.

The cotton mill industry of Alabama is not large compared with other Southern states. The whole number of children employed in the mills of the entire state is 3,734, and of these 1,779 are 14 and under, so we find that the number engaged in this form of industry is very small. We find the mills obeying the law as to age, 12 years, and as to hours, 60 a week; but in the requirement of eight weeks' schooling great laxity is shown. Where the children attend the public schools of the city, as they do in all the large towns, the certificates are sent in, but where the mill owns the school the report of the factory inspector shows that little attention has been paid to this requirement of the law. As the only proof of age required is the affidavit of the parent, and as the parent is often so ignorant as not to know what year the child was born, manifestly this proof is not worth much; yet if the inspector removes a child who he thinks is not the required age, he cannot prosecute, for the parent's word is supposed to be all that is necessary.

The sanitary conditions in the mills are not good. Indeed, in the smaller mills they are very bad. Only public opinion can correct this, as the inspector is not given power over it. We find no medical inspection in any mill of the state and wonder why the mill children should not need this fully as much as the children in the public schools. The humid air of a cotton mill is known to be fertile soil for tuberculosis, and it would seem wise for the state to safeguard the community by having medical inspection of these mills.

Not Reached by the Law.

The cotton mill has so long been the target of attack in regard to child labor, largely because children are there found in sufficient numbers to make an impression, and too, because the long hours of monotonous work are so bad for the children.

But in the investigations which our state committee has been making this year, the evils existing in the moving picture shows and soft drink stands are so much greater and the moral atmosphere surrounding the children at work selling newspapers and carrying messages so much worse, we feel the eyes of Alabama should be turned away from the cotton mill, where good inspection is provided, to these other occupations. In some of the soft drink stands we found children 12 years of age, working 12 or 13 hours a day, during which they were not allowed to sit down.

It is not unusual to find a boy of 12 delivering bundles at 11 o'clock at night for the department stores. These boys very rarely have been beyond the third or at most the fourth grade in school. The newspapers employ a large number of very young sellers, many not over ten years of age, on the streets at six in the morning. In Birmingham we have recently passed a newsboy's ordinance which will in a large measure correct this evil, but in the rest of the state it will continue.

With the help of the school nurse and the probation officer, we have been making a careful study of the records of the working children who go to school. We find them, without exception, way below average in their studies, irregular in attendance and frequently in the Juvenile Court. Out of 60 newsboys appearing before this court in the past year 42 were habitual sellers, all under 16 and most of them under 15. They had been selling for years. Their school records showed habitual tardiness or truancy. Out of the entire number, only 16 had a record of good attendance and very little trouble, and these were far below the average in school standing.

In the messenger service all over the state we find boys working, not many under 16, but with a record of having been at work for years, and with absolutely no schooling. The boys who work at night have no place to lie down and may be found on the tables, under benches, or wherever they can snatch a wink of sleep while waiting to be called. It is from this class of boys we get a history of crime and physical and mental degeneracy so great as to make us feel that in this line of work the age limit should be 21 years!

Alabama has, like most Southern states, the double problem of two races to provide for. We find the colored children in the large cities going to school in large numbers; but in the rural districts a condition of absolute illiteracy obtains among them—again accounting for our large percentage of illiterate children.

By far the greatest wealth-producing industry in the state is the mining industry. Here we find the operators themselves have, for self-protection, gone ahead of the state law and require that no child under 16 shall be allowed in or about the mines; they employ an inspector to see that this law is enforced, and generally speaking, it is obeyed. Exceptions are found among the colored miners, where a man will take his boy in as a helper.

Encouraging Outlook.

Such are some of the conditions obtaining in Alabama among the industries employing children. Dr. Oates, our State Factory Inspector, tells elsewhere in this publication some of the remedies needed. Bad as the conditions are with no compulsory education law, no adequate system of birth registration, no protection given to the child in any form of industry other than mills and factories, I still think the optimistic outlook at the opening of this paper is justified; the awakened conscience of the people does not wish to see Alabama remain first only alphabetically, and the awakened conscience, with a real knowledge of the facts, will kindle into real action. This is almost a "bromide."

Then, too, we are fortunate in having a Governor who states in writing "that he is in favor of reforming the child labor law so as to put Alabama in line with the most advanced states in the Union, and will recommend such legislation at the next session of the legislature." This is most encouraging.

With all this in mind, we believe Alabama's motto "Here we rest" shall not be spoken longer in derision, but shall mean what the splendid old founders of the state intended it to mean—a land of fairness, liberty, justice to all.

II. MISSISSIPPI.

Mrs. E. L. Bailey, Jackson, Miss.,
Member Advisory Board, Mississippi Child Labor Committee.

Irwin Russell, a Mississippian and the father of negro dialect poetry, laments that "some folks ain't got de presence of min' for to see

"Dat ole Mississippi's jes ober de fence
Dat runs aroun' Hebben's sarcumferyence."

While perhaps the child labor situation in Mississippi does not quite measure up to the ideal suggested by the poet, I gladly comply with the request to outline the steps by which we attained our present position.

Because Mississippi is an agricultural state, the problem of child labor did not confront us so early as it did the manufacturing states. The first suggestion of child labor legislation for Mississippi was made at the annual meeting of the King's Daughters in 1902. The committee appointed to consider a suitable law, recognized the latent possibilities of Mississippi as a manufacturing state; and, appreciating the importance of passing a law before the cotton mill interests became a dominant factor in Mississippi politics, prepared a bill which was presented to the 1904 legislature. Inexperience in legislation on the part of the committee, ignorance of the need of such law on the part of the majority of the legislators, and general indifference, may be cited as the reasons why this bill never emerged from the committee room.

This experience taught the friends of the measure the importance of first educating public sentiment, and the United Daughters of the Confederacy, the Woman's Christian Temperance Union, and the Women's Federation of Clubs, were asked to assist in an educational campaign preparatory to our appeal to the next legislature. These organizations responded promptly and earnestly. They appointed press committees, who, to a woman, rushed into print with exhaustive (or exhausting?) arguments favoring a drastic child labor law, setting forth pitiable conditions which might exist in cotton mills—fondly believing, each one, that every honest voter would read her discourse in his county paper, accept her view and demand the passage of her pet law (at least that is the way I felt, and the others wrote much as I did).

While this effort to arouse public sentiment was essential to success, it resulted also in awakening violent antagonism. When the bill came before the 1906 Legislature, it met well-organized opposition by the mill owners. Paid lawyers were on the ground to convince the legislative committees, that this agitation of child labor had no rightful place in Mississippi—that "it was a scheme on the part of New England mill owners to put Mississippi mills at a disadvantage," an effort on the part of "pseudo-philanthropists to earn their salaries," etc. The result: The bill passed the lower house and was defeated in the senate, where the opposition concentrated its forces.

This defeat did not discourage its advocates, but demonstrated that the measure had been lost through lack of organization, failure to appreciate the strength of the opposition, and want of definite, available information regarding conditions in Mississippi. We appealed to Dr. McKelway, Secretary for the Southern States of the National Child Labor Committee. He advised effective methods and sent Dr. Alfred H. H. Seddon to investigate conditions in our factories. Dr. Seddon's report showed that each of the twenty-one cotton mills of Mississippi employed children under twelve years, many working more than twelve hours a day in unsanitary surroundings.

In December, 1907, a call for all those interested in child labor legislation in Mississippi to meet in Jackson, resulted in the organization of the Mississippi Child Labor Committee, auxiliary to the National Committee. A legislative committee was appointed, composed of distinguished churchmen, eminent jurists, broad-minded school officials, men of recognized political influence and philanthropic women. A state senator submitted a bill for consideration, modeled after the form prepared at the Nashville Southern Textile Conference. The bill provided for a fourteen-year age limit and an eight-hour day, was approved and introduced in the 1908 Legislature. The opposing forces were prepared, and fought every section, offering possible and impossible amendments—resorting to every known means to defeat the bill or to destroy its effectiveness. Despite these tactics, there passed, the last day of the session, the much mutilated McDowell bill, Code 1908.

Reorganization.

In 1911, the Mississippi Valley Secretary called upon our committee and urged revision of our inadequate law. A vigorous pamphlet by Dr. McKelway exposed the deplorable condition of children in the Gulf Coast fish and oyster canneries, and showed that the existing law made no mention of such canneries but specified only cotton mills and factories. In December, 1911, the committee met. Political conditions in Mississippi had changed materially since the committee was organized in 1907. While we have but one political party, we sometimes have several political factions. Remembering that in politics, as in "the art of navigation, we must set our sails to catch the breeze," we deemed it the part of wisdom so to reorganize our Child Labor Committee as to bring it into harmony with the dominant political faction. Results demonstrate the fitness of our chosen leaders. An eminently successful lawyer, having no political aspirations, but wielding large influence, generously accepted the chairmanship and wisely directed the campaign.

New Law in 1912.

Careful consideration of the Uniform Child Labor Law convinced us that the doctrine of political expediency demanded elimination of such sections as did not apply in Mississippi. For example, Mississippi being devoid of mining interests, we did not care to hear facetious members of the opposition discourse sarcastically on the hardships endured by Mississippi children in Mississippi mines—by way of killing time and incidentally the bill. Again, compulsory education is a question Mississippi legislators are not ready seriously to consider. Because of our large negro population, competent, thoughtful students of local conditions, regardless of belief or non-belief in negro education, oppose the injection of this question into our politics, since it could but provoke dissension. Omitting, therefore, all provisions which seemed for any reason inexpedient, a bill, covering as briefly as possible our local needs, was compiled and introduced into both houses of the 1912 Legislature. The fight which ensued, while perhaps less bitter than that which confronted the McDowell bill, was persistent and determined. Two days prior to date set for adjournment found the bill held up in the lower house. A strong personal appeal to the Speaker obtained the promise that our floor manager should be recognized and the bill considered. At this stage some of our committee members did the lobbying of their lives. We remained in the house to hear the roll called, and on its passage rushed the bill to the Governor for signature, and Senate Bill 166 became a law—Code 1912.

The characteristic provisions of our present law are:

1. Girls under fourteen and boys under twelve years are not allowed to work in cotton mills, manufactories, canneries, etc.
2. Girls under eighteen and boys under sixteen years are not allowed to work in such establishments more than eight hours a day, and not between 7 p. m. and 6 a. m.
3. No child under sixteen years to be employed without consent of guardian and certificate of age, health, school grade, etc.

Enforcement.

Permit me to say in a spirit of conscious state pride, that the citizenship of Mississippi is, in the main, law-abiding. Many members of the legislature honestly believed that in our zeal for a child labor law we were misguided, and that said law would indeed and in fact work a serious hardship on the "poor widow"—of whom some of you have heard. The mill men who fought the bill to the limit of their ability for ten years had convinced themselves that its passage would cripple the infant industries of our commonwealth, that those favoring such law were influenced solely by sentiment which the situation did not justify, and that they themselves, by giving employment to poor children, were doing philanthropic work. But when the fight was over these men accepted the result and obeyed the law.

Due to the strong prejudice which existed in the 1912 legislature against creating additional offices, the provision for a state inspector was omitted and the following provisions for the enforcement of the act were made:

1. It shall be the special duty of the sheriff to visit each mill, factory, cannery, etc., in his county not less often than twice each month, and to see to the enforcement of this act.

2. It shall be the duty of the county health officer to visit each such establishment without notice, at least twice each year, and see to the enforcement of sanitary regulations and health of children employed and to report violations.

3. It shall be the special duty of Circuit Judges to charge the Grand Juries to investigate violations of this act.

Replies from personal letters to sheriffs, health officers and judges, give assurance that there is no disposition on the part of mill owners or officials to disregard or evade the law. So far as we can determine, the observance of the law has not handicapped in any way the mill interests nor reduced their dividends. To the best of our knowledge and belief the law has proven very nearly satisfactory, and has been strictly enforced in cotton mills and factories.

Present Problem.

Mississippi's most difficult child labor problem at present, is that of the little oyster shuckers on the Gulf Coast. These children are nomads, coming on oyster luggers from the North Atlantic Coast to the Southern Coast for the winter oyster packing season, and returning to the Chesapeake Bay canneries for the summer. The children are with their parents—parents without mental or moral standards, having no conception of right living nor interest beyond their daily food supply. While our law forbids their employment, their cases are difficult to deal with because the parents in many instances live in the oyster sheds, where the children also eat, sleep, play or work around the mothers. They are here to-day, gone to-morrow, often leaving in the night.

While paternalism is a term to make Mississippians hesitate, we cannot fail to accept responsibility toward children whose natural guardians are devoid of any sense of parental obligation. We have not, however, evolved a satisfactory method of dealing with the oyster cannery situation. Whether the case is for the law or the gospel, local charities or national philanthropies, I confess I cannot determine. Perhaps a measure of responsibility rests on each. True it is, however, that humanity not less than Christianity demands that intelligent effort be put forth in behalf of "the least of these our little ones."

III. SOUTH CAROLINA.

J. A. McCullough, Greenville, S. C.,
Chairman, South Carolina Child Labor Committee.

The mills situated in my territory are perhaps among the best in the South. The homes are comfortable and sanitary as a rule, and the mill conditions are, with few, if any, exceptions, favorable to the employes. Before discussing further the topic assigned, permit me to make a few general observations.

The present age limit under the statute of South Carolina is 12 years. No child under 16 is permitted to work between the hours of 8 o'clock p. m. and 6 a. m., but there is a fatal provision to the effect that children under 16 may be permitted to work after

8 p. m. in order to make up lost time caused by some temporary shut-down of the mill on account of accident or some break-down of the machinery; and provided that under no circumstances shall a child under 16 work later than 9 p. m. The act makes it a misdemeanor for any owner, superintendent or other party in charge to knowingly violate its provisions. It is also made a misdemeanor for any parent or guardian to misrepresent the age of the child and requires, before the employment of any child under 14 years, that the parent or guardian should furnish a sworn statement as to name, age, etc.

A bill is now pending in the state legislature to raise the age limit to thirteen from and after July 1st, 1913, and fourteen after July 1st, 1914. This bill has received an unfavorable report at the hands of the Senate Judiciary Committee. It was deemed advisable not to make a fight at this session for its enactment, in view of the fight which was being made for the enactment of a compulsory education bill, and in view of the promises made to the Child Labor Committee by the representatives of the South Carolina Cotton Manufacturers' Association, that if the compulsory education bill was enacted they would unite with us in securing the passage of a bill raising the age limit in South Carolina.

A local option compulsory education bill has passed both houses, but in the opinion of the writer it is more or less loose and inefficient. It is, however, a step in the right direction and gives promise of a more stringent law at some time—we trust, in the near future.

With reference to the physical conditions in the cotton mills of South Carolina, I quote from the fourth annual report of the Commissioner of Agriculture for South Carolina:

"When factory inspection was resumed in the spring of this year, and the new child labor law was in force, as soon as the first 71 mills had been inspected a comparison of the child labor statistics in those 71 mills for the years of 1911 and 1912 to that date, June 5, was made. These mills worked during the year of 1911, 4,211 children under 16 years of age, of which 168 were under 12. During 1912 they showed a total of 2,734 children, all between 12 and 14, 1,524 of whom were between 14 and 16, or a decrease of 1,387, or 33 1/3 per cent. The 71 mills were taken at random and in the regular order of inspection work. . . .

"Considering the condition as to child labor, it is very gratifying that there are 468 less children employed in the textile mills in this state to-day than a year ago, and all of them are now over 12 years of age. This has occurred notwithstanding the increase in the number of people employed. In 1909 there were 8,432 children under 16 years of age employed; in 1910 there were 8,312; in 1911, 7,958; and in 1912, 7,490. There has been during the year a decrease of 517 boys and the increase of girls has been only 49; that class of employment having been kept practically at a standstill. I might call attention to the fact that just three years ago, in the year 1909, we had 726 children under 12 years of age at work in the textile mills. The next year, 1910, that number had been reduced to 620. Last year the number had been further decreased to 410, only 169 of those being girls. Then the new law striking out all of the old exemptions and making it impossible for a child under 12 years of age to work for any cause, became effective, and this year there is not a single child under 12 years of age employed as far as we can find through inspection, though there may be an occasional case that has escaped the inspectors. It is of much gratification to me, notwithstanding the rapid growth and development of the textile industry, that in three years' time, with the average number of employed people steadily increasing, we come to the end of the year 1912 with 944 less children under 16 years of age at work than we had at the beginning of that period. I am gratified, too, that without the use of extensive child labor the textiles are this year able to pay nearly two million dollars more to the employes in wages, and show an increase in the value of their annual product of over two and one-half million dollars.

"The labor cost percentage, about 8½ per cent., is not yet quite up to the average percentage for the textile industry in the United States, which is approximately 28 per cent. . . .

"Frequently during the year operatives wrote to the Governor of the State complaining chiefly that the mills here and there were exceeding the hours of labor allowed by law, and not a few complaining to the chief executive in regard to holding back of wages. In each and every instance these complaints were promptly investigated, inspectors being taken from other work in order to do so. In only one instance could any evidence whatever be obtained to warrant a prosecution, and that case is pending as this report is written. The inspectors' reports on these cases will show that the law as it is now written, is worse than useless, for it gives rise to continual complaint from operatives, without the possibility of obtaining any evidence that would stand in law. In regard to the matter of holding back wages, there is no law that would enable this Department to act . . ."

The annual report of the inspectors, dated December 31st, 1912, contains the following statements:

"We have inspected 164 cotton mills, made 340 regular inspections, and made several inspections to investigate special complaints, usually made by mill operatives. We have also made several night inspections of cotton mills.

"We have issued 283 orders for children to file statements, giving name, place and time of birth, and place of residence; given 110 orders for children to get transfer permits from mills where they had previously filed statements, to the mills that they were working in at the time of the inspection. Sixty-one orders have been served for the immediate discharge of children under 12 years of age.

"Altogether, for lack of permits, transfer permits, and being under legal age, we have given 134 orders that children be sent out of mills.

"We have given fifty-three orders for closets to be kept in better condition, nineteen orders for notices in regard to sex to be placed on closets, and have given two orders for new systems to be installed.

"We have given also twenty-seven orders for posting notices in regard to cleaning machinery while in motion, and several orders for placing guards on dangerous machinery. . . .

"In inspections of textile plants we have met with the hearty co-operation of mill presidents and superintendents. Only on one occasion has an inspector been treated disrespectfully, and upon his return to that mill with a written order, he was shown due courtesy. It has been our policy to suggest and give reasons rather than to give written orders, and we have found that this plan has worked admirably. Our suggestions have been carried out promptly; and, in many cases, more fully than our suggestions warranted. . . ."

Child Labor.

"This being what we considered the most important part of our work, we have paid special attention to the enforcement of the law in this matter. On account of the lack of factory inspectors for the previous year, we found that some of the mills had become careless in this matter. By this we mean to say that the mill authorities in these cases had not intentionally broken the law in working children under the legal age, but that they had simply grown negligent in this matter. We are glad to report, however, that when their attention was called to this, they gladly co-operated with us in the enforcement of the law.

"During our inspections of the mills of this State, we have in many instances found children with papers properly filled out but who do not seem to be of legal age. In some instances we have looked into the family records and found this to be correct; but in many cases there were no family records, father and mother illiterate, and the date of birth merely a matter of guess work. As a remedy for this condition, we beg to call your attention to our recommendation for birth registry. . . .

"The enactment of a law requiring the registration of births should be made and enforced. . . ."

It appears from the report of the Commissioner of Agriculture that there are now 4,253 male children under 16 years of age and 3,237 females employed by the textile industries of this state; 2,848 male children and 2,225 female children from 14 to 16 years and 2,164 male children and 1,455 female children from 12 to 14, are thus employed. Mr. Dawley and other enthusiasts of the system say that all the children employed in the cotton mills are remarkably healthy specimens. At least, this is an inference. The charge is made that Dr. McKelway and others have photographed and pictured only the anæmic ones. This charge admits that there are anæmic ones. If so, these anæmic ones are entitled to the protection of the law.

Our Needs.

1. Our effort to raise the age limit in South Carolina is not intended as a reflection upon the humanity of the mill presidents. We recognize the fact that as a rule they are men of broad sympathies and kind hearts, and they do a great deal for their employes in the way of providing comfortable homes and providing for their intellectual, spiritual and social welfare. Perhaps it is not to be expected that they should voluntarily enforce a higher age limit, since they have not done so heretofore, and for that reason *legislation* is necessary.

2. It is not a question as to whether the children have better homes and more advantages than they had in their mountain homes. This may be granted, and yet that does not justify working little children of tender years in a cotton mill or any other place of constant confinement. Our system of slavery in the South was a civilizing agency to the negro of the South and he was much better cared for and had many more advantages as a slave than he had as a free man in the jungles of Africa; and yet, this fact did not justify the institution of slavery.

3. We freely admit that to work a child in a cotton mill where the sanitary and other conditions are favorable, and the work not too arduous, is better for the child than to loaf on the streets, smoke cigarettes and shoot craps. It does not necessarily follow that all the children turned out of the mills by legislative act *would* do these things. Many of them would seek the schools. It is the purpose, however, of the Child Labor Committee to endeavor, by the enactment of a compulsory education law, to provide the child with a better environment than the mill can afford.

4. The enactment of a vital statistics law is absolutely essential for enforcing a child labor law. We have no such law in South Carolina.

5. The enactment of a medical inspection law, applicable not alone to school children, but to factory employes and especially the children, is also essential in my opinion to a proper solution of the problem.

IV. THE DEMORALIZING ENVIRONMENT OF NIGHT MESSENGERS IN SOUTHERN CITIES.

EDWARD F. BROWN, New York,
Special Agent, National Child Labor Committee.

The messenger service, as carried on at night in the larger cities of the South, has been the subject of inquiry by the National Child Labor Committee since the summer of 1910.

It has been found that calls for night messengers are divided into two groups which might be termed: (1) legitimate, and (2) demoralizing calls. In the first classification there fall calls from

(a) Business houses open at night.
(b) Hotel calls.
(c) Newspaper offices.
(d) Private home calls.
(e) Hospitals.

Were it not for the fact that work at night for children is frequently fatal to proper physical development, our objection to the night messenger service would rest there. But a study of the business in the principal cities of thirty-two states, including the South, has shown us that the majority of calls for boys after nine and ten o'clock at night is confined to our second group, which includes

(a) Calls to houses of ill fame.
(b) Service to disreputable hotels.
(c) Carrying of notes to drinking places of assignation.
(d) Gambling house calls, etc.

Intimate Contact with Underworld.

A careful study has disclosed young boys in the principal cities of Georgia, Alabama, Tennessee, Louisiana and Florida being used nightly as go-betweens among the lawless elements mentioned.

Inmates of notorious places call messengers to deliver notes to their patrons; carry meals to their rendezvous and even serve them; purchase liquors during legal and forbidden hours, and to purchase cocaine and opium and liquors in states where the sale of these things is prohibited.

Frequently young boys are called to police station houses for the purpose of carrying notes from arrested unfortunates to their companions to arrange bail. It is hard to think of a more vicious system which brings young growing boys into intimate contact with a scheme of life where they see strong men living easily on the earnings and degradation of erring women. The young night messenger lives in an atmosphere of vice at an age when he is most likely to plunge into its secrets before an understanding reveals its dangers to warn him.

A Blighted Life.

In Memphis I met a boy who at nineteen years had drifted from a night messenger to a companion of street women. At nineteen he had become a confirmed opium user. To show me how freely a night messenger circulates in the criminal groups of the underworld he brought to me a quantity of opium, which, among other exhibits, is now on file in the office of the National Child Labor Committee.

But usually the night messenger in the South is younger than the lad who at nineteen became a vile master and a drug fiend. In Memphis a fifteen-year-old night messenger whom I met had in his pocket a box of cocaine he was about to deliver to an inmate of a house of ill fame. "I get it for them from ten to fifteen times a night," he boasted. In delivering telegrams and notes and contraband articles to these women, the night messenger is frequently permitted to go directly to the private room of the courtesan. The stories these boys tell of the debauches they witness are of such a nature that they can neither be written or spoken, with propriety.

When these boys reach thirteen or fourteen years they are

frequently contaminated with most horrible diseases. A Jacksonville fifteen-year-old night messenger told me the other day that he was barely fourteen when he first visited a woman of the underworld.

It is not long before the diseased boy, frightened and morose, falls a victim to the vile practitioners who loudly advertise cures which aggravate the loathsome ailment.

Familiarity with Vicious Resorts.

The impression of visits to houses of ill fame by young night messengers is shown in the remarkable memories they have for recalling each place. A nine-year-old night messenger in Montgomery boasted that he knew every haunt of vice in the city. In Savannah a thirteen-year night messenger wrote from memory a list of twenty disorderly resorts to which he is called. In Memphis a fifteen-year night messenger wrote out fifteen houses he became acquainted with while on his rounds as messenger at night. In Nashville a boy wrote twenty-three houses of ill fame. In New Orleans a sixteen-year night messenger wrote twenty addresses. In Mobile a fourteen-year night messenger remembered fourteen places to write down.

In Tampa a sixteen-year night messenger wrote down eight notorious resorts. Another Tampa boy of eleven years wrote six addresses. In Jacksonville a night messenger of 16 years wrote a list of ten addresses. Another Jacksonville night messenger gave us a list of eight places of ill fame. The two last-mentioned boys told us that the element with which they came in contact was so vicious that they had to carry guns for protection at night.

An Industrial Blind Alley.

It is not to be supposed that the office managers of the telegraph and messenger companies are not familiar with these conditions. It has frequently been found that they know exactly the source of the call on which they deliberately send these children. Frequently it has been found that the office of the company during the dull hours of the night becomes a centre of demoralizing practices.

Child Employing Industries in the South 141

The occupation of night messenger is not only an industrial blind alley, but a training school for degenerates and criminals.

There has not been found, except in the city of Pittsburgh, any systematic attempt to train these boys for a future of industrial efficiency. They are seldom taught telegraphy. An eleven-year-old Tampa night messenger summed it up well when he said, "They (the managers) don't care what you do, so long as you deliver the messages."

The uniform of the messenger frequently serves as a pass word to the forbidden places where under cover of darkness debauchery and licentiousness run riot. A fifteen-year-old Jacksonville night messenger bore testimony on this point when he said: "The police don't allow kids in the 'red light' district. Once I was sent to take a telegram to a woman in a house down the line. When I delivered the message a policeman was waiting for me outside. He came up to me and asked me what I was doing in the house. I told him I was delivering a telegram. He said I was lying. I showed him my badge and he said 'alright' and let me go."

Successful Efforts for Regulation.

The need for a strict regulation of the night messenger service is too obvious to require any special brief. Since the National Child Labor Committee undertook this campaign, the states of New York, New Jersey, Massachusetts, Rhode Island, Wisconsin, Utah and Arizona have passed laws prohibiting the employment of any one under twenty-one years of age in the night messenger service after ten o'clock at night and before five o'clock in the morning. The eighteen-year age limit prevails now in New Hampshire, Maryland, Indiana, Ohio, Michigan, Minnesota, Oregon, South Carolina and Delaware (effective January 1, 1914).

Nowhere in the Union is the night messenger service more in need of attention than in the South where it has been found that children, some as young as nine years of age, are subject to the demoralization and ruin of life at night in large cities.

AN EIGHT-HOUR DAY IN A TEN-HOUR STATE.

Henry Nichol,
General Manager, Volunteer Manufacturing Co., Nashville, Tenn.

I give my views on this subject from personal experience, having been connected with some of the largest factories in my city and having hundreds under my employ, and I refer particularly to the work of girls.

The last factory I was superintendent of, for eleven years, worked ten hours a day. I always figured on 5 per cent. of the girls being out. In my present factory, I figure on only one per cent., and my books will show that while we work only eight hours a day, instead of falling off in production I am turning out from 10 to 15 per cent. more work and better work.

I have taught my girls not to think of me as the "Boss," but as the head, letting them feel free and easy, as if they were part of the concern, teaching them a smile is better than a frown and keeping them in harmony with one another. I will not hesitate to say I have the best disciplined set of girls to be found in Tennessee.

Having been a superintendent for 19 years, I advocate the short eight-hour day from my personal experience. Twenty years ago I was cutter for the largest clothing house in our city. The owner, a fine man, never hesitated about working the cutting department overtime to 10 and 11 o'clock at night, and as many as eighteen and twenty nights a month. The mornings after night work I was not fit to commence a day's work. My health was impaired and I thought I would never get it back. I made a secret pledge that if I was ever in position I would have the hours reduced as my first move.

When I first became foreman I stopped work at 12 o'clock on Saturday. I saw the difference at once and the girls looked forward to the half holiday. So, when I started the present concern, my first thought was to make short hours. I have never worked over eight hours since I have been in business for myself—five years. I believe, if the different concerns throughout the country would let their help off every Saturday afternoon, they would get better results. Their help would go about their work with a vim and could get out better work.

I never employ a girl under 17 without the consent of her mother, and then only in rare cases. Young girls are not settled in their ways and do not understand the responsibility of the work they undertake, as the older girls.

To accomplish the best results there should go, hand in hand with shorter hours, oversight from a foreman who issues his orders in a plain, simple manner, insists on their being carried out, shows no partiality and recognizes tact as an invaluable asset in dealing with his workers.

I have visited several plants where they work long hours and the workers go about their work with no life. To have the hours of work most beneficial I would suggest: commence at 7.30 in the morning, stop at 12 for lunch, start at 12.30, quit work at 4.30 (that gives the girls plenty of time to attend to other business and pleasure) and close at 12 o'clock Saturdays, so they can go to the park or amusements and enjoy themselves. I never make ironclad rules about getting to work promptly at 7.30 for the reason that I have a few women who must get their children off to school. The other girls understand the situation and do not say anything.

Union Labor.

With regard to unions and union labor, I believe you can get better results with union labor. All the hands are on the same footing and are paid the same price for what they do. If a girl does not do her duty, all I have to do is to appeal to the shop chairman and the matter can be settled in a few minutes without any trouble. Another feature is, the price for making the garment is fixed once a year and the manufacturer is protected for one year in advance, and that keeps down strikes.

The present legislature of Tennessee is working on a law to shorten the hours in the state, but its success depends on what interest the friends of the movement take to see that it becomes a law.

Tennessee is providing more money for education than ever before in the history of the state, and compulsory education[1] and free text books will be one way to keep the children out of the factories and put them in the schools, where they belong. Then, in ten years, there will be a wonderful change and girls and boys will be able to go forth in the battle of life and not be chained to machines, as is the case at present. Each would be on the same footing, and they could not say they did not have a chance.

I have gone through all the hardships a boy could have, starting at the age of 10 years to work after school, and I now see what I could accomplish if I had a good education to back up my energy. With a national eight-hour law, many a man will be enabled to look on the bright side of life and say "I have something to live for and my family can enjoy some of the fruits of my labor, like the families of other men."

Those are my views on the situation I met as workman, foreman, superintendent and owner. I have never regretted any move I have made for the welfare and comfort of the help under my supervision. I will always believe that with an eight-hour day and taking the children out of the factories, you not only get more and better work, but better citizens.

My factory is open for inspection at any time, so any one can see for himself the results of an eight-hour day in a ten-hour state.

[1]NOTE.—Since this article was written, Tennessee passed a compulsory education law for children under 16 if unemployed.

PROCEEDINGS OF THE NINTH ANNUAL CONFERENCE ON CHILD LABOR UNDER THE AUSPICES OF THE NATIONAL CHILD LABOR COMMITTEE.

Jacksonville, Fla., March 13-17, 1913.

The first Annual Conference of this Committee was held in New York City, February 14 to 16, 1905. The second was held in Washington, December 8 to 10, 1905, with supplementary sessions in Philadelphia and Chicago; the third in Cincinnati, December, 1906; the fourth in Atlanta, April, 1908; the fifth in Chicago, January, 1909; the sixth in Boston, January, 1910; the seventh in Birmingham, March, 1911; the eighth in Louisville, January, 1912.

At the ninth Annual Conference, held in Jacksonville, Fla., March 13-17, 1913, by invitation of the Jacksonville Board of Trade, Jacksonville Woman's Club, Florida Children's Home Society, Associated Charities, and other Civic Organizations, the following program was carried out:

GENERAL TOPIC: CHILD LABOR AND POVERTY.

I. Thursday Afternoon, March 13, 3.30 o'clock.

CHILD LABOR AND CHARITABLE RELIEF.

General Discussion by Chairman and Secretaries of State Child Labor Committees, School Attendance Officers, and Secretaries of Charity Organization Societies.

Sherman C. Kingsley, Director, Elizabeth McCormick Memorial Fund, Chicago, Ill., Presiding.

Questions for discussion:
Is the immature child a proper object of charitable relief?
Shall the state pension the widows?
Shall the school support the child?
Shall charitable societies relieve family distress by finding work for children?

Delegates leading the discussion:
Jean M. Gordon, New Orleans, La.
Mrs. W. L. Murdoch, Chairman, Alabama Child Labor Committee, Birmingham, Ala.
Mrs. Florence Kelley, Secretary, National Consumers' League, New York City.
A. T. Jamison, Connie Maxwell Orphanage, Greenwood, S. C.
R. T. Solensten, Associated Charities, Jacksonville, Fla.
Leon Schwartz, President, District Lodge No. 7, Independent Order B'nai B'rith, Mobile, Ala.
Mary H. Newell, Associated Charities, Columbus, Ga.

II. Thursday Evening, March 13th, 8.15 o'clock.

THE DUTY OF THE STATE TO THE WORKING CHILD.

Dr. Samuel McCune Lindsay, Vice-Chairman, National Child Labor Committee, Presiding.

Addresses of Welcome by Judge William H. Baker, representing the Governor, and Mayor W. S. Jordan, for the City of Jacksonville

1. Ancient Standards of Child Protection. Rabbi David Marx, Atlanta, Ga.
2. The Textile Industry and Child Labor. Richard K. Conant, Secretary, Massachusetts Child Labor Committee, Boston, Mass.
3. The Campaign in North Carolina: The Mountain Whites, by One of Them. W. H. Swift, Greensboro, N. C.
4. Developing Normal Men and Women. Jean M. Gordon, Former Factory Inspector, New Orleans, La.

Reception in charge of Reception Committee, Banquet Hall, Board of Trade Building, immediately following this session.

III. Friday Morning, March 14th, 9.30 o'clock.

SURVEY OF CHILD LABOR SITUATION IN THE SOUTH.

A. J. McKelway, Secretary for Southern States, National Child Labor Committee, Presiding.

1. Conditions in Child Employing Industries.
   Five 10 minute reports.
   - (a) Mrs. W. L. Murdoch, Chairman, Alabama Child Labor Committee, Birmingham, Ala.
   - (b) Hon. J. A. McCullough, Chairman, South Carolina Child Labor Committee, Greenville, S. C.
   - (c) Mrs. E. L. Bailey, Jackson, Miss.
   - (d) Mary H. Newell, Columbus, Ga.
   - (e) Edward F. Brown, New York, Special Agent, National Child Labor Committee.
2. Programs for Improvement.
   Five 10 minute reports.
   - (a) W. H. Swift, Greensboro, N. C.
   - (b) Dr. W. H. Oates, Montgomery, Ala.
   - (c) Mrs. J. W. McGriff, Jacksonville, Fla.
   - (d) Dr. A. J. McKelway, Washington, D. C.
   - (e) Josephine J. Eschenbrenner, New York, Membership Secretary, National Child Labor Committee.
3. Address: Social Welfare and Child Labor in Southern Cotton Mills. Rev. C. E. Weltner, Columbia, S. C.

Proceedings Ninth Annual Conference 147

IV. *Friday, March 14th, 12.30 to 2 o'clock.*

LUNCHEON CONFERENCE.

Luncheon for the Women Delegates, arranged by the Woman's Club, at the Club Building, 18 East Duval Street. Addresses by prominent speakers.

V. *Friday Afternoon, March 14th.*

PARLOR CONFERENCES.

These Jacksonville homes and clubs were open for reception to out-of-town delegates from 3.00 to 5.00 o'clock, and the speakers noted discussed informally the topics of the Conference:

Mrs. Harrison Reed, South Jacksonville.
   Harvey P. Vaughn.
   Mrs. W. L. Murdoch.

Mrs. L. G. Moore, 3006 Main Street.
   John A. Kingsbury.
   Edward F. Brown.
   Kate Holstead.

Mrs. G. H. Dodson, 834 W. Monroe Street.
   Lewis W. Hine.
   Dr. W. H. Oates.
   Grace Strachan.

Mrs. J. E. Cohen, 604 Laura Street.
   Dr. Samuel McCune Lindsay.
   Mrs. Florence Kelley.

Mrs. P. W. Dunk, 1426 Laura Street.
   John C. Campbell.
   Anna Herkner.

Mrs. J. Durkee, 308 Ocean Street.
   Jean M. Gordon.
   Sherman C. Kingsley.

Miss Caroline Bailey, Highway Mothers' Club.
   Mrs. G. H. C. Williams.
   Mary H. Newell.
   A. T. Jamison.

Mrs. W. W. Cummer, 960 Riverside Avenue.
   Owen R. Lovejoy.
   Julia C. Lathrop.

Miss Anna Stockton, Milldale Mothers' Club.
Dr. C. E. Weltner.
Anna Rochester.

Fairfield Improvement Association, Talleyrand Avenue.
W. H. Swift.
Mrs. E. L. Bailey.

Mrs. F. P. Conroy, 231 East Adams Street.
Dr. A. J. McKelway.
Josephine J. Eschenbrenner.

VI. Friday Evening, March 14th, 8.15 o'clock.

CHILD LABOR AND WAGES.

Dr. Samuel McCune Lindsay, Presiding.

1. From Mountain Cabin to Cotton Mill. John C. Campbell, Asheville, N. C., Russell Sage Foundation.
2. Child Labor and Poverty: Both Cause and Effect. John A. Kingsbury, General Agent, Association for Improving the Condition of the Poor, New York City.
3. The Federal Children's Bureau. Julia C. Lathrop, Chief of the Bureau, Washington, D. C.
4. The Eight-Hour Day in a Ten-Hour State. Henry Nichol, Manager, Volunteer Mfg. Co., Nashville, Tenn.
5. The Burden on Children in Shrimp and Oyster Canneries. Illustrated by stereopticon. Lewis W. Hine, Staff Photographer, National Child Labor Committee, New York City.

VII. Saturday Morning, March 15th, 9.30 o'clock.

CHILD LABOR AND HEALTH.

Owen R. Lovejoy, General Secretary, National Child Labor Committee, Presiding.

1. Child Labor and Health. Dr. W. H. Oates, State Factory Inspector, Montgomery, Ala.
2. Child Labor and Need. M. Louise Boswell, Cincinnati Bureau of Vocational Guidance.
3. How to Make Child Labor Legislation More Effective. Dr. Samuel McCune Lindsay, Columbia University, New York City.
4. Neglected Human Resources of the Gulf Coast States. Edward F. Brown, Special Agent, National Child Labor Committee.

Proceedings Ninth Annual Conference 149

VIII. *Saturday Morning, March 15th, 10 o'clock.*

MEETING FOR CHILDREN.

Imperial Theatre.

Under the direction of Mrs. Thomas Palmer, Jacksonville, Fla.

1. Hymn for the Working Children, by Fanny J. Crosby—First Stanza.
   The Audience.
2. The Story of the Medicine Bottle.
   (Illustrated with Lantern Slides of the Glass Industry.)
   Master J. B. Sparks, Jacksonville, Fla.
3. Hymn for the Working Children—Second Stanza.
4. The Story of My Cotton Dress.
   (Illustrated with Lantern Slides of the Cotton and Tenement Home Industries.)
   Miss Muriel Bland, Jacksonville, Fla.
5. Moving Picture Film, "Children Who Labor."
6. Child Labor Verse.—Recitation.
   Miss Hattie Spencer, Jacksonville, Fla.
7. Song, "The Story of Old," Miss Katherine Wilson, Jacksonville, Fla.
8. What Mr. Coal Tells Us.
   (Illustrated with Lantern Slides from the Coal Industry.)
   Miss Nell Wrigley, Jacksonville, Fla.
9. Hymn for the Working Children—Third Stanza.

IX. *Saturday Afternoon, March 14th.*

Excursion on St. Johns River, arranged by the Entertainment Committee, Mrs. J. W. Spratt, Chairman.

X. *Sunday Afternoon, March 16th, Mass Meeting, 3.30 o'clock.*

Senator Frederick M. Hudson, Presiding.

1. Child Wages in the Cotton Mill: Our Modern Feudalism. A. J. McKelway, Washington, D. C.
2. Child Labor and Low Wages are Corollaries. Jerome Jones, Editor and Manager, The Journal of Labor, Atlanta, Ga.
3. The Child Breadwinner and the Dependent Parent. Mrs. Florence Kelley, Secretary, National Consumers' League, New York City.
4. Where American Children Work. Owen R. Lovejoy, General Secretary National Child Labor Committee, New York City.

XI. Monday, March 17th, Workers' Conference and Questionnaire.

In response to many requests it was decided to continue the Conference over Monday, taking the day for special consultation among workers in child labor reform and agencies for charitable relief.

No fixed program was announced, but opportunity was given to discuss informally and in detail the many questions that arose at the regular sessions.

CONFERENCE NOTES.

Exhibit. The National Child Labor Committee exhibited its large collection of charts, photographs, and articles the children have made, in the Board of Trade Building, 209 Main Street, during the days of the Conference. Miss Marie J. Franchowitz in charge, under the direction of the local Exhibit Committee, Rabbi Samuel Schwartz, Chairman.

Delegates. The Governors of all states and the Mayors of many cities were invited to send delegates. The National Child Labor Committee invited the general public to attend and participate in the discussions.

Registration. At Board of Trade Building, 209 Main Street, under direction of Mrs. W. H. Baker, Chairman, Registration Committee. Miss J. J. Eschenbrenner, Membership Secretary, National Child Labor Committee, assisted in registering delegates and in enrolling friends in the membership of the newly organized Florida Child Labor Committee.

Entertainment, as noted in the program, was provided by the local organizations at whose invitation the Conference convened.

FIRST SESSION.

The first session, Thursday afternoon, March 13th, in the Board of Trade Auditorium, was called to order by Hon. Frank E. Jennings, Chairman of the Jacksonville Committee on Arrangements. After a few words of greeting, Mr. Jennings introduced Sherman C. Kingsley, Director of the Elizabeth McCormick Memorial Fund, Chicago, who presided at the opening discussion on Child Labor and Charitable Relief.

Mr. Kingsley said: "It is not easy for us who are in charitable relief work to tell others just what we want, for it is such an enormous question that we hardly know ourselves. We go from one stage to another making discoveries and trying different remedies, and it is hard to formulate a good program. But we do make some progress and out of the discussion this afternoon we hope something will emanate that will make us more sure of our ground. Moreover this problem is taking new forms. In many states there is a question of putting into effect some kind of scheme whereby the state, through the municipality, or the state itself, shall give mothers, who have little children, money to provide for these children shelter and nourishment and something to wear. It is a great big question and some believe in it and some do not believe in it, and a good many people do not know what they believe. They are pretty well agreed that it takes some money to run a family and they are also agreed that there are families that cannot earn enough to live on. But there comes the question how, in these broken families, income sufficient to give nourishment and shelter to the family shall be provided. Here are four questions propounded for discussion this afternoon:

"Is the immature child a proper object of charitable relief?
Shall the state pension the widows?
Shall the school support the child?
Shall charitable societies relieve family distress by finding work for children?"

Jean M. Gordon protested that she did not like the way the first question was put. "If for any reason the child is deprived of its natural supporters through the death or delinquency of either father or mother, the state simply has to take care of it. It is not a matter of charity. But the question is, how is it best to take care of the child? Are we going to adopt the old method of the asylum which has been condemned from one end of the country to the other, or are we going to recognize the mother's right to stay at home with the child and give it training and influence? Certainly, I am in favor of the state pensioning the mother. Naturally, there would have to be a great many safeguards put around it."

Mrs. W. L. Murdoch of Birmingham, Chairman of the Alabama Child Labor Committee, said: "I think Mr. Lovejoy sounded the keynote in the conference last year when he said we had no more right to look at the child of thirteen as an economic asset to the family than we had at the child of three. At least we should not furnish relief for the family by finding work for the child, if the child has not received a certain amount of education. We have an employment agency in Birmingham where the boys looking for situations come daily. And in examining those children for the last five months as to why they were looking for situations, we have found perhaps one out of fifteen of them really needed to go to work. The rest were going to work largely because they were tired of school.

"Where there is an economic necessity in the family (and we certainly know that in a cotton mill district life is desperately poor) if a child can earn six dollars a week in the mill, it is very difficult to tell the father and mother that that child must not be allowed to earn. But they should be told that a child who goes into the cotton mills and earns six dollars a week, will twenty years later be earning six dollars a week. His earnings do not increase.

"The mothers' pension seems to be a red flag to so many that I question whether it is the best way. But certainly some means should be devised to keep the child in school at least five years and to meet the dreadful condition which we have in our state."

Mrs. Florence Kelley said that mothers' pensions from state funds should not be used as a substitute for adequate compensation and a living wage.

(See text of Mrs. Kelley's address on "The Child Breadwinner and the Dependent Parent," delivered at a later session and printed in full in this volume.)

A. T. Jamison, Superintendent of the Connie Maxwell Orphanage, Greenwood, S. C., gave four reasons why a charitable society should not relieve family distress by finding work for children. It is unjust to the family because of danger to the child's health and efficiency. It is not the child's greatest need; it is expensive and it is short-sighted. The community should realize that it is economy to support the widowed mother for a while, in order that the child may have an opportunity to get such training as will enable him to support her in all the years of the future. "The Swiss have set us a fine example in a law they have, requiring that at the end of each successful week in school the child of a widowed mother shall receive a stipend or scholarship. And the Swiss do not regard this as a charity in any sense of the word, but as an advantage to the state. The child shall be sent to school in order that he may be a worker when he is big. Miss Addams has observed that it often happens in America, that the oldest child in the family of a widow goes to work prematurely, before he has had an opportunity to learn a trade, and in the end his mother comes back on the community for support, and all the younger members of the family are objects of charity because his childish strength is quickly exhausted; in addition to her other burdens the mother has an invalid to care for."

Leon Schwartz, President of the B'nai B'rith of Mobile, Ala., said in regard to the second question under discussion: "I would promptly and emphatically say, as a model citizen paying taxes, as a soldier, that if you propose to provide not for widows but for dependent mothers, as suggested by Miss Gordon, I say at once there is more justice for the state to pension women for bringing beings into the world than to pay men for putting beings out of the world."

The Chairman pointed out that not only in the South but in all the states, the job that is open to the immature child is not a job that is getting him anywhere.

R. T. Solensten* of the Associated Charities, Jacksonville, Mary H. Newell* of the Associated Charities, Columbus, Georgia, Mrs. Julia Clark Hallam of Sioux City, Iowa, and Miss Grace Strachan of New York, also contributed to the discussion.

SECOND SESSION.

The second session was held in the Board of Trade Auditorium on Thursday evening, March 13th. Mr. Jennings called the meeting to order and introduced Judge W. H. Baker of Jacksonville.

Judge Baker: "Delegates to the Ninth Annual Conference of the Child Labor Committee, Ladies and Gentlemen, Governor Trammell has requested me to extend to you his most sincere regret that it is impossible for him

---

* Papers marked thus (*) are printed in full in this volume.

to be here this evening. He also requests me to assure you of his hearty sympathy with the objects for which this Conference has assembled. On his behalf and on behalf of the people of the State of Florida, he bids me extend to you a most hearty welcome, not only a welcome to Jacksonville, but a welcome to all of Florida. However attractive and beautiful you may find Jacksonville, you should always remember that Jacksonville is only a gateway to a great and beautiful state. Florida has not only many picturesque and interesting places, but great industrial possibilities. And above all we have a people who are progressive, and wish to be among the foremost in the matters for which this convention has assembled. Florida has not the industries that in the past have utilized child labor; we have no great cotton and woolen mills. Child labor has not been so profitable in this state as in other states. Before it becomes profitable, before our city asks that the children should be used in the industries, it is well that we should consider the subject, because after money has been invested in the industries we will not only have to contend with the natural indifference of the people, but we will have to fight against active opposition as people of other cities have had to fight.

"The world has changed. Men's thoughts and ideas have changed. In the past we thought we could raise children upon maxims and rules of thumb. To-night we have with us from all parts of the country those who will show us that there is a new, a better, and more progressive and Christian way to train children, not only those children who have been committed to us, as their guardians or parents, but children who are homeless, friendless, and poverty stricken. We expect as a result of this Conference that the people of Florida will have this great subject laid upon their conscience and that they will devise practical means to meet the situation and protect our state from the dangers and evils that have come to other states. We welcome you to Florida to-night, not only for the attractions Florida is able to offer to you, but we welcome you because we feel your presence will be a blessing."

Mr. Jennings then introduced Hon. W. S. Jordan, Mayor of Jacksonville, who on behalf of the city extended a cordial welcome to the delegates. After Mayor Jordan's address, Mr. Jennings yielded the chair to Dr. Samuel McCune Lindsay, Vice-Chairman of the National Child Labor Committee.

Dr. Lindsay: "Ladies and Gentlemen, it is indeed a very pleasant duty that falls to me in the absence of the Chairman, Dr. Adler, to thank you for the gracious welcome to Jacksonville. From what I have heard I am not sure but we are bringing coals to Newcastle. I gather that your idea about this Child Labor Conference is, that so far as its practical application to the State of Florida is concerned, you are seeking to remedy your child labor evils before they become too large and too strong to regulate or abolish.

"Now that was precisely the chief purpose in view some nine years ago when this Child Labor Committee was formed. One of the basic ideas about which the group who constituted the National Committee were assembled, was the idea that in the experience of other countries that had been employing child labor longer than the United States, and in the experience of some states whose manufacturing industries had started a little earlier than others, there might be something we could carry through the clearing house of the National Committee, from one state to another; and we might get hold of some of those evils of child labor before they had grown too big to be easily overcome.

"Now there are a great many kinds of reforms being agitated in the North, the South, the East and the West; and I take it that one of the peculiar advantages we have in our deliberations is that this organization is devoted to a reform about which there is practically no difference of opinion. We are united, no matter what particular 'isms' we are advocating, in the sentiment that child labor must cease, for the children of the nation are its chief asset; and that to conserve its wealth we must open the door of opportunity as wide as possible for every child.

"Personally I consider myself especially fortunate, in that I have been privileged to have a part in this child labor work from the very beginning, for it has brought me a little closer than perhaps any other line of study or any other line of effort would have brought me to your own Southern country. Through it I have come to know some of your best people and to appreciate that feeling of chivalry, that eagerness to accomplish something for the good of the whole community, that is so characteristic of the people of the Southland. And I congratulate you upon the opportunity that this particular reform affords you, to show the best that is in Southern life, to bring out the real spirit of the South—coming as it is to-day into a place of greater power and dominance in the affairs of the nation—and to make this one reform one of the great vital issues, one of the forward movements that is to characterize the next few years of American history. I know this is no vain appeal to the people of this state and this community. I am glad that some of us who come from other sections are privileged to work with you; and I hope the spirit of service in this great cause may characterize and dominate all the meetings of this great Conference."

Mr. Lovejoy then read the following telegrams from the President of the United States and the Chairman of the National Child Labor Committee:

"I would be glad to have you express to the Conference my best wishes for the success of its deliberations. Woodrow Wilson."

"I am more disappointed than you can possibly be, but imperative duties force me to remain here. Please express to the people of Jacksonville my infinite regret at not meeting them now and my hope to do so in the future. You will, I know, deeply commend to them the National Child Labor Committee. It is truly the most progressive issue now before the country, on which all are united. It means better citizenship to come, the conservation of the children. With best wishes for an enthusiastic meeting, Yours sincerely, Felix Adler."

Dr. Lindsay introduced Rabbi David Marx of Atlanta, who spoke on "Some Ancient Standards of Child Protection,"* Richard K. Conant, Secretary of the Massachusetts Child Labor Committee, who spoke on "Child Labor in the Textile Industry,"* and William H. Swift of Greensboro, N. C., who spoke on "The Campaign in North Carolina: The Mountain Whites, by One of Them."*

Dr. A. J. McKelway offered the following resolution, which was unanimously adopted:

"*Resolved*, that we, the members of the National Child Labor Committee, in National Conference assembled at Jacksonville, Fla., Thursday, March 13, 1913, with delegates present from all Southern States as well as from the North, East, and West, twenty-six states in all, and supported in this action by the unanimous vote of a mass meeting of the citizens of Jacksonville, hereby declare that we view with apprehension and alarm the report from Washington that the confirmation of the nomination of Hon. Charles P. Neill as Commissioner of Labor will be withheld by the Senate, upon the request of certain Senators because the Report upon the Condition of Woman and Child Wage-Earners in the United States prepared under Dr. Neill's direction was unfair to the South. We affirm our belief that the Government report referred to was an impartial, conservative and scientific presentation of facts, collected with scrupulous care, and that in so far as it referred to Southern mill conditions the investigation was conducted under the immediate direction of a Southern man, who knew and understood the South, and by Southern agents for the most part.

"Although it did not in all respects sustain the findings of our own investigators, nor go so far in revealing the worst conditions of child labor as we believe the full publication of facts would warrant, we have found the report fair and trustworthy. It would be little short of a national disgrace if a faithful servant were punished for speaking the truth because it does not please individual Senators or offends the sensibilities of a few persons who would rather that ugly and unpleasant facts be suppressed than unite in correction of evils that we all deplore and propose to remedy. We unite in demanding Dr. Neill's prompt confirmation in order that the integrity and prestige of the important work of the Department of Labor may be unimpaired, and we hereby instruct the Secretary of the National Child Labor Committee to file a copy of this resolution with the Senate Committee on Education and Labor, and to use his best efforts to secure the confirmation of Dr. Charles P. Neill as Commissioner of Labor."

After the last address of the evening, "Developing Normal Men and Women,"* by Jean M. Gordon, New Orleans, the delegates adjourned to the banquet hall, where a reception was given by the Jacksonville Committee on Arrangements.

THIRD SESSION.

The third session, Friday morning, March 14th, was devoted to a Survey of the Child Labor Situation in the South. Dr. A. J. McKelway, Southern Secretary of the National Child Labor Committee, presided.

Mrs. W. L. Murdoch,* Chairman of the Alabama Child Labor Committee, and Dr. W. H. Oates, State Inspector of Prisons, Almshouses, and Factories, reported for Alabama.

Dr. Oates said that most of his time for the past few years had of necessity been devoted to prison reform in Alabama, but that from now on he would be able to give more attention to the child labor problem. He considered the present child labor law of Alabama ambiguous and inefficient, and he hoped with the aid of Mr. Lovejoy and Dr. McKelway to present to the next legislature a new set of laws which would be adequate for present needs. As the law stands to-day, children under twelve may not work in any mill or factory in the state. Practically this includes only cotton mills. Department stores, messenger service, and all other occupations are open to children of any age, but they should be included in the child labor law. "In trying to enforce the child labor law I have depended largely on diplomacy and by keeping in touch with the manufacturers have persuaded them to co-operate. Hitherto I have been unable to get a conviction or indictment of any one for any violation of the child labor laws; our grand juries need education."

Harvey P. Vaughn, Special Agent of the National Child Labor Committee, speaking of his experience in Arkansas and West Virginia, said:

"There is no limit to the hours that children can work in West Virginia, and no prohibition of night work. Almost the only people that have been interested in getting children under sixteen out of the mines are the labor unions. But the labor unions have been engaged in a bloody conflict which the state is spending fifteen million dollars to quell. The other coal miners in West Virginia, outside of the unions, are a lower, more ignorant type, who seem to be indifferent about child labor. In fact, I think, many of them would rather take their children into the mines. A few of the operators believe they would not have so many explosions if there were no children in the mines under sixteen, and they would like to have an effective age limit law. But there are not many operators who feel this way, because after all, explosions do not cost very much when the courts are ready to free the operator from liability, if he can prove 'contributory negligence.' The Socialist Party stands against child labor and the Progressive Party is making some advance. The women's clubs are beginning to take an interest in politics, and had more lobbyists at the legislature than any other organization except the corporations.

"When I tried to get the child labor law introduced, every man I spoke to in the legislature said: 'Of course, we will vote for a child labor law, if you get it up.' That meant that they would not let it come to a vote, but would kill it in the committee. They had a large committee, fifteen or so, and no matter how hard one worked, one could not get that committee to meet if they did not want to. One member of the committee was the man who accepted $20,000 to vote for a United States Senator and $50,000 to furnish seven other votes beside his own. Mr. W. J. Burns and his detectives got those seven men and they are now awaiting trial. I might add that the same day, a bill was introduced in the Senate and was barely defeated, abolishing the court before which they were to be tried for bribery.

"In Arkansas, the situation was different. The industries are not very well developed and we hoped we might be able to pass the Uniform Child Labor Law. One man, who I had thought was open-minded, asked me if we really intended to limit the hours of work at night and by day as well. When I told him we did, he said: 'This state has got to develop and we will not pass that law.' The legislative session of Arkansas was reduced to sixty days and they had no time to pass any bills except appropriation bills and one bill on which they spent half a day, prohibiting tipping in hotels."

Mrs. E. L. Bailey* of Jackson, reported for Mississippi.

Speaking for Georgia, Mary H. Newell of Columbus, said: "The Georgia law says that no child under ten, under any circumstances, shall be employed or labor in or about a cotton mill. And no children under fourteen shall work between 7 p. m. and 6 a. m.

"One day a little boy of nine in the second grade at school, had been doing his lessons so badly that the teacher began to ask questions. She found that the boy had been working in the mill every day before and after school, and he had been there until half past ten the night before. Besides, the boy had a little sister of six, in the first grade, who went along and helped. The teacher got interested and went through the school, asking questions. She found one child of four in the kindergarten who was a helper in the mill." Miss Newell spoke of the special permits given to children ten to twelve years old, if parents are disabled; she told of several cases that illustrated how permits are procured under false pretenses and also how many children under twelve get into the mills without permits. "The law says that children under fourteen and over twelve can go into the mills provided they have attended school for three months, six weeks of which shall be consecutive. The principal of the school at which I live has issued just four affidavits in the last four years saying that a child has attended regularly; and yet, last year alone, 350 children under fourteen left that school to go to work."

Referring then to the immoral surroundings of the girls, she said: "A young married woman who was working in the mill told us that one of the bosses had sent her an improper proposal by a boy under fourteen. 'I just slapped the boy's jaws and I came awfully near losing my job.' She did not tell us as if the proposal itself was so bad as the fact that she had come near to losing her job!

"It just seems to me that I want to say to this National Child Labor Committee, one and all, as the Macedonians did, 'Come over and help us.' For we must get some good child labor laws passed in Georgia."

Edward F. Brown, Special Agent of the National Child Labor Committee, spoke on "The Demoralizing Environment of Night Messengers in Southern Cities."*

Mrs. J. W. McGriff of Jacksonville, said: "The Florida Child Labor Committee was organized at the State Conference of Charities and Correction in Tampa last fall. So far our one great achievement has been to bring this Child Labor Conference here. But we are not going to rest upon our laurels, for we have a tremendous work before us. We are going to try next month for a child labor bill as near like the Uniform Law as we can possibly get. Then we need members in the State Child Labor Committee so that we can have something in the bank and go ahead with our educational work. I think you will all agree that we need to be educated."

In reply to a question from Mrs. McGriff, Miss Gordon told the details of the scholarship fund in New Orleans. Miss Gordon said: "When we found the need for some fund, I carried it myself till it became too much of a burden. Then some members of the Era Club subscribed, and later we went before the budget committee of the City of New Orleans and asked for five hundred dollars a year, which they gave me and have continued to give us. Now we have a membership of four hundred in New Orleans who all pay a dollar a year, and when we run short we have half a dozen men and women who will advance us twenty-five dollars or fifty dollars until the appropriation comes in from the city. We spend about one thousand dollars a year and we have had no trouble in raising it, for the minute you ask a man or a woman to give five dollars or ten dollars to enable a child to go to school, you generally loosen the purse strings. We have never had more than seven children at one time on the scholarship fund, and we administer it through the school teacher. Most of the children come to my house every Saturday morning to get their checks. I arrange it this way so as to keep in touch with the children; and I like to get them to talking, for we find out a great many things from the children. If Johnnie Jones knows a neighbor who is working under age he is very apt to tell. In fact our factory inspection work in New Orleans depends partly on the espionage that children who are not working, and not allowed to work, keep on others."

Mrs. McGriff then asked for practical advice about better organization of the Florida Child Labor Committee and the Chairman introduced Josephine J. Eschenbrenner, Membership Secretary of the National Child Labor Committee, who spoke, from the national view-point, on the need for strengthening the work of local state committees. She reviewed the fact that the National Committee was called into existence in 1904 by the three state child labor committees then operating in Alabama, Pennsylvania and New York. Their work had been hampered by a lack of national moral support, and because other, especially adjoining, states made no effort for better child labor laws. The cry of competition was being effectively used as an excuse for opposing the legislation these committees advocated.

Miss Eschenbrenner pointed out that just as local committees need the National Committee, the national organization needs the active work of each of the twenty-nine state child labor committees now in existence. The force of the local state committee, with its local branches, lies in its opportunity to foster local sentiment, watch local conditions and the local enforcement of the law—all of which can be done so easily in a community spirit. The local committee must dispel the false tradition, still fondly offered by apologizers for child labor, that early work means early industry and the learning of a trade. It must also dispel the time-worn argument about parents' need. This it can do effectively when armed with local facts, just as the New York Vocational Guidance Survey has been able to prove that out of 406 positions for 237 children investigated, 314 positions offered no training whatever; while 24 per cent. of 69 boys left one school for work, not because of economic need, nor even because of their parents' desire, but because *they disliked* school or "wanted something to do." The local committee's opportunity then, is quite as much to better the schools and to develop interest in school work among the children as to keep young children out of the factory.

Again, the same study by the Survey showed only 20 per cent. of 306 children in one group had left school because of economic pressure. A "scholarship" provision for the children of the comparatively few needy families, is more far-reaching than to place on these children, already handicapped by poverty or lack of parent, a burden from which the state finds it necessary to protect the average child. The scholarship plan must be worked out and developed through local initiative—at least until such time as Mrs. Kelley's hope of a compensation fund from the industry that crippled or killed the father, is realized.

Miss Eschenbrenner urged the need for local sub-committees in the larger towns and cities, under the local state committee, such as the Alabama Child Labor Committee has developed recently; and the need for *active workers* as chairmen, secretaries and members. The success of the Child Labor League of Warren, Ohio, was reviewed. School superintendent, truant officers and factory inspector were all induced to become members of the League; and the active interest of all in seeing that the laws were properly enforced, that the children attended school regularly, and that working certificates were required of all children, while the poorer families were given appropriate relief, resulted in making Warren a town clean of child labor, while children as well as needy families were properly cared for. Similar work by a small organization in Mount Vernon, New York, was also detailed.

Membership in the National Committee on the part of all members of local child labor committees was urged, especially for the sake of the inspiration and broader view-point that the publications of and the "co-partnership" in the National Committee brought its members

"It is not because we are New Jersey people that we should be interested in New Jersey children, or New Yorkers, that we should be interested in New York children, or Floridians, that we should be interested in Florida's children; it is because they are *our* children, the nation's children, that we should be interested. Jean Gordon told me yesterday she had 41,000 children. I am sure if she had stopped to consider she would have claimed not only Louisiana's children, but all the children of all the country as her own. She is doing what she can for everyone of them, whether they live in the city of New Orleans, or the State of Louisiana, or in any other state."

The Chairman, Dr. McKelway, regretted that Hon. J. A. McCullough[*] of Greenville, Chairman of the South Carolina Child Labor Committee, who was to have spoken for that state, had been detained at the last moment. Dr. McKelway said that a bill raising the age limit in South Carolina to fourteen had been unfavorably reported by the senate committee and there the matter had been dropped, so far as the present legislature was concerned. "We hope to make Mr. Swift, who is now our agent for North Carolina, agent for the Carolinas. If he is able to talk to the people of South Carolina about child labor, the next legislature will perhaps be more amenable to reason.

"Arizona has passed substantially the Uniform Child Labor Law, and Oklahoma stands almost beside Arizona, except that we had not discovered the dangers in night messenger service when the Oklahoma law was passed.

"In Virginia, we have a fourteen-year age limit for the employment of children in factories only, and a twelve-year limit for children of dependent parents and orphans. The Virginia legislature meets next year and through the strong Child Labor Committee in Virginia, we shall be able to improve the law.

"The Tennessee legislature has just now increased the number of factory inspectors from one to four (one of them a woman), and passed a compulsory education law for the whole state. It requires attendance at school until fourteen, or until sixteen unless the child is at work. Tennessee has taken a long stride forward in this matter.

"I never saw a larger crowd of earnest young men trying to do what was right, than the members of the Texas legislature that assembled this year. The Uniform Child Labor Law, practically complete, was unanimously reported by a joint committee of house and senate. Unfortunately just as they were about to take up that bill an epidemic of spinal meningitis broke out. Three members of the legislature died and the legislature scattered. They have come together again, but whether they will have time to take this up before the next session I have not been informed.[1]

"New Mexico, I think, is the only Southern State that has not been touched upon. They have a territorial law with a twelve-year age limit for factories and mines. We hope to improve the situation there. A better child labor law passed the house at this session and so far has failed to pass the senate.

"I now take pleasure in introducing to this audience a Lutheran minister, who, while he is not able to see the faces of his fellow-men, has a great interest in this work. It is said of Senator Gore, the blind Senator of the United States, that he sees a great deal further than some of his fellow Senators, and that is true of Pastor Weltner, a Lutheran minister who has been engaged for many years in welfare work in the cotton mills of Columbia, South Carolina."

Dr. Weltner spoke on "Child Labor and Welfare Work in Southern Cotton Mills."*

Mrs. Kelley pointed out with reference to Dr. Weltner's words about the need of organization among the mill workers of the South that when the great co-operative movement and the great trade union movement began in England in the 40's, the working people of England were as isolated and

---

[1] The Texas bill was lost in the senate.

as illiterate as the mill people of South Carolina and Georgia are now; that the strongest unions in the world had been built up in England before compulsory education began in 1870; that our people in South Carolina and Georgia are surrounded by a friendly nation, while the textile workers of England were in the heart of a hostile nation when they entered upon the work of organizing themselves.

"Now it seems to me that this appeal ought not to fall on deaf ears, but that we ought to give whatever moral support is possible to every effort that can be made to organize them; I think we are guilty of moral cowardice if we flinch from this duty, as one of the most essential things to be done before the child labor evil really can be rooted out in the southern textile states."

FOURTH AND FIFTH SESSIONS.

The women delegates were entertained at luncheon, Friday, March 14th, by the Woman's Club of Jacksonville. Informal addresses were made by Mrs. W. B. Young, President of the Club; Mrs. W. A. Hocker, President of the Florida State Federation of Women's Clubs; Julia C. Lathrop, Chief of the Federal Children's Bureau; Josephine J. Eschenbrenner, Membership Secretary of the National Child Labor Committee, and others.

Informal receptions were held on Friday afternoon, March 14th, in eight Jacksonville homes and at three local organizations. Each was addressed by two or three delegates and all meetings were largely attended.

SIXTH SESSION.

The sixth session, Friday evening, March 14th, was presided over by Dr. Lindsay. The first speaker was John C. Campbell of the Russell Sage Foundation: "From Mountain Cabin to Cotton Mill."*

The Chairman then introduced John A. Kingsbury, General Agent of the Association for Improving the Condition of the Poor, New York City, who spoke on "Child Labor and Poverty: Both Cause and Effect."*

Before presenting Julia C. Lathrop, who spoke on the "Federal Children's Bureau,"* of which she is Chief, Dr. Lindsay briefly reviewed the large part the National Child Labor Committee had played in the campaign for securing the establishment of the Bureau.

At the close of Miss Lathrop's address, the Chairman said: "While Miss Lathrop has not made any plea for your support of the Children's Bureau, I know she feels that it needs the support not only of the people here in Florida, but of those all over the United States, in order that there may be larger appropriations for, and more general interest in, the important work the Bureau must undertake. I think I may speak not only for the National Child Labor Committee officially, but for all who are participants in this Conference, in assuring her that we are not going to forget the Children's Bureau, but will co-operate with her in extending its activities."

A paper by Henry Nichol, a manufacturer of Nashville, Tenn., on "The Eight-Hour Day in a Ten-Hour State,"* was read by title. The last speaker of the evening was Lewis W. Hine, Staff Photographer of the National Child Labor Committee, whose address on "The Burden on Children in Shrimp and Oyster Canneries,"* was illustrated with stereopticon.

SEVENTH SESSION.

The seventh session, on Child Labor and Health, was held Saturday morning, March 15th. Mr. Lovejoy called the meeting to order and asked Mr. Vaughn to take the chair. The first address was by Dr. Lindsay on "How to Make Child Labor Legislation More Effective."*

The Chairman in introducing the next speaker, Dr. Oates of Alabama, contrasted him with the factory inspector of another state. "Every time that factory inspector goes on an inspection tour he lets the factories know he is coming; and if by chance he gets into the wrong town on the wrong day, he calls up the office and tells them that he will be out in a certain number of hours. Of course they are ready for him when he gets there. If they are not, they shut down and wait until they are ready for him. It is certainly gratifying to go into any state and find an inspector like Dr. Oates who is doing his duty."

After Dr. Oates' address on "Child Labor and Health,"* Miss Gordon asked how it is possible to have fresh air in cotton mills, since it is said to be absolutely necessary for both the spinning and the weaving of cotton to have moist, hot atmosphere. Dr. Oates replied: "It need not be hot but it must be moist. Fresh moist air can be provided by the use of ventilators and humidifiers, such as are found in many modern mills, and which cost about five hundred dollars to install." Miss Gordon quoted the opinion of a manufacturer who believed that a humidifier was essential to good cotton, in fact an economy because it meant fewer "seconds."

Kate Holstead of Columbus, Ga., said: "In my school we have possibly three hundred and eighty children during the year. Almost every one of those children is so susceptible to colds that even during the weeks they are in school they lose one-third of the time through sickness. Has humidity in the mills anything to do with that?"

Dr. Oates: "It lowers their vitality and their power to resist diseases. But the chief factor in the cotton mill is the lack of fresh oxygen to breathe."

Mr. Swift: "I understand that some mills do not have either humidifiers or ventilators because the mere fact of putting these in the room would tend to make the room worse for the operators than though they were not there. It was impressed upon us in our state that the old way was very beneficial for the operators. The mills were classed with the churches and schools in North Carolina!"

Miss Strachan spoke of the advantage it would be to children in mill families if they might attend open air schools. Dr. Weltner suggested that there would be little chance of good ventilation in any schools provided by the mill authorities, but Dr. Oates did not agree with him. "They do furnish adequately ventilated school buildings. It is all a matter of the dollar mark, and they have nothing at stake in the school buildings, but if they deprive themselves of the moisture in the mills they are going to lose some money."

In the absence of M. Louise Boswell of Cincinnati, Ohio, her paper on "Child Labor and Need"* was read by title. Edward F. Brown spoke on "The Neglected Human Resources of the Gulf Coast States."*

Dr. McKelway said: "We should remember that the problems involved in this discussion of southern conditions are comparatively new to the South. For a long time it seemed to me that I was about the only man from the South who was trying to tell the whole truth about southern conditions. But since I have heard at this Conference so many frank expressions of opinion from the people of the South, I have got into a rather defensive and apologetic frame of mind about these conditions; and I am very hopeful that in the course of a few years we shall have splendid legislation to protect the children, and adequate appropriation for the employment of officials to enforce it.

"Let me give a brief history of our legislation in Florida. My first Florida legislature was eight years ago. I was rather new to the business then but I remember that our bill for a fourteen-year age limit had passed both the house and the senate. On the last day of the session a conference report was brought in for adoption in one house, and just as it was on the point of adoption somebody got up and moved to table the conference report. It went to the table and the bill just died there. An oyster packer of Florida afterwards told me that he was responsible for having the motion to table introduced and passed. And the curious thing about it is that for the last five or six years he has not been employing children in the oyster packing industry in Florida, because he has not been employing anybody. It is with the hope of employing them in the future, it appears, that he has been opposing the bill steadily the last few years, or perhaps because of his interest in the packing houses of other states and in a cotton mill in Georgia.

"At the next session of the legislature we introduced the same bill, with a fourteen-year age limit, sixteen for night work, with certificates for children under sixteen, and with a nine-hour day for children under sixteen. The bill passed one house in that form, as I recollect, and then in the other house, wherever they say anything above twelve they cut it down to twelve. So we have now this unique product of legislation for Florida: children under twelve years of age are forbidden to work in certain specified occupations; then children under twelve years are forbidden to work at night in these specified occupations; then children under twelve years are forbidden to work more than nine hours a day; and finally, certificates are required for children under twelve years of age to work in these occupations. That was six years ago. Two years ago we failed to improve that law, and our friend, the oyster packer, who hopes to employ children in the future, claims he has each time defeated the bill. I do not suppose the state is always going to submit to the domination of one man, and I think we have some facts now that are going to militate against his influence. I believe we have more public sentiment than ever before, and now is the time to prevent evils."

Mrs. F. J. McCormick of Dayton, Ohio: "We have in Ohio some excellent child labor laws on our books, and we have had that comfortable 'I am better than thou' feeling in regard to child labor conditions. But just before I left home I read the report of the State Labor Commissioner and was shocked to find that, even with our laws and our machinery for enforcement, conditions were very bad. We have children working under age, and children working twelve hours a day. And I believe the only way to take care of children north or south, is to arouse public sentiment, because, after all, it is upon the will of the citizens that the enforcement of law depends."

Mrs. Murdoch: "May I say on behalf of Alabama that we have such a short bit of coast line that there are probably thousands of people all over the state that have not the faintest idea that children are working in fish canneries. We need a campaign of education in these Southern States and it seems to me nothing could be so helpful as to have the National Child Labor Committee send us some of these young men and women who have been making investigations, to tell us about the conditions they have found.

"I do not think Alabama will be niggardly about spending money to keep children out of oyster and shrimp canneries when they know something about it. We simply must wake the people out of their indifference and I believe he is the truest friend who tells us our faults in the blackest way."

Replying to a suggestion that compulsory school laws must precede child labor laws, Dr. McKelway said: "I read a book the other day by Scott Nearing and as I recall his summary it was something like this: that we ought to have a minimum wage first before we do anything else; then we ought to have widows' pensions; then we ought to have compulsory education and then we ought to have child labor laws to take the children out of industry. That is the theory and I think that is logical. But I do not believe we can do it that way. We must first eliminate the children from industry by the passage of child labor laws. That forces compulsory education and it is my opinion that we will not have state-wide compulsory education in the manufacturing states in the south up to fourteen years of age, until we have a law forbidding the employment of children under fourteen years of age."

EIGHTH SESSION.

The meeting for children held Saturday morning, March 15th at the Imperial Theatre was so popular that scores of children could not gain admittance. After the meeting was over, the theatre was filled a second time by those who had waited outside and the moving picture film "Children Who Labor," which had been part of the program, was repeated. "The Story of the Medicine Bottle," "The Story of My Cotton Dress," and "What Mr. Coal Told Us" will be printed in the next Child Labor Bulletin.

NINTH SESSION.

The delegates spent Saturday afternoon on St. John's River, which was not only a beautiful and interesting experience in itself, but offered a delightful opportunity for the delegates to become better acquainted with each other and with the people of Jacksonville.

TENTH SESSION.

The tenth session, Sunday afternoon, March 16th, was called to order by Mr. Jennings, who introduced as Chairman of the meeting Senator Frederick M. Hudson of Miami.

Senator Hudson said in part: "We people of Florida look upon the work of the National Child Labor Committee as a work of good citizenship and therefore I would like to consider briefly this afternoon the question we often hear asked, 'What is the test of good citizenship?' The spirit of good citizenship has actuated every great man in history. It is identical with the spirit that we call patriotism when it is applied to the defense of our country; it is the same spirit that in another form underlies practical religion. Often it appears in such humble garb that we pass it by, in our quest for something bigger, something higher and more glittering, for the underlying principle of good citizenship is nothing more nor less than the spirit of sacrifice. Whether in public life or in private life, if we be not actuated by the spirit of sacrifice we are not good citizens.

"Sometimes that spirit demands that we stand patiently waiting and submit. So General Lee, after the failure of the Gettysburg campaign, said, 'I assume the whole responsibility for this campaign,' although he was of the absolute profound conviction that the campaign had failed because his orders had been disobeyed.

"More often, good citizenship calls for courage when cowardice would be accepted or condoned. That was evidenced in the course pursued by General Grant after the surrender of Lee. General Grant went to Secretary Stanton and said, 'I understand you have given orders for the arrest of General Lee.' The answer was, 'I have.' General Grant said, 'General Lee is my prisoner of war. He is out on parole and I am bound to protect him.' Stanton said, 'The order for his arrest has been given and he will be arrested.' General Grant's answer was, 'I start for the army to-night. I propose to put General Lee as near where I found him as I can.'

"But it is not in time of war the call for the exercise of good citizenship is most sure to come to you and to me; rather in time of peace when there is no glory attaching to our heroism. Citizenship calls us to see justice administered among our fellow men.

"If we analyze the opposition raised against the work of the National Child Labor Committee and its members, we find that it comes from those who are hurt or claim to be hurt. And the Committee summons them as good citizens to suffer hindrance and practice self-sacrifice for the sake of justice to those children whom they wish to employ.

"In another way the Committee summons us to good citizenship by its aim to give every boy and every girl an even chance to develop into strong, able, efficient men and women. And surely the perfecting of the development of the childhood of the land is the highest aim that we can set before ourselves as citizens."

The addresses of the afternoon were delivered by Dr. A. J. McKelway on "Child Wages in the Cotton Mill: Our Modern Feudalism,"* Jerome Jones, Editor of the Journal of Labor, Atlanta, on "Child Labor and Low Wages are Corollaries,"* Mrs. Florence Kelley, General Secretary of the National Consumers' League, on "The Child Breadwinner and the Dependent Parent,"* and Owen R. Lovejoy on "Where American Children Work."

The following resolution of thanks was offered by Dr. McKelway and unanimously adopted:

"*Resolved,* That the thanks of the National Child Labor Committee in Conference assembled representing more than six thousand members throughout the nation are hereby tendered to the citizens of Florida and of Jacksonville, who have not only made the holding of our ninth Annual Conference in Jacksonville possible, but have contributed so generously towards its complete and gratifying success.

"We make special mention of the Board of Trade, the Woman's Club, the Florida Children's Home Society and the Associated Charities among the civic bodies of Jacksonville, and of the Committee on Arrangements and the other special committees, whose efficiency has been as conspicuous as their hospitality has been gracious.

"Our thanks are also due to the newspapers of Jacksonville, which have contributed to the education of the public by full and intelligent reports of our meetings, to the churches whose pulpits have been open to our delegates, to the press associations, for the news carried to the press of the country, to Sewell Ford, author and publicist, who gave the services of his gifted pen to the cause of publicity, and to all the speakers whose faithful descriptions of child labor conditions in the various states have added a mass of valuable information to our child labor literature. And the Committee hopes that its visit to Jacksonville shall not have been in vain in interesting anew the good people of Florida in the effort to protect children now at work within the state and to prevent the exploitation of yet greater numbers in the years to come."

Dr. McKelway offered a second resolution appealing for the co-operation of all national organizations, including the National Manufacturers' Association, in the campaign against child labor. This also was unanimously adopted.

"*Resolved,* that the National Child Labor Committee in Convention assembled at Jacksonville, Florida, March 16th, 1913, recognizes that upon it has been laid the chief responsibility for bringing about the abolition of child labor in the United States, fully appreciates the magnitude of its task and because of the meagreness of its resources realizes the deplorable fact that thousands of American children, many yet unborn, will never secure the protection of child labor laws unless there is a greater awakening of interest throughout the nation in the cause of child labor reform.

"That we, therefore, appeal not only to the citizenship of the nation to increase the resources at our command and thus our opportunities for service, but also to all other national organizations which stand for the welfare of society in their respective spheres of education, health, industry, and social service for their co-operation.

"That this Committee asks especially that there be supplied for the promotion of child labor reform not only the active sympathy of the membership of these organizations, but that special investigations of child labor conditions be conducted from the different points of view which these organizations have taken in their respective spheres of work; and we mention among them, while excluding none, the National Education Association, the American Medical Association, the American Academy of Medicine, The National Association for the Prevention of Tuberculosis, The American Red Cross, The American Bar Association, The Russell Sage Foundation, The General Federation of Women's Clubs, The National Council of Jewish Women, The Social Service Commission of the Federation of Churches, The Conference of Catholic Charities, The National Conference of Charities and Correction, The American Association of Labor Legislation, The American Federation of Labor, and finally, since the child employing industries while forming only a small percentage of industrial establishments have brought the reproach of child labor upon American industry itself, the National Manufacturers' Association."

ELEVENTH SESSION.

The closing session, Monday morning, March 17th, was an informal discussion conducted by Mr. Lovejoy.

Mrs. Murdoch told of the newsboys' ordinance recently passed in Birmingham, and asked whether it would be wise to try to cover other forms of child labor by city ordinances, especially in Alabama where the legislature convenes only once in four years. One member thought that to regulate conditions in any way possible would be just so much gained, and that the success of a local ordinance would do away with local opposition to a state law covering the same points. Mr. Brown said his experience led him to believe that, on the contrary, people were inclined to argue that local ordinances made state action unnecessary, and that abuses were likely to develop unchecked outside of the few districts covered by local ordinances. Mr. Swift said that local ordinances would be dangerous in his state because they would encourage North Carolina's bad habit of excepting certain counties from the operation of a state law.

The difficulties of enforcement of street trades regulation were briefly discussed. The enforcement of them has in most places been left to the school attendance officials and the juvenile courts. This brought out the question whether any effectual local enforcement of state child labor laws was possible. Dr. McKelway said: "Any private citizen has a right to move for the enforcement of law. While there is never any enforcement worthy of the name without state factory inspection, private prosecutions advertise the need for it. If we have a statutory officer to enforce the law, it is usually better to get after him and make him do it, than to attempt a private prosecution. I would suggest that in some cases the best time to put a good law on the statute books is when the poor law is not enforced. Recent experience in Maryland has illustrated this point. There had been little enforcement up to last year. Then with almost no opposition we passed one of the best child labor laws in the country and afterwards proceeded to revolutionize the factory inspection department in order to enforce it."

The rest of the morning was devoted to discussion of the present situation in Florida. It was reported that during the Conference seventy-eight members had joined the Florida Child Labor Committee bringing its membership up to one hundred.

Of these, seventeen were present at the meeting, and they proceeded to elect Dr. J. W. Stagg of Orlando, as chairman of the Florida Committee, to succeed Senator Hudson, who resigned. The other officers previously elected are Mrs. F. E. Jennings and Mrs. M. E. Randall, Vice-Chairmen, Marcus C. Fagg, Secretary, and Mrs. J. W. McGriff, Treasurer.

Dr. McKelway was asked to give a synopsis of the proposed Florida law as it had been under discussion at the informal meeting of the Florida Child Labor Committee a few days before. He said: "The Uniform Child Labor Law is the basis upon which we are building. It has a fourteen-year age limit for certain specified occupations and provides that no child under fourteen may be employed in any service whatever during school hours. These two principles are already embodied in the Florida law with a twelve-year age limit and we should not find it difficult to raise the age limit to fourteen years. The Uniform Law has a sixteen-year age limit for dangerous occupations. We have tried to shorten the enumeration of these occupations to processes connected with acids and dangerous processes generally, and to eliminate anything that does not apply to Florida, and will not apply to Florida in the near future.

"The employment certificate occupies a good part of the bill and this could not be shortened very much without weakening the efficacy of the law. The difficulty is the matter of ascertaining the age of the child and the Uniform Child Labor Law provides that employment certificates shall be signed only after definite information has been secured. In case there is no documentary proof of age, then we ask for the physicians' certificate saying, 'To all appearances the child is of the given age and he is fit for the work in which he is going to engage.' It makes the bill cumbersome and we have to face that objection, but I do not know any way to avoid it if we wish to establish the age of the child.

"Then we have almost decided to ask for prohibition of the night messenger service under eighteen instead of twenty-one. I have a good deal of reluctance even in stating this, and I almost feel we had better not agree upon it until we are able to present the evidence we have secured in Florida and let the legislative committee decide as to whether it shall be twenty-one or eighteen.

"As to the length of the working day we decided that we would ask for a nine-hour day instead of eight for boys under sixteen and girls under eighteen.

"With regard to inspection, I understand that the labor organizations have already secured pledges from the members of the legislature for the creation of a Bureau of Labor with a Commissioner of Labor and one or two assistants in charge. It is our business to see that the provisions for factory inspection and the enforcement of the child labor laws are included in that bureau, and then join in urging its creation."

Mr. Lovejoy: "May I suggest to the officers of the Florida Committee that if the Committee is to be effective in preparing for the legislative session, in securing the passage of the bill, and, after you get the bill through, in seeing that it is enforced, you must have a Committee that is strong numerically. You must get a number of leading citizens from different sections of the state, men and women who will have influence with their own legislators, so that when the bill comes up and some man proceeds to oppose the bill you will be able to telegraph to that man's chief constituent, and ask him to stimulate his representative a little and get him on the right side.

"To the members who are here I would like to suggest that you can greatly help Mrs. McGriff, the Treasurer of the Florida Committee, if you will give her the names and addresses of your friends. Mrs. McGriff will prepare a letter asking them to join the Florida Child Labor Committee and she will send it to you to forward with a personal letter from yourself.

"In this way you can build up a State Child Labor Committee so strong that you will surely win in the legislature, for if the legislature finds that a majority of people of the state want child labor laws, the legislature will want it too."

Mrs. McGriff asked for a discussion of the following subject: "Even when the best child labor law has been passed and enforced, the condition which forced the child to work (whether it be ignorance, necessity or indolence on the part of the natural guardian) remains unchanged. And in so far as need is responsible for child labor it seems to me that we must assume some responsibility for the people whom we have deprived of support. If we are not prepared to face this, we shall just be throwing a big problem on the Associated Charities, which they are not in a position to solve. Do you consider that mothers' pensions offer the best solution? If so, should we not include them in our campaign?"

Miss Gordon: "From our experience in New Orleans we have found that most of the children who go to work do not actually need the money they earn. The first few months after our child labor law was passed we investigated five hundred homes to learn why the children had been working, and we found only five children that needed our scholarship fund. The parents were working and in many cases the children were just spending the money they earned on themselves. But it was a habit of mind among those people for the children to go to work as soon as they had learned the catechism and made their first communion. Then, too, the parents had themselves started early and were really worn out and tired men and women at forty years of age, and they felt that if the children didn't go to work they were lazy. Very often in a family where there seems to be real need, you will find a relative who will come forward and help if the matter is laid before him.

"Then there are other parents who would be glad to keep their boys at home, but they cannot control them. These parents would welcome a child labor law, especially if it applied to newsboys.

"I think a scholarship fund can meet the need until the time comes for a mothers' pension. If you appealed to the churches of this community and told them, 'You have got to contribute to this child labor fund and help us right in our own midst before we will contribute anything to foreign missions,' I do not believe you would have any trouble in raising the money for scholarships."

Dr. McKelway: "We must discriminate between the general problem of relief and those cases where it is made necessary because we have raised the age limit from twelve to fourteen years. Senator McDowell of Mississippi, who had charge of the bill there, said when this question of the poor mothers was raised, 'Just refer all these cases to me.' And he never had a single case. In New York City, at one time when the child labor law was so amended that many children were put out of work, a member of the New York Child Labor Committee offered five thousand dollars to take care of the families that suffered because of losing the children's wages. This fact was widely advertised but only ninety cases were found in the great City of New York during a year and a half."

Dr. McKelway referred to similar evidence from Little Rock, Ark. Mr. Vaughn said that in Wheeling, W. Va., the Associated Charities had taken charge of the matter and found that they had not had to increase their budget at all in order to answer the calls that came from families where children had been thrown out of work. Miss Holstead reported that out of a group of one hundred children under fourteen who had at some time worked in the mill in Columbus, Ga., there were only three for whom it had been necessary to work.

Mr. Hine: "It seems to me that Florida is the most fortunate of all our states. For three or four years we have been following the factories in different lines in Florida, and we have found very few tendencies towards child labor. There are some children in the department stores. That is one strong tendency, but it can be easily overcome.

"Your newsboy and your night messenger are other tendencies, but the situation in Florida is not bad and you should be encouraged that you can put your energies into preventive measures and do not have to cure a disease deeply rooted in your system."

Mrs. Murdoch: "In Alabama we have been trying to educate the mothers and that is where the individual work of the members of your Child Labor Committee must come in. You should have a big strong Committee of young men and young women who will go into the homes and carry on a campaign of education. During the last two months, we have put twenty-four newsboys in Birmingham back in school by personal visits to their homes. And I would suggest that in your child labor campaign you do not commence to talk of scholarship funds unless you find it necessary."

Marcus C. Fagg, Secretary of the Florida Child Labor Committee: "The school question is even more serious in Florida, I think, than the question of relief. We are sorry to have to confess that if all the children who ought to go to school in the city of Jacksonville, were going to school, we should have a hard time to take care of them."

F. E. Hoyt, Jacksonville, pointed out that taking the state as a whole, there are no school districts in the South that are in better shape than Florida's; that Duval County has grown rapidly in the last ten years and taken upon itself increased burdens which in other parts of Florida or of the United States would be hard to duplicate; that the population of Jacksonville has jumped in ten years from fifteen thousand to approximately eighty-two thousand; and that Duval County is carrying an educational debt of about three hundred thousand dollars. Mrs. Sutherland, Jacksonville, spoke of the new school building that opened in Riverside last year with ninety-five pupils, and this year had two hundred and forty. It is now crowded to its utmost capacity so that it must be enlarged before next year, although the building is not yet two years old.

Mr. Hoff, Chicago, suggested that the Board of Trade be called upon to meet the school problems created by their aggressive campaign to bring industries to Jacksonville; that they also be urged to discourage industries that intend to employ children from settling in Florida.

J. H. Kaplan, Selma, Ala.: "The fact is that we in this country are not alive to the real interests of education. The way we give our money always shows our appreciation of the things to which we give. When I went to New Mexico a school teacher was paid nine hundred dollars or seven hundred or six hundred dollars, while a sheriff made as high as twenty thousand dollars. In other words we appreciate the dignity of sending a man from the gutter to the prison more than we appreciate educating the children. There is no problem here in Jacksonville any greater than in any other city. No city of this country is yet alive to the value of education. We have money to build monuments and charitable institutions and the finest prisons and the finest churches, merely because we appreciate the value of these propositions. Only when our people know the real value of education will these questions be settled, and in the meantime we must keep working on the child labor problem."

Mr. Lovejoy: "It seems to me that this discussion has raised two very important questions. The first is, what is to be done with those children who are taken out of industry? The second is, how will a needy family be compensated for the loss of the child's earnings?

"Now, in order to get school facilities that are adequate to meet the needs of the children, you must first put the problem on the conscience of the community. We are a great people for correcting big abuses; but we have no interest at all in keeping the abuse from arriving. We do not pass good fire laws till the whole town is swept away. We do not provide for education until the children become a nuisance yelling and playing in our streets. I like to tell of our experience in Rhode Island, because it is such an excellent illustration of what I mean. We were trying to interest the cotton mill operatives in passing a law to raise the age limit from ten to fourteen, and they were indifferent about it because there was no school house in their little town. The mill corporation had given two private dwellings for school purposes, and there the kindergartners were in school, but as soon as the child got big enough to tie a knot it was in the mill. When we began to agitate for a higher age limit, the community exclaimed, 'You are going to throw these children out in the streets and they will become idlers and loafers and bums, and it will be worse for them than to be in the mills.'

"Their argument was logical; there was no school in the town because the children worked in the cotton mills and they had to work in the cotton mills because there was no schoolhouse. But we kept on with our campaign and when the bill passed it broke the vicious circle and inside of six months there was a schoolhouse in the town.

"Then there is another point in regard to education. When I was presenting the child labor problem to the National Association of School Superintendents recently, they questioned whether we should not get more schoolhouses and compulsory education laws before we pass child labor laws. I said, 'Gentlemen, the public school system of the United States spends over four hundred million dollars annually. We spend only sixty-five thousand dollars. I submit that the educational problem of America is up to the four hundred million dollar crowd instead of to the sixty-five thousand dollar crowd.' One of the greatest services we can render is to keep putting it up to the educators—local boards of education, state boards of education, superintendents and teachers—that their educational system is not adequate.

"I believe that during the next few years education will largely solve the other problem under discussion—poverty. But in the meantime we must meet this matter of family distress. Now the problem of caring for the poor widow who has a two-year-old child is recognized as a problem of local charity, and I submit that the problem is not changed one bit if the child instead of being two years old is thirteen years old or twelve years old; he still has not had the opportunity of laying the foundation of an American education; he is just as helpless, just as much an object of social supervision and social control as though he were two years old.

"I am not prepared to say that I should like to see a system of pensions for dependent mothers established in all our states at the present moment. There are a great many problems of administration in working out such a system, that must be experimented upon. But charity organization societies and other relief agencies are taking up this whole matter of the relief of dependent parents, and they are going to handle it. It is not our problem; it is theirs. The educators are going to handle the educational problem.

It is not ours; it is theirs. We can help stimulate these other organizations to work out their part of these problems. But there is just one thing on which we must keep pounding away; we have our one specific job, and that is the elimination of the child from wage-earning industry."

Mr. Fagg: "Before this meeting adjourns I want to say that this Conference has been a tremendous help to the people of Florida and the cause of child welfare in this state; and from the bottom of our hearts we want to thank everybody who has been here, both the speakers and the delegates, because you have left us with an inspiration to activity, which is going to make it possible for us, I believe, to put Florida on the map with the other states that protect their children."

Mr. Lovejoy expressed his appreciation of Mr. Fagg's words and personally thanked the members of the Florida Child Labor Committee and the people of Jacksonville for the large part they had played in making the Conference a success. Upon motion the Conference then adjourned.

The pulpits of many Jacksonville churches were occupied on Sunday March 16th, by prominent speakers and delegates.

Residents of Jacksonville active in co-operating for the success of the Conference were:

Committee on Arrangements.—Frank E. Jennings, Chairman; Mrs. Walter P. Corbett, Treasurer; R. T. Solensten, Secretary.

Executive Committee.—M. C. Fagg, Chairman; W. A. Lloyd, Dr. Junius French, Mrs. W. B. Young, Mrs. J. W. McGriff.

Reception Committee.—Mrs. Richard Marks, Chairman; Miss Carrie Locke, Mrs. J. H. W. Hawkins, Mrs. J. R. Tysen, Mrs. George Fred. Parsons, Mrs. Franklin Russell, Mrs. Frederick Bowen, Mrs. P. C. Perry, Mrs. Frank N. Stormont, Mrs. F. O. McCuen, Mrs. Julian Prewitte, Mrs. James W. Archibald, Mrs. W. S. Jennings, Mrs. R. B. Archibald, Mrs. Beverly Nalle, Mrs. James Y. Wilson, Mrs. Windle Smith, Mrs. John L. Doggett, Miss Delia Meigs, Mr. and Mrs. Cecil Willcox, Mr. and Mrs. W. E. Cummer, Judge and Mrs. W. B. Young, Mr. and Mrs. George Drew, Mr. and Mrs. Frank E. Jennings, Mrs. W. A. Hocker.

Publicity Committee.—W. A. Lloyd, Chairman; B. F. Miller, Mrs. J. W. McGriff, John L. McWhorter, M. C. Fagg.

Finance Committee.—Mrs. Walter P. Corbett, Chairman; C. H. Mann, George R. DeSaussure, Mrs. A. G. Cummer, Mrs. J. W. Spratt.

Children's Meeting Committee.—Mrs. Thomas Palmer, Chairman; Miss Bertha Adams.

Decoration Committee.—Mrs. J. W. McGriff, Chairman; Mrs. T. P. Denham, Mrs. Stephen Foster, C. D. Mills, Mrs. Frank Brock, Mrs. E. F. Elkins.

Registration Committee.—Mrs. W. H. Baker, Chairman; Miss Delia Meigs, Miss Clementine Douglas, Mrs. George Byrnes, Miss Fanny Holt, Miss Frances Anderson.

Child Labor Exhibit Committee.—Rabbi Samuel Schwartz, Chairman.

Committee on Halls.—H. H. Richardson, Chairman.

Entertainment Committee.—Mrs. J. W. Spratt, Chairman; Mrs. R. C. Turck, Mrs. W. E. Cummer, Mrs. A. E. Acker, Mrs. J. G. Coxetter, Mrs. Edward L'Engle, Mrs. C. S. Adams, Mrs. J. P. Middlemas.

Women's Luncheon Committee.—Miss Louise Meigs, Chairman; Mrs. P. J. Croghan, Mrs. Ralph Smith, Mrs. Jas. H. Randolph, Mrs. W. A. Evans, Mrs. Marshall Stewart.

Parlor Meetings.—Mrs. J. D. Douglas, Chairman; Mrs. I. A. Zacharias, Mrs. Harrison Reed, Dr. Ellen Lowell Stevens, Mrs. Henry Clark, Mrs. Frederick Bowen, Mrs. J. Durkee, Mrs. S. E. Fields, Mrs. C. E. Austin, Mrs. T. P. Denham, Mrs. C. D. Rinehart, Mrs. L. G. Moore, Miss Anna Stockton.

CHILDREN AND YOUTH
Social Problems and Social Policy

An Arno Press Collection

Abt, Henry Edward. **The Care, Cure and Education of the Crippled Child.** 1924

Addams, Jane. **My Friend, Julia Lathrop.** 1935

American Academy of Pediatrics. **Child Health Services and Pediatric Education:** Report of the Committee for the Study of Child Health Services. 1949

American Association for the Study and Prevention of Infant Mortality. **Transactions of the First Annual Meeting of the American Association for the Study and Prevention of Infant Mortality.** 1910

Baker, S. Josephine. **Fighting For Life.** 1939

Bell, Howard M. **Youth Tell Their Story:** A Study of the Conditions and Attitudes of Young People in Maryland Between the Ages of 16 and 24. 1938

Bossard, James H. S. and Eleanor S. Boll, editors. **Adolescents in Wartime.** 1944

Bossard, James H. S., editor. **Children in a Depression Decade.** 1940

Brunner, Edmund DeS. **Working With Rural Youth.** 1942

Care of Dependent Children in the Late Nineteenth and Early Twentieth Centuries. Introduction by Robert H. Bremner. 1974

Care of Handicapped Children. Introduction by Robert H. Bremner. 1974

[Chenery, William L. and Ella A. Merritt, editors]. **Standards of Child Welfare:** A Report of the Children's Bureau Conferences, May and June, 1919. 1919

The Child Labor Bulletin, 1912, 1913. 1974

Children In Confinement. Introduction by Robert M. Mennel. 1974

Children's Bureau Studies. Introduction by William M. Schmidt. 1974

Clopper, Edward N. **Child Labor in City Streets.** 1912

David, Paul T. **Barriers To Youth Employment.** 1942

Deutsch, Albert. **Our Rejected Children.** 1950

Drucker, Saul and Maurice Beck Hexter. **Children Astray.** 1923

Duffus, R[obert] L[uther] and L. Emmett Holt, Jr. **L. Emmett Holt: Pioneer of a Children's Century.** 1940

Fuller, Raymond G. **Child Labor and the Constitution.** 1923

Holland, Kenneth and Frank Ernest Hill. **Youth in the CCC.** 1942

Jacoby, George Paul. **Catholic Child Care in Nineteenth Century New York:** With a Correlated Summary of Public and Protestant Child Welfare. 1941

Johnson, Palmer O. and Oswald L. Harvey. **The National Youth Administration.** 1938

The Juvenile Court. Introduction by Robert M. Mennel. 1974

Klein, Earl E. **Work Accidents to Minors in Illinois.** 1938

Lane, Francis E. **American Charities and the Child of the Immigrant:** A Study of Typical Child Caring Institutions in New York and Massachusetts Between the Years 1845 and 1880. 1932

The Legal Rights of Children. Introduction by Sanford N. Katz. 1974

Letchworth, William P[ryor]. **Homes of Homeless Children:** A Report on Orphan Asylums and Other Institutions for the Care of Children. [1903]

Lorwin, Lewis. **Youth Work Programs:** Problems and Policies. 1941

Lundberg, Emma O[ctavia] and Katharine F. Lenroot. **Illegitimacy As A Child-Welfare Problem, Parts 1 and 2.** 1920/1921

New York State Commission on Relief for Widowed Mothers. **Report of the New York State Commission on Relief for Widowed Mothers.** 1914

Otey, Elizabeth Lewis. **The Beginnings of Child Labor Legislation in Certain States;** A Comparative Study. 1910

Phillips, Wilbur C. **Adventuring For Democracy.** 1940

Polier, Justine Wise. **Everyone's Children, Nobody's Child:** A Judge Looks At Underprivileged Children in the United States. 1941

Proceedings of the Annual Meeting of the National Child Labor Committee, 1905, 1906. 1974

Rainey, Homer P. **How Fare American Youth?** 1940

Reeder, Rudolph R. **How Two Hundred Children Live and Learn.** 1910

Security and Services For Children. 1974

Sinai, Nathan and Odin W. Anderson. **EMIC (Emergency Maternity and Infant Care):** A Study of Administrative Experience. 1948

Slingerland, W. H. **Child-Placing in Families:** A Manual For Students and Social Workers. 1919

[Solenberger], Edith Reeves. **Care and Education of Crippled Children in the United States.** 1914

Spencer, Anna Garlin and Charles Wesley Birtwell, editors. **The Care of Dependent, Neglected and Wayward Children:** Being a Report of the Second Section of the International Congress of Charities, Correction and Philanthropy, Chicago, June, 1893. 1894

Theis, Sophie Van Senden. **How Foster Children Turn Out.** 1924

Thurston, Henry W. **The Dependent Child:** A Story of Changing Aims and Methods in the Care of Dependent Children. 1930

U.S. Advisory Committee on Education. **Report of the Committee, February, 1938.** 1938

The United States Children's Bureau, 1912-1972. 1974

White House Conference on Child Health and Protection. **Dependent and Neglected Children:** Report of the Committee on Socially Handicapped — Dependency and Neglect. 1933

White House Conference on Child Health and Protection. **Organization for the Care of Handicapped Children, National, State, Local.** 1932

White House Conference on Children in a Democracy. **Final Report of the White House Conference on Children in A Democracy.** [1942]

Wilson, Otto. **Fifty Years' Work With Girls, 1883-1933:** A Story of the Florence Crittenton Homes. 1933

Wrenn, C. Gilbert and D. L. Harley. **Time On Their Hands:** A Report on Leisure, Recreation, and Young People. 1941